Archaeology Africa

Archaeology
Africa

**MARTIN
HALL**

James Currey
London

David Philip
Cape Town

First published 1996
David Philip Publishers (Pty) Ltd,
208 Werdmuller Centre, Claremont 7700,
South Africa

James Currey, 54B Thornhill Square,
Islington, London N1 1BE

ISBN 0 86486 302 0 (David Philip)
ISBN 0 85255 735 3 (James Currey)

Artwork design: Dominique Fulton
Text design & layout: Dee Murch
Cover design: Ingrid Küpper

Cover photo of australopithecine trackway
at Laetoli, Tanzania by courtesy of the
Getty Conservation Institute, California

CIP data is available upon request from
the British Library

Printed by The Natal Witness Printing &
Publishing Co., 244 Longmarket Street,
Pietermaritzburg, 3201, South Africa

Contents

Contents

Acknowledge-
ments

The first draft of this book was tried out at the University of Cape Town on the AGE101F class of 1995, particularly tutorial groups A and F; they should know that all their comments were taken seriously. I am grateful to the following colleagues for their close and constructive readings of earlier drafts of this book: Yvonne Brink, Hilary Deacon, Simon Hall, Carolyn Hamilton, Ian Hodder, Aron Mazel, Duncan Miller, John Parkington, Judy Sealy, Gavin Whitelaw, Royden Yates. Brenda Cooper, as usual, provided particularly consistent and thorough support. Dominique Fulton joined our group at a critical stage in this project and contributed her considerable design skills. Gavin Lucas, Wendy McKeag and Fiona Wilson helped put the manuscript together in its final form.

Illustrations by Tina Coombes: Figures 134, 162, 169; by Dominique Fulton: Figures 3, 7, 8, 9, 13, 17, 18, 20, 21, 25, 29, 33, 41, 43, 48, 49, 50, 52, 53, 55, 56, 67, 68, 69, 70, 71, 72, 73, 79, 80, 81, 83, 84, 84, 85, 87, 90, 91, 92, 93, 94, 95, 99, 106, 107, 109, 112, 113, 115, 119, 121, 122, 123, 124, 125, 129, 130, 133, 145, 147, 148, 150, 153, 163, 165, 172, 173, 178, 181; by Wendy McKeag: Figures 6, 108, 116, 117, 118, 131, 140, 141, 142, 143, 144, 152, 161, 166, 179, 180, 187, 192, 193 and 196. Photographs by Martin Hall: Figures 2, 5, 12, 19, 24, 26, 27, 37, 45, 46, 64, 65, 98, 120, 137, 146, 164, 174, 175, 176, 185, 186, 212.

Grateful acknowledgement is made to the following for photographs or illustrations supplied, or for permission to reproduce previously published illustrations: **Africana Museum** (Johannesburg), 'Les curieux en extase au les Cordons de souliers', AM 55/543 (Figure 1); Trustees of the **Albany Museum** (Grahamstown): figure 7 from Z. Henderson, 'The context of some Middle Stone Age hearths at Klasies River Shelter 1B: implications for understanding human behaviour,' *Southern African Field Archaeology* 1(1), 1992 (Figure 203); **Archaeology Contracts Office**, University of Cape Town: photographs of excavations at Coburn Street, Cape Town (Figures 16, 111); **British Institute in Eastern Africa** (Nairobi): figures 11 and 22 from P. Robertshaw, 'Gogo Falls. A complex site east of Lake Victoria', *Azania* 26, 1991 (Figures 88, 89); **Cambridge University Press**: figures 6.7 and 6.8 from G. Connah, *Three Thousand Years in Africa: Man and his Environment in the Lake Chad Region of Nigeria*, Cambridge, Cambridge University Press, 1981 (Figures 100, 101); figure 3.4 from J. Parkington, C. Poggenpoel et al., 'Holocene coastal settlement patterns in the Western Cape', in G. Bailey and J. Parkington (eds.) *The Archaeology of Prehistoric Coastlines*, Cambridge, Cambridge University Press, 1988 (Figure 151); figure 5.8 from G. Connah, *African Civilizations. Precolonial Cities and States in Tropical Africa: An Archaeological Perspective*, Cambridge, Cambridge University Press, 1987 (Figure 195); **Community Education Resources**, Centre for African Studies, University of Cape Town: illustrations from Rushdi Nackerdien, *Faizal's Journey: Discovering the Past through Objects* (Figures 34, 35, 36); **David Philip** (Cape Town) for plan of the central town, Great Zimbabwe, from Martin Hall, *The Changing Past: Farmers, Kings and Traders in Southern Africa, 200–1860* (Figure 54); **Hilary Deacon**: photograph of edge damage to stone tool (Figure 128), photographs of Main Site, Klasies River Mouth (Figures 197, 199); **Janette Deacon**: illustration on page 391 of J. Deacon, *The Later Stone Age of Southernmost Africa*, Oxford, British Archaeological Reports, 1984 (Figure 127); **James Denbow**: Botswana aerial photograph (Figure 66); **Getty Conservation Institute** (California): photographs of the australopithecine trackway at Laetoli, Tanzania (Cover and Figure 204); **Department of History of Art Slide Library**, University of Cape Town (Figures 15, 28, 102, 138); **Simon Hall**: photographs of Koonap River Valley (Figure 154), excavations at Welgeluk (Figure 155) and the burial complex at Welgeluk (Figure 156); **David Lewis-Williams and the Rock Art Research**

Unit (University of the Witwatersrand): figures 72, 2 and 14 from J. D. Lewis-Williams and T. Dowson, *Images of Power*, Johannesburg, Southern Book Publishers, 1989 (Figures 168, 182, 183, 184); **Tim Maggs**: photograph, excavations in the Thukela Valley (Figure 86); **Ann Markell**: photograph of the reburial of Flora of Vergelegen (Figure 51); **S. K. McIntosh and R. J. McIntosh**: photographs of the Inland Niger Delta (Figure 188), excavations at Jenne-jeno (Figure 190), ceramics from Jenne-jeno (Figure 194); Executor of the estate of **Chickenman Mkize**, *Butisi Tart*, private collection (Figure 208); **Duncan Miller**: photograph of iron from KwaGandaganda (Figure 135); **Natal Museum** (Pietermaritzburg): aerial photographs, Mgoduyanuka (Figures 77, 78); figure 5 from T. Maggs, 'Msuluzi Confluence: a seventh-century Early Iron Age site on the Tugela River,' *Annals of the Natal Museum* 24(1), 1980 (Figure 62); figure 13 from T. Maggs, *Iron Age Communities of the Southern Highveld*, Pietermaritzburg, Natal Museum, 1976 (Figure 136); **National Museum and Art Gallery** (Botswana): 'Zebra on Wheels', *The Zebra's Voice* 10(3), 1983 (Figure 40); **Newark Museum** (New Jersey) for photograph of the sculpture *Yoruba Village Dignitary with Bicycle* (Figure 213); **John Parkington**: photographs of Dunefield Midden excavations (Figures 11, 82, 139); Robert Broom excavating at Sterkfontein (Figure 103); replicating stone tools (Figure 126); artefacts (Figure 159); **John Parkington and Cedric Poggenpoel**: figure 2 from J. Parkington and C. Poggenpoel, 'A Late Stone Age burial from Clanwilliam,' *South African Archaeological Bulletin* 26, 1971 (Figure 177); **Pijpenkabinet** (Leiden): illustration on page 35 of D. H. Duco, *De Nederlandse Kleipijp. Handboek voor Dateren en Determineren*, Leiden, Pijpenkabinet, 1987 (Figure 105); **Plenum Publishing Corporation** (New York): figure 5 from R. G. Klein and K. Cruz-Uribe, 'The bovids from Elandsfontein, South Africa, and their implications for the age, palaeoenvironment, and origins of the site,' *African Archaeological Review* 9, 1991 (Figure 59); figure 7 from D. Stiles, 'Early hominid behaviour and culture tradition: raw material studies in Bed II, Olduvai Gorge,' *African Archaeological Review* 9, 1991 (Figure 60); figure 11 from J. D. Clark and K. D. Williamson,

'A Middle Stone Age occupation site at Porc Epic Cave, Dire Dawa (east-central Ethiopia). Part I,' *African Archaeological Review* 2, 1984 (Figure 61); figure 4 from A. I. Thackeray, 'Changing fashions in the Middle Stone Age: the stone artefact sequence from Klasies River main site, South Africa', *African Archaeological Review* 7(33), 1989 (Figure 202); **John Rogers**: photograph of part of a deep-sea core (Figure 104); **Routledge** (London): figures 2 and 3 from S. K. McIntosh and R. J. McIntosh, 'Initial perspectives on prehistoric subsistence in the Inland Niger Delta (Mali)', *World Archaeology* 11(2), 1979 (Figures 189, 191); **Sharma Saitowitz**: photograph of trade beads, Mapungubwe (Figure 170); **Andrew Sillen**: photograph of bone samples (Figure 63); **Andrew Smith**: photograph of nomads in North Africa (Figure 14); **Anne Solomon**: drawings of San rock paintings (Figures 32, 75); **South African Archaeological Society**: figure 6 from S. Saitowitz, U. Seemann et al., 'The development of Cape Town's waterfront in the earlier nineteenth century: history and archaeology of the North Wharf,' *South African Archaeological Society Goodwin Series* 7, 1993 (Figure 44); figure 17 from T. M. Evers, 'Excavations at the Lydenburg Heads site, Eastern Transvaal, South Africa,' *South African Archaeological Bulletin* 37, 1982 (Figure 57); figure 5 from I. Plug, 'Some research results on the Late Pleistocene and Early Holocene deposits of Bushman Rock Shelter, Eastern Transvaal,' *South African Archaeological Bulletin* 36, 1981 (Figure 58); figure 3 from B. Werz, 'Maritime archaeological project Table Bay: aspects of the first field season,' *South African Archaeological Society Goodwin Series* 7, 1993 (Figure 97); table 1 from I. Plug, I. and R. Engela, 'The macrofaunal remains from recent excavations at Rose Cottage Cave, Orange Free State,' *South African Archaeological Bulletin* 47, 1992 (Figure 149); figure 9 from S. Hall and J. Binneman, 'Later Stone Age burial variability in the Cape: a social interpretation,' *South African Archaeological Bulletin* 42, 1987 (Figure 157); figure 3 from S. Hall, 'Pastoral adaptations and forager reactions in the Eastern Cape,' *South African Archaeological Society Goodwin Series* 5(42), 1986 (Figure 158); figure 1 from J. D. Lewis-Williams, 'Science and rock art,' *South African Archaeological Society Goodwin Series* 4, 1983 (Figure 167); figures 4, 5 and 9 from H. J. Deacon and V. B. Geleijnse, 'The stratigraphy and sedimentology of the Main Site sequence, Klasies River, South Africa,' *South African Archaeological Bulletin* 43, 1988 (Figures 198, 200, 201); **South African Archives** (Cape Town): plate from Guy Tachard's *Voyage de Siam*, London, 1688. M1/314 (Figure 30); 'Bushman' anatomical photograph (Figure 114); Vergelegen (Figure 160); **South African Museum** (Cape Town): photograph of Lydenburg Head (Figure 4); San group in Botswana (Figure 31); school education (Figure 38); Malawi wood carving (Figure 207); **South African National Gallery** (Cape Town): *Face Value* (Figure 39); Willie Bester, *Challenges Facing the New South Africa*, 1990 (Figure 205); Irma Stern, *Arum Lilies*, 1951 (Figure 211); **Spatial Archaeology Research Unit**, University of Cape Town: photograph, removing graffiti from rock paintings (Figure 42); recording rock paintings (Figure 74); rock-art tracing (Figure 209); **Irma Stern Museum**, University of Cape Town: photograph of West African carved stool (Figure 210); **Transvaal Museum** (Pretoria): photograph of leopard damage to a hominid skull, Swartkrans (Figure 47); **Elizabeth Voigt**: photograph of bone points from Mapungubwe (Figure 132); **Lyn Wadley**: photograph of excavations at Rose Cottage Cave (Figure 22); **Bruno Werz**: photograph, excavations in Table Bay (Figure 96).

chapter 1

Archaeology in Africa

Archaeology is a form of history writing that takes a long, wide view of the past. Archaeologists study human communities from the time, more than 2 million years ago, when the first rough stone tools were fashioned, to the very recent past, recovering the traces that city dwellers have left behind them.

The archaeological story is often detailed, picking out, for example, different activities that took place across a long-abandoned campsite. But broad comparisons, made sometimes from one side of a continent to another, are also ways in which the dynamics of our past may be mapped out.

> **archaeology** the study of the material remains of the human past, ranging from the earliest bones and stone tools to things that are buried or thrown away in the present day

This book focuses on Africa, from the earliest evidence for humanity onwards. At times, Africa has made a formative contribution to global history, while at other times the continent has been the victim of the greed of others. To take a long, wide view of Africa's history is to see a continent that is both unique and a key element in world history.

The chapters that follow are concerned with the practice of archaeology – with the ways in which men and women collect material evidence for the ways in which other men and women lived before them, sometimes only a few years earlier, sometimes at the dawn of humanity.

The focus is on archaeological practice in Africa, particularly southern Africa. This is not because Africa can lay claim to a discipline of its own or because those working in the continent should dissociate themselves from the rest of the world. On the contrary, one of the most important results of archaeological work has been the demonstration that all people, wherever they live, share a common ancestry in Africa. Precisely because all humanity is African, it is not possible to be human and to be dissociated from Africa.

Rather, the focus on archaeology in Africa is a re-spinning of the globe that would put Africa in the centre of the world, rather than leave it as an exotic place on the periphery of Europe and North America: a correction of one part of the manifold legacy of colonialism.

Why should this be necessary?

Pick up almost any introductory textbook on archaeological practice and it is clear that examples of archaeology in Africa are an afterthought. This is not because archaeology is new in Africa. Stone tools were recognised as things made by people (rather than natural phenomena) in Africa as early as in virtually any other part of the world. Archaeology in Africa has had its own traditions of archaeological practice for several generations. Today, research is conducted in Africa that is as advanced and sophisticated as elsewhere.

Why the marginal status? Is it because Africa is still the mysterious, timeless continent, a place without history or science – the Heart of Darkness and the home of the Lion King?

The chapters that follow deal with how archaeologists frame questions, the ways in which archaeological sites were formed, techniques of surveying and sampling, methods of dating the past, ways of interpreting technology and social behaviour and, perhaps most challenging of all, understanding the ways people thought.

These are all cosmopolitan issues of practice, as familiar to archaeologists in London, New York or San Francisco as to those in Lagos, Nairobi or Cape Town. But as issues of prac-tice, they have been modulated by the contexts in which they have been used. Archaeology in Africa has been given its own quality by the experience of research in Tanzania's Olduvai Gorge; or on the edges of the Sahara, where cattle were first domesticated in Africa; or at the pre-colonial city of Great Zimbabwe; or at the tip of the continent, where the first herders in this area grazed their sheep almost two thousand years ago.

Despite the homogeneous view of Africa that is so often held in the West – a vast jungle of colourful tribes and ancient practices – Africa is, of course, a continent as diverse in its history, culture and environment as Europe and North America. Consequently, there are many possible archaeologies of Africa, of which this is only one, coloured by my own experiences in working in southern Africa and within the time frame of the last two thousand years – in a small part of a large continent, and at the tail end of a vast span of time.

> 'The idea that Africa is an idea has an origin. Knowing what this is must be part of the process by which we understand how Europe reached backwards in time or outwards in space to discover what Europe is not ... In their identification of an object called Africa, Euro-peans experienced a fantasy of fulfilled desire in which the distinction between dream and reality was abolished. As a consequence the dogma emerges that Africa was the epitome of economic backwardness and the antithesis of European economic dynamism ...
>
> Certain priorities in African archaeology need to be re-thought. One of these is the need for an historical archaeology of Africa that would address itself more cogently to understanding the origins of the contemporary economic and political conditions that beset the continent ...' (Rowlands 1989: 262–82).

Benchmarks: archaeology's adolescence in Africa

Any form of inquiry rests, inevitably, on what has gone before, on the history of its own practice. Here are some benchmarks that can serve as a framework for the more detailed case studies to follow.

1798: Napoleon's invasion of Egypt leads to the collection and description of Egyptian antiquities and the widespread looting of Egyptian archaeological sites.

1822: The Egyptian system of hieroglyphic writing is deciphered; this provides the basis for the development of Egyptology as a distinct discipline.

1851: A description of archaeological finds in Senegal is published.

1858: The earliest known collections of stone tools are made from the Eastern Cape, South Africa.

1884: The Berlin Conference recognises the Congo Free State, with King Léopold II as its sovereign.

FIGURE 1 THE HOTTENTOT VENUS. European prejudices about Africa developed early, and were based on the widely held assumption that Africans were inherently inferior to Europeans. Between 1810 and 1815 (the year she died in Paris) a southern African woman known as Saartje Baartman (or the 'Hottentot Venus') was exhibited in public in a number of European cities for the amusement and amazement of the public. Parts of her body are still preserved in the collections of the Musée de l'Homme in Paris, despite a number of protests. Concepts of race are discussed in Chapter 8.

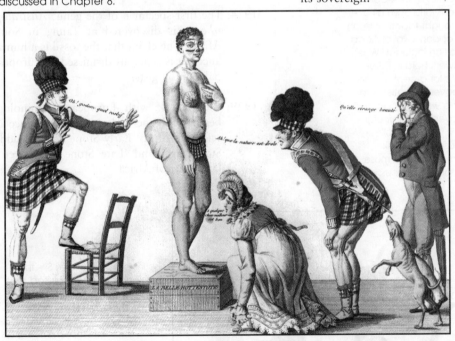

1893: The first known collections of stone tools are made in East Africa.

1897: The destruction of Benin City by a British invasion force, and the plundering of more than 2000 brass works, bring the quality of West African artworks to European attention.

FIGURE 2 'AFRICA: THE ART OF A CONTINENT'. In 1995, artworks from all over Africa were brought together in an exhibition at London's Royal Academy. The exhibition included West African metalwork held in European museums for a century. The catalogue's cover illustration is a brass figure of a woman, cast in Benin in the seventeenth or eighteenth century, from the collections of the Museum für Völkerkunde, Berlin. The role of museums in archaeology is discussed in Chapter 3.

1897: The King of Belgium, Léopold II, opens an exhibition to advocate the colonisation of the Congo, in Tervuren in Belgium. This becomes the basis for a permanent museum collection, and for the publication of archaeological finds from the Congo.

1919: Combined geological and archaeological research begins in East Africa and would lead to the argument that Africa had a series of wet and drier climatic phases ('pluvials' and 'interpluvials') that coincided with glacial advances and retreats in Europe. This would be the basis of archaeological dating in Africa for more than three decades.

1923: The first university lecturer in archaeology is appointed in South Africa.

1924: The first specimen of the genus *Australopithecus* is discovered at Taung in South Africa. The claim that the fossil is a human ancestor is generally dismissed by European palaeontologists.

1929: The break with European terminology begins with the widespread acceptance by scientists of an 'Early Stone Age', 'Middle Stone Age' and 'Late Stone Age' over a large part of Africa.

FIGURE 3 CHARLIE BROWN SHELTER. It has long been recognised that Africa's rock paintings are of major importance in understanding the history of the continent, and in comprehending systems of thought and belief. It is now known that this art is among the earliest in the world. Cognitive archaeology – including the study of rock art – is described in Chapter 12. This group of women, painted for the most part in red, is at Charlie Brown Shelter in the Clanwilliam district of the Western Cape, South Africa.

1931: Excavations begin at Olduvai Gorge, in Tanzania (then Tanganyika).

1935: The Bureau of Archaeology (later the Archaeological Survey) is established in Johannesburg.

1936: More australopithecine fossils are discovered in South Africa, strengthening the claim for human origins in Africa.

1937: First university lecturer in archaeology appointed in Ghana.

1938: The Institut Français d'Afrique Noire (IFAN) is founded in Dakar; an archaeology section is added three years later. This provides an African base for archaeological research in the French West African colonies.

1947: Sixty-one delegates attend the first Pan-African Congress of archaeology in Nairobi, bringing together archaeologists from all parts of Africa for the first time.

1947: The first professional archaeologists are appointed in Zimbabwe (then Southern Rhodesia).

1948: National Party government is elected in South Africa, institutionalising racial discrimination in the form of apartheid. The new government indicates that a planned meeting of the Pan-African Congress of archaeology in Johannesburg will not be welcome; the conference is rescheduled in Algiers.

1953: Excavations begin at Kalambo Falls, on the border between Zambia and Tanzania.

1957: Ghana becomes the first sub-Saharan colony to achieve independence from colonial rule.

1957: Stone tools are discovered in association with australopithecine fossils at Sterkfontein, near Johannesburg.

FIGURE 4 LYDENBURG HEAD. One of archaeology's major achievements in Africa has been to track the origin of the continent's first farming communities in sub-Saharan Africa, and their spread southwards. The life-size ceramic head shown here is one of a group from Lydenburg, near the South Africa–Mozambique border. The methods archaeologists use to study technology, including the manufacture of ceramics, are discussed in Chapter 9, while research into early foodways is the subject of Chapter 10.

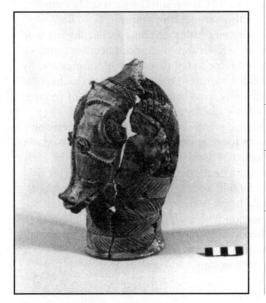

1959: Two separate hominid species are discovered in association with stone tools at Olduvai Gorge, leading to the recognition of the earliest species in the genus *Homo*.

1960: Fourteen French colonies are granted independence, as well as the Congo (Zaire) and Nigeria.

1960: The establishment of the British Institute in Eastern Africa, based in Nairobi, leads to increased research of the Iron Age and of historical settlements along the East African coast.

1961: The first potassium–argon dates from Olduvai Gorge massively expand the span of prehistory and human evolution. At the same time, the increasing availability of radiocarbon age estimations begins to provide African archaeology with an independent dating framework.

Why stop in 1961?

Archaeology is, above all else, the study of people through time. Although important work has been done in fields such as environmental relationships (Chapter 8), early technology (Chapter 9), past economies and diets (Chapter 10), social networks and geographical relationships (Chapter 11), and the way people think (Chapter 12), the results of such studies are invariably set in a time frame.

Moreover, although some archaeologists work within periods for which documentary sources are available to tell them how old things are, by far the majority of the people whom archaeologists study lived before the invention of writing or of calendars.

Consequently, modern archaeology rests on the sturdy foundation of scientific methods of dating, principally potassium–argon dates (for the early human career) and radiocarbon dating (for the last 50 000 years). In the 1960s, archaeologists could begin to move on from their necessary obsession with the age of their sites, and turn instead to interpreting what people were actually doing in the past.

Archaeology had come of age.

FIGURE 5 ZINJ. 'Zinj', the first robust australo-pithecine to be found in East Africa (by Louis Leakey at Olduvai Gorge), dated to between 1.7 and 1.9 million years before the present day. Because of its enormous teeth, the fossil was named the 'nutcracker'. Australo-pithecines are discussed further in Chapter 2, and dating methods in Chapter 7.

The scope of archaeology

There are many different definitions of archaeology. In their book *Archaeology: Theories, Methods and Practice*, Colin Renfrew and Paul Bahn give a descriptive account of the discipline:

'Archaeology is partly the discovery of the treasures of the past, partly the meticulous work of the scientific analyst, partly the exercise of the creative imagination. It is toiling in the sun on an excavation in the deserts of Iraq, it is working with living Eskimos in the snows of Alaska. It is diving down to Spanish wrecks off the coast of Florida, and it is investigating the sewers of Roman York. But it is also the painstaking task of interpretation so that we come to understand what these things mean for the human story' (Renfrew & Bahn 1991: 9).

This range of activities is as characteristic of African archaeology as it is of archaeology in other parts of the world. African archaeology encompasses the discovery of the riches of Tutankhamun's tomb on the Nile, the study of the chemistry of human bones to find out what people ate in the past, and reconstructions of the ways in which people lived from the slightest fragments of evidence. Discovering the archaeology of Africa has included excavations in the Sahara Desert and in Lesotho's snowbound mountains, as well as underwater excavations near the southernmost tip of the continent. But above all else, archaeology in Africa is the careful interpretation of history.

Other definitions of archaeology have been more classificatory, seeking to map out a field of study within the broader domain of the humanities. William Rathje and Michael Schiffer offer the following definition:

'Archaeology is a specialized field of study within anthropology, which itself is a behavioral science that studies human societies and the culture, language, and biology of their people. Languages are studied by linguists and human biology by physical anthropologists. Culture – a society's distinctive behaviors, artifacts and beliefs – is the province of both cultural anthropologists and archaeologists. Cultural anthropologists investigate living societies and focus on belief and behavior. Archaeologists study both modern and ancient societies, emphasizing the relationship between artifacts and human behavior in all times and places' (Rathje & Schiffer 1982: 5).

This definition can be visualised as a tree (see Figure 6). The trunk is the broad field of anthropology – the study of all human societies and the culture, language and biology of their people. There are three main branches of this tree: language (the world of the linguist), human biology (the work of the physical anthropologist) and culture. This third branch is further divided into two smaller branches. The first of these is cultural anthropology (also known as social anthropology). The second is the practice of archaeology.

Rathje and Schiffer's classification works well enough in placing archaeology within the big picture of the humanities. But it is decidedly fuzzy in distinguishing between cultural, or social, anthropology and archaeology. And

FIGURE 6 ANTHROPOLOGY: BRANCHES OF KNOWLEDGE.

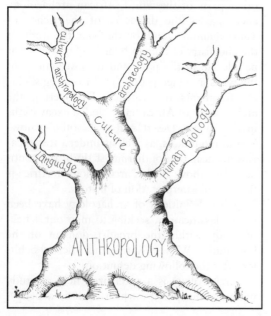

since their book was published in 1982, this distinction has become even fuzzier.

Many social anthropologists are interested in the beliefs and behaviours of past societies, and in seeing how these have changed through time – in other words, they are writing history. Many archaeologists are interested in the lives of people living today or in the very recent past – they are writing cultural anthropology. Some of the most exciting new work in African archaeology involves social anthropologists, historians, archaeologists, linguists and physical anthropologists collaborating and blurring the boundaries of their disciplinary fields.

David Clarke, taking a cue from the novelist Gertrude Stein, has dealt with this definitional morass succinctly. 'Archaeology', Clarke wrote (1968), 'is Archaeology is Archaeology.' In other words, archaeology is simply what archaeologists do and, like all dynamic fields of study, this is changing all the time.

But despite the attraction of leaving the problem of definition and moving on to more interesting subjects, there is a kernel of common identity that leads one archaeologist to recognise another, even if their fields of study are on opposite sides of the world and a million years apart. This is captured in Rathje and Schiffer's phrase 'emphasizing the relationship between artifacts and human behavior in all times and places'. The core of archaeologists' work is the study of artefacts: things fashioned by human agency, whether these be stone tools, pottery vessels, houses, ships or landscapes.

> **artefact** something fashioned by a person or people, ranging from the smallest tools to entire landscapes

Different kinds
of artefacts

One of the most intriguing and difficult questions for archaeologists working in Africa is the definition of humanity itself.

It is now accepted that the first humans evolved in Africa between 4 and 6 million years ago. Most physical anthropologists working in this field group the fossil bones of these first humans into two different groups – known as 'genera' (singular, 'genus') – on the basis of their physical characteristics. One of these genera has been called *Australopithecus* (or 'southern ape'). The first australopithecines were small, with adults less than 1.5 m tall, and weighing between 25 and 45 kg. Later australopithecines were more heavily built. The other genus is our own: *Homo*. The earliest hominids of this type, *Homo habilis*, probably evolved from the lighter-built australopithecines more than 2 million years ago. *Homo habilis* had a larger-sized brain than its australopithecine forebears, and hands and teeth that were more human in their characteristics (Figure 7).

The australopithecines and *Homo habilis* walked upright and lived in social groups. But this alone is not enough for us to consider them fully human. Archaeologists look for additional evidence that they were able to pass on learned ways of living to their children – in other words, that important aspects of their behaviour were not genetically transmitted. The best evidence for the acquisition of such skills, and for the translation of knowledge to others, is collections of stone tools from archaeological sites – that is, the earliest artefacts.

It is not completely clear whether the very first artefacts were made by both genera of hominids, or whether they were the work just of *Homo habilis*. But it is apparent that starting from about 2 million years ago, our ancestors chipped off rough flakes from stone cobbles to make implements. Most of these were probably general purpose tools, used for hacking at animal carcasses that had been scavenged or hunted, or for digging up plant foods (Figure 8).

Humans continued to make and use stone tools for tens of thousands of years, although

FIGURE 8 ARTEFACTS: HAMMERING AND CUTTING. Simple tools for basic tasks can be made from a wide variety of raw materials. From the earliest years of humanity, people fashioned stones to make suitable working edges.

FIGURE 7 HOMINIDS. Left, a gorilla, and right, the skeleton of a modern person. In the centre is a reconstruction of the skeleton of an adult *Australopithecus afarensis*, based on fossil bones more than 3 million years old, discovered in Ethiopia.

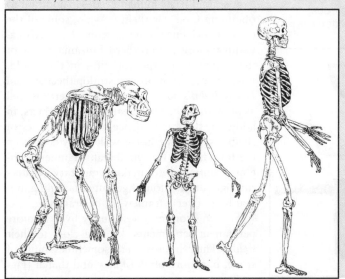

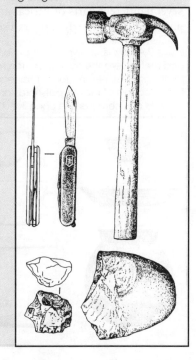

the shape, size and technical expertise that lay behind the manufacture of these artefacts changed considerably with the passage of time. Early people also worked wood, grass, leather and bone, but these less durable artefacts rarely survive on archaeological sites. Because the evidence that we have is so often in the form of collections of stone tools, archaeologists refer to this long initial period of Africa's history as the 'Stone Age'.

Except in unusual circumstances, most people in the Stone Age were nomadic, moving around the country with the changing seasons. This way of life is known as 'hunting and gathering'. There are still hunter–gatherers living in parts of Africa today; probably the most widely known are the San communities of Botswana's Kalahari Desert.

It was only in the last ten thousand years that new ways of living were developed. In several widely separated parts of the world, people began to experiment with planting fields and taming (or 'domesticating') wild animals. This was a long process of change that took many generations to effect. But because it had such a dramatic impact on human history, it is often referred to as the 'agricultural revolution'.

The new farming way of life developed in several different parts of Africa, and the plants and animals that early farmers used depended

FIGURE 9 ARTEFACTS: STORING AND COOKING. Fired clay and metal were the most common raw materials for storage vessels and for containers to cook food. Scatters of broken potsherds are often clear markers of where people once lived.

on local possibilities and conditions. But certain new kinds of artefacts were appropriate for the new way of living, and the use of these eventually spread over much of the continent, marking the end of the long years of the Stone Age. One category was ceramics – fired clay vessels that were used for carrying water, storage, cooking food, and other domestic tasks (Figure 9). Like stone tools, pottery sherds are artefacts that survive the passage of time well, and are often preserved on archaeological sites.

A second new category includes artefacts made of iron. The earliest iron implements were made in Africa some three thousand years ago. Iron tools were needed for agricultural purposes: hoes, axes and other implements for clearing the savanna to cut new fields. Remains of these artefacts are found much less frequently than potsherds. But because of the importance of the new technology, farming sites are grouped together as belonging to the 'Iron Age'. Archaeological sites from the Iron Age are found throughout Africa in those areas where rainfall and soils were adequate for a farming way of life.

The kinds of artefacts studied by archaeologists are not, however, limited to small, portable objects such as stone tools, ceramic vessels and iron tools. Any raw material that a person has fashioned in some way is an artefact, and imaginative archaeological work involves taking into account the full breadth of human ingenuity.

A second basic human need – in addition to obtaining food – is shelter. Again, some of the earliest evidence comes from East Africa. Olduvai Gorge, in northern Tanzania, is one of the richest archaeological sites in the world. Fossil bones from both australopithecines and *Homo habilis* have been preserved here, as well as numerous clusters of early stone artefacts. In addition, there is evidence for simple types of shelter: settings of stones which may have been the foundations for windbreaks. Hunter–gatherers continued to make temporary shelters throughout the Stone Age, often fastening animal hides over a framework of branches.

Farming communities usually lived in more permanent settlements, keeping close to their fields. Their houses were sometimes built of stone, but more often of clay and thatch (Fig-

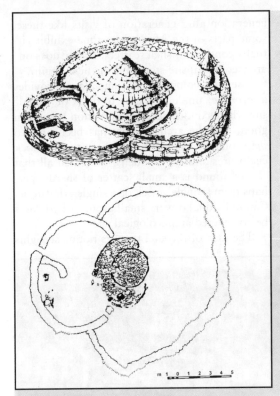

FIGURE 10 SHELTER: A BASIC HUMAN NEED. Archaeologists often find the remains of places where people once lived. This is a reconstruction of a house on the high grasslands of southern Africa – part of a village built long before colonial settlement of the area. The archaeological evidence on which the reconstruction has been based consists of the building's foundations, shown in plan in the lower part of the drawing.

ure 10). Typically, all that survives in the ground for the archaeologist to discover is the clay of the house floor and the outlines of what once were holes, dug originally for the uprights holding up the roof. Although this evidence may seem unpromising, it is often possible to work out what houses (and, indeed, whole villages) would have looked like from these architectural fragments.

Buildings, of course, were made in a wide variety of forms in order to satisfy many different needs. Pre-colonial farmers built livestock enclosures in different styles as well as the monumental architecture that marked out high-status areas. The first colonial settlers put up fortifications, warehouses and dwellings that were mixtures of many architectural traditions. All these structures can be considered as artefacts and within the orbit of archaeological study.

From the earliest times, human activities such as these have modified the landscape in different ways. Sometime between 3 and 4 million years ago, a group of early hominids walked across a muddy pan in present-day Tanzania, leaving a set of footprints which were preserved under the ash from a later volcanic eruption. In the mid-seventeenth century, the Dutch East India Company marked out the grid of Cape Town's streets – the foundations for a landscape now entirely of human agency. In between these extreme examples there are many various circumstances in which the landscape itself has become an artefact.

African Archaeological Review publishes papers on all aspects of African archaeology.

Azania is an archaeological journal that concentrates on East African archaeology.

Journal of African History publishes occasional review articles of new archaeological results.

South African Archaeological Bulletin includes papers on southern African archaeology.

West African Journal of Archaeology specialises in the archaeology of West Africa.

A lot of archaeological writing deals with the details of individual artefacts or groups of artefacts of a particular kind. The pages of specialist journals are full of such reports, which may be highly technical and esoteric. But papers such as these are not the main purpose of archaeological research. Rather, the aim is to bring the results of detailed study together in broader syntheses that map out major themes of Africa's history through space and time.

Concepts:
site and assemblage

In order to generalise beyond particular details, archaeologists make use of a number of abstract concepts that serve to group information together. These concepts are often defined loosely and used differently by individual archaeologists. Their validity is frequently debated. This flexibility is appropriate, for abstract concepts are part of the language of interpretation, rather than of the past itself, and their suitability and meaning have to be continually reviewed as the methods and theories of archaeological research change and develop.

generation after generation of visits like these, some parts of the African coastline exhibit virtually continuous shell scatters. Where does one archaeological site stop, and the next begin?

The archaeology of farming villages provides a second example. It is easy to think of a single site where conditions of preservation have been good, and the archaeologist has been able to map out the positions of houses, livestock enclosures and ash middens. But often all that can be found is a small scatter of sherds, perhaps from a single vessel, or a single grindstone. Can individual or very small groups of artefacts be considered archaeological sites?

The idea of the site, then, is not as straight-

FIGURE 11 DUNEFIELD MIDDEN. This site, on South Africa's west coast, was made when a small band of hunter–gatherers made camp for a few weeks, collecting plant foods, trapping and hunting animals, and collecting shellfish from the nearby beach. Sites such as these are commonly known as 'middens'.

One of the most widely known of these concepts is the 'site'. At first glance, the idea of the archaeological site seems unproblematic. But in practice, it is often difficult to determine where a site begins and ends. For example, many coastal areas were visited repeatedly, through many generations, by groups of hunter–gatherers. People would stay near the shore for a while, collecting shellfish and other foods, and then move away, perhaps following game animals as they moved to inland summer pastures. These hunter–gatherer bands would leave heaps of shells behind them (known as 'middens'; see Figure 11). Some shell middens would be left on top of the middens of previous visits, while others would be on fresh ground. As a result of

forward as it may first have seemed. Considered against the range of possible archaeological circumstances, it can be defined only in the loosest of terms, as a cluster of artefacts that may range from one or two objects to a whole city.

Another way of thinking of the site, which is more pragmatic and perhaps more useful, is simply as a place where an archaeologist has chosen to work. Many (but by no means all) of the artefacts that archaeologists study are buried beneath the ground. Archaeologists excavate in order to find artefacts. Sites are places where archaeological work has taken place: they are rather like holes that have been cut into a box to see what is inside.

FIGURE 12 THE CASTLE, CAPE TOWN. Here, archaeologists are excavating the foundations of kitchens built in the seventeenth century to look after the needs of officers in the Dutch colonial garrison.

Karim Sadr faced the problem of defining an archaeological site in his study of early pastoralists in the southern Atbai region of northeast Africa (Sadr 1991). In this arid environment, the wind is constantly moving the sandy soil about, leaving artefacts scattered around the modern land surface. These artefacts are clearly important evidence for the lives of early nomads, but how can sites be identified and plotted in such confusing circumstances?

Sadr's solution was to measure the varying density of scatters of artefacts. Places where there were less than 25 potsherds in every square metre were defined as 'low density sites', areas with between 25 and 100 sherds/m² were called 'medium density sites', and areas with more than 100 sherds/m² were designated 'high density sites'. This was an arbitrary division by the archaeologist: potsherds were scattered widely, and separate density areas merged into one another in a complex mosaic. But looking at the landscape in this way allowed Sadr to move into the next phase of his research and ask whether these patterns on the windblown ground surface reflected what he couldn't see – more intact sets of artefacts preserved beneath the surface of the desert. Excavation showed that this was indeed the case. High-density potsherd scatters proved to be the fallout from substantial campsites, while low-density scatters reflected short stays in one place.

Sadr's Atbai research shows that although the definition of an archaeological site may be an arbitrary decision, it can also be an essential stage in the process of teasing apart complex and confusing evidence to get at the history beneath.

FIGURE 13 THE SOUTHERN ATBAI AREA.

FIGURE 14 NOMADS IN NORTHERN AFRICA. Nomads have few possessions, leaving only the faintest of archaeological traces behind them.

Another widely used archaeological concept is the 'assemblage'. The term 'assemblage' is often used to designate a group of artefacts that were made at one place and in a specific time period. For example, an archaeologist may talk about the assemblage of artefacts from the lowermost part (or 'layer') of a rock-shelter site. But the term is also used to distinguish between different kinds of artefacts from the same place and time period. So, for example, an archaeological site report may include sections on the ceramic assemblage, the stone tool assemblage or the iron assemblage.

Again, it is important to remember that the notion of the assemblage is an analytical abstraction that is used so that the archaeologist can summarise and generalise complex details more easily. People do not think of their possessions as assemblages of, for example, clothes, crockery, glassware or furniture. Thus people leaving a campsite alongside an East African lake two million years ago did not think of themselves as abandoning an assemblage of stone tools. Likewise a person breaking a pot in a farming village in southern Africa two thousand years ago did not think of the ceramic assemblage that had been created.

A term that is often used alongside the notion of the assemblage in describing an archaeological site is 'feature'. Features are artefacts, in that they have been made by people. But they are also non-movable attributes of archaeological sites: hearths, wall foundations, pits, soil stains that mark where posts once stood in the ground, iron-smelting furnaces and so on.

Archaeologists also make use of abstractions beyond the scale of the individual site, bringing together information from several different sites in an area, and from sites that were used by people successively through time. These larger-scale concepts include the notion of 'culture'. Earlier this century, archaeologists working in Europe and North America began to employ the working assumption that assemblages made up of similar artefacts had been left by members of a common society, whether this was a band, tribe, chiefdom or state. They called these archaeological units 'cultures' or 'traditions'. At the time, deterministic notions were generally fashionable in the social sciences: anthropologists and historians believed that people's identities were fashioned by their environments and were essential features of an

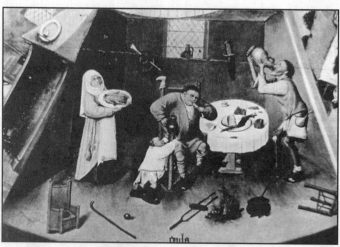

FIGURE 15 ASSEMBLAGES IN THE MAKING. The people in this detail of a fifteenth-century painting are clearly intent on eating and drinking; they are taking the dishes, jugs and other household objects around them for granted. But we can see that a number of different archaeological assemblages are being formed. Before long, the revelries will result in pot-sherds, while furniture already lies broken on the floor. The meat which is being consumed with such gusto will result in an assemblage of animal bones. The small cooking fire in the foreground (with an iron pot next to it) will leave a heap of ash and charcoal – an archaeological feature.

FIGURE 16 EXCAVATING A GRAVE. This nineteenth-century burial – an example of an archaeological feature – is being removed before modern building construction begins in Cape Town.

individual's make-up, rather like hair or skin colour. Although these social concepts have now been completely discredited, the idea of the archaeological culture has proved to be remarkably resilient, and is still used to group together sites in regional syntheses. An archaeological culture is often named after a specific site, either because this was the first place where the particular type of artefact was found, or because the collections from this 'type site' are particularly rich.

Because archaeological cultures are known from the assemblages that define them, they are often said to be made up of 'material culture' – 'the buildings, tools and other artefacts that constitute the material remains of former societies' (Renfrew & Bahn 1991: 489).

The ideas of the archaeological culture and material culture are thus convenient shorthand expressions that allow complicated sets of information to be described and mapped out through space and time; but they can also be easily misinterpreted. This is particularly the case in Africa, where colonialism implanted the old racial assumption that Africans were bounded by primitive cultural practices that set them apart from more civilised Europeans.

In a study which brings together archaeological evidence, oral traditions and written documents, D. Kiyaga-Mulindwa has used the archaeological concept of 'culture' in order to reconstruct the broad history of the Birim Valley in southern Ghana between about AD 1450

FIGURE 17 THE BIRIM VALLEY, GHANA.

and AD 1800 (Kiyaga-Mulindwa 1982). Kiyaga-Mulindwa argues that the potsherds excavated at sites in the valley fall into two categories: 'Earthworks Ware' and 'Atwea Ware', both of them 'cultures' in the sense employed by archaeologists (Figure 18). He suggests that the period when Earthworks Ware was made came to an end as a result of the devastation of the slave trade: 'it is therefore quite possible – the evidence seems to tilt in this direction – that the Birim Valley population of earthwork builders ... was a victim of ethnocide, caused by the Atlantic slave trade, evidence for which has until now been lacking' (Kiyaga-Mulindwa 1982: 76–7). Later, new people moved into the now-empty land, leaving as a trace of their settlement the broken sherds of their distinctly different pottery, labelled by archaeologists as Atwea Ware. Oral traditions identify these people as Twi-speaking communities who called themselves Atweafo:

'The resettlement of the Birim Valley by groups we have associated with "Atwea Ware" was a complex process of migration and settlement. Here, the traditions told today by the descendants of Atweafo contribute considerable evidence to a reconstruction of the history of this period ... The early Atwea settlers appear to have had a problem of finding spous-

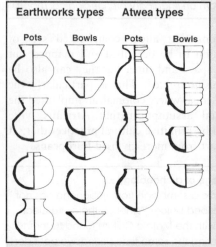

Earthworks types		Atwea types	
Pots	Bowls	Pots	Bowls

FIGURE 18 EARTHWORKS WARE AND ATWEA WARE. In this study of a formative period in Ghana's history, the various shapes of ceramics have been used to identify different archaeological cultures, and these have then been correlated with oral histories and documentary evidence.

es as the area, so their traditions claim, was completely empty of other people, and the original Atweafo group was forced to split up some time after their settlement at Asantemang or Osokore so that they could intermarry without committing incest ...' (Kiyaga-Mulindwa 1982: 77).

Kiyaga-Mulindwa's work shows how the archaeological concept of a culture, defined by a particular category of artefacts (all that now remains of a once-rich and varied set of artefacts in everyday use), can help us reconstruct regional histories when the archaeological evidence is fully integrated with other forms of evidence.

The concept of culture

'The idea of culture as it is used in the modern period acquired the main features of its meaning in the nineteenth century. It shares a complex intellectual history with the ideas of "society", "nation" and "organism", all of which appeared with their contemporary sense around the beginning of the nineteenth century. They have in common the idea of self-contained and self-regulating *wholeness*. Several intellectual sciences developed around these ideas, and today form the content of the academic disciplines of anthropology and/or ethnology, sociology, political economy and/or political science, and biology. The powerful ideas that these sciences have contributed to the world have transformed it completely in the two centuries in which they have been current.

'These ideas have interacted with each other too. The idea of "culture" has frequently been fused with that of "society", and they have been used interchangeably to refer to a general social state of affairs or to a more or less clearly recognisable group of people. Ideas about "cultures" and "organisms" have also influenced each other in the development of theories of evolution, both cultural and biological.

Sometimes people have argued that cultures are like organisms, or even that cultures are a *kind* of organism or "super-organism". Such notions have supported the idea that nations are endowed with unique cultures – something like the genetic component of an organism – which must be protected in order to preserve "society". Unfortunately, these ideas are confused and contribute nothing to a useful understanding of culture.

'Worse still, these ideas have been used to justify repressive and brutal forms of government by arguing that, like an organism, a culture or a nation must defend itself against internal, as well as external, enemies. If the initial premise that cultures are "owned" by nations is accepted, the activities of repressive state bureaucracies may be justified as a form of political hygiene. But in many cases the apparent similarities that exist between ideas of "cultures", "organisms", "nations" and "societies" are the result of the historical development of these ideas in a common intellectual and political context, and not the expression of genuine insight into the human condition ...

'Today, culture is best thought of as a resource. Like other resources, such as energy, sunlight, air and food, it cannot belong exclusively to any particular individual or group of individuals. All groups and individuals must have access to at least some of these resources to survive. Similarly, culture is the *information* which humans are *not* born with but which they need to interact with each other in social life. It must be learned during the long process of education, socialisation, maturing and growing old. Like other kinds of resources, culture can be – and is – controlled by the environment, which places limits on what can and cannot be done. But the physical environment can never determine the content of culture. Unlike other physical resources, however, culture is never "used up", but can only grow, change or even disappear in use. It is people who create cultural resources and control access to them' (Thornton 1988: 19–24).

Environmental archaeology

The study of artefacts (and their collection together as assemblages and cultures) by no means defines the discipline of archaeology. Understanding the past requires more than studying the things that people made: it also requires analysing the environments in which people lived, the ways in which these environments were changed through human intervention, and the things people ate.

'Environmental archaeology is now a well-developed discipline in its own right. It views the human animal as part of the natural world, interacting with other species in the ecological system or *ecosystem*. The environment governs human life: latitude and altitude, landforms and climate determine the vegetation, which in turn determines animal life. And all these things taken together determine how and where humans have lived – or at least they did until very recently' (Renfrew & Bahn 1991: 195).

A comparison between this clear manifesto for the determining role of nature, and the reservations that have been expressed about this view, reveals one of the tensions that run through the practice of archaeology: what is the extent of environmental influence on the ways in which people behave?

Those plant and animal remains and geological and geomorphological features that are relevant to understanding the ways in which people lived in the past are sometimes called 'ecofacts'. This archaeological neologism expresses well the important role of environmental archaeology. Ecofacts include food waste abandoned on archaeological sites (animal bones, or faunal assemblages, and plant assemblages); fossilised pollen, which is evidence for the plants and trees growing near to a site in the past; and sediments, which may indicate climatic conditions.

FIGURE 19 ECOFACTS. Excavation forms only a small part of archaeological research. Here, marine shells from a midden assemblage are being sorted into different categories so that they can be identified and measured. Information such as this is a basis for working out how people made a living in the past.

Africa's changing environment

We are used to thinking of Africa as a mosaic of different environments: the tropical forests of West Africa, the dry sand dunes of the Sahara, East Africa's savanna grasslands, the Mediterranean climate of the Cape. We are also used to seeing these as unchanging – the 'eternal' desert, the 'timeless' wilderness of the bush. But in reality, climate and the distribution of animals and plants across the continent are changing all the time. Some of these changes are small-scale and quite rapid; study of the annual growth rings of trees, for instance, has shown that in parts of southern Africa rainfall fluctuates in cycles of between 10 and 20 years. Other changes are more dramatic, but take place over very long time periods. Around parts of Africa's coast, for example, changes in the height of the sea-level have either inundated lower-lying areas or opened up vast plains across what is today the sea-bed.

Archaeologists make use of the geological time-scale as a general framework for understanding the changes in Africa's environment. This system originated in the nineteenth century, when geologists discovered that there had been a series of 'ice ages' during which ice sheets and glaciers expanded outwards from the colder northern and southern parts of the globe, taking up vast quantities of water and causing sea-levels to fall. In between the ice ages were warmer periods ('interglacials') when the ice sheets melted back and the sea-level rose again. Today, geologists know that these changes were far more complex than was first thought; nevertheless, the earlier terms still provide a useful general framework.

The last of the ice ages started in a geological period known as the Pleistocene, and lasted from about 1.6 million years ago until about 10 000 years ago. The period that followed the Pleistocene – which is the period in which we live today – is known as the Holocene.

In understanding Africa's changing environments through the Pleistocene and the Holocene, rainfall ('precipitation') and temperature are the most important factors. Together, they determine the extent of rivers and lakes, the densities and types of plants that can grow, and therefore the species and numbers of animals that can live in different parts of the continent.

'Climate influences every component of the environment – hydrological and biochemical cycles, plant cover, animal life and human activity. Since most of Africa lies within 30° of the equator, temperatures are generally above the global mean and adequate for plant growth throughout the year except at high altitudes and in the extreme north and south of the continent. On the other hand, evaporation losses are everywhere great, exceeding 1000 mm for the rainforest and 3000 mm from lakes in arid regions. So, availability of water at the surface and for replenishing aquifers depends on adequate rainfall; precipitation is the most important of the climatic elements' (Grove 1993: 32).

As with the rest of the world, the story of Africa's changing environment has become increasingly complicated as more and more research has been conducted. It used to be thought that there were general changes that affected the whole continent; now it is clear that global changes in weather patterns affected different areas in various ways.

During the Pleistocene, snow-lines on Africa's high mountain chains came further down the slopes, and it was generally colder. In North Africa, average temperatures were about 9°C less than today, and to the south some 5°C less. Winds were stronger. Between the tropics of Capricorn and Cancer (from present-day Sudan, southwards to Zimbabwe), there was much less rainfall than today: the Sahara extended 500 km south of its modern limits. But in other areas, such as the northern Kalahari in Botswana, there were extensive lakes that have since dried up.

The end of the Pleistocene brought marked changes in these climates. The most striking of these was the amount of annual rainfall between the two tropics, which was much higher in the early part of the Holocene than it is today. Between about 9500 and 8500 years ago, closed basins were flooded by lakes, some of which rose as much as 100 m above their present-day levels. But at the same time, the southern part of the continent became drier

The language of archaeology ...

'In addition to the material culture assemblage, Feature 22a at Bobonong also contained a substantial faunal assemblage, comprising domestic cattle and a variety of wild animals. The pollen profile shows that at the time Bobonong was occupied, there were extensive grasslands close to the village, rather than the near-desert conditions of modern times. This reconstruction of the early environment is confirmed by the analysis of sediments from the now-dry river course near by.'

(Extract from an imaginary archaeological report)

than today (Figure 20).

By 7500 years ago, this intertropical wet phase was ending, and there is evidence that lake levels had begun to fall (although there were complex oscillations caused by short periods of renewed high rainfall). But north and south of the tropics conditions were again different. In Botswana's northern Kalahari area, for instance, rainfall peaked between 5000 and 6000 years ago – at a time when the Sahara had become markedly drier.

By about 3500 years ago, Africa's present-day climate had set in over most of the continent. There were, however, phases of higher rainfall after this date in several places, and evidence for climatic instability exists today. Rather than being an immutable characteristic of an area, the weather is, and always has been, liable to change.

What are the implications of these climatic changes for Africa's human communities? The earliest hominids (the australopithecines and *Homo habilis*) lived in Africa before the beginning of the Pleistocene, when the overall climate was probably warmer and wetter than today. Through many generations, the average size of the hominid brain increased and the skeleton became better adapted to a life away from the forests – the habitats of the great apes, with whom we share common ancestors. Early people were able to walk and run more easily than their predecessors. In recognition of these

FIGURE 20 RAINFALL IN AFRICA BETWEEN 8500 AND 9500 YEARS AGO.

Wetter than now
Drier than now

0   1000   2000 km

changes, physical anthropologists talk about the evolution of a new species within the genus *Homo*. This new species is called *Homo erectus*, and was the direct descendant of *Homo habilis*. It is important to bear in mind that this species distinction is a convenience which helps to organise the complicated fossil record into general categories. The real history of our genus is one of long, continual change that links us directly with the first, tool-using hominids who lived in Africa 2 million years ago.

In comparison with its ancestors, *Homo erectus* was a remarkable creature. Through much of the cold, dry Pleistocene, these early people spread outwards to live in most parts of Africa, and then on into Europe and Asia. Our knowledge of the Pleistocene environment serves to emphasise the importance of social behaviour. Without the ability to control fire, build shelters and fashion artefacts, it is difficult to see how *Homo erectus* could have adapted to the varied and often challenging environments of the Pleistocene world.

Just as *Homo erectus* developed from *Homo habilis*, so our own species, *Homo sapiens*, evolved in its turn from *Homo erectus*. Well before the end of the Pleistocene, all people were like us physically.

The changes in climate that marked the beginning of the Holocene in Africa had major consequences for the continent's people. With the wetter phase in the central African latitudes between 8500 and 9500 years ago, new wetland and lakeside habitats developed and were used by hunters and gatherers. The later, much drier climatic phases stimulated changes that were closely connected with the development of the farming way of life in the continent.

The Saharan lakes and river banks were settled by hunter–gatherer bands, who made distinctive bone harpoons and pottery, often decorated with wavy lines. By identifying the animal and fish bones from these sites ('faunal analysis'), archaeologists have been able to work out what these people were eating. Fishing was naturally important, but nearby grasslands were a source of wild animals as well. Collections of excavated bones also show that crocodile and hippopotamus were then living in what is now the heart of the desert.

'Fishing and the exploitation of other aquatic food resources now played a much larger part in the economy of a vast area of the central and southern Sahara from the Nile Valley at least as far to the west as Mali. Sites were now concentrated on the shores of rivers and lakes which were significantly higher and more extensive than those of today. Although at most sites hunting and grain collecting were continued on a reduced scale, the pre-eminence of fishing now allowed larger populations to remain for longer periods of time at individual sites' (Phillipson 1985: 106).

But the drier conditions that had well set in by 6000 years ago must have made life difficult for the descendants of these fishing communities. As the lake levels fell, the rich shoals of fish declined, and as the rainfall decreased, the grasslands diminished in carrying capacity, resulting in the steep decline in density of the animal populations. People needed new ways of living. A solution was to specialise: to concentrate on a particular animal species, taming the animals and controlling their access to grazing and water. In this way, the environment could be made more productive, and the effects of the deteriorating climate counteracted. By studying and measuring animal bones from these early herding sites, archaeologists have been able to track this process of domestication. Some of the earliest evidence for the domestication of cattle in Africa comes from Uan Muhuggiag in the central Sahara, where the skull of a short-horn ox has been dated to about 7000 years before the present day. This is backed up by the skeleton of a domestic cow, excavated from the site of Adrar Bous in Ténéré, and dated to about 6500 years ago (Figure 21).

'Ecofacts' such as these, although often widely separated in space and time, provide vital evidence for the changing environments of Africa, the opportunities that such changes offered (as well as the constraints they imposed), and the ways in which human communities adapted their behaviour to the climate and to the resources that were available to them.

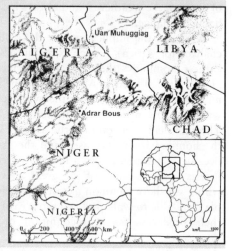

FIGURE 21 SAHARAN ARCHAEOLOGICAL SITES WHERE EVIDENCE FOR THE EARLY DOMESTICATION OF CATTLE HAS BEEN FOUND.

Context

The language of archaeology ...

'It was clear that Feature 22a at Bobonong had not been disturbed, and that the assemblages were in their original contexts. This demonstrates that the people who made the pottery herded domestic stock and hunted wild animals. On other parts of the site, however, artefacts had been turned up by ploughing; these collections have not been included in the analysis because they are, unfortunately, out of context.'

(Extract from an imaginary archaeological report)

Artefacts and ecofacts form the basic material of the story that archaeology has to tell. But, as should be clear from some of the examples that have already been given, their relationships with one another are just as important as the objects themselves.

For instance, it is only possible to say with certainty that the people who made beautifully fashioned bone harpoons some 8000 years ago used them to spear fish, because both harpoons and fish bones have been found in close association with one another at the spot where they were dropped by the person who last handled them. It is only possible to argue that early hominids living in Olduvai Gorge were making windbreaks, because the stone foundation blocks were found in their original positions, and were mapped and photographed before they could be disturbed.

Archaeologists refer to the associations between objects on a site as their 'context'. Although it is often necessary to work with artefacts that have been casually collected, or have been turned up by farming or construction work, it is always better to work on a site that has not been disturbed. Many countries have legislation that protects archaeological sites, and specifies that only qualified archaeologists may carry out excavations. The detailed recording of context is one of the things that differentiate archaeology from treasure hunting.

FIGURE 22 ROSE COTTAGE CAVE. This site, on the border between South Africa and Lesotho, and close to Maseru, was visited by hunter–gatherer bands for tens of thousands of years. The recovery of this history has depended on close attention to the contexts of the different assemblages: a precise record of where each artefact was found, and the sort of deposits in which it was buried.

Context, however, is more than the situation in which an artefact is discovered. Context is also the whole set of beliefs and perspectives in which an archaeologist frames a question, pursues a research project and, eventually, writes history. And, as such, this broader context has a past which is just as important as the present. Like all historians, archaeologists work in the shadow of their own past, either continuing previously established lines of reasoning and interpretation, or reacting against them.

Early archaeology in Africa

The history of archaeology in Africa can best be understood as an interplay between approaches developed and tried out in Europe, and the archaeological record of the different parts of the continent as it has been increasingly developed over the past century and a half. This dynamic has been driven by two overwhelming characteristics of African archaeology: its implication in Europe's colonisation of Africa, and the fact that until quite recently, all professional archaeologists, including those born in Africa, have been trained either in Europe or in North America. It is only in recent years that specifically African approaches to writing archaeology have begun to develop, and the intellectual hegemony of the West has been challenged (Trigger 1990).

'The whole Expedition is a fascinating turning point in European attitudes to the East. In many ways the elaborate surveys, maps and drawings, and the stealing of objects and cultural monuments to embellish France, were an early example of the standard pattern of studying and objectifying through scientific enquiry that became a hallmark of European imperialism and a basis of the 19th-century "Orientalism" described so well by Edward Said. On the other hand, there were still many traces of the older attitude towards Egypt, and among the scientific members of the Expedition there was the belief that, in Egypt, they could learn essential facts about the world and their own culture and not just exotica to complete Western knowledge – and domination – of Africa and Asia' (Bernal 1991a: 184).

The first part of the continent to attract the West's attention was Egypt. Early interest was given great impetus by Napoleon's invasion in 1798, and the record of Egyptian antiquities, published in the *Description de l'Egypte* between 1809 and 1813. The consequence was widespread popular knowledge and extensive looting, which had an irreparable effect on Egypt's cultural heritage (Fagan 1977).

In 1799 a French officer dug up an inscribed, black basalt stone, just over a metre long, at Rashîd (Rosetta) about 50 km from Alexandria. After the French surrendered Egypt in 1801, the Rosetta Stone, as it had become known, passed into British hands and to the British Museum, where it is housed today. The inscriptions, written by the priests of Memphis in 196 BC in two languages – Egyptian and Greek – and three writing systems – hieroglyphics, demotic script (a cursive form of hieroglyphics) and the Greek alphabet – were finally translated by Jean François Champollion in 1822, forming the basis for the distinct discipline of Egyptology (Aldred 1984).

Other parts of Africa had, of course, experienced the impact of European colonialism long before Napoleon sailed for the Nile. But archaeological evidence remained largely unrecognised because there was no intellectual framework for conceptualising the continent's early history. The standard interpretation of the Bible still held that the world had begun in 4004 BC. It was developments in the disciplines of geology and natural history that allowed prehistoric archaeology to emerge as a field of study.

In geology, it was argued, first by James Hutton (whose *Theory of the Earth* was published in 1785) and then by Charles Lyell (in his *Principles of Geology*, 1833), that ancient geological processes were the same as (or 'uniform' with) processes that could be observed happening in the present day: the deposition of sediments into stratigraphical layers, and the erosion of rocks and soils by wind, water and other agencies. This principle, known as 'uniformitarianism', now seems so self-evident as to be hardly worth stating. But in the early nineteenth century it was revolutionary, challenging the Bible as the only authority on the history of the world and opening up the possibility of a distant past (Renfrew & Bahn 1991).

It was one thing to have a radically extended concept of the past, but how was it to be ordered and conceptualised without the apparatus of conventional history, such as lists of kings, dates and documentary sources? A scheme was almost immediately supplied by the Danish scholar C. J. Thomsen, in his guidebook to the National Museum of Copenhagen, published in 1836 and translated into English in 1848. Thomsen proposed three technological phases in human development: the Stone Age, Bronze Age and Iron Age. Later, the Stone Age was divided into the Old Stone Age (the Palaeolithic) and the New Stone Age (the Neolithic). Then in 1841, Boucher de Perthes, a French customs official, showed that shaped stones, found in ancient river-gravel deposits with fossil animal bones, had been fashioned by humans. Prehistoric archaeology was now launched as a discipline (Daniel 1980).

The contribution of natural history to the new discipline came from the theory of evolution. This had developed over a number of years, and was synthesised by Charles Darwin in *The Origin of Species*, published in 1859. Evolutionary theory provided a basis for recognising and classifying human fossils (Gowlett 1990). It also stimulated ethnographers to develop classifications of living societies, which were seen as representative of the various stages that European civilisation had passed through before attaining its cultural superiority. At the base was 'savagery' (hunting), followed by the higher order of 'barbarism' (simple farming) and, ultimately, 'civilisation' (Renfrew & Bahn 1991). Social evolutionism of this kind was to provide a major buttress for colonial ideologies: by arguing that Europeans brought preordained progress and enlightenment to the 'dark continent' it justified expansion into Africa and the destruction of indigenous customs and systems of social organisation. Ironically, social evolutionism also had a major influence on Karl Marx's philosophy of history.

Early archaeological work in Africa has to be understood against this background in European studies. Colonial collectors saw themselves as representatives of their home countries, rather than of their colonies, and often sent specimens back to Europe for study. During periods of home leave, they visited colleagues in London or Paris or Vienna, and exchanged views. Africa, however remote, had become an extension of the Victorian drawing-room, rather than a place in its own right.

Some of the earliest descriptions of African antiquities outside Egypt came from Senegal in 1851 (de Barros 1990), and from the Eastern Cape, South Africa, where the British settler T. H. Bowker built up and described a collection in 1858 (J. Deacon 1990). The first known collections from East Africa came somewhat later, in 1893 (Robertshaw 1990). These amateur archaeologists – often colonial administrators – worked within the European classificatory systems, describing their finds as 'Palaeolithic' or 'Neolithic'. It was generally assumed that these collections provided evidence for prehistoric migrations into Africa from Europe.

Other developments in archaeology stemmed more directly from the politics of colonial expansion. In 1890 Mashonaland (later to become Southern Rhodesia and then Zimbabwe) was occupied by the British South Africa Company; shortly thereafter the first archaeological expedition set off to the site of Great Zimbabwe. In 1897 a British invasion force captured and destroyed the ancient West African city of Benin, plundering more than 2000 works in brass. This hoard drew European attention to the riches of West African art (Kense 1990).

Thus, by the end of the century, archaeology was established in Africa, but as an accomplice in colonial expansion and domination. Controlled, careful excavations had begun with the work of Flinders Petrie in Egypt (O'Connor 1990), but further south fieldwork was driven by the wish to prove either outside stimulus for Africa's past or the primitiveness of Africa's prehistory. Thus G. W. Stow, summarising his view of the continent's past, could write in 1905 that 'the seething mass of equatorial life' had been hemmed in by Mediterranean civilisation to the north, 'until amid internal heavings and internecine wars another storm wave rose which, beaten from the north, would naturally expend its fury in the opposite direction ... until they came into contact with strange white-faced men still more invincible than they imagined themselves to be, against whom, with many minor fluctuations, the tidal wave of rude barbarism beat in vain' (Stow 1905: 233-5).

Great Zimbabwe: rumours and prejudice

The first European power to colonise Africa in modern times was Portugal. In 1415 Portuguese forces captured the North African town of Ceuta, and in the following decades fleets sailed regularly from Lisbon to establish trading connections down the West African coast. Early in the new century, the Portuguese founded permanent garrisons on the East African coast, and in the 1530s the first trading posts were set up inland, along the Zambezi River.

The Portuguese, along with many other Europeans, believed that a fabulously wealthy Christian king, called Prester (or Priest) John, lived somewhere in Africa's interior. These stories were run together with myths about the lost wealth of the biblical characters King Solomon and the Queen of Sheba. A travel account called *Da Asia*, which had first been circulated in 1552, summarised the prevalent myths of the time. *Da Asia* told of reports of abandoned gold mines and stone buildings (known as 'Symbaoe') in the interior, that had been built on instructions from Prester John. These were the ruins which were later to become known as Great Zimbabwe. In the belief that Prester John's kingdom was the source of the gold that had previously reached coastal towns through indirect trade, the Portuguese mounted laborious expeditions, often sweltering in heavy suits of armour. Their men weakened by fever and picked off by defending tribesmen, such incursions were invariably disastrous.

For two more centuries, expeditions such as these ended only in frustration: it is testimony to the power of the legend that the search continued at all. But in 1871 tangible evidence at last came to light. Carl Mauch, an energetic and credulous explorer, came across the ruins of Great Zimbabwe. In his journal Mauch assumed a posture that Hollywood was to adopt for its image of the archaeologist a hundred years later. Working alone, with sketch book and revolver at the ready, he struggled 'through thick grass intertwined with leguminous creepers' while keeping 'well hidden from possible observers by the tall grass'. Applying an extremely tenuous chain of reasoning, Mauch noted that splinters of wood from a cross-beam were very similar to the wood of his pencil, indicating that both were cedar.

FIGURE 23 CARL MAUCH'S SKETCH OF GREAT ZIMBABWE.

'It can be taken as a fact that the wood which we obtained actually is cedar-wood and from this that it cannot come from anywhere else but from the Libanon [*sic*]. Furthermore only the Phoenicians could have brought it here; further Salomo [Solomon] used a lot of cedar-wood for the building of the temple and of his palaces: further: including here the visit of the Queen of Seba [*sic*] and, considering Zimbaye or Zimbaöe or Simbaöe written in Arabic, (of Hebrew I understand nothing), one gets the result that the great woman who built the *rondeau* could have been none other than the Queen of Seba' (Burke 1969: 190).

Although Mauch's journal was not published at the time, his theories were known to his contemporaries. According to Theodore Bent, who was himself to work at Great Zimbabwe twenty years later, Mauch maintained that the Hill Ruin was a copy of King Solomon's temple on Mount Moriah, while the lower ruins were a copy of the palace in which the Queen of Sheba stayed while in Jerusalem. Thomas Baines's 'Map of the Gold Fields of South Eastern Africa', published in 1873, showed the ruins of Great Zimbabwe and labelled them as 'the supposed realm of Queen of Sheba'.

In 1890, when Mashonaland was occupied by Cecil Rhodes's British South Africa Company, Great Zimbabwe became an imperial possession. Rhodes became obsessed with the place, acquiring Mauch's finds and equipping expeditions to dig for evidence. In 1891, the first archaeological expedition to Great Zimbabwe left England, under Rhodes's patronage and with the support of the Royal Geographical Society and the British Association for the Advancement of Science. It was led by Theodore Bent, an antiquarian who had travelled extensively in the eastern Mediterranean, and who was considered an expert on Phoenicia. The results of his excavations were published in 1892 under the title *The Ruined Cities of Mashonaland*.

Bent's book was the first to devise that ambivalent combination of collision and collusion with popular mythology that would characterise subsequent archaeological work at Great Zimbabwe. In it Bent dismissed popular opinion and asserted the need for proper scientific work if the truth was to be found. 'From Fort Victoria', he reported, 'came over during our stay a whole host of visitors to see how we were getting on. Prospecting parties going northwards tarried at Fort Victoria for a rest, and came over to see the wondrous ruins of Zimbabwe. Englishmen, Dutchmen from the Transvaal, Germans, all sorts and conditions of men came to visit us, and as temporary custodians of the ruins we felt it our duty to personally conduct parties over them, thereby hearing all sorts and conditions of opinions as to the origin of the same ... The names of King Solomon and the Queen of Sheba were on everybody's lips, and have become so distasteful to us that we never expect to hear them again without an involuntary shudder' (Bent 1969: 64).

But although Bent dismissed King Solomon and the Queen of Sheba from his stage, he retained and strengthened the structure of the mythology that had sustained them for so many years. Bent used his authority as an Orientalist, buttressed by the expert evidence of Professor Müller of Vienna, 'the great Austrian authority on Southern Arabian archaeology', to show that Great Zimbabwe was the work of Sabaean Arabs garrisoned in enemy territory and mining gold for Mediterranean and Asian merchants. The influence of Phoenicia was marked by the evidence at the site for phallic worship, while the 'Temple' served as a solar calendar. Proof of northern connections was given in the orientation of the monoliths on the Temple walls. 'It is remarkable', Bent felt, 'that only stars of the northern hemisphere seem to have been observed at Zimbabwe ... This, of course, points to a northern origin for the people ...' (Bent 1969: 174).

Bent saw this early Mashonaland civilisation as overrun by the dark forces of barbarism – the ancestors of the 'Karanga'. Their past, 'like all Kaffir combinations', was the story of 'a hopeless state of disintegration'. They were little more than animals, to be classed together with 'a tribe of baboons', 'more closely allied to one another than they are to the race of white men, who are now appropriating the territory of both' (Bent 1969: 33, 43).

The dark continent

Extravagant claims for Africa's indebtedness to outside influences continued to be made well into the twentieth century. In West Africa, for example, Maurice Delafosse spent most of his life trying to establish the extent of Egyptian and Phoenician influence on the Ivory Coast. Delafosse's work had the virtue of illustrating the importance of early Arabic sources for African archaeology, as he used them for their descriptions of the various towns and capitals of the Ghana, Mali and Songhai empires. However, his claim that the Kingdom of Ghana was established by Judaeo-Syrian invaders was nothing but speculation (de Barros 1990).

A similar diffusionist claim, this time for deep prehistory, was made by Oswald Menghin in his synthesis of the Stone Age of Central Africa, published in 1925. Menghin developed the notion of a widespread 'Tumba Culture', with global connections, covering the Belgian and French Congo as well as Angola. His associations with Nazism brought to him both the rectorship of the University of Vienna and exile, after the Second World War, in Argentina from where he continued to look for global diffusionist connections (de Maret 1990).

There are direct links between claims such as these and present-day representations of Africa as the 'dark continent' – a place where history must always come from outside, where immigrants bring enlightenment to people stuck in permanent conditions of savagery and barbarism (M. Hall 1995).

'Centuries before tall ships were ever dreamed about, long before the dawn of a western civilization, a nomadic tribe from northern Africa set out to seek a new world, a land of peace and plenty. The tribe wandered for many years in search of such a magical place, and at last their quest was rewarded. The land they discovered to the south became the legendary valley of the sun, known today as the Valley of Waves. Not only did they bring with them a rich culture, but also architectural skills which were exceptional even by today's standards. Something special was created: from the jungle rose an amazing city with a magnificent Palace, a world richer and more splendid than any they had ever known ... Then a violent earthquake struck this idyllic valley, the survivors fled, never to return and left it to be found and restored by archaeologists centuries later. We have today restored it to its former glory ...

'Discover the most extraordinary hotel in the world ...'

(Visitor information sheet, The Palace at Sun City, North-West Province, South Africa)

Great Zimbabwe Robbery

Theodore Bent, the first to excavate at Great Zimbabwe, found Africa a 'mysterious and awe-inspiring continent'. It was also a fitting object of study for the archaeologist, 'almost the very last person who a short time ago would have thought of penetrating its vast interior' (Bent 1969: 42). Stories of Great Zimbabwe's artefacts spread quickly, and Cecil Rhodes moved to turn antiquarianism to profit, promoting Rhodesia Ancient Ruins Ltd as a company with exclusive rights to work the sites for treasures. Involvement in this licensed depredation gave a local journalist, Richard Nicklin Hall, the opportunity to present himself as an antiquarian and scholar. His *Ancient Ruins of Rhodesia*, published in 1902 in collaboration with W. G. Neal, a local prospector, offered an archaeological periodisation: a 'Sabaean Period' (2000–1100 BC) followed by a 'Phoenician

FIGURE 24. ENTRANCE TO THE GREAT ENCLOSURE, GREAT ZIM-
BABWE. The construction of Great Zimbabwe
involved the highly skilled use of drystone walling,
both for coursing and for features such as door-
ways and steps. This quality of work was ignored
by many writers, intent on portraying Africa as
the 'dark continent'.

trespassing in forbidden precincts possesses
one'.

'Large bats and night-moths fly unpleasantly
close to one's face ... A frog in some dark and
dank corner startles one with a loud croak of
"*Work!*" ... A low moaning, soughing wind
now springing up sweeps round the temple and
rustles in the upper branches of the trees. The
temple is now lovely in the extreme. The shadows on the walls are now in quick movement.
Fireflies swing their tiny lamps over dark enclosures. The white radiance of the moonlight
completely invests the conical tower, its intense
whiteness being heightened by the large, thick,
and dark-foliaged trees on either side ...'

From this unambiguous sexual allegory the
writer moves to interpretative speculation:
'Amidst such surroundings a score of ancient
scenes are pictured in one's mind – the
approaching priests with processual chant
emerging through the north entrance from the
Sacred Enclosure, the salutation to the emblems
of the gods, the light of altar fire and torch
reflected upon the walls and upon the sacred
golden fillets bound round the brows of the
priests, the incense-laden air, the subdued mur-
murings of the waiting crowd of worshippers,
the invocation of the deity by priests who stand
upon the high raised platform in front of the
conical tower, the mystic rites, dark enchant-
ments, and the pious orgies' (R. N. Hall 1905:
23, 24).

Hall widely reflected the beliefs of his times.
The list of subscribers to his later *Prehistoric
Rhodesia* (1909) reads like the invitation list for
a colonial ball: His Excellency the High Com-
missioner for South Africa, His Excellency the
Governor of the Cape Colony, His Worship the
Mayor of the City of Cape Town, Professors
from the South African College, Judges of the
Supreme Court and many others. Hall was also
an 'enthusiast', digging trenches with an aban-
don which showed none of Bent's declared

Period' (from the start of the Christian era), a
transitional period, and a final 'decadent period', when descendants of the first builders
mixed with the local population (R. N. Hall &
Neal 1902). In the same year that his first book
was published, Hall was appointed curator of
Great Zimbabwe. Having dug the site extensively, he published his results in a second book,
Great Zimbabwe, in 1905.

Hall closely followed Theodore Bent's interpretations of the site, dedicating the book to his
mentor and recalling phallic worship, the celebration of the sun and the moon, and the
destructive force of the 'Kaffirs'. But *Great
Zimbabwe* was as much a work of romance as
an attempt at scholarship. Despite the detailed
descriptions of artefacts, there are useful hints
for the visitor and Gothic descriptions of the
ruins by moonlight. Here is Hall's invitation to
his Temple. The natives are preparing to celebrate the full moon, with fertility signs exposed
on their bare stomachs: '... the noise of the village drums, the blowing of horns, and the deep
wild choruses of crowds of men, mingled with
the voices of women and girls, were waxing
louder and more incessant as midnight
approached.' The 'Temple', in contrast, is silent
– a place where 'an inexplicable sensation of

respect for method, and advancing his claims for the lost civilisation with none of the dry caution of the scholar. Under his curatorship, extensive and irreparable damage was done to the site, damage which still scars Great Zimbabwe and has seriously inhibited later archaeological research.

The first professionals

There was a complex interaction between the ideology of European colonial expansion and the consequences of some of the research that colonisation promoted and supported. 'While African archaeology has been powerfully influenced by its social and political milieu, its often unanticipated findings have altered entrenched interpretations of African history. Because of this, archaeology has played a significant role in helping to promote the decolonisation of Africa. It is more than a passive reflection of social, political and economic conditions, but must be seen as a discipline that plays an active role in helping to bring about social changes' (Trigger 1990: 309–10).

With a momentum that accelerated through the years, twentieth-century archaeology in Africa became professionalised and increasingly independent of direct government control. Individual archaeologists often held strong liberal views that were opposed to racism and discrimination, and were sympathetic to the goals of African nationalist movements. And, not surprisingly, a growing rift developed between most of the continent and the south, where the winds of change were slow to blow.

The basis for the increasing professionalisation of the discipline was improved institutional support. This came first in francophone West Africa. In 1897, an exhibition devoted to the Belgian colony of the Congo had been opened at Tervuren as part of King Léopold II's efforts to convince Belgians of the value of colonialism. This exhibition had included both ethnography and prehistoric archaeology, and formed the basis of a permanent museum collection. Through the years that followed, Tervuren became an important centre for African studies (de Maret 1990). In 1923 the first university appointment in archaeology was made in South Africa (at the University of Cape Town). In 1935 the Bureau of Archaeology (later the Archaeological Survey) was set up in Johannesburg; it was to acquire extensive influence in

> **Thurstan Shaw (appointed to a lectureship in Ghana in 1937):**
>
> 'I suppose at the beginning I had two principal aims, which in fact fed into each other. The first was to gather, as systematically as possible, all the archaeological evidence already obtainable which I could lay my hands on. The second was to create, and increase as widely as possible, an awareness of the "archaeological dimension". These two aims contributed to each other inasmuch as the more archaeological evidence there was to present and disseminate, the greater was likely to be the archaeological awareness: and the greater the archaeological awareness among people throughout the country, the more information about finds and sites was likely to come in ...
>
> 'The dissemination of "archaeological awareness" was pursued by the displays in the museum, by talks and lectures to schools, clubs and societies, groups of teachers and teachers' colleges, and by articles in the press and local magazines; and when Radio Accra came into being, by broadcast talks ...' (Shaw 1990: 208–9).

other African colonial countries (J. Deacon 1990). Two years later, the first university-level appointment in archaeology was made in Ghana (Kense 1990). In 1938 the Institut Français d'Afrique Noire (IFAN) was founded in Dakar; an archaeology section was added in 1941 (de Barros 1990). Professional archaeologists were first appointed to positions in Zimbabwe (then Southern Rhodesia) in 1947 (M. Hall 1990).

It is important to bear in mind that all of these institutional developments took place before 1957, when Ghana's independence began the surge of political change that was to transform much of Africa within a decade. Increasing knowledge of Africa's deep past came to develop in tandem with nationalist sentiments.

Nevertheless, archaeologists were often widely spread, and were forced to work in comparative isolation. Their first task usually had to be primary fieldwork in an area then virtually unknown. Consequently, the first Pan-African Congress for archaeology, which was held in Nairobi in 1947, was particularly important in bringing its 61 delegates from all over Africa together in one place. In Desmond Clark's words:

'When I arrived in Africa there were only two or three professional archaeologists in the whole of the continent south of the Sahara, who were separated by hundreds of miles and only met on rare occasions. So we all worked, or tended to work, in watertight compartments, so to speak. The danger of this is that one's own material tends to assume greater significance than it really deserves, if it is not looked at within a broader spectrum. Louis Leakey recognised the importance of this and, in 1947, brought together in Nairobi for the first time prehistorians, Quaternary geologists, human and animal palaeontologists, all actively working in the continent. The Pan-African Congress on Prehistory and Quaternary Studies, as it came to be called, was a milestone in prehistoric research in the continent as it broke down the geographical barriers and provided a forum for exchange of information about recent discoveries and research as well as for informal discussions, the establishment of collaborative research projects and the opportunity to visit the sites and examine the collections on which the regional sequences had been built up' (Clark 1990: 193–4).

Great Zimbabwe: reaction

R. N. Hall's careless and cavalier approach to Great Zimbabwe's history attracted a backlash in the form of the British Association's decision to support a second expedition to Great Zimbabwe.

The Association's candidate for the controversy was David Randall-MacIver, an archaeologist with considerable experience in Egypt. Randall-MacIver excavated at Great Zimbabwe in 1905 and published his results in the following year. He is generally recognised as the first to carry out modern fieldwork at the site. In Peter Garlake's assessment, his 'approach had been faultless, his excavations careful and his assessment of the basic culture of the occupants of Great Zimbabwe unassailable' (Garlake 1973: 78). Indeed, Randall-MacIver's *Mediaeval Rhodesia* comes as a bucket of cold water after Hall's *Great Zimbabwe*. Biblical interpretations, 'popular opinion', 'romanticists' and the work of 'untrained amateurs' are all dismissed. The 'temple' is interpreted as a 'fort', combining the 'Great Chief's Kraal' with a ceremonial centre in which the conical tower symbolised the head of the Monomotapan state. Randall-MacIver suggested that it was the 'patriotic duty' of Rhodesians to accept a recent, indigenous attribution of Great Zimbabwe, and to study the ruins as part of the ethnography of the native population (Randall-MacIver 1906).

Randall-MacIver was without doubt a fine archaeologist, but the element of collusion, characteristic of Bent's opinions, is evident in Randall-MacIver's writing as well. Thus he made his case not by elevating the 'Makalanga' to a higher cultural status, but by bringing the workmanship of Great Zimbabwe down to the 'native' level. 'The building, fine as it is,' he wrote, 'has been executed in exactly the same spirit as all the other "ancient monuments" in Rhodesia. Laborious care has been expended on the most conspicuous and effective parts, but elsewhere the workmanship is slipshod. Probably several gangs were engaged on different parts of the wall at the same time, and, like clumsy engineers boring a tunnel from different ends, they failed to meet at the agreed point of junction.'

Within this frame of reference, Bent's and Hall's phallic objects and fertility rites posed no interpretative problems. Randall-MacIver had seen it all before: 'That these negroes, like all other negroes, revelled in obscenity is probable enough. That they had orgiastic rites, like every other primitive people, from China to Peru, we may well believe. And the phallic emblems may well be charms connected with such rites' (Randall-MacIver 1906: 68, 73).

But Randall-MacIver's fieldwork fuelled rather than settled the controversy. Rhodesia's small but noisy settler community could hardly accept that one of the most basic tenets of their new history could be swept away by an outside 'expert'. Eventually, in 1929 the British Association for the Advancement of Science commissioned a third archaeological investigation of Great Zimbabwe, this time by Gertrude Caton-Thompson.

Like Randall-MacIver, Caton-Thompson had had previous experience excavating in Egypt. And like Randall-MacIver, she has been credited with a formative status in modern archaeological work in southern Africa. 'In her approach to the archaeological problem, Caton-Thompson was systematic and professional. She ignored the temptation to range widely across the rich archaeology of the region, and concentrated on Great Zimbabwe itself and a small set of nearby stone ruins ... By carefully excavating deposits, Caton-Thompson

FIGURE 25 GERTRUDE CATON-THOMPSON'S DRAWING OF A PASSAGEWAY AT GREAT ZIMBABWE. In her fieldwork, Caton-Thompson paid close attention to detail and to recording architectural features of the site.

was able to classify pottery by its colour, texture and finish – a standard archaeological technique then, as today' (M. Hall 1987: 7).

Caton-Thompson claimed to be free of prejudice: she had 'no germ of preconceived ideas as to the ruins' origin and age', was 'unconcerned with speculations', and was 'unencumbered by *a priori* hypotheses as to who might have done what, who sacrificed to the morning star, and who worshipped the new moon'. These, she declared, were 'subjects which have no place at all in the earlier chapters of archaeological research, and which lead, unless firmly tethered by chronological data, to wildernesses of deductive error' (Caton-Thompson 1931: 2). In contrast, she emphasised the need for careful analysis and unequivocal chronological evidence.

After starting excavations in April 1929, Caton-Thompson delivered her report to the British Association, meeting in Johannesburg, on 2 August. She argued that 'instead of a degenerate offshoot of a higher Oriental civilisation, you have here a native civilisation unsuspected by all but a few students, showing national organisation of a high kind, originality and amazing industry. It is a subject worthy of all the research South Africa can give it. South African students must be bred to pursue it' (Caton-Thompson 1983: 132).

But as with Randall-MacIver's writing, there is an underside to Caton-Thompson's work that does not conform comfortably to the image subsequently put into circulation, both by herself and by others. Caton-Thompson follows Randall-MacIver in seeing her 'Zimbabwe Culture' as not up to much: 'The architecture at Zimbabwe, imitative apparently of a daub proto type, strikes me as essentially the product of an infantile mind, a pre-logical mind, a mind which having discovered the way of making or doing a thing goes on childishly repeating the performance regardless of incongruity'. Inevitably she sees the trend as downhill – 'unbroken through retrogressive continuity of custom down the ages since Zimbabwe was erected ... away from the best towards deterioration ...' (Caton-Thompson 1931: 103)

Apartheid

Ironically, the first Pan-African Congress in Nairobi was also the last time that professional archaeologists from all parts of Africa were to meet for almost fifty years. In the following year, the National Party was elected in South Africa on a platform of institutionalised racism. The new administration was suspicious of archaeology's challenge to the biblical version of creation, and of evidence that suggested Iron Age settlement before white colonial expansion. The government intervened in the proposal to hold the Second Pan-African Congress in Johannesburg in 1952, and the meeting was rescheduled in Algiers, with no South African delegates present (J. Deacon 1990). In the years that followed, archaeology in southern Africa developed in increasing isolation from the rest of the continent, with its own particular politics of coping with the dichotomy between the results of archaeological research and the political aims of white minority governments seeking to deny indigenous progress in history (J. Deacon 1990, M. Hall 1990).

Property and Finance Magazine, **Rhodesia, November 1972:**

'In these days of deliberate subversion of civilised authority, the international New Liberalism attempts to mould all aspects of life including the sciences, to the glorification of the Negro. Archaeology, the study of antiquities, is a natural victim, for it can be used as a means of creating an artificial cultural respectability for Black nationalism and, accordingly, a justification of Black rule. Against all objective evidence, Zimbabwe is again being promoted as a Bantu achievement' (Quoted by Frederikse 1982: 12).

FIGURE 26 A WALL JUNCTION ON THE HILL, GREAT ZIMBABWE. The walls of Great Zimbabwe form architecturally complex features, reflecting in turn the complex political and social life in this pre-colonial city.

chapter 3

Public archaeology

It is clear from Chapter 2 that archaeology is often political. Today, it is easy to look back at the early years of the colonial scramble for Africa, and to see how many interpretations offered by ethnographers and prehistorians fitted in well with the need of colonial governments to justify their territorial conquests historically and morally. But, at the same time, there were often contradictions in the way that writing about Africa's past developed. Although some archaeologists were unambiguous apologists for racist policies, others were opposed to the juggernaut of European domination. The only way to fully understand the complexity of archaeology's historical context is to look closely at the work that was done and at the reports and syntheses that were written.

Politics and the past

An example of this complexity is the set of reactions that greeted Gertrude Caton-Thompson's first report on her work at Great Zimbabwe. Her presentation to the British Association for the Advancement of Science in Johannesburg in August 1929 was greeted by the academic community in very varied ways. Some fully endorsed Caton-Thompson's argument that Great Zimbabwe was 'essentially African', while others insisted on holding on to the old ideas of a lost civilisation from Europe and Asia. Ironically, some of the most vigorous and vociferous objections came from Raymond Dart, who five years earlier had discovered the first australopithecine fossil, paving the way for the modern view that all humans are 'essentially African'. As we have seen, Caton-Thompson held views about the nature of African societies that would today be regarded unambiguously as racist; in 1929, some academics clearly

THE ZIMBABWE MYSTERY

MISS CATON-THOMPSON'S INVESTIGATIONS

WORK OF AFRICAN RACE

PROBLEMS THAT REMAIN UNSOLVED

PROF. DART MAKES HEATED SPEECH

(From Our Special Correspondent.)
JOHANNESBURG, Friday

Predominant interest in today's proceedings of the British Association has centred in Miss Gertrude Caton-Thompson's lecture on the Zimbabwe ruins. It has undoubtedly been a great event, and the reason is not only the interest of the subject-matter, but also the personality of Miss Caton-Thompson herself. It was a memorable experience to watch the little bird-like woman with the soft voice and the red cheek, leaning on the long wooden pointer which lantern lecturers always use, with the nonchalance of a punter on his punt-pole, and solving with gentle logic what has been regarded as one of the mysteries of the ages.

The deduction she advanced as the result of her recent investigations was that the ruins are the work of 'a vigorous native civilization', and herein her view coincides with that of Dr. Randall MacIver. More surprising was her assertion that the ruins are not more than 1,000 years old, and probably not as old as that …

A WORD OF WARNING

Professor Myres said Miss Caton-Thompson's work seemed to him conclusive, but he put in a word of general warning as to the difficulty of basing archaeological dates on stratification of deposits. On a complicated site it was quite as possible for objects of an earlier date to be washed into a given stratum as it was for objects of a later date …

In the debate which followed the address, the Rev. S.S. Dornan stated that during his wanderings in Rhodesia he had fallen in with an aged witch-doctor in the Umtali district. All that the witch-doctor told him tended to support Miss Caton-Thompson's conclusions …

PROFESSOR DART INDIGNANT

Dr. P. Wagner, while adding his voice to the chorus of congratulations, said he had been much struck by the laying of the stone steps in the Zimbabwe Ruins – a technique which, as far as he was aware, was quite foreign to the African. Without attempting to date the ruins, he put forward the hypothesis that they were the temple of a priesthood which grew up during the immense period represented by the gold working of the locality.

Professor Dart, in a fierce outburst of curiously unscientific indignation with the whole course of the discussion, charged the chairman with having called upon none but supporters of the Caton-Thompson theory to speak.

The chairman (Mr. Henry Balfour) rose to point out that the whole object in the investigations was to stimulate interest. He reminded Professor Dart that a general invitation had been given for discussion.

Professor Dart then proceeded to add that Miss Caton-Thompson's investigations had pushed Dr. MacIver's dating back from the fifteenth or sixteenth century to 600 AD. He ventured the opinion that further investigations would push back Miss Caton-Thompson's date an equal distance into the remoter past.

After a few further remarks, delivered in tones of awe-inspiring violence, Professor Dart sat down very hard on his chair.

Miss Caton-Thompson disposed of him allusively and effectively in a brief reply, and so closed a discussion of the widest interest and the deepest significance.

(Cape Times, *Saturday 3 August 1929*)

regarded her as a dangerous radical.

Just as earlier archaeology had its politics, so does the practice of the discipline in the present day. These perspectives and preferences, which interplay subtly with the way the past is written, are more difficult to tease apart the closer we come to the present. It is sometimes claimed that archaeology is 'above' or 'outside' politics, and should be 'detached' and 'objective'. While it is quite possible for archaeologists to distance their work from explicit political positions, it is inevitable that, just as archaeologists today look back critically at work written fifty years ago, so archaeologists in fifty years' time will look back critically at the archaeology of the present day.

One way of assessing the politics of contemporary writing about the past is to think in terms of 'public archaeology'. Most professional archaeologists are accountable in some way: to a museum's board of trustees, or a university council, for example. In turn, such controlling bodies are accountable themselves, perhaps to a government department or, in a democratically ordered society, more directly to the wider community. Although in many cases archaeologists will have a lot of individual latitude in how they design research projects and put together their interpretations, ultimately they are writing about the past *for* someone else.

> 'Why, beyond reasons of scientific curiosity, do we want to know about the past? And whose past is it anyway? These issues very soon lead us to questions of responsibility, public as well as private. For surely a national monument, such as Great Zimbabwe or the Athenian Acropolis, means something special to the modern descendants of its builders? Does it not also mean something to all humankind? If so, should it not be protected from destruction, in the same way as endangered plant and animal species? If the looting of ancient sites is to be deplored, should it not be stopped, even if the sites are on privately owned land? Who owns, or should own, the past?' (Renfrew & Bahn 1991: 463)

The place of African archaeology in the wide domain of public affairs was highlighted in 1985. For some years, the International Union of Pre- and Protohistoric Sciences (IUPPS) had been planning its next world congress in Southampton, England. The organising committee was particularly anxious to have participation from many countries, including the 'third world', and sessions had been planned that would involve participants from an unprecedented range of countries. By the middle of 1985 the list of archaeologists who had indicated they would attend the congress the following year included more than twenty working at universities and museums in South Africa (Ucko 1987).

For some time, archaeologists working in many parts of the world had been uneasy about collaborating with colleagues inside apartheid South Africa, and a significant minority of South African academics felt that they should support an academic boycott in order to put additional pressure on their own government. But others felt equally strongly that academic freedom – the right to teach, carry out research and collaborate without political intervention –

must override boycott politics, however abhorrent South Africa's political policies might be. In the words of Peter Ucko, National Secretary for the World Archaeological Congress to be held in Southampton:

'As the State of Emergency of 1985 was announced in South Africa (July 20), and some of the events were shown on television (more than 1,200 people detained without trial and at least 15 killed in clashes with the police and army during the first week and at least 129 killed by the middle of August), Jane kept asking how this was going to affect the Congress. The first real indication of trouble came from the Anti-Racism Committee of Southampton University's Students' Union, in early March and, slightly later, the South African issue was raised officially at one of our Local Community Committee meetings. As the evidence grew of local preoccupation with the issue of South Africa, and as the international news, including the USA's and Britain's veto of the UN's call for mandatory sanctions, grew more and more disgraceful, so I was becoming clearer and clearer that it was indeed the most vital of all the political issues that confronted us, for the demands were for the imposition of an academic ban on South Africa/Namibia. The UN adopted a resolution calling for voluntary sanctions (with Britain and the USA abstaining), and the Commonwealth Group of Eminent Persons issued its damning report on South Africa ... Quite separately from the local pressures, and much more significant to me personally, was the growing evidence that some countries, particularly in Africa, would not let their nationals participate if South Africa was represented at our Congress' (Ucko 1987: 54).

The debate between those who advocated political contingency and those who insisted on inalienable academic freedom became a public issue in the UK and the US, with newspaper columnists and leaders taking different positions. Major sponsors of the Congress, such as the Southampton City Council, also became involved as representatives of the public interest. In the end the invitations to South African archaeologists were withdrawn, resulting in angry responses, both from within South Africa and from academics in Europe and North America. A letter written by Philip Tobias of the

University of the Witwatersrand is an example of one widely held point of view. The letter from Professor Tobias is reproduced in full in Ucko 1987:

Dear Professor Ucko

Re: Rejection of South African participants in the World Archaeological Congress

I have received your letter of 9 September 1985, informing me that 'the Executive Committee ... has decided that it cannot accept your participation in the above 1986 meeting' and that 'this decision reflects the policy of numerous organizations who call for a total academic boycott of South Africa'...

Nothing in the Statutes of IUPPS gives authority to national organising committees to make such a decision, as a study of Section VII of the Statutes makes clear. Indeed, it is implicit in the Statutes of the International Union that its congresses will be open to delegates of all countries ...

The reason for the Executive Committee's decision given in your letter is that 'this decision reflects the policy of numerous organisations who call for a total academic boycott of South Africa.' I am unable to comprehend, let alone condone, that a national committee, charged with organising a congress *on behalf of an International Union*, could allow itself to be influenced by any other than the policy of the International Union on whose behalf it is acting ...

I am sorry to say that this is the first occasion known to me when *one's fellow-scientists* have taken a decision to exercise political discrimination against a group of their fellows ... Another implication of the Committee's decision is that, by keeping out all South African participants, you are in effect identifying all those researchers with the policies of South Africa. To being so identified, a number of colleagues and I take exception. Some of us, like myself, have spent decades opposing racism and apartheid; we work for institutions like the Universities of the Witwatersrand and Cape Town which are non-segregated, whose policies are predicated upon non-racial admissions of students, non-racial appointment of staff members and strong opposition to apartheid in educational matters ...

But despite dire predictions about the consequences that this 'politicisation' of archaeology would bring, the World Archaeological Congress proved to be a milestone in the history of the discipline. Archaeologists attended from a far wider spectrum of countries and continents than they had at any previous IUPPS congress, and the papers that were delivered resulted in

FIGURE 27 ONE WORLD ARCHAEOLOGY.

the publication of a series of 22 books: the *One World Archaeology* series (Figure 27). The last of these books, titled *The Archaeology of Africa: Food, Metals and Towns*, included 44 contributions on many different aspects of Africa's past but not, of course, South Africa (Shaw et al. 1993). Subsequent to the 1986 Southampton convention, the World Archaeological Congress has become an international organisation, meeting every four years (in South America in 1990, and in India in 1994).

The issues raised in 1985 and 1986 are complex, and have by no means been solved by the success of the World Archaeological Congress or by South Africa's move towards democracy and non-racialism. Few countries institutionalise injustice to the extent of South Africa's apartheid regime. But in many parts of the world, including the 'first world', there are systematic violations of basic human rights.

Is academic practice above such issues (and, if so, why), or should academic workers be as involved as everyone else (and, if so, how)?

One of the reasons why the South African issue was so complex and emotive, and why it was probably impossible to have any truly international meeting of archaeologists if South African delegates had participated, was that apartheid had come to stand for the collective injustices and legacies of the colonial era. But, of course, most public archaeology is not cast in negative terms, and the flip side of the rejection of racism has been the assertion of national identity – using archaeology to claim the rich cultural heritage that many colonial administrators tried so assiduously to deny.

Resolution of the African participants at the World Archaeological Congress, Plenary Session, 1986

'That the organisers of this Congress be congratulated for successfully organising a truly WAC. Our feeling is that this has been a most meaningful Congress because the organisation has: i) achieved truly worldwide representation; and ii) addressed themes of worldwide interest and relevance. With these achievements, it is clear that the WAC has made a breakthrough in discussing and finding solutions to the practical problems of man understanding fellow man' (Ucko 1987: 192).

Museums and national identity

For many people in Africa, museums are inescapably part of the colonial legacy:

'There is no denying the fact that the museum in its current form and structure is an alien institution in Africa. It was introduced by the colonial master. Despite arguments to the contrary, it is generally believed that the intention was to collect and preserve the culture of the colonized peoples. As such, it was to be the store house for the past and an educational resource centre from where scholarly information can be obtained. However, the averagely or less educated African did not see the museum in this light. Many saw it as a place for storing antiquated objects, others thought it was an elitist institution whose collections and displays required special training to be able to under-

FIGURE 28 EATING TOGETHER IN ABIDJAN, IVORY COAST.

stand and appreciate them ...' (Asombang 1990: 189).

But following independence from colonial rule, many saw in museums the possibilities for establishing national identity and for awakening a 'national consciousness'. 'Many countries began to see the museum in a new light. It became an important cultural institution to support and project the newly won political independence. It was consequently fully embraced and developed towards this objective. It was at this time that the National Museum (*Musée National* in Francophone countries) was born (for example, in Nigeria, Kenya, Niger, Equatorial Guinea, Benin, etc.)' (Asombang 1990: 189).

This new role for the museum has introduced tensions of a different order. Should national museums stress cultural unity, seeking to smooth over historical differences in the interests of one perception of the future? Or should they mirror cultural diversity, protecting minority traditions from being lost from memory? Writing about a project to establish a new national museum in Cameroon's capital city, Yaounde, Raymond Asombang stresses the need to protect diversity:

'Cameroon, like many African nations, is endowed with a rich and diversified cultural heritage which she can exploit to boost her development. Cultural pluralism has often been given a negative image by those who exploit it for partisan politics. On the contrary [it can be argued] that cultural pluralism can and does enrich the cultural capital of a nation.

'How can the would-be National Museum of Cameroon enrich the country's cultural capital? To achieve this, it has first of all to be loved and visited by the community at large. The people should feel that the museum would be loved and visited by people of all social classes or ethnic and cultural groups, only if it reflects the cultural diversity of the country rather than a national culture where one cultural group dominates. Given our cultural background, any attempt to create a national culture runs the risk of leading to cultural integration of less dominant cultures. The National Museum which aims at projecting the idea of a national identity and national unity should portray the cultural multicentricism of the nation rather than dominant cultures. Though this may sound paradoxical, it is nevertheless true that a National Museum which portrays a national culture whereby some cultures have lost their identity, will help to destroy rather than promote national unity' (Asombang 1990: 195–6).

Archaeology and nationalism

The colonisation of Africa by Europe resulted in territorial divisions of the continent which often bore no relation to the pre-colonial boundaries of states and chiefdoms. With independence, most of these arbitrary boundaries became the borders of new nations (Figure 29).

Nationalist movements, both while fighting for liberation and while seeking to consolidate post-independence identities, needed to find unifying historical themes which encouraged national pride. At the same time, it was vitally important to replace the stultifying racist myths of colonialism – which asserted that Africa had no past worthy of being called 'history' – with a sense of the richness of Africa's vibrant past.

The interplay between nationalism and archaeology has been particularly marked in West Africa. 'Negritude' writers, members of a literary movement that began among French-speaking African and Caribbean writers as a protest against French colonial rule, stressed the superiority of African culture, with its mystical connections with the past and with the land, over the corrupt materialism of Europe. A leading figure in the Negritude movement was the poet Léopold Senghor, elected first President of the Republic of Senegal in 1960. It was natural that Negritude's emphasis on the richness of the African past should lead to an interest in archaeology. This was most prominently expressed in the work of the Senegalese intellectual, Cheikh Anta Diop.

Diop argued that there had been a close relationship between black Africa and ancient Egypt. Diop stressed the achievements of Egyptian civilisation and pointed out that the ancient Egyptians had been black. He asserted that the Nile Valley was the point of origin for African people ranging from the Fulani to the Zulu, and used archaeological evidence to trace migration routes, arguing for instance that the 'burial mounds' of the Inland Niger Delta were West African versions of the pyramids (Diop 1979; Holl 1990).

Many archaeologists have been unhappy about Diop's work. They point out that his synthesis of Africa's pre-colonial history depends on precisely the same reasoning as that used by nineteenth- and early twentieth-century white supremacists, who also held that everything good in the world originated in Egypt. Critics of Negritude history argue that his notion of African origins suffers from the same weakness as all diffusionist theory: by relying on often-slight similarities between buildings, languages

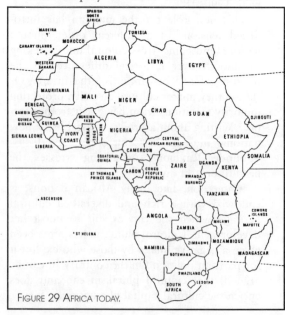

FIGURE 29 AFRICA TODAY.

and customs that are widely separated, it violates the basic principle that the full context in which an artefact is found is of primary importance.

But at the same time, the work of Negritude historians such as Diop has been highly effective in demolishing the tenets of colonial histories of Africa. It has highlighted the richness of the African past, and the importance of research and writing that are free from the fetters of racist assumptions. In particular Diop's writing has emphasised the importance of Egypt's past in understanding the full sweep of Africa's history, and of Africa's contribution to the history of the Mediterranean and Europe. His critique of earlier historical writing about Africa has recently been taken up again by Martin Bernal. Bernal's close examination of the literature on Egypt has shown the full extent of the racist and anti-Semitic assumptions that have burdened African and European historiography (Bernal 1991a, 1991b).

Subsequent to the earlier interest of Negritude writers, a distinctive brand of archaeology developed in post-colonial West Africa. This work has remained closely connected to issues of national consciousness and ethnic identity, and has stressed the continuities between past and present, often providing a 'charter' for the present day that is given authority by reference to the past (Holl 1990). Bruce Trigger, in an overview of the history of archaeology in Africa, has contrasted the situation in West Africa, where there is wide popular interest in archaeology, with that in South Africa. In Trigger's view South African archaeology is 'the most colonial of all African archaeologies ... its relationship to the majority of South Africans remains highly ambiguous' (Trigger 1990: 316).

'West African archaeologists ... are interested in the precolonial history of their countries and of the region as a whole. They address problems of ethnic origins and prehistoric economic, social and cultural development. Many students carry out research in their home territories that combines oral traditions and ethnographic data with archaeology by means of ethnoarchaeology and the direct historical approach. The archaeology that is practised in Nigeria and Ghana is simultaneously intensely anthropological and intensely historical, even though in the universities it has avoided institutional affiliations with documentary history, which is seen as using different methods to study the past. While archaeology remains much more closely affiliated with history departments in the countries of former French West Africa, growing involvement with researchers from many different parts of the world is promoting an internationalization of archaeological methods.

'Throughout West Africa problems arise as to how archaeological research should serve regional, national and local or ethnic goals. Sites of historical importance have become the focus of special study and preservation and museums are being developed as centres of public education. In some situations it is feared that by strengthening local loyalties archaeology may weaken national ones; in others this contradiction is not regarded as a serious issue. Political control of archaeological research and interpretation has been indirect and achieved through the allocation of funding where it has occurred at all. Above all, the general goal of strengthening pride in West Africa's precolonial achievements is one that is not seen, by West Africans or outsiders, as creating a contradiction between "objective" or "scientific" canons of archaeological research and serving social and political ends. Archaeology is providing West Africa with a far more detailed, dynamic and exciting past than did Diop's ethnographically based speculations. West African archaeologists take pride in their research and believe that, by enhancing respect for their past, they are playing a significant role in the economic and social development of their region' (Trigger 1990: 317).

Gender and archaeology

We have seen that a major theme in public archaeology is the way in which the past has been used in the construction of identities. But although the reassertion of African culture after the long, dark interlude of colonialism has been a major concern since the early 1960s, when many African countries achieved independence, nationalism is not the only area in which perceptions of the past interplay with the politics of the present. More recently, gender has become an important issue, and feminists have developed a critique of patriarchal society that cuts across previous political boundaries.

> **androcentrism** an attitude which assumes that men must be central in society and history

Gender, in fact, has become an issue surprisingly late in archaeology – in comparison with the other social sciences. Why? Meg Conkey and Ruth Tringham believe that the development of an archaeology of gender has been held back by archaeology's continuing empiricism – by the concentration on finding and describing things, rather than on interpreting them. But after an initial conference in 1988, gender issues have now become a major field of debate in archaeology, forming a bridge between academic interpretations of the past and the politics of the relative positions of men and women in the modern world (Conkey & Tringham 1995).

Most feminist archaeologists do not recognise a distinction between the way in which the discipline works – who gets appointed to which jobs in universities, museums and other institutions – and the way the past is read academically. Their approach challenges the divide that others would make between public archaeology and academic practice, and is consistent with the broader direction of 'post-processual archaeology', which insists that the way research is carried out is intimately connected with the way in which archaeology is written (see Chapter 4).

For example, feminists point out that a male-dominated (or 'androcentric') image of archaeological fieldwork is still prevalent: the 'hard', masculine occupations of site surveying and excavation are contrasted with the 'soft', feminine tasks of laboratory work and curatorial tasks. It has been shown that these patriarchal assumptions in archaeological practice spill over into writing. Extrapolations are made into the past which see men's roles as cattle herding, iron smelting or hunting, and women's work as cultivation, pottery manufacture and plant gathering, even when there is no evidence either way for gendered specialisation of labour.

> 'Archaeology has consistently been told to us from a male perspective that adopts "male" as the norm and proceeds from the male experience. In the received view, art is male, with females sometimes as subjects/objects; males take over agriculture because agriculture is the more critical activity. Tools, their production and use, are male concerns and are intimately involved with the evolution of "man". Empires are made by men, and the underlying labor and energy directly attributable to women lies hidden' (Conkey & Gero 1991: 18).

Stereotypes

Carl Mauch's description of Great Zimbabwe launched at least one literary career. Henry Rider Haggard lived in South Africa between 1875 and 1881, after which he returned to England and, in 1885, found commercial success with his third novel, *King Solomon's Mines*. Haggard was inspired by the newly discovered Mashonaland ruins, as well as by other elements in his African experience. His romance was immediately successful, selling extremely well by the standard of the times.

Three adventurers – Sir Henry Curtis, Captain Good and the narrator, Allan Quatermain – set off into the African interior in search of Curtis's lost brother and King Solomon's diamond mines, marked on a parchment map. They take with them a servant who turns out to be the rightful ruler of the Kukuana, a tribe which has long occupied King Solomon's lost country though ignorant of the details of its history. After a bloody battle, the rightful king is

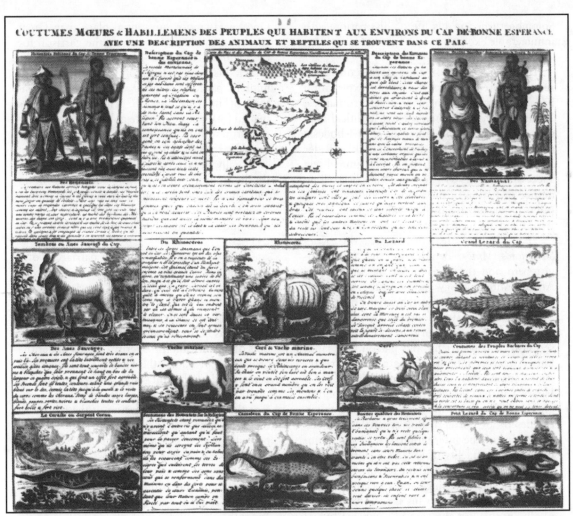

FIGURE 30 AFRICA, THE 'DARK CONTINENT'. A page from Guy Tachard's *Voyage de Siam*, published in London in 1688. Tachard visited the Cape on his way eastwards, and recorded his impressions of Africa's animals and people, each with a drawing and a descriptive caption. His representations of the 'Hottentots' and 'Namaquas' (top left and right of the illustration) conformed with contemporary stereotypes of southern Africa's indigenous pastoralist communities, and were published repeatedly by travellers and adventurers through the years.

restored, Sir Henry's brother (as well as the diamonds) is found, and the adventurers return to safety and prosperity.

Haggard's land of the Ancients is a place of harmonious cornucopia. There are possibilities of sexual licence, and Haggard is at his most erotic in his descriptions of the landscape of this long-lost paradise. Kukuanaland lies beyond 'Sheba's Breasts', the slopes of which mountains 'swell gently from the plain, looking at that distance perfectly round and smooth'. In case the reader has not grasped the point, Haggard continues with the metaphor. Around the mountains 'the mists and shadows ... take the form of a recumbent woman, veiled mysteriously in sleep', while each of Sheba's Breasts is capped by 'a vast hillock covered with snow, exactly corresponding to the nipple on the female breast'. To complete the analogy, Haggard has Sir Henry Curtis (a scholar as well as warrior, and an archetype of the archaeologist in the field) deduce that the weathered, monumental statues of Kukuanaland are associated with 'phallic worship' – the idols to which King

Solomon turned in his life of dissipation with innumerable exotic wives and concubines (Haggard 1885: 66).

This stereotype of the 'dark continent' revealed by enlightened European exploration has been continued in more recent romances. Wilbur Smith's *The Sunbird* is a political allegory that mourns the fading days of Rhodesia through images of the past. And, like Rider Haggard, Wilbur Smith has been immensely successful: in 1981 he was the bestselling author of fiction in the world. *Sunbird* clearly offers its readers what they want to hear about Africa and about its past.

The Sunbird leans heavily on *King Solomon's Mines*. Ben Kazin, the archaeologist–hero and the Director of the Institute of African Anthropology and Prehistory in Johannesburg, believes that Carthaginians had a formative influence on southern Africa's past, though the academic world has yet to take him seriously. Kazin's friend and patron, the fabulously wealthy mining magnate and entrepreneur Louren Sturvesant (a re-embodiment of Sir Henry Curtis), shows Kazin an aerial photograph which reveals the outline of a lost city in the deserts of northern Botswana. Despite the scepticism of the international academic community, the infidelity of Kazin's beautiful assistant Dr Sally Benator, and the terrorist activities of Kazin's one-time linguistic specialist, Timothy Mageba, Kazin finds his site, to the acclaim of all. But this lost city carried a curse: a fungal infection kills Sturvesant and takes Kazin into a prolonged dream of the past, in which the destruction of this earlier civilisation is enacted.

The Sunbird intertwines several long-established stereotypes: big game hunting, historical romance, the despised male hero made good, and discovered treasure, all spiced with some sex and a good deal of violence. Smith plays to a standard gallery of prejudices, calling up lesbian priestesses, pederastic Arabs and sexually voracious blacks.

Ben Kazin is the custodian of 'the legend of the ancients', 'a race of fair-skinned golden-haired warriors' who had come from across the sea and had 'mined the gold, enslaved the indigenous tribes, built walled cities and flourished for hundreds of years before vanishing almost without trace'. Their capital had been Opet, a far more substantial place than Great Zimbabwe (which was merely the garrison for the 'Middle Kingdom'). Like the Ophir of the Bible, this was a land of fabulous plenty, a hunter's paradise teeming with game, a repository of immense wealth. The economy was fuelled by Opet's extensive gold mines, and subject tribes from the rest of the subcontinent brought tribute. The 'treasury of Opet', when eventually discovered by Kazin and Sturvesant (in the tradition of both *King Solomon's Mines* and Tutankhamun's tomb), is found to contain elephant tusks, amphorae, linen, silk, metals, diamonds and tons of gold (Smith 1972: 14, 31, 241–2).

Opet is subject to the benign patriarchy of a hereditary king, the 'Gry-Lion', and an oligarchy of nine noble families. Their power is buttressed by a religious authority that would have delighted Theodore Bent and R. N. Hall. The city is adorned with 'phallic towers', 'symbols of fertility and prosperity', and is under the protection of Baàl – the Phoenician male deity personified by the sun – and of Astarte – whose symbol is the moon, the cycles of which represent the 'symbolic subjugation of the female to the male, repeated in the human female by the periodic moon-sickness' (Smith 1972: 114, 329).

All this was swept away by the dark disaster of the 'Bantu migration', an episode of 'diabolical fury', 'an almost superhuman destructive strength', 'a solid mass of black humanity' (Smith 1972: 163, 175). Here, in the narrative, Wilbur Smith plies back and forth between his imagined history and his political present. The attack on Opet is lead by Manatassi, King of the Vendi, while the attack on white Rhodesia is under the command of Major-General Timothy Mageba, of the People's Liberation Army. Kazin, historian and archaeologist of Africa, sums up the connection for the reader: '... it came to me then that this man was not unique, Africa had bred many like him. The dark destroyers who had strewn her plains with the white bones of men, Chaka, Mzilikazi, Mamatee, Mutesa, and hundreds of others that history had forgotten. Timothy Mageba was only the latest in a long line of warriors which stretched back beyond the shadowy, impenetrable veils of time' (Smith 1972: 231).

The ruins of Opet are there to be discovered – 'something to rank with Leakey's discoveries at Olduvai Gorge, something to startle and dazzle the world of archaeology.'

Wilbur Smith wrote *The Sunbird* before Steven Spielberg took the theme of archaeological adventure and discovery and gave it the slight additional exaggeration needed for farce. The legend of the lost city received this treatment in the 1984 film version of *King Solomon's Mines*, filmed on location in Zimbabwe with the cooperation of the Ministry of Information and the National Museums and Monuments of Zimbabwe. Rider Haggard's story has been adapted to accommodate a female lead, a dumb-blonde archaeology student, Jesse Huston (Sharon Stone), who has hired a younger and handsome Quatermain (Richard Chamberlain) to look for her lost father, Professor Huston. The setting has been brought forward to the First World War, to allow a scramble for the lost mines between Quatermain and German soldiers under the command of the archetypal Hun, Colonel Bockner. The adventure starts from somewhere in the Sudan (permitting the inclusion of the archetypal Turk, Dogati). The 'map' is a statue of Sheba, with breasts and belly representing the topography of the region of the lost mines. Quatermain, Jesse and their faithful servant Umbopo encounter archetypal cannibals, and end up as prisoners of the Kukuana and the despotic witch Gagoola, who tries to feed Quatermain to her pet crocodiles. They are saved by Umbopo, who declares himself the rightful ruler of the Kukuana. Gagoola carries Jesse off to the mines, and everyone chases after them. In a cavern they discover the fossilised bodies of the queens of the lost kingdom, including the Queen of Sheba, and it becomes clear that the savage tribes have believed Jesse to be a reincarnation of one of their own past rulers. After a chase around the mines, Gagoola, Bockner and Dogati get their just deserts, Umbopo gets his kingdom, Quatermain gets Jesse and Jesse gets the diamonds.

Both *The Sunbird* and the 1984 film version of *King Solomon's Mines* bring stereotypes of Africa's archaeology into the mass system of circulation of modern popular culture. Wilbur Smith's political agenda is quite clear. Brought up in Zambia under colonial rule, and a Special Constable in the rebel white outpost of Rhodesia, he told the *Weekend Argus* in February 1983 that 'when history is counted out', 'the British Empire will be seen as the most altruistic ever. Whatever else it did, it brought peace, education and the ideal of fair play to warring tribes.'

Appropriately then, *The Sunbird*'s ending is a lot less confident than the conclusions to Rider Haggard's tales. Although Africa gets its early history, and Kazin finds glory and the woman he loves, Timothy the terrorist slips away from the Rhodesian security forces, and his historical counterpart, Timon, destroys the city of Opet. Timothy–Timon personifies the rampant threat of black nationalism, and Ben Kazin – vilified by the international community but vindicated in the end – is an inspirational figure for beleaguered white Rhodesians.

The film of *King Solomon's Mines* is more slippery. Packaged as light entertainment, it combines slapstick and special effects with a fast-moving story. It could be argued that by exaggerating the antics of its stereotypes, the script explodes them as serious portrayals. And yet behind all of this, the old mythology is repeated without challenge. At the heart of Africa is the Queen of Sheba and her fabulous diamond mines. The Kukuana are absurdly barbaric and Umbopo is a diminished, rather cowardly version of Rider Haggard's Umbopa/Ignosi. The Hun is bombastic and the Oriental is devious and unreliable. Given that many people who see this film find it very funny, it seems perverse and stuffy to argue that this is the representation of Africa at its most reactionary – precisely the sort of response that would be expected from one of Wilbur Smith's 'debunkers' or 'politico-archaeologists'. But is it not a particular strength of the 'Indiana Jones' *genre* to have immunised its reactionary images through their presentation as comedy and farce? (M. Hall 1995)

Women and the Late Stone Age

Looking again at the past with an emphasis on gender often leads to a completely different interpretation. This can be illustrated by the examples of histories that have been written about the Late Stone Age in southern Africa.

Late Stone Age (or 'LSA') communities were bands of hunter–gatherers who moved about the landscape, living by collecting plant foods and snaring and hunting animals. Over the years LSA archaeology has attracted a variety of interpretations, emphasising in particular stone-tool technology and the role of the environment in providing food resources and framing human behaviour. But more recently, some archaeologists have argued that these older ways of reading the past are unduly restrictive and deterministic, and that an approach is required which stresses the social aspects of the LSA.

Working from ethnographic accounts of hunter–gatherers who still live (or have recently lived) in southern Africa, Lyn Wadley has argued that gender tensions between marriage partners and kin members play a major role in the dynamics of hunter–gatherer life. These are played out through an annual cycle, as people come together in large camps (an 'aggregation phase') and later move apart in smaller groups (a 'dispersal phase'). Wadley sees this gender dimension expressed in material objects: arrows, for instance, are associated with male ritual activity, while bored stones (used as weights on digging sticks) are particularly associated with women. In other words, artefacts reflect gendered social relations, and these can be 'read' from archaeological sites (Wadley 1987).

Southern Africa's LSA communities also left us a remarkable collection of art, painted on the walls of rock shelters and other surfaces in the subcontinent's mountainous areas. There have been different interpretations of this painting, but in recent years many archaeologists have accepted that it was the work of medicine men and women, probably in a state of trance, and that the art was closely connected with rain-making and rituals of social renewal (Lewis-Williams 1981).

Again, the recent interest in the role that gen-

FIGURE 31 SAN IN BOTSWANA. By taking into account the way in which hunter–gatherers live today, feminist archaeologists have shown that people's behaviour is fundamentally structured by relations between genders. For example, the ways in which food is obtained and shared during meals, and the mythology surrounding food, govern the day-by-day relationships between men and women. Feminist archaeologists argue that the lack of importance often ascribed to such gender relationships is a consequence of the androcentric bias of 'mainstream' archaeological research.

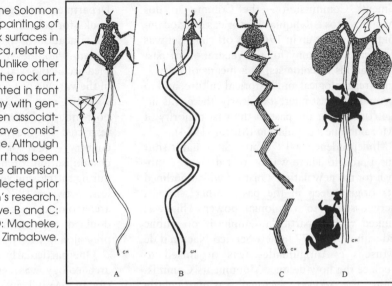

Figure 32 MYTHIC WOMEN. Anne Solomon has shown how these paintings of women, found on rock surfaces in many parts of southern Africa, relate to fundamental San beliefs. Unlike other images of people in the rock art, 'mythic women' are painted in front view, with legs splayed, many with genital emissions. They are often associated with objects known to have considerable ritual significance. Although southern African rock art has been studied for many years, the dimension of gender was largely neglected prior to Solomon's research.
A: Charter, Zimbabwe. B and C: Marondera, Zimbabwe. D: Macheke, Zimbabwe.

A   B   C   D

der plays in social organisation has led to a revision of interpretation. While acknowledging that trance rituals were important for LSA communities, Anne Solomon has shown that the interlinked themes of gender, sexuality and rain were also important (Figure 32). By looking at the art from this point of view, Solomon has found new evidence for the role of women, giving us a far richer perspective on this aspect of the past (Solomon 1992).

Public archaeology in Mozambique

'Archaeology is one means of collection, interpretation and transmission of historical information in specific social contexts and not merely a way of accumulating knowledge of past human behaviour. The focus and frame of reference should be susceptible to discussion. What is the object of study? For whom? What emphasis should be placed on which set of meanings embedded in material culture? How should the work be implemented – mass involvement or small, highly trained technical teams? Should research be oriented academically towards theoretical advances or should resources be redirected to convey an awareness of the existence and characteristics of the pre-colonial past to Mozambican peasants and workers? Some of these questions may well be superseded, for it is to be hoped that a situation develops in Africa in which there is no contradiction between academic interest, both foreign and local, and development needs' (Sinclair et al. 1993a: 428).

Mozambique's independence in 1975 from Portuguese colonial rule brought about a marked change in public archaeology in the country. This change highlights the need faced throughout Africa to find an appropriate balance between the requirements of academic research and the obligation to make information about the past widely available.

Before 1975, there had been little interest in Mozambique's pre-colonial past. Although rock paintings had been reported early in the eighteenth century, very few sites had been systematically investigated, and no stratified rock shelters had been excavated. The Salazar regime, which came to power in Portugal in 1932, promoted racially oriented ethnography, and in 1936 an anthropological institute had been established in Maputo – the Missão Antropológica de Moçambique – with the tasks of investigating the racial characteristics of colonial subjects and of categorising their beliefs and customs. This had stimulated some peripheral interest in the Stone Age, though knowledge of the results of these studies did not spread beyond academic circles. When a Monuments Commission – the Commissão dos Monumentos e Relíquias Históricas de Moçambique – was set up in 1943, its official brief was to 'act as testimony for the veneration of past generations of colonists, as a means of providing archaeological and historical culture, and to promote tourist interest'. Clearly, there was little concern for the past of the vast majority of Mozambique's population (Morais 1984).

Independence in 1975 brought a major shift in approach. There was a great drive to establish for the new nation a history which outlined its origins deep in the past, rather than its servile status to a colonial power. This was linked with a particular emphasis on public education. In 1977, a new Serviço Nacional de Museus e Antiguidades was organised to replace the now-defunct Monuments Commission. The Serviço Nacional was particularly concerned with cultural resource management, and identified as the key to this the creation of a national resource inventory of archaeological sites. The project involved educational goals on a national scale. By the following year the archaeological survey programme was sufficiently well established to gain financial support from the Swedish Agency for Research Cooperation and, later, from the Swedish Board of Antiquities.

These new archaeological goals were further strengthened in 1980 with the establishment of a Department of Archaeology at the Eduardo Mondlane University in Maputo. Apart from conducting research and teaching, staff in the Department concentrated on producing textbooks for schools. They were also involved in the education of *agentes de cultura* at the secondary school level, and the education of qualified archaeological technical assistants to work in the various provinces.

Sadly, many of the initial public goals in post-independence Mozambique have been restricted by the protracted civil war in the country – part of the campaign of regional destabilisation orchestrated by South Africa during the closing years of apartheid. Nevertheless, between 1976 and 1983 the number of archaeological sites known in Mozambique doubled and understanding of the country's pre-colonial past was dramatically improved.

One particularly notable example of public archaeology was centred on the stone-walled site of Manyikeni, located in Mozambique's south-central region (Figure 33). This settlement – an outlier of the Zimbabwe Culture, architecturally connected with Great Zimbabwe – was first excavated by a foreign team involving traditional techniques and practices that led to the publication of results in academic journals. Subsequently, additional areas of the site were excavated by Mozambique-based archaeologists. By 1978, some 400 local people had participated voluntarily in the fieldwork at the site, and in the following year a site museum was opened in an attempt to make a continuing educational contribution to the local community.

In the archaeologists' words, 'the implementation of the project at Manyikeni in an area which was adversely influenced by the war situation symbolized for a wider audience in Mozambican society the people's determination both to comprehend and to affirm their historical role in the struggle for nationhood ... it is this reservoir of public concern which must be tapped for the further development of the archaeological discipline in Mozambique' (Sinclair et al. 1993a: 429).

FIGURE 33 MANYIKENI, MOZAMBIQUE.

Archaeology in Nigerian education

Nwanna Nzewunwa, reviewing archaeology in Nigerian education in the late 1980s, has written:

'The absence of archaeology in the informal education sphere has made it impossible to tap the popularity that archaeology could well enjoy among Nigerian people.

'The absence from the primary and secondary schools of programmes in archaeology has kept archaeology away from the grassroots of Nigerian cultural education. As a result, interest in archaeology is delayed until a much later stage when students enter university. This is too late. Since only a very small percentage of the population benefits from university education, the knowledge of archaeology is further restricted to a tiny group of Nigerians. It is, therefore, an inescapable conclusion that archaeology in Nigeria is exclusive and elitist.

'This is what archaeology should not be in Nigeria, nor indeed in any African setting, because of its place in local Nigerian history. Since Africans view history as a continuum made up of the past, no matter how remote, the present and the future, archaeology that enhances the recovery and interpretation of this history should have an elevated status, and should be shared by a larger sector of the Nigerian society. This is what archaeology in Nigerian education should now aim to achieve. To do this requires the collective responsibility and collaboration of policy-makers in accepting archaeology into the curriculum of these lower levels of education. It also requires the recognition by Nigerian archaeologists that they must begin to popularise archaeology, make it more accessible, less mystifying, and devoid of the jargon that can only appeal to academic professionals' (Nzewunwa 1990: 40–1).

Taking archaeology to schools

Rushdi Nackerdien, an archaeologist working with the University of Cape Town's Community Education Resources group, wrote a story about archaeology for primary-school children (Nackerdien 1993).

His book is in two parts. In the first part Faizal is told about archaeology by his older sister Zaida, a university student. They find some stone tools, and Faizal has a dream about meeting a boy called Ukwane, whose family made stone tools of the kind that Faizal and Zaida had found.

The second part of the book is an account of what archaeologists do – the use of sources, excavation and laboratory work. Rushdi Nackerdien worked with children and teachers at a local school to make sure that *Faizal's Journey* was pitched at the right level. Here are some extracts.

It was a glorious sunny day on the beach as Zaida chased Faizal playfully across the sand. Just as she was about to catch him, he fell. Laughing, he struggled to his feet and stubbed his toe on a stone half-buried in the sand. 'Ouch!' he shouted, rubbing his foot and staring at the stone. 'Hey,' he said, 'Look at these funny stones.' Zaida stooped down. 'Why, these look almost like stone tools …

'People in the past could make and shape ordinary pieces of stone into very delicate tools, just like this. Look at how carefully this piece of stone has been chipped to this shape.' She showed him a fragment of stone that looked like a half-moon. 'Hmm,' Faizal thought, 'those tiny marks all along the edge do look very reg-

FIGURE 34 'Join Faizal in discovering more about the past'.

Join Faizal in discovering more about the past.

Turn the page to learn more!

ular, but I still don't believe that people made them.'

By the time night came, they were both exhausted. Faizal had asked so many questions that Zaida could not answer all of them. That night Faizal had trouble falling asleep. He was still excited about what they had found that day. He had finally drifted into a deep sleep, when he started to dream …

He was walking in a narrow valley in the Cederberg. There were luscious green plants and bushes as far as the eye could see. He could hear a river and walked tentatively towards the bubbling sound. The river snaked through a clearing in the bushes. He drank the clear fresh water and looked around curiously. There was a rocky overhang several metres above the river. He decided to climb to it, so that he could see further.

Nestling in the stony shelter, he sat down to rest … Slowly, Faizal became aware that there was something different about this shelter. He turned round expectantly. The back wall was covered with rock paintings!

The drawings looked like they had been painted very recently. That was strange … Could it be that he was in the past?

Suddenly, he heard soft footsteps approaching. He tried to hide, but the footsteps were too close. He turned to face the stranger. It was a boy … 'Who are you?' the boy asked. Although he spoke a different language, Faizal understood what the boy was saying. 'My name is Faizal,' he answered. 'Where do you come from?' enquired the boy again. 'I am from a different time, the future.' The boy did not act surprised at all. 'I'm Ukwane. I live here.'…

Ukwane was saying that he was learning to be a healer in his community. He was learning from his father and when they danced, they went into a dream-like state. In this dream, they spoke to good spirits and fought the bad ones in order to cure the sick or to bring goodwill and happiness to the community. Sometimes they succeeded in their attempts, sometimes they did not. Often they would show their families what they saw in their dream-state by painting it on the walls of caves or shelters like this one …

'Are all these paintings dreams?' Faizal asked, gesturing to the shelter wall behind them

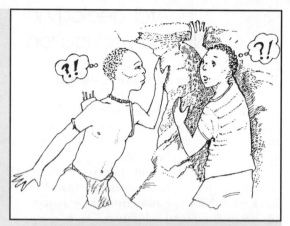

FIGURE 35 'He turned to face the stranger'.

… 'Oh yes! My family and our ancestors painted them here long before Old Mother Tu was born. She does not know when my ancestors first came here.' Pointing to a faint outline of an animal covered by many paintings, he said: 'Old Mother Tu says that this eland was the first painting by our ancestors. Each time we dance, we touch it and enter into the spirit world, where our ancestors live. When we paint our dreams, we always try and paint close to it, so that our paintings can also become powerful. Each generation, one of my family is chosen to repaint the eland, renewing its power …'

Faizal woke up with a start. The cat had knocked one of his books off the table. He lay awake for a long time thinking about his dream and Ukwane and the important stone tools they had found … While he was getting dressed, Faizal decided to spend his holiday finding out more about archaeology.

FIGURE 36 'He lay awake thinking about his dream'.

Kenyan archaeologist Karega-Munene has outlined some of the difficulties which he and his colleagues face in disseminating information about archaeological work in East Africa.

- There is a strong tradition of publishing virtually all research results in Europe or North America. The only exceptions are dissertations written by local students, the journal *Azania*, and a local newsletter, *Kumbuka*.
- Almost all publishing houses in East Africa are foreign-owned, and have no interest in financially risky, specialist books.
- The number of indigenous archaeologists in Kenya, Uganda and Tanzania is small, as are the numbers of students studying archaeology in East African universities. This has limited the development of a viable local market for archaeological publications.
- The price of books in East Africa is high.
- Archaeologists and libraries are centralised in a small number of cities. This makes it virtually impossible for people in rural areas to get access to archaeological information.

As a result of difficulties such as these, very few people hear about archaeology, and archaeologists find it ever harder to mobilise support for their profession: they are locked in a spiral of diminishing resources. 'The problem in East Africa is not democratization of archaeological data *per se*, but democratization of the already available information' (Karega-Munene 1992: 46).

Karega-Munene considers the expansion of computer networks one possible solution for problems such as these. He points out that computers can counter the inaccessibility of publications and the high cost of books, and can help to make archaeological information far more available both to members of the public and to professional archaeologists. Although computer resources are still very limited in East Africa, this is a potentially important area of development for the future.

Schools, museums and other public institutions have a vital role to play in the dissemination of knowledge about the past. In earlier years, archaeologists often felt that their tasks were research and technical writing for the benefit of their colleagues. Fortunately, this view was never universal, and people such as Thurstan Shaw in Ghana and then Nigeria, and Ray Inskeep and Revil Mason in South Africa, insisted that public education must be central to the development of the discipline. Today, their view is widely shared. This change in attitude is partly altruistic and partly pragmatic: in an era of diminishing resources for research, increasing public accountability is being demanded for expenditure on research. But in addition, archaeologists are also finding that there are considerable benefits in working with a wide range of people: there is a lot of valuable knowledge in the public domain.

Public archaeology and history in Kenya

The development of archaeology in Kenya has been closely tied to historical studies. Although this has the advantage of encouraging a holistic view of the past, archaeologists working in Kenya have also found that their discipline has acquired something of a second-string status. Simiyu Wandibba remembers the way archaeology was taught at the University of Nairobi until the early 1970s. 'Prehistory of the World' formed part of the History syllabus:

'Of all the "history" courses, archaeology was the only one to which the students were introduced for the first time at university level. I personally had never heard the term archaeology before I joined the university. To make matters worse, the subject was full of tongue-twisting scientific words. This was especially true of the lectures on human evolution. Additionally, one came across many prehistoric sites that were not only difficult to pronounce, but also to spell, especially those in Hungary and China ... The course tended to be a mere catalogue of prehistoric sites and cultures. Consequently, it turned out to be not only difficult, but also quite dull. There was very little that could excite the students ... For the first seven years of the course's existence, only the present author, among the many hundreds of history students, was interested enough to indicate his desire to become an archaeologist, and actually went on to do so' (Wandibba 1990:44–5).

Not surprisingly, given the place of the discipline in the university syllabus, archaeology had only a slight role in primary- and secondary-school teaching, even though archaeological research has occupied a central place in the writing of Kenya's precolonial history.

This situation began to change in 1980, when the introduction of a new university curriculum gave students the chance to obtain a degree in archaeology for the first time. But in Wandibba's opinion, the focus was still overwhelmingly historical:

'Kenyan archaeology is still considered as part of history. Students in both primary and secondary schools normally learn bits of archaeology by way of background to their history classes. Textbooks for such courses are usually written by historians who, because they see archaeology as part of history, do not bother even to consult archaeologists. The result is disastrous in that such books end up containing information that is generally out of date and also downright inaccurate ... At university, archaeology continues to be taught as background to the history of Africa, or to whatever African region is being studied. Historians normally do not ask their archaeology colleagues to give such lectures, merely assuming that they know enough to give the lectures themselves. This practice has been, in my view, one of the main obstacles preventing the development of a viable archaeology programme for university education in Kenya' (Wandibba 1990: 47).

To some extent, the consequences of this neglect have been mitigated by the role of the national museums of Kenya. Museums play an important part in educating the general public about the importance of archaeology, and supporting research and training of archaeology students. In addition, the government of Kenya has made it a condition that all foreign research workers who come to explore the country's rich cultural heritage include in their programmes training opportunities for Kenyan students.

'Many people in Kenya remain ignorant of what archaeology is. This lack of archaeological awareness is in part due to the paucity of coverage that the profession receives from the mass media, which only rarely report on archaeological work. Thus the National Museums have to rely on their Education Department to publicize archaeological activities. This is done through lectures to primary school children as well as to students of post-primary institutions. But this outlet is still insufficient to promote archaeology adequately in Kenya' (Wandibba 1990: 49).

The museum: temple or forum?

'Every museum exhibition, whatever its overt subject, inevitably draws on the cultural assumptions and resources of the people who made it. Decisions are made to emphasise one element and to downplay others, to assert some truths and to ignore others. The assumptions underpinning these decisions vary according to culture and over time, place, and type of museum or exhibit. Exhibitions made today may seem obviously appropriate to some viewers precisely because those viewers share the same attitudes as the exhibition makers, and the exhibitions are cloaked in familiar presentational styles. We discover the artifice when we look at older installations or those made in other cultural contexts. The very nature of exhibiting, then, makes it a contested terrain' (Lavine & Karp 1991: 1).

In introducing a symposium held at Washington's Smithsonian Institution, Steven Lavine and Ivan Karp suggested that museums fall into two categories. A museum may be a 'temple' – a place where objects are displayed and venerated, and are claimed as timeless models of taste or as unassailable historical evidence. Alternatively, a museum may be a 'forum' – a place where there is confrontation, experimentation and debate.

Many people working in museums today would assert the 'forum' role. But they would also know that moving away from older ideas is often challenging. Conceptualising alternative perspectives can be difficult and new displays may take a long time to complete, making them seem obsolete by the time they are ready for presentation to the public. Despite the best intentions of their curators, museums become elite places by virtue of diverse language preferences, illiteracy, poverty and the inaccessibility of towns and cities to largely rural populations. Finally, museum visitors themselves are often conservative, seeking authoritative statements rather than debate, or the confirmation of ideas already held rather than new concepts.

Many museums in Africa originated in the days of colonial rule. Dawson Munjeri, reviewing the pre-independence history of museums in Zimbabwe, has traced the inception of the present National Museums and Monuments organisation back to 1899, when a society was formed to make a collection of the 'natural and human sciences' (Munjeri 1991). Museums in Southern Rhodesia were geared to serve the settler community, and until the 1950s Africans were discouraged from entering their doors, and were often restricted to a single visiting day in each week. Similar policies were ubiquitous in other parts of colonial Africa.

But at the same time, museums have often provided bases from which seminal archaeological research projects were conducted. Much of the Stone Age sequence of southern Africa was initially mapped out from the results of long-term, systematic excavations carried out by museum-based archaeologists. Similarly, the first sequences of pottery decoration styles used by early farming communities were determined on the basis of museum-sponsored research work. Museums store and create large collections of stone tools, potsherds, animal bones from excavated sites and organic remains, and their archives contain original site notes and drawings and inventories of excavated collections. Because archaeological excavation is a basically destructive process, museum collections have often themselves become the primary evidence for thousands of years of early history.

Museums also have a particularly important role in public education. Because archaeology is often not a major part of the school syllabus, the museum becomes the primary medium through which people learn about

the more distant past. Then again, archaeology offers its public objects: stone tools, potsherds and other things which can be seen and, under some circumstances, handled – visual and tactile qualities that are educationally stimulating. And unlike animals, plants and birds that may be displayed in a museum, archaeological objects cannot easily be seen in the 'wild'. Most museum displays consist of objects that have been unearthed by means of the mediating hand of the archaeologist. They can have the appeal and excitement of detection and discovery.

A major goal for archaeology in museums is taking into the present what is good and useful from the past – in particular, established traditions of research and important collections of material. How can archaeologists move from being 'temple' custodians to 'forum' facilitators?

This issue is being widely discussed, particularly in South Africa, where apartheid has left an enduring legacy in the organisation and facilities of public institutions. In Cape Town, this colonial heritage is set in stone and mortar. The monumental South African National Gallery, traditionally the repository of 'art', is placed on one side of the old Company Gardens, originally established by the first colonists in the mid-seventeenth century. To its right,

FIGURE 37 BEHIND THE SCENES IN THE MUSEUM. Archaeological excavations result in large collections of artefacts that remain primary sources of evidence about the past. Museums have an important role in the storage and conservation of these collections.

FIGURE 38 ARTEFACTS CAN BE PUT TO IMAGINATIVE USE IN MUSEUM EDUCATION.

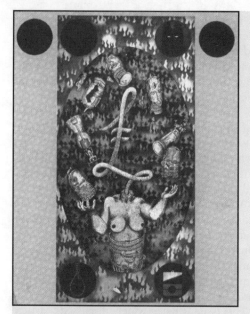

Figure 39 'FACE VALUE'. This exhibition in the South African National Gallery, Cape Town, challenged the boundaries between 'archaeology' and 'art'. The invitation to the exhibition opening featured a copper-plate etching in which a headless woman juggles clay sculptures from Lydenburg ('artefacts') and similar sculptures made by the artist himself ('works of art').

beyond the Houses of Parliament and the President's residence, and at the bottom of the Gardens, is the South African Cultural History Museum, first a slave house, then the Supreme Court and thereafter the repository for colonial 'culture'. At the top of the Gardens is the South African Museum, home of natural history, archaeology and ethnography.

In 1993 the South African Museum organised a symposium to explore ways of change – an exercise in self-critique which illustrates the importance ascribed to these issues by its staff. The core problem was summarised by Bryan Krafchik, who coordinated the meeting: 'at the South African Museum, the grouping of artefacts from indigenous African people with natural history has given rise to the criticism that the Museum is inherently racist. The exclusion, until recently, of African material from the South African Cultural History Museum has lent support to the argument that both institutions justified apartheid by portraying society as being divided along tribal and racial lines. The current challenge is to find ways of using museum resources to renegotiate these classificatory and institutional divisions' (Krafchik 1994a: 2).

One approach is to contest distinctions such as 'art', 'culture' and 'ethnography'. At the symposium Marilyn Martin, Director of the South African National Gallery, described a recent

exhibition, 'Face Value', which had included tenth-century clay sculptures from the archaeological site of Lydenburg in the province of Mpumalanga alongside work by Malcolm Payne, a present-day Cape Town artist (Figure 39). The Lydenburg finds have been housed in the South African Museum, and were loaned to the Gallery for the duration of the exhibition. But this was not without controversy. Archaeologists at the Museum felt that other material from Lydenburg should be displayed in the Gallery in order to set the archaeological sculptures in their context, but the artist was adamant that this would interfere with the integrity of his exhibition (Martin 1993).

There is not, and should not be, a general consensus about the 'correct' way to display archaeological objects such as the Lydenburg Heads, about whether they are 'art' or 'ethnography', or about an artist's right to appropriate and reinterpret them. The point is rather that there is contested terrain, that the museum has become a 'forum' rather than 'temple', a place for discussion and debate rather than the arbiter of taste or the authority on meaning.

Another approach is to breach the enclosing walls of the museum – to take objects and interpretations to the people. Here, there is great potential in site museums, which usually offer stimulating possibilities for conveying the contexts in which artefacts were once used. At Vergelegen, an early eighteenth-century farm about an hour's drive from Cape Town, Ann Markell excavated the building used for housing slaves, unearthing new evidence for aspects of the daily lives of those people at the very bottom of the colonial social order. She then was given the opportunity to design an exhibition that would tell the story of the excavation and the analysis of excavated material. As a result, visitors can both learn about slave life and get a sense of the rural setting in which people lived and worked. There are many other similar opportunities for 'living archaeology'. Examples include rock-painting sites, excavations left open so that visitors can gain a sense of the ways in which archaeological work is conducted, and monumental sites such as Great Zimbabwe.

But some of the most effective improvements in museum education may prove to demand far less of an investment in time and money than is required at a permanent site museum. One particularly successful enterprise has been the Botswana National Museum's 'Zebra-on-wheels'. Founded in the year of its country's independence, this museum faced a daunting task. Little money was available, and Botswana's population was spread thinly over a vast area with a rudimentary communications network. It was clear that only a very few, better off people would be able to benefit from museum displays if they were confined to galleries in the capital of Gaborone. The solution was a mobile museum, loaded in the back of a van. Today, there are 4 four-wheel-drive vehicles, equipped with generators, film projectors and display collections and painted with the zebra's stripes. The Zebras-on-wheels move around the country continually, visiting each school at least once a year. When it arrives at a village, the mobile museum is set up in the meeting place, the *kgotla*, encouraging the participation of the entire community (Metz 1994). It is difficult to imagine a greater contrast to the traditional museum, with its treasures protected by glass, its watchful attendants and its church-like atmosphere.

FIGURE 40 ZEBRA-ON-WHEELS.

Teaching the past to posterity

Mr Peter Shinwin Atanga lived at Akum, a few kilometres from Bamenda on the Bafoussam–Bamenda road in Cameroon. A farmer and bookshop-keeper, Mr Atanga started a private museum collection in the late 1940s when his daughter asked him what men used to shave with before there were razor blades. This led him to realise that knowledge of the past was being rapidly lost, and such questions would not be answerable in the next century. The purpose of his collection was, in his opinion 'teaching the past to posterity and providing material for research for Cameroonians, Africans and people of all races'.

Atanga called his collections the International Museum and Library, and established them in four rooms of his house. Apart from books, he collected world currencies and stamps, cinematographic equipment from the years before independence, musical instruments, pottery, basketry and beadwork. He purchased everything himself, apparently to the irritation of his eight children, who would have preferred him to develop his business interests. Such was the value of Atanga's collections that a case has been made for their purchase by the government of Cameroon as the nucleus for a proposed National Museum in Yaounde (Asombang 1990).

51

Archaeology and development

One of the effects of the widening scope of public archaeology has been the growth of specialist areas – the promotion of special methods and approaches to deal with new aspects of archaeological practice. One example of such an approach can be labelled 'applied archaeology'. This assumes that archaeological knowledge about the past has a direct, practical relevance to present sociological and ecological problems. For example, modern pastoralist communities in southern Africa have faced a succession of crises in recent years. With the transition from commonage to deeded ownership of the land, these communities have found themselves occupying besieged enclaves in Namaqualand, the Richtersveld and Namibia. In some of the areas from which indigenous pastoralists have been displaced, there is strong evidence for ecological deterioration caused by commercial ranching. How does archaeology come in? Simply because, without the archaeologist, there can be no history of pastoralists stretching back beyond the short term. 'Pastoral cultural ecology needs to embrace a concept of history, a past that over thousands of years has developed the close relationship between people, animals and the land' (Smith 1992: 257). In this approach, archaeology becomes part of the broader field of development ecology, contributing to practical solutions for managing resources effectively over long periods of time.

'With the growing literature on pastoral societies within the context of post-colonial governmental frameworks, we are aware of the changes taking place in traditional herding societies. The exploitation interests of outside forces, such as mineral wealth, absentee landlords, etc., put new pressures on pastoralism but there is no evidence that pastoralism is diminishing. What, perhaps, is becoming smaller is the area of commonage formerly used by herding people.

'The complexity of relationships of man to the land and animals underlines the importance of an ecological approach in prehistory. Here we have a methodology for studying the dynamic interaction between man and the varied aspects of his environment. The physical environment is only one aspect of the total model, and since the political and economic environments are often very difficult, if not impossible, to detect in early prehistoric societies, these elusive components are generally ignored in attempts to reconstruct former societies …

'Of the various components of cultural ecology, archaeologists can, to a certain extent, control for the biological systems, i.e. the plants and animals eaten or inadvertently brought onto a site. By extrapolation of these food resources, along with palaeo-environmental and geomorphological data, a picture of the physical systems can emerge. The relationship of the focal subject prehistoric society with

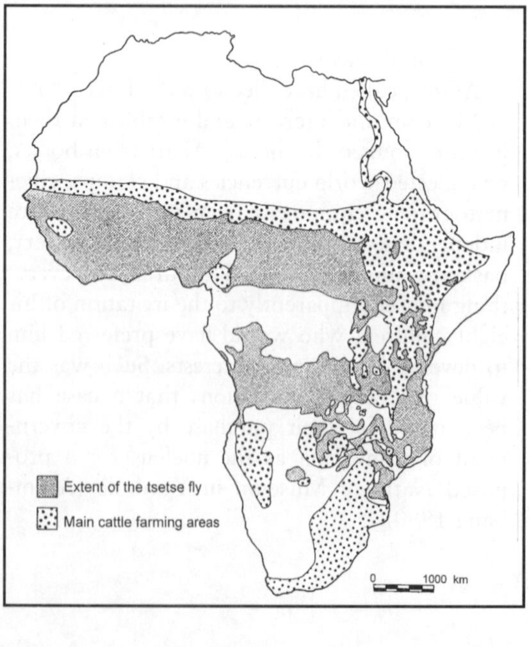

Figure 41 Pastoralism in Africa. Pastoralism is a way of life across wide areas of Africa. An archaeological perspective allows us to study the adaptations between pastoralist communities and the environments in which they live, through time – a vital perspective if ecological factors are to be properly understood. For example, the extent of the areas in which tsetse fly is endemic has a major impact on cattle keeping. In turn, tsetse is affected by the density of vegetation, and therefore by the activities of farming communities. Applied archaeology, leading to the identification of cause and effect relationships in the environment, has a major role in contemporary development studies. Ecological approaches to archaeology are discussed further in Chapter 8.

Extent of the tsetse fly

Main cattle farming areas

0   1000 km

other cultural groups can be obtained at a gross level from the material culture differences that appear in the archaeological record, and, of course, the technological and material culture aspects of the subject society are the bare bones of any archaeological analysis. It is the internal system which is usually lacking, particularly the psychological or world view that the society under study conceives in relation to the land and animals' (Smith 1992: xii-xiii).

FIGURE 42 REMOVING GRAFFITI FROM ROCK PAINTINGS. Although legislation may exist to protect archaeological sites, it may not be effective or adequately enforced. For example, many rock-art sites have been damaged by people who feel a compulsion to write their names over the painted surfaces. Here, archaeologists use specially tested chemicals to remove graffiti from an important set of images. Conservation work such as this is an important part of Cultural Resource Management.

Cultural Resource Management

Developmental problems such as these can be regarded as special cases of the broader field of Cultural Resource Management (CRM), almost a discipline in its own right in North America, and a specialisation that is becoming increasingly important in Africa.

Two very different projects – at different ends of the continent, widely separated in scale and at polar extremes in terms of public interest – serve to illustrate further the scope of CRM, and to conclude this overview of public archaeology: Egypt's Abu Simbel and Cape Town's North Wharf.

Cultural Resource Management (CRM)

'Most nations of the world now recognize that it is the public duty of a government to have some policy of conservation. That policy will apply to natural resources and wildlife, but it will also apply to archaeological remains. So most nations now have protective legislation – not all equally effective – for their ancient sites, minor as well as major … ' (Renfrew & Bahn 1991: 470).

Case Study: Abu Simbel

Abu Simbel, on the west bank of the Nile near to the Sudanese border, is the site of two temples built by the Egyptian king Rameses II, who reigned between 1279 and 1213 BC. The complex includes four colossal statues of Rameses, each 20 m high, carved in a sandstone cliff. They guard the entrance to the temple, which is dedicated to the sun gods Re-Amun and Re-Horakhti. This extends more than 50 m into the cliff face, and is decorated with more images of the king and with painted reliefs illustrating his life and achievements (Aldred 1984).

In the early 1960s, the construction of the nearby Aswan High Dam threatened Abu Simbel with flooding. The Egyptian government and the United Nations Educational, Scientific and Cultural Organization (UNESCO) sponsored a project to save what was possible of the tem-

ple. Between 1964 and 1966 an international team of engineers, supported by funds from more than 50 countries, dug away the top of the cliff and disassembled both temples, reconstructing them again on higher ground a short distance away.

FIGURE 43 ABU SIMBEL.

FIGURE 44 CULTURAL RESOURCE MANAGEMENT AT CAPE TOWN'S NORTH WHARF.

Case study: Cape Town's North Wharf

Through the years, the shoreline of Table Bay has been extensively modified by land reclamation projects, with the result that the heart of Cape Town is now considerably further from the sea than it was a century and more ago. During this process of urban expansion, some early features were buried beneath landfill. Now, with urban renewal and redevelopment proceeding, some of these features are being exposed again during construction work.

One example is Cape Town's North Wharf (Saitowitz et al. 1993). Construction of this important feature of the city's commercial development began in 1839, and the new jetty was opened for use in 1842. It was an iron and timber structure, with piping to carry fresh water to the ships moored alongside. Archaeological excavation, ahead of redevelopment of the site, was commissioned by Cape Town's Urban Conservation Unit, and resulted in the recording of details of construction techniques, amplifying the sparse documentary sources and photographs. Once the excavation had been completed, the remains of the North Wharf were buried again, and redevelopment was designed to minimise the damage from new foundations.

In a way, archaeology in Africa has turned full circle. African archaeology started with the widespread surge of European public interest early in the nineteenth century that followed Napoleon's invasion of Egypt. During the next hundred years, Europe's domination of the 'dark continent' was asserted, and archaeology helped to buttress the ideologies of colonialism. The first professional archaeologists inherited this regrettable legacy, and reacted by looking inwards and talking to one another, rather than to the 'amateurs' among the colonial bureaucracies and settler communities. But with the consolidation of the post-colonial era in Africa, a very different sort of public interest has arisen, and archaeologists are again looking outwards to their wider communities. It is likely that public accountability will be the key concept in Africa's archaeology of.the twenty-first century.

chapter 4

Questions

Writing about the past involves a constant, and often complicated, interplay between present-day concerns ('politics' in the broadest sense of the term) and archaeological evidence – the collections of artefacts that have survived the passage of time. As the work of several generations of archaeologists in Africa has shown, the study of the past is particularly important when it challenges preconceived ideas (such as colonialist assumptions about the 'barbarism' of the 'dark continent'). In other words, archaeological evidence has the potential to dispel widely held views about the nature of the past.

But at the same time, giving meaning to archaeological evidence depends on propositions about the nature of the past. For example, shaped stones, first described from Africa and Europe in the nineteenth century, could not be recognised as the work of past humans without the geological theory of uniformitarianism and the growing acceptance of biological evolution as an explanation for the origins of all living organisms. This chapter looks at the ways in which questions about the past are framed, and at some of the basic concepts that lie behind archaeological inquiry.

Facts and theories

John Goodwin, whose *Method in Prehistory* (first published in 1945) was probably the first handbook on archaeological methodology written for Africa, stressed the importance of this interplay between theory and evidence. 'A theory', Goodwin wrote, 'has been described as a policy; perhaps it might better be regarded as a systematic framework into which facts can be fitted ... A theory can never affect the validity of a fact. Smash a theory and the facts will remain awaiting an alternative explanation. A stubborn fact will, however, kill a theory. The one is absolute, the other hypothetical ...' (Goodwin 1953: 13).

Today, it would be generally accepted that Goodwin's formulation is incomplete. The interplay between theory and evidence is constant and central to what archaeologists do. Without theories about the nature of the past, there can be no archaeology. But the standing of the 'fact' has become less secure.

This can be illustrated by turning again to the history of excavation at Great Zimbabwe. Theodore Bent, in keeping with the fieldwork methods of his times, was interested in 'special'

FIGURE 45 AN ABSOLUTE FACT? Architectural detail at Great Zimbabwe. This upright stone still stands in the slot specially made for it in a stone-walled enclosure in the 'valley' area of Great Zimbabwe. But is it part of a doorway or a phallic symbol? Differing interpretations of such archaeological evidence are discussed later in this chapter. In archaeology, there is rarely such a thing as an 'absolute fact'.

finds, and would have considered lunatic the modern practice of collecting and curating every potsherd. R. N. Hall took Bent's approach to its extreme, discarding most of what he considered 'native' and 'recent' in his search for artefacts that proved the presence of Phoenicians or other long-lost settlers. Gertrude Caton-Thompson arrived in southern Africa with a completely different outlook and an approach to excavation which she had developed under Flinders Petrie's guidance in Egypt. She was interested in evidence for a 'Zimbabwe Culture' indicated by pottery design, and deemed highly relevant those same ceramic sherds that Bent and Hall regarded as a mere nuisance. Later archaeologists realised that the controversy about Great Zimbabwe's age could be resolved by using the new technique of radiocarbon dating, and excavators searched painstakingly for fragments of burnt charcoal. It was also realised that animal bones could reveal a great deal about the nature of the site's economy, and some of the dumps from earlier digs were then patiently re-excavated (Garlake 1973).

Thus, there is not one immutable set of facts about Great Zimbabwe, but rather a series of observations, with each set modulated by theories about the nature of the past. Each new interpretation has to take into account previous constellations of observations, in this way making archaeological interpretation ever more complex. It must follow that the observations made in our own time cannot be a final 'truth' about the site. They are, rather, further contributions in an ongoing dialogue. Facts, like kings, are no longer absolute.

Archaeologists understand the relation between what they write and the evidence they write about in various ways. At one end of the spectrum are 'empiricists', who hold that archaeological evidence has objective patterning, irrespective of which archaeologist is carrying out the research, and that describing and explaining this patterning is archaeology's legitimate task. At the other end of the spectrum are 'relativists', who believe that all observations are framed and structured by the perceptions of the observer, and that the past can be no more than an image of the preoccupations and prejudices of the present day.

Despite the marked divergence of these theoretical positions, they are both indebted in one way or another to major changes in archaeology as a whole that took place in the middle years of the twentieth century. Confusingly, this is still known as the 'New Archaeology', even though its unreformed proponents have long been the gatekeepers of the establishment, which newer voices are contesting.

The foundation stone for New Archaeology was the reversal of the research procedure that had been seen as fundamental by earlier writers, such as John Goodwin. In *Method in Prehistory*, Goodwin had written that 'there are certain rules or disciplines governing scientific method. It is, for instance, essential to work from the known to the unknown ... The routine of scientific method as applied in our subject can best be epitomized thus: observe, record, remember, compare, interpret' (1953: 12, 15).

New Archaeologists turned maxims such as this on their heads. They argued that working from observation to interpretation *explained* nothing about the way people had behaved in the past; it merely led to rote descriptions of artefacts and contexts. New Archaeologists insisted that true interpretation had to be deductive. The archaeologist had to start with a proposition, a hypothesis, that was formulated before fieldwork began. Next, the archaeologist should construct a 'model' – a set of expectations about how the propositions in the hypothesis could be met. Only after these prior stages should the archaeologist begin to conduct fieldwork. The aim of collecting evidence through survey work or excavation should be to test, as rigorously as possible, whether the original hypothesis could stand, or whether it should be discarded and replaced with a new set of propositions. This attitude to research, adopted from a school of thought in the philosophy of science, was known as the 'hypothetico-deductive method' (Binford & Binford 1968; Clarke 1968).

New Archaeology has been widely criticised. Critics have questioned the philosophical soundness of hypothetico-deductive reasoning as well as the practicality of a laboratory-style, experimental approach to the archaeological record. In particular, the New Archaeologists' search for general, timeless laws of human behaviour has been seen as a goal that takes history out of archaeology (Hodder 1991). But despite all these criticisms, it was New Archaeology that overturned the sovereignty of the fact in archaeological method, opening the doors wide for the myriad interpretative approaches to the past that make archaeology such a stimulating and valuable discipline today.

It is clear that this intellectual revolution in archaeology has major implications for even the most practical aspects of the discipline. When the fact was king, the only imperatives in fieldwork were optimum recovery and accurate observation. As long as artefacts had been recovered in context, the fact could be trusted to speak for itself. But today, the world of archaeology is a less certain place. Despite Hollywood's continuing caricature, merely to drive into the bush and dig a site is to invite trouble of some form or other. Rather than submitting to a rush of enthusiasm like this, we need to contemplate New Archaeology's legacy: the issues of how archaeological facts are formed, and how archaeological questions are framed.

FIGURE 46 HOLLYWOOD'S ARCHAEOLOGY.

Formation processes

In approaching the first of these issues, William Rathje and Michael Schiffer draw a useful distinction between what they term 'cultural formation processes' and 'natural formation processes' (Rathje & Schiffer 1982).

> **cultural formation processes** the ways in which human actions have affected an artefact between the time that it was first used and the moment when it is recovered by an archaeologist; the complex history through which something made and used in the past becomes part of our history
> **natural formation processes** the environmental factors that contribute to the history of artefacts between the time that they are discarded and the time that they are excavated or described by an archaeologist

A cultural formation process is part of the complex history through which something made and used in the past becomes part of our written histories. Rathje and Schiffer suggest that we think of cultural formation processes as having four possible stages.

Firstly, there is the possibility of re-use. Recently, archaeologists researching the Late Stone Age in different parts of southern Africa have begun to notice that people were systematically re-using much earlier stone tools, which they must have collected from long-abandoned camp sites. It has also been shown that superimposition at rock-art sites – the painting of a new image over an earlier one – was often deliberate. Intentionally or otherwise, these hunter–gatherer communities were reworking the archaeological record. A second example is provided by the archaeology of slavery. Slavery depends on systematic deprivation to ensure control of the slave by the overseer. Thus when a slave hid away everyday objects pilfered from the master's table he was offering an effective form of mundane resistance (M. Hall 1992). The artefact thus stolen and later excavated has a complex history of multiple use.

Secondly, there is deposition – the manner in which an artefact enters the archaeological record. Rathje and Schiffer point out that deposition happens in a wide variety of ways. Artefacts may be deliberately buried, either as grave goods or as caches of valued possessions. Objects may be accidentally lost or deliberately discarded. Most artefacts enter the archaeological record for the last of these reasons: people throw away their rubbish, and some of it survives through time to be studied by the archaeologist. Wells are archaeological sites that usually combine a range of different forms of deposition. A good example of this was provided by excavation of a well shaft cut into a backyard in Cape Town's Barrack Street in the closing decades of the eighteenth century. The assemblage that was recovered included everyday food waste, such as fish and mutton bones and broken ceramics, as well as some pieces of fine jewellery, coins, pins, a thimble and a child's porcelain doll that had probably been accidentally lost (M. Hall et al. 1990).

Rathje and Schiffer's third stage in the processes of cultural formation is reclamation:

'Not everything that enters the archaeological record stays there. Some of the survivors of Pompeii returned to dig out their belongings from the volcanic ash. The same process occurs when survivors of floods, hurricanes, and fires return to "dig out". Reclamation processes thus include those activities that move objects from archaeological context back into systemic context' (Rathje & Schiffer 1982: 121).

To take another example, members of the London Missionary Society's expedition to Central Africa in 1877 were presented with bored stones which had been collected and conserved by local people as messages from their ancestors (Roberts 1984). In being reclaimed in this way, these artefacts have acquired at least two sets of archaeological meanings – their original purpose of manufacture, and their later, ritual significance.

The fourth stage is disturbance: human

> 'Archaeologists study artifacts in two states: *systemic context*, where the artifacts are a part of activities within an adaptive system, and *archaeological context*, where artifacts have been deposited and are no longer involved in activities ... The way in which materials are moved between systemic and archaeological context affects the nature of archaeological evidence, or the *archaeological record*. The processes that govern these movements are known as the *cultural formation processes* of the archaeological record' (Rathje & Schiffer 1982).

activities on a site after deposition, but before archaeological excavation. The nature of disturbance varies considerably according to the context of the specific site, but it is usually a factor to be considered. The landscape is an active environment, undergoing constant modification. Some rock-shelter sites in the Western Cape, South Africa, have been extensively disturbed by farmers digging trenches for fertiliser, while painted walls have attracted graffiti, some of it hundreds of years old. The sites of farming villages have, in many areas, been disturbed by ploughing and hoeing; after all, the same fertile soils that attracted farmers hundreds of years ago are valuable today as well. In cities, constant cycles of urban decay and renewal mean that archaeological sites are constantly reworked by human agency.

Finally – despite attempts by many archaeologists to remain scientifically detached from the objects of their research – we should remember that archaeological excavation is itself a stage in the cultural formation process of a site. Increasingly, as archaeology becomes more integrated into the wider public domain, what happens during and after an excavation will become integrated with the complex ways in which the archaeological record has been formed.

Natural formation processes, in Rathje and Schiffer's definition, are the environmental factors which contribute to the history of artefacts between the time they are discarded and the time they are excavated by the archaeologist (Rathje & Schiffer 1982). Natural formation processes may usefully be thought of in terms of the nature of the agency, and the length of time that it has been operating.

A number of different agencies operate on artefacts, whether assemblages are buried or exposed on the surface of the ground. Chemical agents, for example, commonly interact with the material from which an artefact is made, causing metalwork to rust, or bone to be damaged by acidic soils. Biological agents, such as bacteria, work through time to break down organic materials, often leaving few, if any, traces of the original artefact. Physical agents, in particular wind and water, erode and abrade exposed artefacts.

In addition, archaeologists must take into account the length of time – the duration – that

natural formation processes have been affecting artefacts. The degree of chemical or biological decay that takes place, for example, will often be proportionate to the age of the archaeological site. Assemblages from older sites will thus be affected differently from assemblages from younger sites, and if the differential pattern of natural formation processes is not taken into account, interpretations will be biased.

Natural formation processes, particularly when they apply to bones from archaeological sites, are also referred to as the 'taphonomy' of the archaeological site (from the Greek word *taphos*, a grave). Taphonomic re-evaluation of archaeological evidence – understanding natural formation processes properly – can have a dramatic effect on archaeological interpretations. For example, work by C. K. Brain at cave sites in Gauteng, South Africa, has shown that many of the early hominids were victims of carnivores, probably leopards (Figure 47). This taphonomic study has forced a revision of the argument that our earliest ancestors were predominantly hunters, and that they killed one another – the idea of 'man the hunter', which has been one of the most persistent androcentric assumptions in archaeological interpretation (Brain 1981).

Figure 47 LEOPARD DAMAGE TO A HOMINID SKULL, SWARTKRANS. The two small holes at the back of the cranium match the size and shape of leopard canine teeth. Taphonomic studies such as these provide vital clues to the ways in which sites were formed.

'Environmental processes have four basic characteristics: (1) nature, (2) duration, (3) effects, and (4) scale. By defining the characteristics of specific environmental processes, archaeologists can determine their effect on materials in archaeological context ...

'The nature of the process is manifest in the three kinds of agents or forces that act directly on artifacts: chemical, biological, and physical. Chemical agents are among the most common since most materials are not inert, but react with air and with compounds in the depositional environment, the surroundings of artifacts in archaeological context ... Biological agents are plants and animals ... One common physical agent is moving water, which displaces artifacts and deposits sediments on sites ...

'The second characteristic of environmental processes is duration, the length of time an agent acts on artifacts. Some of the most devastating effects are wrought by single events, such as floods, hurricanes, fires, volcanoes, and tidal waves. At the other extreme are the long term processes involved in decay and disturbance by biological and physical agents, such as worms.

'Their specific effects make up the third characteristic of environmental processes. Effects are additive when environmental materials are introduced into deposits and attach themselves to artifacts ... Effects are subtractive when artifacts are deleted.

'The fourth characteristic of environmental processes is scale of effects, and this ranges from whole regions to single artifacts ....'(Rathje & Schiffer 1982: 130–2).

The Adesina Oja decay experiment

One way of studying the interaction of different formation processes is to set up an artificial 'archaeological site', burying artefacts and then studying the effects of human and natural agencies on them over time (an approach which forms part of 'experimental archaeology', described in greater detail in Chapter 9).

Archaeologists at the University of Ibadan in Nigeria needed to understand better what happens to artefacts and food remains buried in soils in tropical climates. They tackled this problem by establishing an 'archaeological reserve' – a small village evacuated by the government as part of a development programme. The recently abandoned houses were fenced off and their structure carefully recorded. An inventory was made of all the debris left behind by the villagers when they had moved out. One house was set alight so that the formation processes acting on a burnt building could be compared with the rest of the village.

As part of the project, B. E. Bassey-Duke of Nigeria's National Commission for Museums and Monuments excavated a 5 m test trench, burying a range of artefacts at differing depths and carefully recording the exact position and condition of each. These were left for five years and then excavated.

'The Adesina Oja Decay Experiment was set up to observe the process of decay or the alteration of organic and inorganic objects buried in the ground so as to provide useful information for the archaeologist on the rate of survival of the most common types of materials often encountered in archaeological excavations in most parts of the world' (Bassey-Duke 1981: 72).

The results were instructive. Cloth and sorghum – essential in tracing trade-routes and early farming – had disappeared completely. 'Cloth being of cellulose fibres would quickly disappear in soils where the pH range is optimal for the survival of micro-organisms. These soil organisms are largely responsible for the breakdown of the cellulose fibres. Sorghum also contains mainly organic matter which is easily degraded by micro-organisms and by the chemistry and temperature of the soils' (Bassey-Duke 1981: 71). Iron nails had rusted, the more so the deeper they were buried in the experimental trench. This was because soil was more acid lower in the ground. Wooden objects had been damaged by soil organisms. By contrast bottle glass, potsherds and animal bones were in the same condition as when they had been buried five years earlier.

Understanding formation processes is vital in interpreting archaeological evidence. Since formation processes vary considerably with environments, detailed studies need to be locally based if possible.

'This experiment no doubt has immense future contributions to make to the archaeology of Nigeria and indeed for the whole of Tropical West Africa. It would perhaps be very significant to set up similar experiments to those of Adesina Oja in different parts of Nigeria where climatic and other environmental factors that aid decay and preservation differ markedly from those in the humid tropics. For example, a decay experiment in the savanna grassland or in the sahelian region of Nigeria would provide valuable comparable data on the survival rate of similar objects in these environments' (Bassey-Duke 1981: 72).

FIGURE 48 LAKE TURKANA.

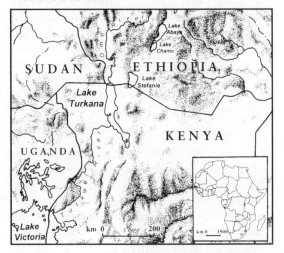

A good example of the challenges in distinguishing between natural and cultural formation processes is Zefe Kaufulu's work in the Karari area near Kenya's Lake Turkana (Figure 48, 49). Kaufulu was faced with the problem of understanding small scatters of bones and stone tools left behind by early hominids almost 2 million years ago. Because the evidence for behaviour is so sparse at this early period, the position of every artefact counts in working out whether a scatter was a place where people lived, or where they cut up an animal carcass, or where they stopped to fashion a stone tool. But what if the positions of these bones and stones were determined by natural agencies rather than by hominid activities? Failure to identify correctly the formation processes at work could lead to much deception (Kaufulu 1987).

'Research focusing on processes of site formation has shown that horizontal and vertical displacements of individual pieces are likely to occur before, during and after burial. This may result in patternings of material debris not directly related to the original hominid activities, or in the mixing of artefacts from an unrelated series of hominid activities. In fact, recent investigations indicate that the archaeological record is inevitably distorted by various post-occupational processes ...' (Kaufulu 1987: 23).

FIGURE 49 NATURAL FORMATION PROCESSES IN KENYA'S KARARI AREA. Two types of floodplain affect how artefacts are preserved. In situation A, the floodplain built up with annual flooding; a slow, shallow river (1) deposited sediments and artefacts (2) in the positions they were left by the early people who made and used them. In other parts of the Karari area, Kaufulu found that different natural formation processes had operated (B). In these cases, annual floods resulted in a fast-flowing river (3) cutting a deep incision through earlier sediments. Here, artefacts from different contexts were exposed and may have been mixed together (4).

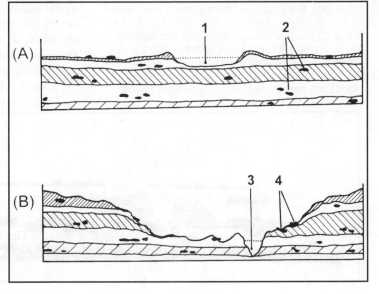

Kaufulu's approach to this problem was to sample in detail the sedimentary outcrops around each archaeological site. These sedimentary outcrops had once been gravel, sand, silt and volcanic ash – the muddy world of our early ancestors, much wetter then than today. By studying these sediment samples closely, Kaufulu was able to work out the conditions under which they had been deposited. In addition, he plotted the alignment of bones and artefacts, looking for evidence that they had been affected by strong river currents.

As a result of this study, Zefe Kaufulu was able to divide the Karari sites into two kinds. First were those sites that had formed in places where sediments were accumulating: 'the archaeological materials at these sites are enclosed within sedimentary layers' (Kaufulu 1987: 24). In these cases, because of the relation between natural and cultural formation, Kaufulu could be confident that the ways in which the artefacts had been abandoned would reflect aspects of hominid behaviour. But other sites occurred in places where natural formation processes had been dominant: 'landscapes that were dominated by processes of channel scouring and soil formation ... Archaeological interpretations which can be based on such sites are restricted to matters of artefact technology and morphology. Issues such as site layout, food refuse and palaeodiet etc., cannot be usefully addressed at such sites' (Kaufulu 1987: 24, 31).

The reburial of Flora of Vergelegen

In recent years, there has been controversy surrounding the excavation, display and storage of human remains. In some parts of the United States, this is a conflict between Native Americans and the archaeological community: the battle has taken on such proportions that excavation of Native American burials for scientific study is no longer possible in many cases. In Australia, Melanesia and New Zealand there has been conflict of the same nature. Similar problems have surfaced in Israel between Orthodox Jews and archaeologists. These conflicts centre on perceptions of the proper treatment of human remains. In the view of many Native Americans, for instance, disturbing the final resting place of the dead is abhorrent, and archaeologists have often been seen as insensitive to the issues involved.

In November 1990 archaeologists working on an eighteenth–century slave house at Vergelegen in the Western Cape, South Africa, discovered the grave of a woman, aged between 50 and 59 at death, that had been dug into the floor of the building while it was still occupied (Figure 50). Today, Vergelegen is corporately owned and operates as a farm, winery and historical attraction. Most of the resident community of labourers can trace their descent, on the one hand, to slaves brought to the Cape from Malaysia, Madagascar, Burma and other areas in the East and, on the other hand, to the indigenous Khoikhoi herders and San hunter–gatherers who were displaced from the

FIGURE 50 THE SLAVE HOUSE AT VERGELEGEN. Excavation revealed the full foundations of this building, constructed in the first years of the eighteenth century. The grave had been dug beneath the floor. Later alterations to internal walls had resulted in foundations running across it.

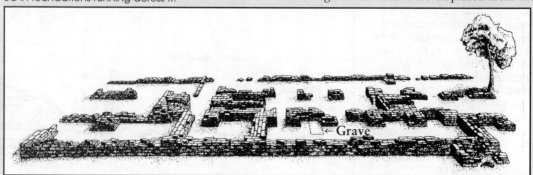

← Grave

Cape by Dutch colonial settlement (Markell 1993). Many have worked their entire adult lives at Vergelegen. Some of them were born on the estate, as were their parents and their grandparents.

There had been interest from this community in the archaeological project from its earliest months. With the discovery of the burial, interest quickened and more people began to visit the site to see the skeletal remains as they were being excavated. A clear change in attitude had taken place. People began to raise questions about the buried woman's identity and, when told that it was unknown, named her 'Flora'. They asked about her race, and then her status. All they could be told was that, because she had been buried in the slave lodge during its occupation, she had probably been a slave.

The skeleton was taken to the University of Cape Town for four months. During this time there were numerous enquiries about the state of analysis and when it would be complete (see Chapter 10). Questions began to arise about a funeral. Opinion held that the woman had probably not had a proper burial to begin with, and it would be appropriate to hold a formal ceremony when she was brought back.

Funeral arrangements were made. A coffin was purchased, and food and flowers were planned. The day of the reburial ceremony, 6 April 1991, was rainy, but the clouds parted in the afternoon, long enough for the ceremony and the refreshments afterwards. Approximately forty people came. One of the local women presided over the ceremony. She spoke, in her eulogy, of the circumstances of Flora's discovery and exhumation. She told of the bits of information that the archaeologists had surmised about Flora, and how she had received her name. She spoke of the history of the estate, and of the slave lodge. She spoke of Flora's humanity, of the fact that though her personal history was unknown, she had been someone's daughter and, perhaps, mother or sister. She spoke of the fact that Flora had walked over the same ground that they walked over, and of her ties to the same land where they lived.

FIGURE 51 THE REBURIAL OF FLORA OF VERGELEGEN.

Functionalism and structuralism

The nature of an archaeological 'fact', then, is far from straightforward. Although good archaeological research involves a constant dialogue between theoretical propositions and empirical evidence, the perception of what constitutes evidence, and how it must be understood, is changing all the time. Theoretical approaches are similarly complicated. In Colin Renfrew and Paul Bahn's words:

'The past 25 years have seen the re-emergence of the use of archaeological theory. For several decades, the whole subject of explanation was in the doldrums. However, with the development of the New Archaeology in the 1960s, and the accompanying "loss of innocence", came the realization that there was no well-established body of theory to underpin current methods of archaeological inquiry. To a large extent this is still true, although there have been many attempts sparked off by the processual approach of the New Archaeology to provide an underlying body of theory. Today there is a superabundance of approaches to explaining "why?" The archaeological literature is awash with polemical discussions between positivists, Marxists, structuralists, "post-processualists", etc., all claiming some special insight' (Renfrew & Bahn 1991: 405).

Despite Renfrew and Bahn's rather cynical view of the resurgence of explicit theory, the world of archaeology is now far more exciting than it was in the first half of the twentieth century. Rather than offering repetitive descriptions of artefacts and archaeological sites, archaeologists now ask a wide variety of questions about the past, structuring their research from different sets of premises about the way history works. Some of these theoretical approaches are complementary, while others are mutually exclusive. The overall effect is one of diversity and controversy – evidence that readings of the past are being constantly challenged and revised.

It is conventional to divide up theoretical approaches into different schools of thought. This is a useful way of summarising a complex situation, although it can be misleading. In practice, different modes of interpretation often merge into one another, while individual archaeologists may profitably use different theoretical concepts as circumstances dictate. And so we should remember that the 'isms' of archaeology, as with any discipline, are arbitrary divisions in a complex and varied theoretical terrain.

It is useful to start with 'functionalism'. Today, this is often used in a derogatory sense, implying a naive belief that societies function like well-oiled machines, with all their varied parts coordinated and interdependent. However, this is a misleading caricature. In a way, the whole discipline of archaeology is predicated on functionalism, for if we are unable to assume that associated artefacts and ecofacts affect one another in cause-and-effect relationships, it is difficult to see how most archaeological sites could be interpreted at all. Functionalist explanations have been characteristic of all modern archaeology, and will continue to be important in the future.

Many archaeologists, however, have come to see functionalist explanations as limited and unsatisfying. Functional correlations between artefacts and aspects of their environments may be the bread and butter of archaeological procedures, but they do not explain the rich diversity of the archaeological record or take us close to the way that people thought in the past. In their search for greater insights into the past, archaeologists have turned to more sophisticated approaches.

One of these approaches is structuralism. Derived ultimately from linguistics, and more

> **functionalism** an approach to interpretation that starts from the proposition that a society is a system of parts that work to maintain one another, ideally in a state of equilibrium. In more limited studies, functionalism emphasises the utilitarian properties of artefacts

FIGURE 52 DIGGING STICKS. 'Functionalism' plays a part in most archaeological explanations. For example, round stones with holes bored through them have been found on many Stone Age archaeological sites. Considered alone, they may be liable to a range of interpretations, some of them improbable and others fantastic (for example, ritual objects from India or thunderbolts). Functionalist principles direct archaeologists to the likely uses to which artefacts could have been put. In this case, analogy with the activities of modern hunter–gatherers points to an interpretation – that the bored stones were used as weights for digging sticks, vital in the daily task of collecting plant foods.

immediately from anthropology, structuralism stresses that human actions are guided by recurrent patterns of human thought, organised as pairs of polar opposites – such as dirty–clean, male–female, left–right, cooked–raw and black–white. In addition, structuralists argue that structures of thought evident in one sphere of life will also be expressed in other spheres. This point is particularly important for archaeology, for it allows the interpreter to move from one body of information (such as an ethnographic account) to 'silent' assemblages of artefacts.

> **structuralism** an approach to interpretation that works from the proposition that human actions are guided by recurrent, innate patterns of thought, which are organised as pairs of polar opposites

For example, the anthropologist Adam Kuper used a wide range of southern African ethnographies to argue that structural oppositions such as male–female, left–right and up–down determined the layout of all villages built by Bantu-speaking people (Kuper 1980). Because structuralism asserts that the model must persist through space and time, structuralist archaeologists have interpreted the fragmentary remains of villages up to 1500 years old as members of the same 'Southern Bantu Cattle Pattern' and have used Kuper's study to determine which parts of the archaeological site were occupied by men and women, and by people of high and low status (Huffman 1982).

The different nuances of functionalist and structuralist approaches to archaeological explanation can be illustrated by recent interpretations of the stone structures that form the centre of the town of Great Zimbabwe. It is clear that these walls were not integral parts of houses, but rather served to shelter some areas from public view and to give emphasis to status and authority. 'The walls of Great Zimbabwe were built primarily to display the power of the state. They symbolize, in permanent and obvious fashion, the achievements of the ruling class. They are therefore essentially a political statement' (Garlake 1982). The relation between the walls and houses in the central town is best revealed by Gertrude Caton-Thompson's 1929 excavations (Figure 53). Her

work showed that numerous small stretches of walling were built up against clay and thatch houses to form sets of dwellings that were surrounded by small stone-walled courtyards (Caton-Thompson 1931). Although no other part of Great Zimbabwe has yet been examined with the same close attention, it would seem that the same concept lay behind other buildings in the town centre.

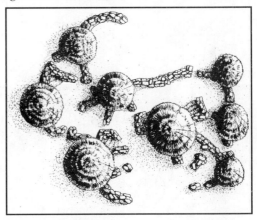

FIGURE 53 WALLS AND HOUSES AT GREAT ZIMBABWE. In this bird's-eye reconstruction, it can be seen how Great Zimbabwe's stone walls framed courtyards and entrances to mud and thatch houses. Today, all that survive are the stone walls and the circular clay floors of some of the houses.

The significance of Great Zimbabwe as a centre of power is further indicated by the size of its central court. This large open space, which lacks any evidence that houses were ever built in it, lies in the centre of the complex. A hill of bare granite rises to the north of this court area. The ruins on top of the hill, once known as the 'acropolis', consist of lengths of stone walling over and between large granite boulders, forming a set of enclosures. Some of the hill enclosures contain debris from many successive periods of occupation, while others were not used for living purposes at all.

To the south of the open court, and spread out across the valley, are numerous stone ruins. The largest of these is the Great Enclosure, once known as the 'temple'. This building is bounded by Great Zimbabwe's most substantial and elaborate walling, and contains a number of smaller enclosures and architectural features, including the well-known conical tower (M. Hall 1987).

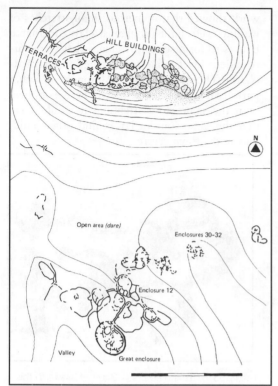

FIGURE 54 PLAN OF THE CENTRAL TOWN, GREAT ZIMBABWE.
The buildings on the Hill, at the north end of the
central town, overlooked a large open area, or
dare. To the south (in the 'valley area') was an
extensive complex of stone-walled enclosures,
the largest of which is today known as the
Great Enclosure. This central town was surrounded by an extensive settlement of mud and
thatch houses, in which commoners lived.

A functionalist explanation for the town
plan of central Great Zimbabwe has been given
by Peter Garlake. Garlake believes that, in its
earlier years as a major centre, Great Zimbabwe's ruler lived on the hill. Later, as the town
expanded, the Great Enclosure was built as a
new royal palace, with the high, elaborate walls
put up to emphasise status and authority. The
smaller house complexes surrounding the Great
Enclosure were where members of the town's
elite lived. With this change, the Hill became
the domain of those who could control the spirit world. Garlake has drawn on Shona ethnography to support this interpretation. 'King and
medium are independent and autonomous.
They maintain entirely separate establishments.
Each however depends on the goodwill and cooperation of the other. And it is not unusual for
their courts to be close together. All told, it
seems reasonable to suppose that, in the later
years, the Great Enclosure was the ruler's residence and the Hill was the seat of a senior spirit medium' (Garlake 1982: 28).

In this reading, Great Zimbabwe's plan is

FIGURE 55 THE GREAT ENCLOSURE, GREAT ZIMBABWE. In
structuralist terms, this building has been seen as
a female initiation centre, with the most important area around the conical tower (partly hidden today by a clump of large trees inside the
enclosure). In accordance with the cognitive
opposition between male and female principles, men and women would have entered the
initiation area through separate doors positioned opposite each other.

interpreted as the imprint of an organic culture: secular and sacred needs were met by the areas set aside for the king and the spirit medium, and changes in one aspect of the society were mirrored by changes in other, connected spheres.

Tom Huffman has also made use of the Shona ethnography. But in explaining Great Zimbabwe, he has started from structuralist principles, looking for the underlying 'model' – the way in which people thought about the world and ordered their concepts.

Using structuralist interpretations of modern-day village plans in southern Africa, Huffman argues that Great Zimbabwe can only be understood as a set of oppositions between male and female elements. He sees the Hill as male, and always the residence of both the king and the royal spirit mediums. In contrast, the valley to the south of the open court was the female part of the site, where the king's wives lived and held court (Huffman 1981).

Huffman has extended this interpretation to incorporate the details of the Great Enclosure's architecture. Using Venda customs as an analogy, he has argued that the Great Enclosure was an initiation school for girls. Different structures, hidden from view behind high walls, represented the essential elements of masculine and feminine roles (Huffman 1984).

In this different reading, then, Great Zimbabwe is seen as the consequence of an innate cognitive structure, shared by all members of the society. The architecture is the expression of a state of mind.

Marxism

A different approach is offered by Marxism. Marxism has a venerable history in archaeology. Gordon Childe, an Australian archaeologist working in England in the first half of the twentieth century, was strongly influenced by Marx's ideas about the nature of history, and argued for a Neolithic Revolution, giving rise to farming, and a later Urban Revolution, resulting in the first towns and cities (Childe 1936). Although modified, these concepts have remained very influential in archaeology through the years. In addition, all archaeological research in China and the former Soviet Union was ordered until recently by Marxist theory.

Marxism is an economic, social and political theory originally formulated by Karl Marx (1818–83), and subsequently elaborated by a wide range of thinkers. Although there are various Marxist approaches, they all privilege economic considerations over other factors in explaining social change and development. Particular importance is given to the 'forces of production' (the artefacts and other resources available to a given community) and to the 'relations of production' (the ways in which people organise themselves in order to use the forces of production). Together, these constitute specific 'modes of production'. To varying degrees, forces of production are seen as controlled by minorities within a specific social formation, resulting in inherently conflictual situations – class struggle.

The influence of Marxist thought is clear, though not explicit, in more recent research carried out in Zimbabwe by Paul Sinclair, Innocent Pikirayi, Gilbert Pwiti and Robert Soper (Sinclair et al. 1993b). This study moves away from the focus on Great Zimbabwe itself to an examination of the archaeology of the early Zimbabwe state as a whole, seeing a wider view of the roles of economy, ideology, and social and political organisation. There is the implication of potential conflict within a hierarchical structure:

'Analysis of Great Zimbabwe tradition sites suggests that the state was organized as a three-tier structure, the different sites belonging to different levels within the hierarchical structure. The stone walls enclosed residential units of small groups of people, probably a ruling elite, and the walls themselves were probably a symbolic expression of power and prestige. Archaeological evidence has indicated that the enclosures known in Shona as *zimbabwe* were surrounded by commoner peasant settlements on whom the elite probably relied for subsistence and other needs' (Sinclair et al. 1993b: 711).

The study examined the landscape around settlements to assess land use, and established the basic structure of the economy. The implication of the study is that the broad base of the Zimbabwe economy provides a more appropriate explanatory starting point than an abstract

FIGURE 56 SITES IN THE THUKELA RIVER CATCHMENT.

cognitive system.

A second example of the Marxist approach to archaeological explanation is Aron Mazel's work in the Thukela Basin, southeast of the Drakensberg range in South Africa (Mazel 1989). Mazel wanted to use the evidence from 20 rock-shelter excavations and the archaeology of 10 open campsites to understand the social dynamics of hunter–gatherer society in the region between 7000 and 2000 years ago, immediately prior to the arrival of Iron Age farmers in the area.

He argued that the stone tools from his sites would have been exchanged as reciprocal gifts between people – in a system of social reciprocity recorded among hunter–gatherers in modern Botswana. If this working assumption was correct, then stone tools could be read as material evidence for the social relations of production within the Thukela Basin mode of production. The forces of production could be identified from the animal bones and plant remains from the excavated sites – the debris from meals which would provide vital clues for the resources available to the community.

Working from this model, Mazel argued that during the 5000 years he was studying, there were three phases of social development. Initially, there was a single network of social relations covering much of the Thukela Basin. People relied relatively heavily on hunting. This was also a period of social stress – hence the need for wide-ranging social connections. Subsequently, the role of women became more important; this brought a greater contribution from gathered plant foods, and reduced social stress. With increased stability, the number of local networks of alliances increased appropriately, a change reflected in the archaeological record by localised styles in artefact manufacture. Finally, population densities in parts of the area increased to the point where stress again developed within the mode of production, leading to wider networks of alliance.

Mazel's interpretation has been criticised for being premature: 'if historical materialist models of the LSA are to be informative rather than speculative, they must be founded on an appropriate data base' (Barnham 1992). But this criticism misses the point that there is always a complex interplay between theory and data collection. It is only by asking specific questions stimulated by the application of theoretical concepts that concrete evidence comes to be collected.

Archaeologists, like all historians, move backwards and forwards between abstract sets of concepts and the actual evidence for what people did in the past, refining theory in the light of new data.

Post-processual archaeology

Functionalism, structuralism and Marxism are systems of thought which start from very different premises about the nature of human societies. But their proponents share the view that there are universal social rules, knowledge of which can be used to explain very varied historical circumstances. For example, in explaining the architecture of Great Zimbabwe as the consequence of a set of cognitive oppositions, Tom Huffman is using exactly the same structuralist principles that James Deetz employed to explain the architecture of European colonial settlement in North America (Deetz 1977). Similarly, in identifying a hunter–gatherer mode of production in the Thukela Basin, Aron Mazel is applying the same model that Randall McGuire has employed to explain the cultural landscape of Broome County, New York, between 1880 and 1940 (McGuire 1991).

In addition, these approaches all tend to see the analyst – the archaeologist – as detached from the object of study. The most pronounced posture of detachment is to be found in the New Archaeology, which explicitly adopted the laboratory approach of the experimental sciences. Other forms of functionalism, as well as structuralism and much Marxist writing, have also taken a position 'out' of history, adopting the role of referee and seeking to make a fair and balanced judgement within the rules of the particular game being played.

But in recent years, there has been a reaction against tenets such as these, in a wide range of cultural studies. Grouped together under the loose rubric of 'post-modernism', these new academic approaches challenge the notion that there can be general theories of human society, and that the analyst can be regarded as independent of her or his field of study.

Post-modernism is more a range of reactions than a school of thought. It is closely connected with a decline in confidence in the West's cultural superiority and colonial dominance of the rest of the world. In Robert Young's words, post-modernism 'can best be defined as European culture's awareness that it is no longer the unquestioned and dominant centre of the world … postmodernism, therefore, becomes a certain self-consciousness about a culture's own historical relativity' (Young 1990: 19). In archaeology, these post-modernist approaches are often labelled 'post-processual' to emphasise distance both from the New Archaeology and from structuralism (Hodder 1991).

Post-processual archaeologists see history writing as inevitably weaving the social position of the archaeologist into the fabric of the past (a philosophical approach known generally as Critical Theory). Characteristically, post-pro-cessual archaeologies are written in the first person, disclaiming the detached, scientific language of the New Archaeology. Post-processual archaeologists also emphasise the importance of individuals and their identities in the past, eschewing the search for general laws of human behaviour that lay behind both functionalist and structuralist approaches. This often leads to an emphasis on the symbolic value of material culture.

Ian Hodder, for example, starts with what has always been a major problem in archaeology: 'It is of course one of the central paradoxes of archaeology that the objects dug up are concrete and real things, yet it is so difficult to ascribe any meaning to them' (Hodder 1989: 67). Hodder's approach has been to build on the association between archaeology and language studies (which was established with structuralism), and sees material culture as a 'text' to be read and understood.

'On writing a text one does,. of course, use rules, structures and grammars. The text may be an article or a book, but we can also talk of spatial texts or material culture texts. Here again, rules and structuring principles (up–down, left–right, inside–outside) are employed in the organization of activities in space and in the production of pots, bone residues, burial ceremonies and so on. However, the creator of any of these texts does not want to be understood in relation to an abstract code. He or she also wants to be believed, respected, distinguished, listened to, or whatever. In other words the text is produced to *do* something and to have some tangible social effect. Thus, the writing of a text is rather like a performance. It is "staged", using the rules, but manipulating them in relation to social ends' (Hodder 1989: 68–9).

'The processualists' response to these ideas is to point out that to follow them seems to imply that one person's view of the past is as good as another's (so-called "relativism"), without any hope of choosing systematically between them. This would open the way to the "fringe" or "alternative" archaeologies … where explanations can be offered in terms of flying saucers, or extra-terrestrial forces or any phantasms which the human mind may conjure up. It is not entirely clear how the Critical Theorists can answer this criticism' (Renfrew & Bahn 1991).

Quantification

These varied approaches to archaeological explanation are very different from one another and, as we have seen, may have radically different implications for the way that the past is written. Nevertheless there are common techniques that may be employed and create a degree of convergence in the questions that archaeologists ask, giving the discipline a feel of unity, despite its increasing theoretical divergence.

These techniques have to do with measurement. Measurement has long been at the core of the enterprise of archaeology. Establishing con-

> 'Quantitative methods should be seen, not as a distinct scientific specialism within archaeology, like pollen analysis, for example, or the various techniques of artefact characterisation, but as part of every archaeologist's mental tool kit. Statistical, mathematical and computer specialists may often be required to cope with particular problems, but archaeologists must have sufficient quantitative awareness to recognise when problems arise which can be helpfully tackled in a quantitative fashion. No one else can do this for them' (Shennan 1988: 3).

FIGURE 57 AN ATTRIBUTE ANALYSIS OF ONE OF THE LYDENBURG HEADS. In this stylised drawing of Head Number 1, the decoration has been broken down into five zones, each of which can be described in terms of the decorative attributes known from Early Iron Age ceramics.

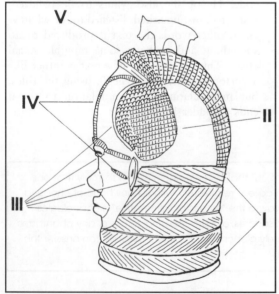

text always involves measurement, and the concern with context is what differentiates archaeology from antiquarianism. In its turn, measurement can be broken down into two fields of application: quantification and archaeometry.

Some archaeological writing is about individual objects. For example, moulded ceramic heads, found at Lydenburg in Mpumalanga, South Africa, and dated to between the sixth and ninth centuries AD, have been described in individualistic terms. Tim Maggs and Patricia Davison, in a paper in the journal *African Arts*, wrote about the aesthetic qualities of these artefacts. Although the Lydenburg Heads are not unique, they are rare objects that can be assessed as art works (Maggs & Davison 1981). But at the same time, the Lydenburg Heads are decorated with a variety of motifs that they hold in common with pottery found from other Early Iron Age farming sites in southern Africa: these have been dated to the same time period. Since decorative 'attributes' such as these have been quantified in other archaeological papers, the Lydenburg Heads can be seen as part of a broad tradition of ceramic decoration (Evers 1982). Almost all artefacts, however unique they may be, have the potential for quantification.

The most effective methods of quantification in archaeology are often the most straightforward, and involve the simple presentation of information in graphic form so that its characteristics are clearly apparent. Representations such as these – known as 'frequency distributions' – are a familiar part of everyday life: bar diagrams, pie charts or graphs indicating changes in the gold price, inflation, or changing crime rates.

Simple frequency distributions group objects in a limited number of categories. So, for example, the frequency of occurrence of different categories of stone tools from Bushman Rock Shelter, in Mpumalanga, has been represented as a bar chart: the different tool classes and technological details are arranged vertically and the percentages shown horizontally (Figure 58).

Simple graphic representations such as these are becoming more respected after a long period during which sophisticated computer-generated approaches to quantification were regarded as the only legitimate form of analysis. The

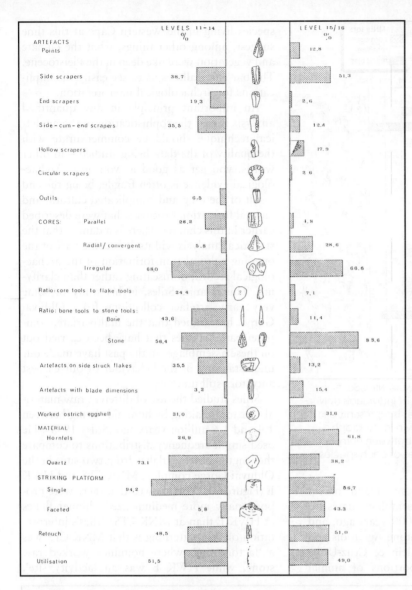

LEVELS 11-14 % LEVEL 15/16 %

ARTEFACTS
Points
Side scrapers 38,7 / 51,3
End scrapers 19,3 / 2,6
Side-cum-end scrapers 35,5 / 12,4
Hollow scrapers / 17,9
Circular scrapers / 2,6
Outils 6,5
CORES: Parallel 28,2 / 1,8
Radial/convergent 5,8 / 28,6
Irregular 68,0 / 66,6
Ratio: core tools to flake tools 24,4 / 7,1
Ratio: bone tools to stone tools:
Bone 43,6 / 11,4
Stone 56,4 / 88,6
Artefacts on side struck flakes 35,5 / 13,2
Artefacts with blade dimensions 3,2 / 15,4
Worked ostrich eggshell 31,0 / 31,6
MATERIAL
Hornfels 26,9 / 61,8
Quartz 73,1 / 38,2
STRIKING PLATFORM
Single 94,2 / 56,7
Faceted 5,8 / 43,3
Retouch 48,5 / 51,0
Utilisation 51,5 / 49,0

FIGURE 58 STONE TOOLS FROM BUSHMAN ROCK SHELTER. A simple graphic presentation of archaeological evidence. This bar chart shows different features of the stone-tool assemblage along the vertical axis: different categories of stone-tools (the top seven categories), followed by other features which describe the assemblages. The percentage occurrences for these features are compared for Levels 11–14 from the site (the Later Stone Age) and Levels 15–16 (the Middle Stone Age). This presentation allows the reader to gain a quick visual impression of the major changes that took place through a sequence spanning many thousands of years (Plug 1981).

idea is not to replace complex statistical analyses, but instead to make sure that they remain subordinate to the archaeologist's interpretation of the evidence. As Stephen Shennan explains, this is known as 'exploratory data analysis':

'... its hallmarks are a far greater concern with visual displays of data than with summary statistics derived from them, and a far lower emphasis on statistical significance tests. Rather, the aim is to explore the data set to hand, defined as relevant to some problem, to see what there is in the way of significant patterning. The idea is, to use the jargon of exploratory data analysis (or EDA, as it is known), that

data = smooth + rough

'In other words, a given set of observations can be divided into two components, a general pattern, the "smooth", and the variations from that pattern, the "rough". The task of the data analyst then is to distinguish the smooth from the rough in the most objective kind of way, being continuously sceptical as he does so' (Shennan 1988: 22).

A second example of the graphic presentation of simple frequency data comes from Richard Klein and Kathryn Cruz-Uribe's study

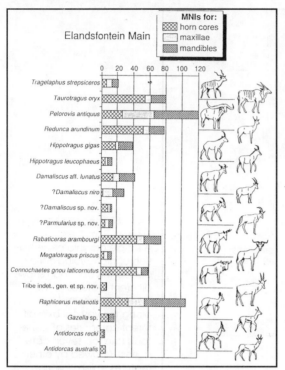

FIGURE 59 BOVID SPECIES FROM ELANDSFONTEIN, SOUTH AFRICA. The Minimum Number of Individuals (MNI) by which each animal species is represented in the faunal assemblage is shown in this graph. The graph also differentiates between horn cores, maxillae and mandibles of each species (Klein & Cruz-Uribe 1991).

of animal bones from the site Elandsfontein (Figure 59). This rich assemblage dates to between 700 000 and 400 000 years ago, and was associated with Early Stone Age tools and human skeletal remains (Klein & Cruz-Uribe 1991). The differing proportions of animal

species living in the Western Cape at this time suggest, among other things, what the climate and vegetation were like deep in the Pleistocene. The bar chart allows us to see easily the implications for archaeological interpretation.

An important principle in any quantified analysis is that the sophistication of the analytical technique should be commensurate with the quality of the data being studied – in other words, you get as good as you give. Archaeological evidence is often fragile, being the end result of the long and complicated cultural and natural formation processes that were described earlier in this chapter. There is a danger that the statistical analysis will itself become part of the ongoing cultural transformation of the archaeological record, obfuscating rather than clarifying. Thus Daniel Stiles, in his study of some very early artefact collections from Olduvai Gorge, has argued that the multivariate, computer-based studies that have been carried out on these assemblages in the past have made our understanding of the behaviour of our earliest ancestors still murkier.

Stiles studied the use of different raw materials for tool-making by hominids living between 1.4 and 1.6 million years ago (Stiles 1991). He used simple frequency distributions to compare the lengths of stone flakes from two sites in the Olduvai Gorge complex, MNK CFS and HWK E (Figure 60). This showed that there were proportionally more medium-sized, thinner flakes at HWK E than at MNK CFS. Stiles's interpretation of this patterning is that MNK CFS was a 'factory site', where hominids worked raw stone, while HWK E was an 'activity site',

FIGURE 60 FREQUENCY DISTRIBUTIONS OF STONE FLAKES FROM OLDUVAI GORGE. These simple frequency distributions show the maximum lengths (in mm) of whole flakes from MNK CFS and HWK E, Olduvai Gorge. The graph compares the percentage frequency of two variables. The vertical axis shows percentage, while the horizontal axis gives 11 size classes for the lengths of whole stone flakes (Stiles 1991).

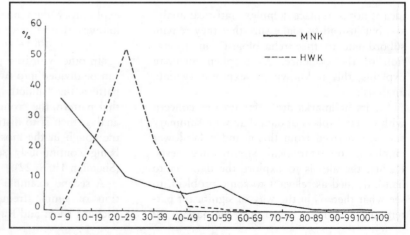

where selected stone flakes were actually used as tools. The implication that tools made at one site were transported to another place for use suggests that hominids were capable of planning and executing a series of activities – one of the defining characteristics of humanity.

'MNK CFS provides evidence for a centre of hominid activity some 1.6 myr ago in which a relatively complex sequence of stone raw material exploitation involving planning, choice and transport was carried out. HWK E was a place to which hominids regularly brought selected chert and lava for use. I believe that these results support a view that early hominids did recurrently use central places as a locus of socio-economic activity' (Stiles 1991: 14).

In many cases, however, simple visual display of archaeological evidence is not an appropriate end in itself. It is then necessary to use statistics in their more traditional role to test ideas rigorously and objectively – what has been called 'confirmatory data analysis' (Tukey 1977). The basis of such tests is descriptive statistics of the amount of variability in a sample. For example, in analysing a ceramic assemblage, an archaeologist may need to describe in statistical terms the set of pot diameters. He or she could start by drawing a bar chart of the measurements, in the way that has already been described. This exploratory phase in the data analysis may show a curved shape distribution of size categories.

Next, the archaeologist could use simple descriptive statistics to characterise the shape of this distribution pattern. One such statistic would be the 'arithmetic mean' – the sum of all the scores in the sample, divided by the number of cases. The 'arithmetic mean' reflects the 'central tendency' of the sample, but not its extent. For this, the archaeologist would specify the 'range' – the smallest and the largest measurements in the sample. The range is a measure of the 'dispersion' of the sample, but it is not sufficient to characterise the shape of the distribution pattern. For this, the archaeologist would commonly use what is known as the 'standard deviation'. This is a formula that takes into account the amount by which each case deviates from the arithmetic mean of the sample.

An example of simple descriptive statistics in use is the published report on excavations car-

ried out at Porc Epic Cave in east-central Ethiopia (Clark & Williamson 1984). This Middle Stone Age site was probably used as a hunting camp at the time of the year when game migrated from the Afar Plains to the escarpment. It was occupied between 61 000 and 78 000 years ago. As with all excavations, the archaeological team was initially faced with a confusing array of stone artefacts. They needed to sort them into categories so that the assemblage could be described and analysed. Following a well-tried approach, they distinguished between unmodified flakes, flakes that showed signs of use, and flakes that had been retouched to make tools.

Next, the archaeologists wanted to compare unused flakes with tools and used flakes, in order to deduce some of the choices that the Middle Stone Age toolmakers had made. To do this, they calculated the basic descriptive statistics for each of the three categories of artefacts (Figure 61). The result showed clear differences between the categories – rather similar, in fact, to the differences that Daniel Stiles has found for the far earlier sites to the south in Olduvai Gorge. 'When one compares flake form in unmodified flakes, tools and edge-damaged flakes it is apparent that there is a significant tendency to select the longer, blade-like exam-

FIGURE 61 FREQUENCIES FOR ARTEFACT CATEGORIES FROM PORC EPIC CAVE, ETHIOPIA. This graph compares the maximum lengths for three categories of artefact: unmodified whole flakes, utilised flakes and all whole tools. The shapes of the graphs ('polygons') allow a quick visual assessment of the patterning in the archaeological evidence (Clark & Williamson 1984).

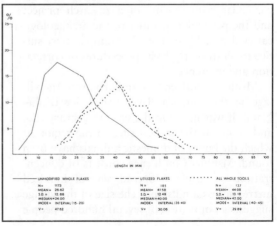

ples for use and retouch' (Clark & Williamson 1984: 58).

A special case of the frequency distribution of a sample is known as a 'normal distribution'. A normal distribution is a particular pattern of symmetrical distribution around a mean, producing a bell-shaped curve that can be defined by a specific equation. It has been shown that a normal distribution results from the cumulative effect of many variables that are independent of one another. For example, the adult body height of a large-enough sample of people will be a normal distribution, since body height is determined by a complex combination of genetic and environmental factors, many of which are independent of one another. If a sample has a normal distribution, or approximates to one, then a sophisticated battery of additional statistical tests can be carried out. However, it is often the case that archaeological samples do not satisfy these requirements. This does not mean that statistical tests cannot be applied. It merely serves to underline the point that all statistical applications have to be chosen with careful regard to the nature of the evidence that they are being used to describe (Shennan 1988).

The full range of uses of statistics in archaeology goes well beyond the formal description of data. Properly used statistics form the basis for comparison, correlation and inference. They help archaeologists to make interpretative decisions in the face of ambiguity in their evidence, and they provide a measure of the significance of such ambiguity.

There is a wide range of higher-order statistical tests available. The appropriateness of using these needs to be assessed in terms of the particular requirements of a research project and the particular qualities of the archaeological evidence. Here, a single example must suffice to illustrate the basic procedures of correlation and inference.

Msuluzi Confluence is an Early Iron Age village in the Thukela River valley, KwaZulu–Natal. It was in use in the seventh century AD, and is one of the earliest sites in the region at which the bones of domestic animals have been found. Msuluzi Confluence consists of concentrations of artefacts spread several hundred metres across a hillslope. The size of the village suggests a population of several hundred people (Maggs 1980a).

Particularly interesting, and relatively unusual, is the occurrence of Late Stone Age stone tools scattered across the site. The villagers living at Msuluzi Confluence were probably some of the first farmers to move into this part of the Thukela valley. Did they happen to build their village on top of an earlier archaeological site – a cultural formation process leading to the mixture of two distinct assemblages – or were hunter–gatherer bands interacting in some way with the newly arrived farmers?

'This raises the question of what sort of interaction might have taken place between Early Iron Age and Later Stone Age peoples and their economies. A number of items other than the flaked stone also imply some sort of interaction – the bone "arrowheads" of this and other sites, the grooved stone that may have been for straightening arrow shafts, and even the practice of making shell disc beads. Some or all of these items could have been incorporated into Early Iron Age technology elsewhere in time and space. On the other hand, San hunter–gatherers survived in neighbouring parts of the Thukela Basin into the later nineteenth century and therefore some interaction must have taken place between them and the Iron Age villagers. By historical analogy one could suggest some form of client relationship, with the San acting as hunters or herders for the villagers, in exchange for food and other items. However, material traces of such clientship have seldom if ever been found on Later Iron Age sites, even those in areas where clientship was known historically. The Early Iron Age evidence, therefore, might indicate a closer pattern of interaction than that known from terminal Iron Age and historic times' (Maggs 1980a: 136).

Tim Maggs's approach to this interpretative problem was to carry out a statistical test for significant correlation between separate sets of artefacts. He counted and weighed three different categories of artefact that occurred in each square of a grid laid out across part of the site: pottery and the debris from metal working, left by the farming community, and stone tools used and left by hunter–gatherer groups (Figure 62). Then, pairs of readings were tested for statistically significant correlations, producing a statis-

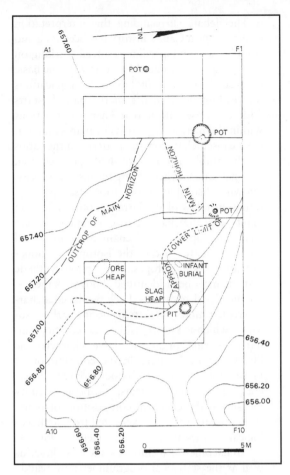

FIGURE 62 SITE PLAN FOR THE EARLY IRON AGE SITE AT MSU-LUZI CONFLUENCE. This shows the grid that was laid over part of the site. The numbers and weights of potsherds, iron slag and stone tools were taken for each square. Statistical tests were used to look for significant correlations (Maggs 1980a).

the techniques of physics and chemistry to archaeology. Archaeometry is a sub-discipline in its own right now, bringing an impressive array of scientific techniques to bear on archaeological problems.

More detailed examples of archaeometric studies will be given later in this book. One comparatively simple, but hugely significant, study serves to illustrate the archaeometric analysis of materials excavated from an archaeological site.

How to control fire was one of the most important discoveries made by our earliest ancestors. Apart from immensely widening the resource base of communities by allowing food to be cooked, the controlled use of fire made it possible for human groups to colonise parts of the world well away from the tropics during the most intense cold periods of the Pleistocene. Without the use of fire, it is difficult to see how *Homo erectus* could have spread widely through the world. Until 1988, the earliest known use of fire was in China about half a million years ago. But then C. K. Brain and Andrew Sillen argued that dark-stained animal bones from Swartkrans cave in South Africa, associated with stone tools and hominid fossils and dated to between 1 and 1.5 million years ago, had been deliberately burnt.

Brain and Sillen's approach was first to experiment with modern animal bones, heating them to temperatures of up to 800°C for thirty

tic known as a 'correlation coefficient'. Although the statistical trend was weak, Maggs felt that it was definite enough to indicate that the stone tools, pottery and iron-working debris were all part of the same site, rather than the result of an unrelated superimposition of occupation. This in itself does not prove that there was economic cooperation. Rather, like all such statistical tests, it indicates a statistical probability, which can be used by the archaeologist to infer the history of the site.

Archaeometry

The second category of measurement in archaeology has become known as archaeometry. Strictly speaking, this term should include statistical analysis as well, since the neologism comes from *archaios*, old, and *metron*, a measure. But in practice archaeometry has become more narrowly understood as the application of

FIGURE 63 BURNT BONE FRAGMENTS – EVIDENCE FOR THE EARLY USE OF FIRE.

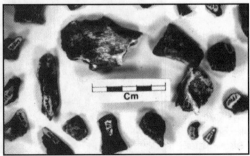

minutes, and then allowing them to cool slowly, in this way replicating conditions in a hearth. Thin sections from these bones were examined by microscope to see how the structure of the bone had been changed. In addition, the changing ratios of carbon to nitrogen were measured in the comparative samples, which allowed the temperatures at which the bone was charred to be plotted. By comparing the archaeological collection with the modern experimental sample, they deduced that these bone fragments had been heated at temperatures up to about 500°C (Brain & Sillen 1988).

Other archaeometric studies have measured the chemical composition of human bones, establishing directly the categories of food that people ate in the past, and addressing questions of general archaeological interpretation. For example, there has been considerable interest in the ways in which Holocene hunter–gatherers in the Western Cape moved between the coastlands and the inland mountain ranges. On the basis of the faunal and floral assemblages from archaeological sites, patterns of transhumance have been proposed. It is believed that people visited the coast for short periods in the winter, and travelled inland with the spring to take advantage of new plant growth in the upland areas.

This proposition has been tested archaeometrically, by measuring the ratios of stable carbon isotopes in bone samples from human skeletons excavated in the research area. The conclusion of the archaeometric study is that the transhumance interpretation needs to be drastically modified or abandoned. In particular it can be argued that some Stone Age hunter–gatherers spent long periods of time at the coast.

The debate surrounding this interpretation of the Western Cape's history has been long and complicated, and is still unresolved (Parkington 1991; Sealy & Van der Merwe 1992). The basic archaeometric concept has wide implications for reading the evidence of the past. It starts with the observation that chemical reactions within the metabolic systems of plants and animals caused characteristic patterns in the ratios of the stable isotopes of hydrogen, carbon, nitrogen and oxygen in organisms – a process known as 'isotopic fractionation'. Isotopic fractionation takes place during photosynthesis in plants, and the characteristic isotope ratios are passed on up the food chain to animals and humans. In the case of the isotopic fractionation of carbon isotopes, three photosynthetic systems have been identified, known as the C_3, C_4 and CAM pathways. Each produced a characteristic ratio between two specific carbon isotopes, which is known as the $^{13}C/^{12}C$ ratio. Similarly, marine organisms have characteristic $^{13}C/^{12}C$ ratios. As a result, the contribution of marine food groups, and foods from the different photosynthetic systems, can be assessed by measuring the chemical composition of bones from human skeletons excavated from archaeological sites (Sealy & Van der Merwe 1986).

Archaeometric techniques such as these, as well as the statistical programmes now readily available through the huge advances in computer hardware and software, provide archaeologists with a formidable set of techniques to use in measuring the varied dimensions of evidence for the ways in which past people lived. But always the answers that are obtained will only be as good as the questions that are asked.

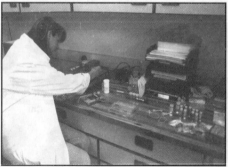

FIGURE 64 PREPARING BONE SAMPLES FOR ISOTOPIC ANALYSIS.

FIGURE 65 ANALYSING SAMPLES IN A LIGHT ISOTOPE MASS SPECTROMETER.

chapter 5

Survey and sampling

Archaeologists ask a wide variety of questions. Their views about the past will have been formed from differing theoretical positions, and the interpretations that they offer can be mutually exclusive of one another. But despite the diversity of theoretical positions that are adopted and argued, the heart of archaeology remains the study of artefacts within their contexts.

> 'In a sense, archaeology is defined by its concern with context. To be interested in artifacts without any contextual information is antiquarianism, and is perhaps found in certain types of art history or the art market. Digging objects up out of their context, as is done by some metal detector users, is the antithesis in relation to which archaeology forms its identity' (Hodder 1991: 123).

Archaeological surveys

Were a New Archaeologist, a structuralist and a post-processualist to carry out fieldwork together, they would spend their evenings arguing passionately about conflicting interpretations of the past. However, come the morning, they should be able to agree on some basic fieldwork techniques and recording methods.

Artefacts, as the case studies in this book have already shown, come in a wide variety of shapes and sizes. But before they can be studied they have to be found, and in order for them to have any interpretative value, their context has to be established. In some situations, artefacts or sites may be far too abundant for the archaeologist to record or collect them all. In other cases, artefacts may not be visible, and the archaeologist must work out an excavation strategy that will result in representative collections. Almost all archaeological fieldwork involves initial questions such as these, which can conveniently be considered together as problems of survey and sampling.

A considerable amount has been written about techniques of archaeological survey. New Archaeologists were particularly concerned to set up rigorous approaches that were of a scientific standard. Some approaches were worked out and tested for dealing with areas previously unexplored – situations where it was the task of the archaeological survey to start from the beginning, formulating information in such a way that it could support sustainable generalisations about human behaviour.

These techniques are today important parts of the archaeological tool-kit, and may be used by archaeologists asking a wide variety of questions about the past. But more often than not, the actual course of an archaeological survey is essentially pragmatic.

In many cases, a survey is initiated because important sites are already known from a region. The Spatial Archaeology Research Unit at the University of Cape Town, for example, has carried out extensive site surveys on the coast and in the coastal hinterland of the Western Cape. This work has developed from the original excavation of the key rock-shelter site of Eland's Bay Cave (Parkington 1981).

In eastern Botswana, an extensive field study was built around previous knowledge of a small group of important hilltop villages (Denbow 1984).

Ideally, the aims of a field survey should be the complete recording of all archaeological evidence considered relevant. In practice, though, this is only achieved under special circumstances: if the survey area is small, or if there are unlimited resources available. Usually the archaeologist must select particular parts of a study area for attention. The manner of this selection is known as the 'sampling strategy'.

> **sample** a set of items (for example, artefacts or sites) selected so that interpretations may be made about the nature of the larger population from which the set has been drawn

> '*Regional survey* is the activity of locating and describing the remains of past settlements as they exist in the landscape today. It is usually the first step toward understanding past regional settlement systems and answering more specific research questions …
>
> Archaeologists have available a large arsenal of survey techniques to use in sampling the archaeological record. The most widely used survey technique is the *pedestrian tactic* – systematically walking over the ground with set intervals between surveyors …
>
> Choices must also be made about the size and shape of the sample units. To determine optimum sizes and shapes of sample units archaeologists have done a number of experiments using information from surveys having 100 percent coverage …
>
> The unit shapes commonly employed in surveys are a square (called a *quadrat*) and an elongated rectangle known as a *transect*. Quadrats provide good information on site clustering and associations among types of sites. Transects, on the other hand, are often easier to lay out and survey …
>
> The bases of decisions concerning intensity and unit shape and size are not simple. No configuration of units and intensity is ideal for all problems and areas. Usually the archaeologist is trying to balance gains in precision against greater field costs. Thus, each decision reflects the application of basic principles in the context of specific field situations' (Rathje & Schiffer 1982: 163–5).

Mapping Botswana's history

For a long time, little was known about the Iron Age in Botswana, for only one site, Toutswemogala, had been documented and dated. But in 1978 a programme of surveying and mapping was begun with the aim of finding out more. James Denbow, who directed the project, believed that there must be much more evidence for cattle-keeping in these savanna grasslands:

'Research was begun in the region surrounding Toutswemogala in order to test the hypothesis that pastorally-oriented economies would tend to develop as a matter of course in semi-arid areas such as the margins of the Kalahari because these environments are favourable to animal production, but experience periods of drought and low rainfall, which subject crop production to increased uncertainty and risk' (Denbow 1984: 24).

Toutswemogala is a hilltop site, and so Denbow started by looking for evidence of settlement on other hilltop locations. He realised that sites were marked by large accumulations of cattle dung, and that these had so altered the local ecology that places once occupied are today marked by dense stands of a particular grass species, *Cenchrus ciliaris*. Stands of *Cenchrus ciliaris* can be seen as small, light-coloured patches from as high as 10 000 m above the ground surface. Denbow was able to use existing trigonometrical aerial photographs as a survey aid (Figure 66).

Later, the field survey was extended to include the lower-lying areas and smaller, less conspicuous sites. Because the survey area had a radius of some 60 km outwards from Toutswemogala, it would have been impossible to search this all on foot. Instead, a smaller sub-region of about 450 km² was taken as representative, and searched closely.

The final result of the field survey was a map of some 300 sites. Although this was in itself a major contribution to Botswana's history, the information had limited value until something could be said about the dates when these places had been occupied, and about the relationships between them. It was clearly impractical to carry out even small excavations at so many sites. Thus it would be necessary to dig at a small number, which would then be taken as representative for the region as a whole. How

should these sites be chosen?

Denbow's approach to this problem was first to subdivide the full set of sites known from the field survey into three categories, based on the substantial differences in the sizes of the dung middens that had accumulated on them while they had been in use. The smallest sites, ranging in size from 1 000 to 5 000 m², were defined as 'Class 1'. The next category, 'Class 2', had kraal middens averaging 10 000 m² in area. The largest sites of all, 'Class 3', were ten times larger again, with kraal middens of between 80 000 and 100 000 m² (Figure 67). Denbow reasoned that, because the differences in size of sites within his study area were so marked, there must have been some sort of political and economic hierarchy in operation. By choosing to excavate sites in various size categories, he could be sure of investigating the full range of settlements.

Excavation proved that the largest sites – belonging to Class 3 – were occupied for long periods of time, with houses and other structures rebuilt as need arose. The middle-size category sites – Class 2 – were used for between 200 and 300 years, while the smaller Class 1 sites were used for a generation or so before being abandoned. All sites had similar pottery – called the 'Toutswe Tradition' by the excavator – which was similar to ceramics from Zimbabwe and the northern Transvaal. Radiocarbon dates showed that this phase in eastern Botswana's history had spanned the period between about AD 680 and AD 1300.

Additional information came from comparing patterns of settlement with the distribution of different types of soil. The Class 2 and 3 hill-

FIGURE 66 AERIAL SURVEY IN BOTSWANA. Archaeological sites are covered by dense stands of a particular grass species, *Cenchrus ciliaris*, which appears as a white spot on the air photograph.

FIGURE 67 TOUTSWE SITES IN EASTERN BOTSWANA.

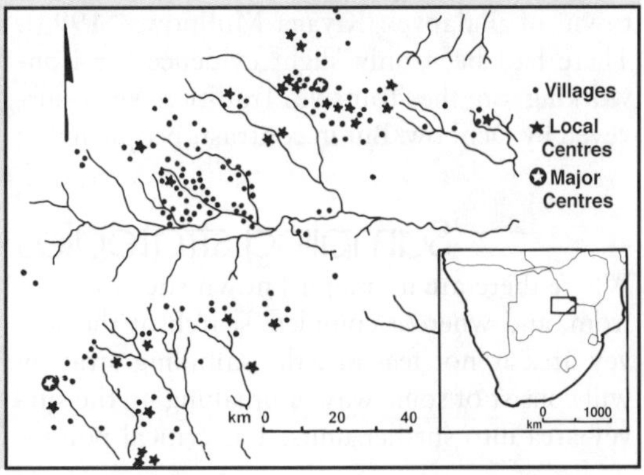

- Villages
- ★ Local Centres
- ⊕ Major Centres

km 0   20   40

km 0   1000

top sites were in areas of poor, sandy soils. In contrast, Class 1 sites – the ordinary villages at the bottom of the hierarchy – were often near to better agricultural soils – the same lands cultivated by Botswana's farmers today. Excavations at Class 1 sites such as Kgaswe B55 showed that there had been storage bins, some of which still contained burnt sorghum and millet seeds. This evidence suggested that political and economic power was marked by ownership of large herds of livestock, and that these were kept in defended kraals at hilltop locations; on the other hand ordinary farmers, living in the smaller villages, were responsible for cultivating crops.

'The archaeological data on settlement patterns and settlement distributions strongly suggest that hierarchical socio-political systems were forming along the fringes of the Kalahari by the end of the 1st millennium AD. The paucity of trade goods and the complete absence of gold in the region, however, would suggest that this process of centralization was based upon control of cattle wealth, and the need periodically to defend this wealth. In such hierarchically differentiated societies, the complexity of socio-spatial exchange networks greatly increases. A meaningful explanation of the origins and development of these networks should require an understanding of both the centripetal forces that linked subordinate to superior institutional levels and the centrifugal forces that may have operated between subordinate communities of equal rank' (Denbow 1984: 37).

Denbow's field survey in the hinterland of Toutswemogala was matched by fieldwork carried out by D. Kiyaga-Mulindwa further to the east, in the Tswapong Hills near the modern town of Palapye (Kiyaga-Mulindwa 1993). There had been only slight evidence for ironworking on the Toutswe Tradition sites surveyed by Denbow. But in contrast, people living at the same time in the Tswapong Hills had mined and worked iron ore, leaving behind them the distinctive evidence of abandoned furnaces and surface mines. Again, small-scale excavations allowed an interpretation which could be extrapolated for the region as a whole.

Moeng 1 was a mining and smelting site dated to between AD 650 and AD 1350, and therefore contemporary with the Toutswe Tradition further to the west. Makodu, about 10 km away, was a craftsmen's village. In Kiyaga-Mulindwa's words, 'the presence of a heavy scatter of faunal remains at Makodu, but without any associated vitrified cowdung deposits in the area, is obvious evidence of exchange networks between the cattle sites and the iron-smelting sites. These sites also shared in the foreign exchange networks, either directly or through the well-established sites of the Toutswe political elite. There must have been many other sites in the area which specialized in other items of trade or subsistence which are still awaiting exploration but, from the evidence available so far, this area of east–central Botswana had both political and economic networks, which sustained these iron age communities at hitherto unimagined levels' (Kiyaga-Mulindwa 1993: 390).

Together, the field surveys around Toutswemogala and in the Tswapong Hills have given a completely new perspective on a formative stage in eastern Botswana's history, connecting the region with the wider dynamics of pre-colonial state formation in southern Africa. 'Communities, having had a close affinity with the Zhizo peoples of Zimbabwe, would have moved eastwards in search of better grazing for their large herds of cattle. This is also the time when the Zimbabwe state was rising in the east, to which the Toutswe emigrants must have been a welcome addition, especially with their massive wealth on the hoof' (Kiyaga-Mulindwa 1993: 389).

Sampling strategies

Where there are no major known sites to work from, and where a complete search of the survey area is not feasible, the sampling strategy will consist of some way of breaking up the survey area into smaller units. The critical point – and the test of the viability of any given sampling strategy – is whether one can reasonably assume that the set of archaeological sites discovered and recorded from these smaller units is representative of the survey area as a whole.

One approach taken is known as 'systematic

sampling'. Typically, a grid of equally spaced sample blocks is set up over the survey area, and each is searched (Figure 68). At first sight, this might seem a logical and bias-free solution. However, in practice the results of systematic surveying can be very misleading. If, for example, the archaeological sites were themselves laid out in a grid-like manner, then the survey could miss – or hit – every case, leading the archaeologist to conclude either that the survey area was devoid of archaeological evidence or that it was all one big site. A systematic sample of a colonial city like Cape Town, laid out as a grid of streets and residential blocks, could yield such results.

An alternative to systematic sampling is known as 'random sampling' (Figure 69). In this method, the sample blocks within the survey area are fixed by coordinates drawn from a table of random numbers. The principle of randomness is that the numbers used bear no relation to the factors determining the distribution of the archaeological evidence, thus avoiding the major drawback of systematic surveys.

It is often thought that sample points select-ed at random within a survey area will tend to be scattered evenly across the landscape. In fact, though, this is very unlikely to be the case, and it is much more usual for random samples to occur in quite tight clusters, with substantial parts of the study area remaining unsampled. This technique often results in the collection of field evidence that cannot take into account the archaeologist's intuitive knowledge of the landscape. For example, it may be quite apparent that important village sites are clustered close to a river bank, but a simple random sample might not select any riverine areas for study. Because of this limitation, many archaeologists prefer to make use of stratified sampling techniques. In this approach, the study area is first divided into zones which the archaeologist considers appropriate. These zones may be based on climate, topography, ecology or any other attribute. Thereafter, random surveys are conducted within each zone (Figure 70). The result combines the benefits of intuitive knowledge and randomness.

FIGURE 68 SYSTEMATIC SAMPLING.   FIGURE 69 RANDOM SAMPLING.

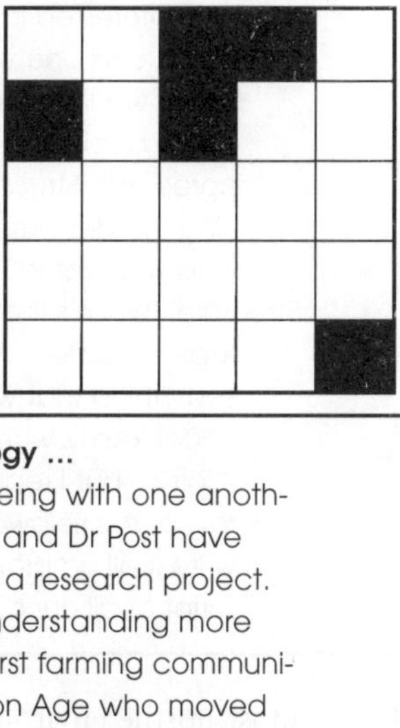

FIGURE 70 STRATIFIED RANDOM SAMPLING.

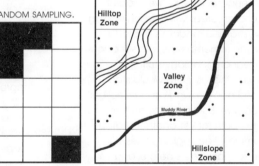

Hilltop Zone

Valley Zone

Muddy River

Hillslope Zone

ical zones. Let's see: probably the sedimentary soils along the river course, and then the lower slopes on the north and south banks, and then the upper catchment areas all the way around the valley – four zones altogether. Here, Dr Post, pass me a sheet of that notebook you're doodling away in, and I'll sketch it out for you.'

Post: 'What results do you think you'll get from such a survey, Dr Function?'

Function: 'I'd be grateful if you'd cut out the sarcasm, Dr Post. You know what I'm looking for – I've published the results of this sort of survey many times before. These early farmers probably had a mixed economy, with fields cultivated close to the river, where there would have been good supplies of water. They would have moved their livestock about with the changing seasons, bringing the animals up here onto the high ground during the spring and early summer, when there was fresh grass. We can expect to find village sites in the riverine zone, and perhaps cattle camps in the upper catchment zone. We can't possibly search the whole valley – we haven't enough time. So we'll search randomly chosen areas within each ecological zone. A stratified random sample, Dr Post. Surely you remember how to set about it – it's first-year archaeology stuff.'

Structure: 'I do wish that you two would stop arguing – and don't yawn, Post – it's deliberately provocative. But I must say that I also don't see the point of yet another stratified random sample of ecological zones. It's been done so many times before, and you do seem to know what the results are going to be, even before we've started, Dr Function.'

Post: 'So how do you propose setting about the job, Structure? What will your research strategy be?'

Structure: 'Well, of course I agree with Dr Function that we must be completely thorough, and plot and record everything that we find – we have to keep up standards, don't you agree? But I'm interested in finding a major village site – one with good preservation and the possibility of excavating a variety of different areas. We know so little about the cognitive system that governed this society. A village plan would be most illuminating. And a good pottery sample, of course. It would be fascinating to see if the structural elements of the architecture are mirrored in ceramic decoration. I really need only one good site …'

Function: 'I really don't see how you can generalise from one site to the whole community. And what about the environment? Surely the ecology of the valley must have had a major effect on how people designed their villages? But I know you'll never agree with me – we've been over this issue time after time. What do you think, Dr Post? How do you propose that we organise our fieldwork?'

Post: 'Oh, I agree with Structure, by and large. I'm only interested in looking at sites in close detail, and one village would probably be all we would have time for, were we to come back and excavate. I'll probably disagree with Structure when it comes to planning the dig, but we'll cross that bridge when we come to it.'

Structure: 'What's that in your pocket, Post? A tape recorder? Why are you recording everything that we're saying? Turn it off at once! Really, what an invasion of privacy!'

Post: 'Sorry – but I really must record the full context of this fieldwork, you know. How can I write it all up properly unless I have a transcript of all our discussions and decisions?'

Low visibility: site surveys in Tivland and Zululand

Landscapes in which there is low visibility pose special problems for archaeological survey. Low visibility can be the result of a number of factors, such as dense vegetation or modern land use. In some respects modern cities can be the most hostile environments of all: rich archaeological resources may be effectively unavailable because they are masked by roads, parking areas or buildings.

Where archaeological sites are difficult to find easily, there is often a trade-off between research strategy and resources. It may be technically feasible to search an area thoroughly, but impractically expensive. In situations such as these, the archaeologist must think of ways of gaining a representative idea of what is there, so that an interpretation of the past can be built up from only a small number of the archaeological sites in the study area.

Two examples of low-budget site surveys illustrate different methods that may be adopted. Both were concerned with plotting the archaeological evidence for early farming in their regions. Whereas the Nigerian study worked back from the present towards the past situation, the South African example sought to make from the partial archaeological evidence inferences that were consistent with modern ecological data.

Tivland is situated in the Middle Benue Valley region of Nigeria (Figure 71). As part of a wider project to study early food production in West Africa, Oluwole Ogundele has been mapping archaeological sites and carrying out selected excavations. His problem has been that conditions of preservation have favoured certain artefacts and not others. Some stone structures survive on hilltops, but the majority of early compounds were made of mud brick, and have not survived the passage of time. The problem is further exacerbated by the Tiv practice of recultivating old village sites. Taken at face value, an archaeological survey would

yield highly skewed results, suggesting that people in the past had lived exclusively in the higher-lying parts of the landscape.

Ogundele's approach has been to work back from the present, seeking to understand modern Tiv villages fully, and to collect oral traditions about where people lived in the past. He has chosen to use a broad definition of what constitutes a settlement: 'Looked at in the context of African and in particular Tiv settlements, we conclude that for our purpose it is best to define an archaeological settlement as the locale or cluster of locales within a given environment where members of a community live and carry out economic, social and political activities in a delineable time-period' (Ogundele 1993: 71).

Using this approach, he has identified a number of places in Tivland which are clearly worthy of further archaeological attention. Excavations at selected sites have also had to be planned around limited fieldwork resources: the archaeological team has sampled sites with test trenches in order to establish an outline of chronology and the basic profiles of subsistence and technology. The result is a framework for understanding the archaeology of Tivland over the last five centuries or so.

'Archaeological fieldwork in the Middle Benue Valley ... has produced a substantial body of oral traditional, archaeological and ethnographic data about aspects of the lifeways of the Tiv from the proto-historic/ historic times to the ethnographic present. Given the paucity of written data of considerable time depth as well as the absence of monumental remains of settlement in the study area, as opposed to places such as East Africa and much of Europe, appropriate oral traditions and ethnographic data have served as an important basis for formulating models to be tested archaeologically and generally as adjuncts to archaeological situations' (Ogundele 1993: 88).

Zululand, part of modern-day South Africa, lies beneath the southeastern slopes of the Drakensberg. Rivers have cut broad deep valleys and formed wide stretches of fertile alluvial soils before reaching the flatter coastal plain. These regions were particularly favoured by early farmers, who began to settle in about AD 250. Unlike farmers living in later periods in the higher grassland areas, lowland farmers built

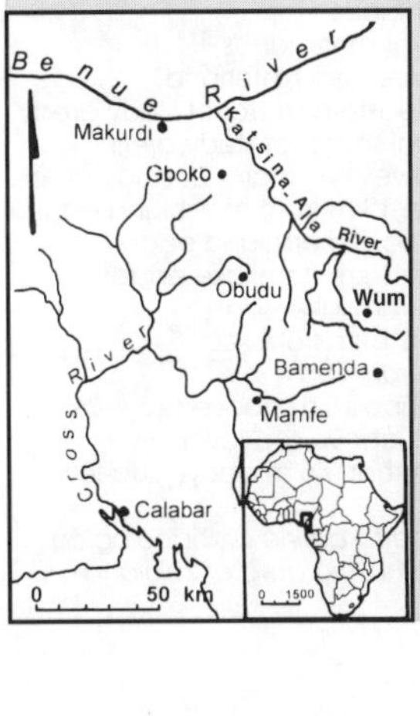

FIGURE 72 ST. LUCIA LAKE.

FIGURE 71 TIVLAND.

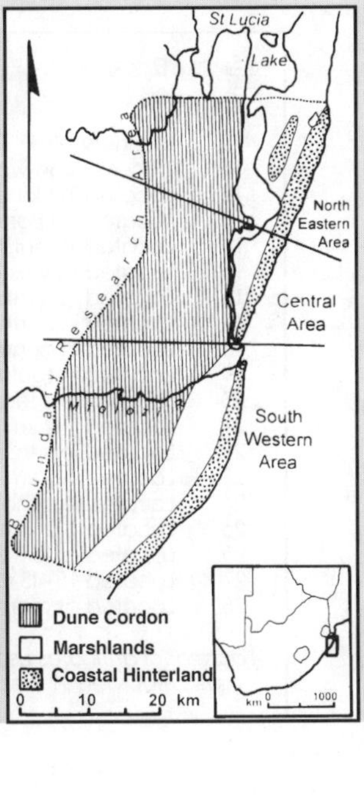

entirely with wood, thatch and clay, with the result that remnants of their buildings are very rarely found above the modern land surface. The sites of their villages are marked by scatters of decorated potsherds and, closer to the shore-line, by broken marine shell. Often these sparse traces are masked by the vegetation: high grasses, commercial plantations of pine trees and extensive sugar-cane plantations.

In contrast with Tivland, there are no modern settlements in these areas that can claim an unbroken line of connection with the past. People have either been moved out of areas designated for commercial farming or nature conservation, or else concentrated in bounded 'home-lands' by apartheid land policies. In this situation, the archaeological sites have (as it were) to talk about themselves.

The approach I followed in investigating the site was, first, to gain a thorough understanding of the way the landscape is structured today. This is best illustrated by the example of the coastal region of part of Zululand. Here, along the coastal plain stretching north from St Lucia estuary, there is a clear northeast–southwest zonation (Figure 72). Immediately behind the shoreline is a cordon of high sand dunes, still masked in places by patches of dense subtropical coastal forest. Because the dunes restrict the outlet to the Indian Ocean for rivers and streams, there are marshlands and estuaries which rise and fall with the seasonality of the rainfall. Further inland is the slightly higher sandy hinterland. Today, much of the area is covered by plantations of pine trees.

Conveniently, firebreaks cut through the pine plantations across this ecological zonation, providing ideal survey transects. In quite a few places, strong seasonal winds had scoured away the grass cover in the firebreaks, further exposing pottery and shell scatters. The result of walking and searching these firebreak transects was a zebra-like site-distribution map, with rectangular empty spaces separating linear clusters.

The question that faced me was, how could these maps be interpreted so as to give a meaningful indication of the places where people chose to live in the past? A first stage in the analysis was to group the sites chronologically. As in Tivland, we carried out small sample

excavations in order to obtain radiocarbon age estimations. In addition, we took into account pottery decoration. A basic division was made between sites belonging to the 'Early Iron Age', dated to between AD 250 and about AD 1000, and sites belonging to the 'Late Iron Age', dated from about AD 1000 to the recent past.

Next, we drew up a list of attributes that, together, would serve to define the location of each site, as well as its basic archaeological characteristics. (As all the sites had scatters of pottery, it was not necessary to include this attribute.) These are summarised in the table below.

The particular combination of attributes taken together for each site served to define its basic locational characteristics. Because there are a large number of potential combinations of the attributes listed in the table below, each site in a relatively small survey zone such as the St. Lucia area could be potentially unique. But at the same time, the individual characteristics of some sites would be more similar to one another than to those of other sites. The problem thus became one of discerning clusters of sites that were more similar to one another than they were to sites in other clusters.

This problem we tackled by using a computer based statistical technique known as multi-dimensional scaling, or MDS for short. MDS is an 'iterative' programme: it looks at all the possible ways in which the sites could be compared

ATTRIBUTE CODE	DESCRIPTION
10	Marine shell
11	Traces of iron-working
12	Located in higher parts of dune cordon
13	Located on northwest slopes of dune cordon
14	Located in marshlands
15	Located to west of marshlands
16	Located in northwestern hinterland
17	Located in northeastern sector of study area
18	Located in central sector of study area
19	Located in southwestern sector of study area
20	Located less than 1 km from marshland edge
21	Located 1–2 km from marshland edge
22	Located less than 1 km from lake edge
23	Located 1–2 km from lake edge
24	Located less than 1 km from sea
25	Located 1–2 km from sea
26	Located at less than 15 m above sea-level
27	Located 15–45 m above sea-level
28	Located at more than 45 m above sea-level

Locational attributes used to define archaeological sites recorded in the St. Lucia area of Zululand

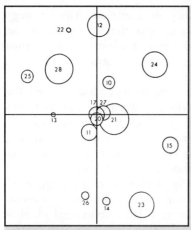

FIGURE 73 COMPUTER PLOT OF SITE LOCATION ATTRIBUTES, ST. LUCIA LAKE REGION. The technique of multi-dimensional scaling, or MDS, has produced a three-dimensional plot which groups together similar locational attributes. This method characterises the choices early farmers made in deciding where to build their villages, thus re-creating aspects of the past directly from the results of archaeological survey.

with one another, and offers the best possible 'fit' from a statistical point of view. In the case of the Zululand coastal study, MDS showed that Early Iron Age sites tended to be clustered in the northeastern part of the study area, close to the seaward margin of the marshlands (Fig-ure 73). Most had evidence for metal-working and for the use of marine fauna. In contrast, there was less consistency in the location of Late Iron Age sites, which tended to be further from the sea. In effect MDS offered us what we would have been able to discover intuitively if the low archaeological visibility in the study area had not impeded our view: a clear patterning in site distribution. The interpretation of such patterning, as with all maps, is a task for archaeological reasoning:

'During the Early Iron Age, the concentration of settlements close to the boundary between the marshlands and the dune cordon probably reflected interest in a specialised niche particularly suited to the colonising stage of agricultural expansion. In the third century, it is likely that the coastal dune cordon was thickly shrouded with forests ... by the Late Iron Age, after almost a millennium of farming settlement, the environment would have been far more open. This is reflected by the dispersal of sites in the second and third (Late Iron Age) groups through the full length of the coastal dune cordon. It can also be argued that the opening of the environment resulted in extensive areas of grassland, which in turn allowed domestic livestock to become more important in the Iron Age economy' (M. Hall 1982: 139–140).

Asking new questions

The example of stratified random sampling raises an important feature of all survey techniques. Despite the search for statistical viability and representativeness, there is always an interplay between the questions that archaeologists ask (as well as the differing theoretical approaches they adopt) and the results of the survey. To start with, the decision about the appropriate size of a survey area is closely connected to what the archaeologist expects to find. There is no point, for instance, in selecting one square kilometre if the research goal is to map the settlement system of a pre-colonial state. And then again, the choice of the method of stratification is, appropriately, a reflection of the archaeologist's research design. An archaeologist interested in ecological adaptations, for instance, would choose a zonation based on ecological regions, while someone interested in ceramic technology might choose to divide up the survey area according to the various types of available clay.

FIGURE 74 RECORDING ROCK PAINTINGS. Rock art is an important source of information about the past. In this photograph, the archaeologist is tracing the painting on a plastic sheet spread over the rock face. Particular care must be taken in rock-art survey work not to use recording techniques that could damage these fragile images.

Good examples of field surveys, illustrating some of these theoretical and methodological aspects, are provided by rock-art studies. Rock-art sites – paintings and engravings on the walls of rock shelters and on free-standing boulders – occur in many parts of Africa. Some of the art is many thousands of years old. Study of the images is particularly important because it gives us the opportunity of understanding what people were thinking in the past, and of learning more about their social lives – aspects of the past that can be approached only indirectly through most other categories of artefacts. Rock-art studies are now a central and integral part of archaeological practice (Lewis-Williams 1983).

Many rock-art sites are readily visible and some have been known about for many years. In several parts of Africa, rock-art sites were the first archaeological occurrences to be noted in colonial reports. As a result, many rock-art surveys have been developed in areas where important sites were already known.

But surviving rock paintings are often spread over large regions where the landscape is rugged and inaccessible, making complete survey coverage impracticable. Therefore most rock-art surveys are stratified samples. Because sites suited to painting are restricted to specific geological formations, such as bands of exposed sandstone where rock shelters have formed, field teams will often concentrate on these zones, giving other parts of the study area

only a cursory examination. This strategy always carries the risk that an important site will be missed, but the trade-off is a high return of site records within the available time and funding limits.

Finally, rock-art surveys illustrate well the subtle interactions between research goals and data recording. Rock-art surveys usually involve extensive recording of the paintings, sometimes by copying and tracing, but more usually by photography. In some cases, field surveys have been planned to photograph all the paintings found in a study area. As a result, there are now very large collections of photographs of rock art in several research centres in different parts of Africa. These are invaluable sources of information, particularly because many rock paintings are being lost as a result of natural weathering and human intervention. But archaeologists who come back to these archive collections with new research questions often find that such records, however thorough, can only be a first stage in their investigation. They may be interested in a specific detail which cannot be seen clearly enough in a photograph, or they may need to know how the texture of the rock surface was used by the artist as part of the painting's effect. In consequence, researchers constantly revisit survey areas, building on earlier fieldwork. There is a constant interplay between theory and empirical field observations.

Rock art and gender

A convincing case has been made for seeing a range of images in southern African rock art as part of shamanism, dances in which medicine people enter trance, and of altered states of consciousness experienced during trance (Lewis-Williams & Dowson 1989). In the course of field surveys, many paintings have been photographed and copied to illustrate these interpretations – ways of understanding which are

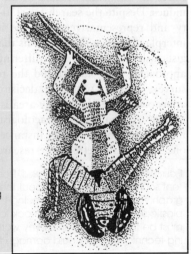

FIGURE 75 NEW QUESTIONS IN ROCK-ART RESEARCH: 'MYTHIC WOMEN'. In archaeological research, new questions are being asked all the time, resulting in a constant interplay between writing about the past and the results of field survey work. Figures like these – this example comes from the KwaZulu–Natal Drakensberg – offer exciting new possibilities in interpreting gender relations in the past (Solomon 1992).

now widely accepted as providing valuable insights into the lives and minds of people who lived centuries ago.

But it is also clear that, taken as a whole, the corpus of rock paintings from a survey area will include images that relate to experiences other than the trance dance itself, even if these experiences were modulated by shamanistic practices. Interest in developing rock-art studies further, and along these different lines, is encouraging researchers to revisit some of the best-known areas, re-recording paintings with attention to details that assume greater significance in the light of new theories.

An example of such revisionism is the work of Anne Solomon. By looking again at key paintings, Solomon has come to the conclusion that the interlinked themes of gender, sexuality and rain are as important in the art as shamanistic elements:

'Although interpretation by reference to trance has been extremely productive in studies of San rock art, many paintings make no obvious reference to trance, and features of the art which have been interpreted primarily in relation to shamanism may also be interpreted in relation to gender ideology. It may be suggested that neither is primary and that both are relevant relations of meaning. Trance performance may be a context of the art; however, this does not entail that the gender and sexual symbolism can be seen as less relevant to the iconography and/or meaning(s) of the art. No doubt other relations of meaning await identification and will contribute to studies of the polysemy of the art. To decentre trance is not to deny its importance, but to permit exploration of other avenues of meaning' (Solomon 1992: 321).

Another specialised branch of archaeological survey work is underwater reconnaissance. In the case of Africa, this has invariably been focused on searches for shipwrecks in coastal waters. The principles of underwater archaeology are the same as those of terrestrial archaeology. However, given the difficulties and expense of working on the sea-bed, underwater archaeologists would be unlikely to contemplate surveys of areas where there is no evidence for wreck sites. It is far more usual for searches to be planned in areas where either an important wreck is known to have occurred, or wreck material has already been reported. Underwater surveys usually aim at recording all visible archaeological material, rather than concentrating on pre-selected sample areas.

Underwater archaeologists are able to make use of a variety of sophisticated technological aids to assist with survey work. The Proton Magnetometer is an instrument that is towed behind a survey boat, detecting iron and steel objects (such as ship's cannon and metal parts of a hull) that interfere with the earth's magnetic field. Sidescan Sonar sends out sound waves through the water, which bounce back and are recorded by the instrument, producing a graphic representation of the sea-bed that will indicate the presence of a major object such as a shipwreck. However, the key to underwater survey, as with work above the ground, is visual inspection by the archaeological team.

Robben Island shipwrecks

Underwater environments pose particular challenges for archaeology. Although principles of survey and excavation similar to those of terrestrial archaeology apply, the difficulties of working underwater necessitate specialist technologies and methods. The results of such 'fieldwork' are often highly rewarding, for although ships invariably become archaeological sites under traumatic circumstances, conditions of preservation of some artefacts on the sea-bed may be excellent.

Africa's coastlines have been regularly navigated for centuries, and many ships have been lost off the continent. Some of these wreck sites have been plundered, both by sport divers and by commercial salvors, and a good deal of invaluable historical information has been lost. There is growing pressure for effective legislation and protection of these cultural resources.

A pilot project code-named *Operation Sea Eagle*, which set a standard for underwater survey, was completed in 1992. The task was to record the shipwrecks along the rocky shores of Robben Island in Table Bay. Robben Island's reefs had been the bane of navigators since the fifteenth century, and were known to have claimed many victims. A systematic survey was

FIGURE 76 SHIPWRECKS OFF ROBBEN ISLAND. This nineteenth-century painting shows the wreck of the *Sceptre* in 1799 (Gordon-Brown 1975).

the prerequisite for any effective management of these wreck sites (Werz 1993a).

Preparatory work was undertaken in the archives, with the aims of compiling an inventory of the ships that had been wrecked off Robben Island, collecting information about these ships that would allow them to be recognised on the sea-bed, and making decisions about the relative historical importance of different wrecks.

The archival study was followed by the underwater survey, involving a qualified maritime archaeologist working with a team of between 12 and 15 Navy divers. Most of the wrecks were known to have taken place quite close to the shore, in waters less than 10 m deep, and where there was often considerable wave action. This made it difficult to use surface support vessels or sophisticated detection techniques such as sidescan sonar survey. Vast beds of giant kelp made diving difficult. Not surprisingly, wrecks had usually become widely fragmented in this hostile environment. In consequence, the most effective survey technique was also the most basic: a close visual search of the sea-bed.

A particular problem in underwater survey is marking a find spot. In the Robben Island survey, 15 datum points were first set up along the shore and related to the trigonometrical grid. Next, additional markers were set up between the cardinal points at intervals of approximately 200 m. Once a wreck site had been located, it was buoyed and surveyed in relation to the terrestrial markers by means of a theodolite.

All in all, there was satisfaction with the results achieved by *Operation Sea Eagle*. A total of 22 shipwrecks had been tracked down in the archives, while 15 wreck sites were found during the survey. Of these, 10 wrecks were identified with a reasonable degree of certainty; the remaining 5 had fragmented beyond recognition.

Aerial survey

Walking and swimming are not the only ways to find archaeological sites: there is also flying. In some situations, it can be easier to find things from above – from the air. Low stone walls, making up terracing or village architecture, may be almost invisible in tall grass, but very conspicuous from above. Human modifications to the landscape, such as ploughed fields and pathways, may leave faint traces across the earth's surface which can be seen only under the right lighting conditions and from the air. This potential has long been realised by archaeologists, and aerial survey has become a specialised field within the discipline.

Again, Gertrude Caton-Thompson was a pioneer for African archaeology, organising an air-force overflight of Great Zimbabwe in

1929. This produced a set of aerial photographs, which helped enormously in mapping the complex stone-wall architecture (Caton-Thompson 1931). During the Second World War the British archaeologist Charles McBurney flew as an airforce pilot in North Africa, subsequently incorporating what he had learned in this aerial reconnaissance into his synthesis of the region's archaeology (McBurney 1960). As research on the continent's Iron Age has expanded in recent years, it has become clear that aerial survey has tremendous potential for locating and plotting village sites over large study areas.

Not all aerial survey requires an aeroplane. Some of the earliest air photographs of archaeological sites were taken from balloons, and this technique has been used more recently to record Iron Age farming villages in Natal (Noli 1985). Any means of getting the archaeologist and camera above a site has the potential of giving worthwhile results.

Today, specifically commissioned aerial photography is invariably too expensive for archaeological field budgets. But where they exist, Government Survey trigonometrical photographs can often provide useful information. Although these may have been taken from 10 000 metres or more, larger archaeological sites are often still visible. One of the best examples of the use of this survey technique is research carried out by Tim Maggs into the farming settlement of the southern highveld, a vast area of grassland that covers much of South Africa's interior plateau (Maggs 1976).

In designing his research project, Maggs wanted to find a way of plotting the distribution of village settlements over a large study area. It would not have been feasible to carry out a ground search of even a sample part of the study zone, since high grass often hid the low stone walling from view. But he found that by examining high-altitude air-survey photographs (taken by the government as the basis for their standard 1:50 000 map series) with a low magnification microscope, he could not only locate sites, but also divide them into different groups on the basis of their architectural style. Once he had completed the aerial survey, Maggs designed a selected ground survey to test the validity of his results, visiting and excavating sites in each of the different architectural groups.

A further form of aerial survey, which has a potential yet unrealised in African archaeology, is satellite photography. LANDSAT satellites orbit the earth frequently and continually, transmitting back a record of reflected light and infra-red radiation from the surface of the earth. This electronic information can be con-

FIGURE 78 AERIAL SURVEY: MGODUYANUKA. In this photograph, taken from a lower altitude, the architectural details of Late Iron Age villages are clearly visible (Maggs 1982a).

FIGURE 77 AERIAL SURVEY IN KwaZulu-Natal, South Africa. This photograph shows a number of Late Iron Age settlements around Mgoduyanuka Hill in the centre, and close to a bend in the Thukela River. On the ground, these foundations are difficult to see in the high grass (Maggs 1982a).

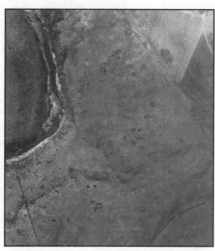

photographs but are in fact impressions of changes in the nature of the earth's surfaces.

Work in South America has shown that archaeological sites can be identified from LANDSAT images. The potential of this technique is probably greatest in arid areas, where there is minimal interference from vegetation cover.

Often, these various techniques of archaeological survey are used most effectively in combination. Sophisticated site surveys can be ends in themselves, enabling the archaeologist to record and interpret artefacts that remain dispersed across the landscape without the need to carry out excavations at all. For example, correlations between distributions of sites and aspects of the environment might suggest clear cause-and-effect relationships, such as the choice by farming communities of combinations of fertile soils and good grazing. By no means all archaeological work involves excavation, and in recent years survey data have achieved respectability in their own right.

Sandwich Harbour

In some cases, archaeologists can learn a lot about the past without needing to excavate; such surveys can be ends in themselves, or they can be preliminary to more detailed fieldwork. A study of the archaeology of nineteenth-century settlements around Namibia's Sandwich Harbour belongs to this type of work.

Sandwich Harbour is on the desolate Atlantic coast, about 50 km south of Walvis Bay (Figure 79). This was once the only safe anchorage with adequate fresh water in Namibia. But shifting sands, which constantly threatened to engulf the settlement, eventually made the harbour unnavigable, and it was abandoned. Today the area is part of the Namib–Naukluft National Park. Archaeological surveys carried out in 1984 and 1988 led to the recording of a diverse range of sites (Kinahan 1991).

The harbour first came into use as a commercial fishery in the second half of the nineteenth century. In 1884 Germany annexed this part of the coast: this led to a dispute with England, a commission of inquiry and a report. The *Proceedings of the Angra Pequena and West Coast Claims Joint Commission of 1885* was published in Cape Town for the information of the public, and is a valuable source of contemporary information for interpreting the archaeological evidence.

Evidence given to the commission by Mrs Carolina Pullman, wife of the manager of one of the fish-drying stations at Sandwich Harbour, outlined both the size and nature of the community and their annual routine. According to Mrs Pullman, the fishery comprised a dwelling house, a storehouse and some drying sheds. Buildings were mostly made of wood, although rushes were used for temporary shelters. An iron ship, the *Eagle*, was permanently moored close to the lagoon's edge for use as a store. There were twelve 'native fishermen' on the books, but only four of these men were kept in regular employment; the others were paid seasonally. Besides these employees, there were always numbers of local inhabitants about, numbering up to 500, who came to the lagoon edge to fish and forage when summer plant foods had ceased to be available. The principal commercial fish was snoek, caught between October and May; harders were also considered important. Two or three boats could catch about 80 tons of fish a year. The catch was then

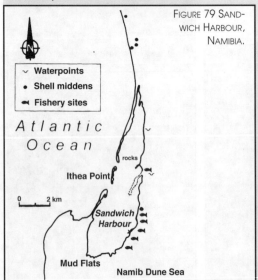

FIGURE 79 SANDWICH HARBOUR, NAMIBIA.

Waterpoints
Shell middens
Fishery sites

Atlantic Ocean

rocks

Ithea Point

0   2 km

Sandwich Harbour

Mud Flats

Namib Dune Sea

dried and sent to Cape Town, from where it was exported to Mauritius. Every two months or so a ship would come from Cape Town with provisions for the fishery.

Further information comes from a watercolour painting by Thomas Baines, who visited Sandwich Harbour in 1864. Baines climbed the dune above the fishery and sketched the fishermen's houses and the fishery buildings, also showing the *Eagle* moored on the lagoon shore.

These documentary sources were used in conjunction with the material remains of the Sandwich Harbour fishery that survive today. During the field surveys, the wreck of the *Eagle* was located (although it now lies 200 m inshore from the high-water mark). The roofs of two sheds, protruding from a sand dune and temporarily uncovered by wind action, were correlated with Baines's sketch.

In themselves, these results would provide only limited historical evidence. But the archaeological surveys also uncovered additional evidence that may add new dimensions to the documentary sources, hinting at some of the social dynamics within the fishery community, and between the small commercial settlement and the indigenous population of this part of Namibia. The survey team found that wind action had uncovered middens – the rubbish of everyday life – leaving the remnants exposed for a while before they were re-covered by the shifting sands (Figure 80). These 'snapshots' of life

a century and more ago were evidence for the very ordinary aspects of life – too unimportant to be recorded in the evidence of the commission of inquiry, or sketched by a visiting artist.

One such midden, made up largely of fish bones, lay close to the rusting hulk of the *Eagle*. A surface inspection during the archaeological survey showed that the bones included those of kabeljou, steenbras, sea barbel, hake and snoek. Steenbras jaws, ribs and vertebrae predominated, which suggests that heads were chopped off and dumped here and the fish eaten somewhere else. There were also bones from whales, cattle and sheep, broken earthenware and bottle glass, rusted iron, bits of copper wire and occasional brass buttons.

The archaeological survey also mapped middens – this time mostly made up of shellfish – that had been left by a local community living about five kilometres to the north at a place called Gorogos – out of Baines's view, and beyond the brief of the commission of inquiry. Apart from shellfish, these middens included quantities of stone tools and potsherds in the long-standing traditions of this part of Namibia. But there were also some European goods such as bits of bottle glass and porcelain and more brass buttons.

Taken together, the Sandwich Harbour and Gorogos middens are evidence for the frontier between the small colony by the lagoon and the indigenous population – a re-enactment of the general process of contact and interaction in southern Africa.

'The fish midden is evidently associated with the *Eagle* and with nineteenth-century commercial fishing activities by its position in relation to the wreck, and by the predominance of material of European origin on and around it. At the fishing establishment, before the catch was salted and dried, the fish-heads would have been chopped off. After curing, the fish were casked and shipped to Mauritius via Cape Town. Although the fish would not have been filleted, the fishermen subsisted partly on the catch, and also gave handouts to local inhabitants who probably contributed to the substantial fishbone midden situated near to the wreck' (Kinahan 1991: 15).

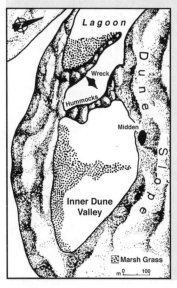

FIGURE 80 ARCHAEOLOGICAL SITES AT SANDWICH HARBOUR.

Whatever approach is used in surveying and sampling a study area for archaeological sites, accurate field recording is essential. Sites must always be numbered systematically, by means of national or regional systems set up by museums and other agencies if these systems are available.

Sites must also be mapped as accurately as possible. This is sometimes not as easy as it may sound. Recently, new techniques of site mapping, known as global positioning systems (GPS), have become available. These hand-held instruments provide map coordinates by locking into signals transmitted by satellites (Figure 81) – a constructive by-product of navigational systems developed by the US to direct nuclear warheads to their targets. Use of GPS in the field, particularly in rugged landscapes, has shown that map positions marked in previous surveys were sometimes very inaccurate, distorting distribution patterns.

In archaeology, as we have stressed before, context is everything. Accurate field recording is essential in establishing the contexts of sites found in field surveys.

FIGURE 81 SURVEYING WITH GPS. Global Positioning Systems have transformed archaeological fieldwork, allowing sites to be plotted with great accuracy. A hand-held instrument picks up signals from navigation satellites orbiting high above the earth's surface.

chapter **6**

Excavation

Many of the techniques that archaeologists use in sampling survey areas are also applied, in modified form, to individual archaeological sites. For example, a dense scatter of artefacts, such as stone tools exposed in a sandy hollow, may be too large to study as a whole. In this situation, the archaeologist will need to develop a sampling strategy in the same way that sampling strategies are devised for searching landscapes. Again, the choice will be between techniques such as systematic, random and stratified sampling.

Alternatively, the archaeologist may be faced

Nwanna Nzewunwa, introducing his study of shell middens in West Africa's Niger Delta, writes:

'Archaeological excavations by their nature and scope are typical of samples and their procedures are part of the wider field of sampling. Even when entire archaeological features or manifestations are excavated, the factors of differential preservation reduce such an exercise to the wider kinds of sampling. As total excavations are prohibitive in time, labour and financial costs it has become the rule in most archaeological excavations to adopt sampling procedures best suited to the problems they are set to solve. The objective in midden sampling is that the total composition of the site be inferred from the samples' (Nzewunwa 1980: 108).

---

with an extensive area of deposit, such as the surface of a deep rock shelter. It is often impractical – and undesirable – to excavate the whole site. How can excavation areas be chosen when there are no features of the site, such as hearths, pits and middens, visible before excavation begins? Similarly, the archaeologist may use sampling techniques to choose where to dig.

But once again, pragmatic considerations often count for more when an excavation is being planned. Particular attention is usually given to the natural formation processes, outlined in Chapter 4. Archaeological sites can be complex physical and organic environments: wind and water action, burrowing animals and insects, plant growth and human interference may create a site history that stands between the material traces left by the original occupants and the archaeological imprint available to the modern researcher. There is not a great deal of point in insisting on a statistically correct, randomly generated sample of excavation areas if a major part of a site has clearly been reworked by a seasonal stream or if a family of aardvarks has made a home in the midden.

FIGURE 82 RECORDING ARTEFACTS FROM A SAMPLE GRID AT DUNEFIELD MIDDEN. During excavation, as in archaeological survey work, sites are often sampled. A careful record of the logic behind the sampling strategy is essential.

Keeping records

John Goodwin writes in *Method in Prehistory*: 'Scientific excavation ... can be likened to the reading of a book, page by page, in contrast to the habits of the book-worm, which bores little holes through its pages, stealing a letter here and there ...' (Goodwin 1953: 86).

What is important, though, is accurate recording, including an account of how choices were made of areas to excavate. The test for adequate record-keeping is replicability. Another archaeologist, working only with site logbooks, maps and drawings, should be able to follow the tracks of a predecessor through all stages of a project, including the site survey, the choice of a site for excavation, the nature of the site before excavation commenced, and the reasons for developing the specific excavation strategy. In several countries, it is now a legal requirement that the full documentation from an excavation is lodged with the artefact assemblages in the cultural institution where the collections are to be permanently housed. Complete, accurate recording is essential in establishing archaeological context.

A good archaeological excavation is as precise as a scientific experiment, and is often described in careful, detached language. As we will see, a battery of scientific techniques can be used to deduce past human activities from such sources as soil stains and fragments of plants and animal bones, or age estimates from samples of charcoal. But this attention to detail does not mean that there is a single, correct way of excavating an archaeological site. As with survey work, there is a continual and subtle interplay between excavation goals, technical developments and theoretical perspectives.

Site 50

The lake basins of the East African Rift Valley were ideal places to live, both for animals and for early humans (Figure 83). There were extensive tracks of grassland and open savanna woodlands, as well as adequate supplies of water. This area was equally ideal for archaeological preservation. The rapid deposition of sediments as lake levels rose and fell sealed scatters of broken bone and stone very much as they had been abandoned; with time, these sed-

iments formed hard rock strata. Volcanic eruptions along the margins of the Rift Valley produced clouds of radioactive dust which periodically settled across the lacustrine sediments, forming distinct layers which can now be dated using the potassium–argon technique. Numerous archaeological sites have been excavated in the Rift Valley, in Ethiopia, Kenya and Tanzania, and more continue to be found.

One particularly rich area, where there have been numerous finds, is Koobi Fora in Kenya.

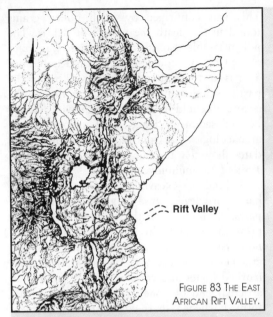

FIGURE 83 THE EAST AFRICAN RIFT VALLEY.

Rift Valley

Here, close examination of the ground surface has led to the discovery of small scatters of fossil bone and stone, revealed as the sedimentary rocks erode under today's harsh climatic regime. Site 50 (formally known as FxJi50) is one such scatter.

'Flying north-eastward from Koobi Fora, one leaves the shores of Lake Turkana and heads across low-lying country towards a sinuous line of hills. These hills form part of the rim of an ancient sedimentary basin into which river systems have been discharging loads of gravel, sand, silt, and clay for several millions of years. In many places these layered deposits preserve a fossil record which includes both palaeontological and archaeological evidence relating to very ancient proto-human ways of life … Looking out of the airplane window at the part of the sedimentary basin that lies inland from Koobi Fora, one sees that today deposition has largely ceased, and the layered deposits that were laid down between 1 and 3 million years ago are being eroded' (Bunn et al. 1980: 109).

Site 50 was chosen for excavation because, in addition to the characteristic scatter of weathered stone tools and fossil bone, there were also bones and stones *in situ* – that is to say, still covered by the sedimentary rocks and volcanic residues that were laid down after the hominid band had left the site and moved on

elsewhere. A crew of ten people from the Kenya National Museum worked at Site 50 for nine months, giving us a unique glimpse of the way in which some of our earliest ancestors lived.

One feature of Site 50 that made it particularly interesting was that, in comparison with other sites in the Koobi Fora area, it had relatively fewer bones and stone tools. This lower artefact density made it more likely that archaeologists would be able to map the traces of particular hominid activities. Dense sites, although important in providing large samples, are often jumbles of superimposed activities that cannot be easily unravelled.

In particular, the Site 50 team wanted to know whether these early hominids had camped around an animal carcass that they had either killed or scavenged (thus behaving like a variety of other carnivores), or whether they had carried meat back to a 'home base' for sharing (behaving more in a human than an animal manner). Cultural differences such as these are part of the way in which 'being human' is defined.

Once excavation had been completed, the archaeologists had an assemblage of 1405 stone items and about 2100 pieces of fossil bone to work with. More than 90 per cent of the stone collection was made up of flakes and parts of flakes, while the remainder was made up of small cobbles and chunks of rock. Some of these tools had damaged edges and signs of battering, hinting at their use. The bones were from a wide variety of animals – most of the species that would have lived in this part of the Rift Valley at that time, with the exception of the carnivores, rhinoceroses and elephants.

During excavation, the position where each piece of bone and stone had been found was recorded. Once they had been cleaned and

FIGURE 84 A RECONSTRUCTION OF THE ENVIRONMENT AROUND SITE 50.

marked, these fragments were then fitted back together as far as possible, and a map built up of the site showing a complex web of connections. Because parts of the same bone or artefact were frequently found at opposite ends of the site, and in the upper and lower sections of the deposits, it was reasonable to deduce that Site 50 had been formed by a single set of interconnected activities over a short time span. It was, in the words of its excavators, 'an indivisible archaeological entity'.

These activities included the making of stone tools (known as 'knapping') – marked by clusters of flakes and cores that could be fitted back together again – and the battering of bones to extract marrow, marked by clusters of refitting pieces of bone with distinctive kinds of damage (Figure 85).

There was also a cluster of hippopotamus rib bones at one edge of the site, alongside what would at the time have been a stream bank: 'Spare rib of hippo would hardly be carried very far, so perhaps the original reason for use of the site was the finding of a hippo carcass in the channel nearby' (Bunn et al. 1980: 128–9).

Other evidence from Site 50 allowed the basic structure of the environment to be reconstructed. The bones and stone tools had been left on the sandy silts of a river floodplain, close to a bend in the nearby stream. In view of the the range of animals that had been food to the hominid group the site 50 team deduced that there were once extensive grasslands nearby.

This was confirmed by fossil pollen grains found just beneath the scatter of debris. The pollen sample also showed that there were trees along the watercourses. Today, the Koobi Fora area is arid and sparsely vegetated, but in the past the environment had been very different.

Site 50 could be dated from the volcanically derived sediments lying above and below the archaeological horizon. These potassium–argon dates show that the campsite was used between 1.5 and 1.6 million years ago.

'During the excavation of Site 50 we have had a privileged sense of gaining glimpses of particular moments in the lives of the very early proto-humans who lived in East Africa 1.5 million years ago. More than anything else this attaches to the discovery of such things as cut marked bones and conjoining sets. Finding an articular end of bone, with marks apparently formed when a sharp-edged stone implement was used to dismember an antelope leg, cannot but conjure up very specific images of butchery in progress. Finding the fitting pieces of hammer-shattered bone shafts invites one to envisage early proto-humans in the very act of extracting and eating marrow ... Equally, the discovery of clusters of conjoinable flakes establishes a sense of connection across time which one lacks in working with disconnected assemblages of debitage, even though it must have formed as the result of precisely similar flaking episodes' (Bunn et al. 1980: 132–3).

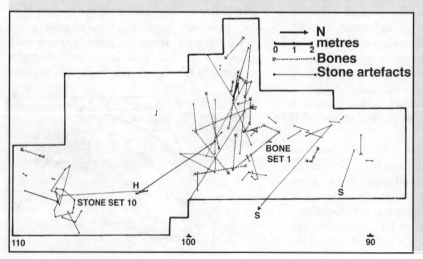

FIGURE 85 BONE AND STONE AT SITE 50. After excavation, the archaeologists working at Site 50 were able to fit together many of the broken pieces of bone and the flakes of stone. This allowed them to identify different working areas on the site.

Stratigraphy

Although archaeological sites have been excavated in many different ways, there is a single, fundamental principle underlying all approaches: control. Excavation is about recovering artefacts in context, and context depends on knowing where the artefact came from.

In turn, it is useful to think of control as comprising two dimensions: the horizontal and the vertical. Most excavations are designed to record the position of an artefact, or an assemblage of artefacts, in relation to the deposit both above and below it, and in relation to the plan of the site as a whole. Although the problems that archaeologists address, and the nature of the sites at which they work, are very varied, it is horizontal and vertical control, and the recovery of artefacts in context, which differentiate archaeology from treasure hunting.

John Goodwin wrote the last edition of his handbook for archaeology in Africa just as the first radiocarbon dates were becoming available. He realised the potential of the new technique, but could not have known the revolutionary effect it would have on his discipline.

In Goodwin's time, as for the whole of the previous century, archaeologists had been completely dependent in their writing of history on the sequence in which artefacts and assemblages were recovered from the ground. Based on geological concepts, particularly uniformitarianism, this concept of layering is known as stratigraphy.

John Goodwin writes in his *Method in Prehistory*:

'Those who (like myself) keep an untidy desk will long ago have learnt that older work tends to lie at the bottom, and the later accumulates above. This is simple *stratification*, and it has happened since the world began. Discarded things tend naturally to build up in layers, the oldest at the base, and dust settles over each layer until it is covered by the next. Here are some unpaid accounts, one is dated early January, the next mid-February, the last is late March. These provide us with *fixed points* in our pile, and the matter that lies between these can be called the lower and upper pile. We may have a shrewd suspicion that certain things happened at certain times between the three fixed points, "This letter must have been written towards the end of January, and this about the middle of March." It is a guess, but a limited guess. But here is a scrap of paper on which ink has been spilt, while here is another in my next pile with a stain that matches the first. This is evidence: we have a *horizon* or *limiting date*, both must have been exposed at the surface at the same time – but when? The stain (ink-horizon) certainly dates from my son's short holidays. All this we can call *chronology*, the study of time and the study of the order in which things happened' (Goodwin 1953: 10).

stratigraphy 'is a chronological ordering of the events and processes responsible for the observed stratification or layering of deposited material' (Rathje & Schiffer 1982: 192).

FIGURE 86 EXCAVATION: HORIZONTAL AND VERTICAL CONTROL. Cedric Poggenpoel excavating the early farming village of Ndondondwane, Thukela River valley, Kwa-Zulu–Natal (Maggs 1984a).

When we look back at the history of archaeology in Africa, it is clear that a concern with stratigraphy (and therefore with the context of artefacts) marked the beginning of professionalisation – the move away from amateur collecting to support wild diffusionist theories, and towards the empirical record which has made the writing of Africa's early history possible. Goodwin had been appointed to the staff of the University of Cape Town in 1923, as the first university teacher of archaeology in Africa. He immediately started the task of rearranging all the disparate bits and pieces of evidence for the Stone Age into a sequence, the key to which would be provided by stratigraphic excavations carried out in rock-shelter sites. Working with C. van Riet Lowe, who was later appointed Director of the Bureau of Archaeology in Johannesburg, Goodwin published the first synthesis of archaeological evidence for the region in 1929: *Stone Age Cultures of South Africa* (Goodwin & Van Riet Lowe 1929). Their careful study of stratigraphies from excavated sites prompted them to suggest a revision of part of the European 'three age system' to better suit the African evidence. These categories of Early, Middle and Late Stone Ages are still in use today (J. Deacon 1990).

Similar developments were happening in other parts of Africa. In 1925, J. Colette began fieldwork in the Belgian Congo, where he also introduced the techniques of systematic stratigraphical excavations (de Maret 1990). In the following year Louis Leakey began his long archaeological career, excavating a number of sites stratigraphically and, like Goodwin, publishing a regional synthesis, *The Stone Age Cultures of Kenya Colony* (Leakey 1931).

---

uniformitarianism the principle that ancient geological processes were the same as (uniform with) processes that can be observed in the present day. Uniformitarianism is largely accepted as self-evident today, but in the nineteenth century it was a key concept in the challenge to the biblical creationist view of the origins of life, and had an important influence on archaeology in its formative years.

As we have seen, any method of independent dating for archaeology was a mere dream at that time. Archaeologists working before the availability of documentary sources had no way of knowing how old their artefacts and assemblages were in calendar years, and often possessed only tenuous means of linking together assemblages from the stratigraphic sequences of different sites. This was one of the reasons why early archaeologists were so interested in the geological contexts of their sites, for example the river gravels of the Vaal and Zambezi rivers. As the principle of uniformitarianism had already established, geological events such as rising and falling levels of lakes and rivers usually took place over wide, and even intercontinental, areas. Therefore artefacts found associated with the same geological event in different areas could be read as having been made and used at much the same time, and individual archaeological stratigraphies could be linked to form a chronological network.

Because of this central concern with chronology, Louis Leakey was strongly influenced by contemporary geologists, who believed that Africa had experienced a sequence of wet and dry periods ('pluvials' and 'interpluvials') which corresponded to the glacials and interglacials of the European Pleistocene, or Ice Age. For many years, this 'pluvial sequence', as it became known, provided a framework for the chronology of much of Africa's Stone Age. It was only in the late 1950s that the scheme was shown to be unfounded. Fortunately, radiocarbon and other forms of independent dating soon became available (Robertshaw 1990).

Over the years that followed, a number of other regional sequences were built up on the basis of the principle of stratigraphy. Gertrude Caton-Thompson had based her interpretation of Great Zimbabwe on knowledge of stratigraphy, learnt from Flinders Petrie in Egypt. Her ideas were taken further by John Schofield, who built up a pottery sequence for much of southern Africa. In 1947, the first professional archaeologists were appointed in Zimbabwe (then Southern Rhodesia). In this area a stratigraphical sequence for the Iron Age was established on the basis of excavations (M. Hall 1990). In West Africa, Raymond Mauny brought together evidence from a wide area in a series of articles published between 1947 and 1961 (de Barros 1990). In work such as this, archaeologists of Africa showed consistency with international trends. Both here and abroad the widespread concern with regional stratigraphic systems and the classification of evidence preceded the dual revolutions of independent dating and the New Archaeology (Willey & Sabloff 1974).

Desmond Clark has written:

'I first arrived in Africa at the beginning of January 1938 and, after a brief stay at the Cape to meet John Goodwin, I took the train to Livingstone in Northern Rhodesia (now Zambia). I was interested in the Stone Age where the emphasis lay throughout the continent at that time and, due to the teaching of Miles Burkitt and Grahame Clark at Cambridge, stone artefacts were something that I believed I was equipped to investigate. At Livingstone, the Zambezi was literally on my doorstep and the Victoria Falls only six miles away. With the Vaal River survey as a model, I set out to try to establish a similar sequence for this part of the Zambezi valley that could be conveniently fitted into a pluvial/interpluvial framework' (Clark 1990: 191).

Gogo Falls

FIGURE 87 GOGO FALLS, KENYA.

Some places are better to live at than others. A location may have a particularly favourable combination of natural resources, for example readily available water, nearby woodlands and grasslands with food plants and animals, and good soils for cultivation. In such circumstances, groups of people may periodically revisit the same place. Hunters and gatherers may set up seasonally occupied campsites. Then, centuries later, farmers may establish a village on the same spot, staying for a generation or two before moving on to find new land to cultivate. Later again, a colonial settler may have been attracted by the same combination of water and grassland. These different groups of people each leave behind the debris of their everyday lives – the remains of meals, ash swept from their hearths, broken pots, stone tools that are no longer required. Rubbish tips like these – 'middens' in the language of archaeology – may be records of many centuries of settlement.

There are hundreds of thousands of middens in Africa, as in all other parts of the world. Their excavation has been central to telling the story of the past. One example is the site of Gogo Falls in the South Nyanza area of Kenya (Figure 87). This site, by the side of the Kuja River and near to both the well-watered Kanyamkago Hills and the drier lowlands along the eastern shore of Lake Victoria, has been occupied time and again over the last five thousand years, and is still cultivated today. Through the centuries, a large midden of rubbish, more than 50 m across and 2 m deep, built up. During repairs to a hydroelectric dam on the Kuja River, a bulldozer sliced through part of the midden, revealing ashy layers, pottery, stone tools and animal bones. The site was excavated by Peter Robertshaw in 1983 (Robertshaw 1991).

Robertshaw was interested in the site because, both in the fields covering the site today and in the cut made by the bulldozer, there were broken pieces of pottery decorated in distinctive styles. From fieldwork carried out elsewhere in Kenya and in the southern Sudan, Robertshaw knew that this pottery had been made by some of East Africa's first pastoralists and farmers. Gogo Falls had the potential to reveal much more about the ways in which these people had lived.

The history of a site like Gogo Falls is rather like an old book: as it is passed down through the years, each generation tears out a handful of pages until random bits of every chapter are all that is left between the covers. When early pastoralists and hunter–gatherers cleaned up camp, they threw much rubbish on the midden: inedible parts of plant foods, worn-out leather clothing, broken pots, ash from the fire, remains from meals, grass baskets and bedding. Some of this debris was a gift to a menagerie of scavengers such as dogs, hyenas, porcupines and vultures. Other rubbish – leather and grass for instance – soon rotted away. By the time that the trace of the site's earlier occupants came to be buried beneath the rubbish left by later visitors, it was already only a fragmentary record of what had originally been left behind.

The partial nature of the archaeological record is further underlined by the practical limitations of archaeological fieldwork. A team of six people from Nairobi and a gang of local labourers worked at Gogo Falls for a month. Even so, they were able to excavate less than one per cent of the whole midden. There were further practical limitations on the analysis of material from this small sample. Plant remains can only be recovered by washing the excavated soil – this is a slow process, and only 350 buckets of deposit could be processed. There was a very large collection of animal bones from the excavated part of the site: only the

teeth could be studied. Similarly, more than 30 000 fish bones were found, but only 5 per cent of this sample could be studied in detail.

The archaeologist's task, then, is to try to reconstruct what was going on at a place like Gogo Falls from a sample of a fragment of the rubbish that people left behind them long ago. Inevitably, things that are frequent, durable and large are well represented, while things that were less frequently used and that deteriorate may not be represented at all.

The most frequent categories of artefacts at Gogo Falls were stone tools and potsherds. Well-established conventions govern the ways in which these finds are sorted and classified (Figure 88). The stone tools were first sorted into the raw materials from which they had been made – quartz, different kinds of volcanic glass, chert and other fine-grained silicas. They were then further divided into the categories of deliberately fashioned implements, named after their shapes or presumed functions (crescents, triangles, awls, scrapers); flakes that had evidence for use; and waste materials, the by-products of tool-making.

If possible, potsherds were first glued back together. Then they were divided into three groups: sherds and parts of pots that showed the shape of the original vessel or hinted at its use (pieces of rims, spouts, bases, and so on); decorated sherds from the bodies of vessels; and undecorated sherds. Accordingly, the collection was described both by the frequency of different types of vessel (pots, bowls and jars) and by the frequency of characteristic types of decoration (Figure 89). On the basis of pottery decoration the collections from Gogo Falls could be grouped with different regional pottery styles, such as the 'Elmenteitan', so named by archaeologists after the sites from which they were first known.

The most frequent category of food debris was bone, both from mammals and from fish (Marshall 1991, Stewart 1991). Again, there are well-established conventions for describing such material from archaeological sites. Bones are first sorted into different species, using comparative collections, made up of complete skeletons, to confirm the identifications. Within each species from the site, a wide range of calculations and measurements is possible, depending

FIGURE 88 STONE TOOLS FROM GOGO FALLS. Archaeologists use conventionalised drawings such as these to aid the description of collections of excavated artefacts. Each stone tool is shown in several perspectives so that its definite attributes can be illustrated.

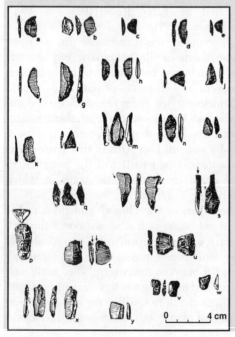

0   4 cm

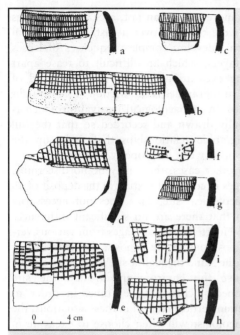

FIGURE 89 POTTERY FROM GOGO FALLS. In this conventional archaeological illustration, the shape and decoration of each potsherd is shown, as well as a profile, giving an indication of the shape of the ceramic vessel before it was broken.

on the answers that archaeologists are seeking from the site. The particular interest in Gogo Falls was early livestock herding, and so the focus fell on the teeth of domestic livestock. Patterns of dental eruption and wear reveal the age of the animal when it was slaughtered. By combining the age estimates for the whole collection, inferences can be drawn about the way in which herds were managed. Study of the fish bones, even though the sample was very small, showed that the site's occupants took advantage of the seasonal spawning runs in the nearby river. Shellfish preserved at the site suggested foraging trips to the shores of Lake Victoria.

Plant remains were disappointingly rare from the Gogo Falls excavation, although at many other sites this has been a valuable source of evidence (Wetterstrom 1991). Nevertheless, it would seem that the site's occupants made use of a wide variety of plant foods. Other plant remains hint at the local ecology: the seed of a weed most commonly found on disturbed ground (*Zaleya pentandra*) reinforces other evidence for cattle-keeping at the site. Grass phytoliths – small silica particles derived from the

cells of plants and surviving after the rest of the organism has decomposed – probably came from cattle dung: further indirect evidence for economic practices.

Other finds from Gogo Falls were less frequent, and were sometimes unique. Nevertheless they were important to the reconstruction of what people were doing at and around this place. There were some iron objects, poorly preserved (as is often the case); these included fragments of bars, some broken bangles and rings, and iron beads. There were fragments of bone points, and shell beads. A single cowry shell pointed to contact with the coast. There was also a human burial, the skeleton lying in a contracted position on its left side beneath several large boulders. The pelvis was too damaged to determine the person's sex, but the pattern of tooth eruption indicated an age between 12 and 15 years.

Fieldwork at Gogo Falls satisfied only some of the archaeologists' hopes. It could not be proved that the people who made the first pottery at the site also kept cattle, and it was difficult to date these earliest layers unambiguously. Future excavations at Gogo Falls – and 99 per cent of the midden remains to be investigated – may well allow a greater understanding of the very earliest phases of food production in Africa. But in the meantime, the site has added considerably to what we know of the lives of somewhat later occupants: the stone tools and pottery that they made and used, the ways in which they made use of wild plant and animal resources, and how they managed their livestock herds.

'Some time between about the first century BC and the fourth century AD Gogo Falls was occupied by pastoralists, whose livestock accumulated dung in a midden that is now in places more than two metres thick. This midden contains dense concentrations of Elmenteitan stone artefacts and pottery, as well as well-preserved faunal remains of both wild and domestic animals, and occasional seeds and other botanical specimens. It is difficult to envisage the onset of this Elmenteitan occupation as anything other than an immigration of new groups of people into South Nyanza, who brought with them the first domestic animals and radically new styles of pottery' (Robertshaw 1991: 170).

The vertical dimension

Although the principle of archaeological stratigraphy is straightforward – artefacts at the bottom of a site are older than those higher up – stratigraphic interpretation is often much more complicated. This is because a suite of the kind of natural and cultural formation processes that were discussed in Chapter 4 may operate at a site between the time that it was first used by a past community and the time it is excavated by an archaeologist.

For example, people revisiting a site might have used only a small part of it, perhaps leaving an ashy fireplace and a small scatter of food refuse in one corner of a shelter before moving on. The archaeological trace of this behaviour will be a change in soil colour that does not cover the whole site. To allow for this situation, archaeologists distinguish between 'layers', which are usually continuous, and 'lenses', which are not (Figure 90).

In more cases than not, archaeological sites that were revisited over a sustained period in the past develop complex sequences of lenses and layers, which are difficult to tease apart during excavation. The key to the record of such stratigraphies is the 'section' – the straight side of an archaeological excavation which is carefully drawn and recorded so that the full stratigraphic relationships that make up the site's history can be properly understood.

In other cases, there may be no discernible changes in colour or texture in the deposit of an archaeological site. This does not necessarily mean that there are no significant differences between artefact assemblages from various vertical positions in the deposit: the deposit may look the same through a site's sequence simply because the environment around the site remained unchanged over time. In order to maintain vertical control in these situations, the archaeologist will often choose to excavate in

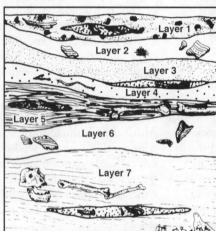

FIGURE 90 THE SECTION: LAYERS AND LENSES. This imaginary vertical section shows seven layers, each with a distinctive soil colour and texture. Smaller, discontinuous patches of deposit, such as the one between Layer 3 and Layer 4, are

FIGURE 92 STRATIGRAPHIC COMPLICATIONS. In this hypothetical example, there are three distinct phases of human activity. Firstly, people have lived at the site, producing the deposition of Layers 7 to 1. Next, a pit has been dug through these earlier layers. Finally, the pit has itself filled up with deposits (Layers D to A). More often than not, archaeological stratigraphies are complicated in ways like these.

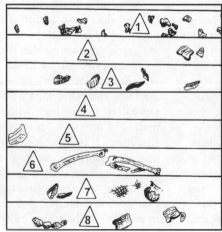

FIGURE 91 THE SECTION: ARBITRARY EXCAVATION UNITS. In situations where it is not possible to make out differences in soil texture or colour, the archaeologist may make use of arbitrary 'spits', often represented conventionally as numbers in triangles.

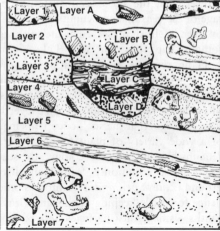

arbitrary horizontal units, known as 'spits' after a Low German word for a spade's depth of earth (Figure 91). Then again, if the natural layers of a site are too thick to maintain adequate control, the archaeologist may elect to excavate in spits within layers. The correct strategy is the one most suited to the specific site, but the aim is always the same – to maintain the control necessary to establish the context of an artefact or an assemblage.

Stratigraphies may be further complicated by the history of a site after deposition has taken place – the cultural formation processes that make up its history. For example, features are often cut down into earlier deposits (Figure 92). People using a rock-shelter site may have dug a pit to store food: this may have its own stratigraphic sequence. Very often, burials were cut down into earlier deposits. If the evidence of these later disturbances of earlier stratigraphic layers is missed, then assemblages of widely different ages will be excavated as if they are in association, and the collections mixed. When this happens, then context is lost, and the evidence from the site is of no historical value.

Such later reworking of a site will often result in what is termed an 'inverse stratigraphy'. When a pit is dug into existing archaeological deposits, the first soil to be removed will form the base of the spoil tip, and the oldest soil from the pit will make up the highest level in the new heap. Inverse stratigraphies, as their name implies, appear to turn the basic principle of archaeological stratigraphy on its head. In reality, they are complicated features rather than true stratigraphies, but unless they are correctly identified during excavation, they will jeopardise the interpretation of the site's sequence.

FIGURE 93 MZONJANI: MAPPING A SITE BY FEATURES. Mzonjani, the site of one of the earliest known farming villages on the southeast African coast, was discovered during the construction of a freeway. The swathe cut by earth-levelling machines (shown as a stippled track on the site plan) exposed a set of features, such as scatters of shellfish remains, potsherds and pit features. Because the site was too large to grid (and time was short in this rescue operation), each feature was mapped and surveyed as a point, shown as triangles on the site plan (Maggs 1980b).

The horizontal dimension

Similarly, methods of horizontal control of an excavation are often adapted to fit the particular requirements of a site. Most archaeologists work within a rectangular grid that has been marked out across the surface of the site and mapped in relation to a fixed marker, or 'datum point'. In its turn, the datum point can be surveyed into the trigonometrical system. This means that any archaeologist returning to a previously excavated site should be able to lay out the earlier excavation grid from the known datum point alone.

Grid systems of horizontal control work well with smaller archaeological sites, and are now almost universally used in rock-shelter excavations. However, they may be cumbersome on larger sites where they can be difficult to map out accurately. In these situations, the archaeologist may choose to define the site as a cluster of features, such as pits, small midden deposits, stone foundations or clusters of potsherds. In this system of horizontal control, each feature is accurately mapped as an individual point, and then excavated independently.

Among the most difficult decisions that have to be made in planning an excavation are those relating to appropriate vertical and horizontal scales. This is because archaeological sites pre-

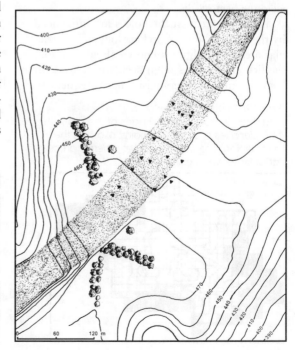

sent a paradox: really secure decisions about how to dig can only be made on the basis of a comprehensive knowledge of what is in the ground; but what is in the ground cannot be established before the dig takes place.

This paradox is particularly marked when it comes to decisions about scale. There would be little point, for instance, in excavating a city in a 25 x 25 cm grid system with 5 cm horizontal spits: the end result of a long and expensive field season would be a very detailed understanding of a very small, unrepresentative part of the site. Equally, it would be negligent to

choose a 5 x 5 m grid system and 50 cm spits for a rock-shelter site, as deposits spanning thousands of years would be lumped together in a single assemblage and all meaningful information about context would be lost. It is always possible to excavate on a fine scale and amalgamate units later, but this can be very expensive in fieldwork costs and time. One of the most difficult decisions in archaeological fieldwork is deciding when a shovel or a bulldozer, rather than a trowel or a dental pick, is the appropriate tool to dig with.

Dunefield Midden

The way that an excavation is planned will have a marked effect on the sorts of questions that can be successfully asked. If, for instance, the archaeologist wants to gain an outline of the long-term history of a place, and knows of a site with deep deposits, then a small sounding through from the modern land surface to the natural soils pre-dating the first evidence for human occupation may be the appropriate strategy. But if the archaeologist is interested in the layout of a camp or village, and in trying to establish where different activities took place, then a shallow but extensive excavation may yield the best results.

To some extent, such choices are influenced by the general state of archaeology in a particular area. When little is known about a region, the first concern has often been with long-term history, and archaeologists have tended to

choose sites with deep deposits, excavating small, deep holes to obtain samples of artefacts from successive time periods. Later, when basic regional sequences have been established, people may ask more sophisticated questions about what was going on in the past. At this stage, more extensive sites become more attractive.

Dunefield Midden (DFM), near the mouth of the Verlorenvlei on the Cape west coast, is a particularly attenuated example of an extensive archaeological site: most of it consists of the debris left behind by a single camp about 650 years ago (Figure 11). When the site was abandoned, the thin scatter of debris and a low midden were buried by wind-blown sand, today forming a protective blanket up to 2 m thick (Parkington et al. 1992).

The archaeology of Dunefield Midden is rather like a hazy and indistinct old snapshot. With care and patience, it is possible to discov-

FIGURE 94 DUNEFIELD MIDDEN: DISTRIBUTION OF MARINE SHELL. The 'contours' identify parts of the site with high densities of shellfish remains, allowing the archaeologist to suggest places where particular activities were carried out.

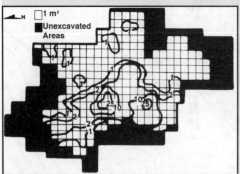

FIGURE 95 DUNEFIELD MIDDEN: ASHY FEATURES. Plotting concentrations of ash shows where people once made domestic hearths, or where they used fire for other tasks, such as roasting larger pieces of meat or preparing shellfish to eat.

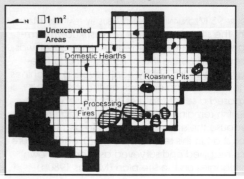

er where people made their hearths, sat to work stone tools, and where they tossed the remnants of their meals.

John Parkington, who began excavating here in 1988, started by laying a metre-by-metre grid over the entire area. Within each square, artefacts and features such as hearths were mapped in, and the deposit sieved through a fine mesh to recover the smaller items. A computer-based mapping technique known as GIS ('Geographical Information Systems') has been used to record all the locational information, and to produce maps of different aspects of the campsite at varying scales. This method has allowed the occupation to be simulated on the computer, and to be analysed from various perspectives with emphasis on, for example, hearths and stone tools or on abandoned food waste.

'In order to phrase our histories of pre-colonial people in more social terms we need methods that focus on social issues and processes. But the generation of method has been difficult because most archaeological sites are palimpsests, blurred overprinted images of repeated occupations. We suggest that social interpretations depend on our ability to resolve person as well as time and place ...' (Parkington et al. 1992: 64).

The results from Dunefield Midden have justified this approach. A shell midden, about 25 m long and 5 m wide, ran along one side of the site (Figure 94). Hearths and patches of ash formed a swathe approximately parallel to the shell midden, and about 5 m from it, suggesting an overall campsite layout similar to some used by present-day hunter–gatherers in the Kalahari Desert (Figure 95). Small stone tools (made from quartz) were fashioned next to the hearths, leaving behind tell-tale patches of stone chips. Food was provided by shellfish, particularly limpets, and by seals, tortoises and small antelopes. Plant foods must also have been important even though, as is often the case, their remnants have not survived the passage of time. There were also a number of eland bones scattered around the campsite, and the argument has been made that these all came from a single animal, butchered and divided up amongst people living around the different hearths.

'Looking at the measurements on the eland from the DFM northern site, as well as the pattern of body part representation, we are sure that only one eland, an adult, is represented. As might be expected in the case of a large animal, body parts are widely distributed about the camp including rear satellite and main dump areas, a pattern we think relates partly to the distribution of meat but mostly to the disposal of bone already processed for marrow. We ascribe some considerable significance to the presence of an eland not only because by its size it is the equivalent of 50 steenbok or 20 seals, but also because as a meat parcel it would obviously have been obtained at one single moment ... It may well be that a prime reason for occupying this piece of the landscape was the good chance of taking an eland' (Parkington et al. 1992: 69).

Underwater archaeology

FIGURE 96 EXCAVATING THE WRECK OF THE *OOSTERLAND*. The archaeologist is recording the locations of artefacts. Horizontal control is as important on the sea-bed as on land.

Underwater sites, where there may be little or no surviving stratigraphy, provide examples of excavations where horizontal control is vitally important: it marks the distinction between scavenging and archaeological research (Figure 96). Excavation of the *Oosterland*, a Dutch East India Company ship that was returning to the Netherlands from the East and was lost in Table Bay in 1697, illustrates the point.

'Excavation of the *Oosterland* site and related research involves many different aspects. The basic motivation is to collect information which is relevant to current international maritime research, focusing on the history of the

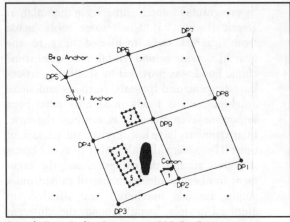

FIGURE 97 THE *OOSTERLAND* WRECK SITE. The site plan shows the grid, consisting of four squares each 10 m², anchored to the sea-bed, the position of the smaller working grid, and major archaeological features, such as a patch of concretion (shown as a dark shape on the site plan) and (lying to the right of it) a cannon.

Dutch East India Company (VOC). By excavating the wreck and studying recovered materials, which include textiles, dye, tropical woods, earthenware, porcelain and spices, aspects of intercontinental trading and the demand for Asiatic products in seventeenth-century Europe can be studied in more depth. As the VOC was instrumental in the shaping of the settlement at the Cape of Good Hope, the results of this project can also add to a better understanding of part of South Africa's past. Because the site provides material for comparative studies, and because this material can be dated accurately, it is possible to improve and expand on results of land excavations in Cape Town and environs' (Werz 1993b: 33).

The *Oosterland* lies in the eastern part of the Bay, about 280 m offshore and at a depth of between 5 and 7 m. The sea-bed is sandy, and very exposed to westerly and northwesterly winds, conditions that accentuate the strong currents. As a result, visibility underwater can be extremely poor, and parts of the site may be buried rapidly by deep sediments, only to be exposed again when conditions change.

The first stage in the project was a sidescan sonar survey of the sea-bed to establish the general topography of the site. Next, a grid was laid over the wreck site (Figure 97). This consisted of a 30 m rope square, held in place by concrete sinkers. An additional concrete sinker in the centre of the square divided the site again into four quadrants. These datum points were buoyed and mapped from the shore by means of a theodolite. Periodic checks were made from land to ensure that the outline grid had not shifted.

Smaller, rigid grid frames, each 3 m square, were used within the larger rope grid. Hooks had been welded on to the rigid frame at metre intervals so that tape measures could be firmly attached to the grid. This system allowed any artefact to be located in the grid by means of a set of coordinates – a simple but effective method of surveying, particularly suited to these difficult sea-bed conditions.

Over parts of the wreck site, large amounts of sand had to be dispersed before artefacts could be plotted and taken to the surface. This overburden was removed either by 'hand fanning' to disturb sediments, which were then swept away by the current, or by using a 'blower', a large suction tube which was driven from a boat on the surface and which airlifted the sand out of the grid unit.

By plotting larger artefacts lying on the sea-bed, the team could reconstruct the last hours of the *Oosterland*, and work out how the wreck was positioned. Two bronze cannon were lying on an east–west axis; there was a row of iron

FIGURE 98 FINDS FROM THE SEA-BED. This small Chinese porcelain teacup is still intact, embedded in concretion.

guns on a north–south axis; and a large iron anchor was found on the northern part of the site. By using archival documents that detailed how ships like these were equipped, the team could identify the port (left) and starboard (right) sides of the wreck. The *Oosterland* seems to have come in under a westerly gale and touched bottom with its bow before being pushed around by the waves. The ship probably took the full strength of the wind on its port side, capsizing and setting on its starboard side.

Excavation revealed a diverse selection of finds, a number of which provide information about activities on board. Some objects were characteristic of the armament store, while other equipment was typically used by the barber-surgeon. There was also a collection of Chinese and Japanese porcelain, probably part of an illegal cargo smuggled on board by one of the sailors.

'The excavation showed that accurate surveying can be achieved underwater to the same standards as on land sites. The principles applied and the approach which was followed indicate that there are no major differences between maritime archaeology and terrestrial archaeology. Techniques of fieldwork, however, are different as a result of the environment in which excavation takes place' (Werz 1993b: 38–9).

At the opposite extreme to horizontally dominated excavations of sites such the *Oosterland* wreck are archaeological sites with long, complicated sequences. These need to be excavated in ways that maximise the amount of stratigraphic information that is recovered. In these cases, the system of vertical control defines the way that the site comes to be written.

Daima

Lake Chad, Africa's largest lake, which lies to the south of the Sahara at the borders of Niger, Nigeria, Chad and Cameroon, has long been a focal point for human settlement. There are various local environments around the lake, offering different possibilities for ways of living. These include the *firki* lands to the south: extensive black clay soils which dry hard and crack in the dry season (*firki* is a Shuwa Arabic word meaning 'splitting' or 'cracking'). *Firki* clays are self-fertilising. Dry grass as well as other vegetation is caught in the cracks in the dry months and mulched into the soil when the rains waterlog the ground. Towards the end of the rainy season, shallow flood waters from Lake Chad cover the *firki* plains and farmers practise 'falling flood' cultivation, delaying the retreat of the flood waters with low mounds and planting and harvesting crops. When the dry season eventually sets in, livestock can be grazed on the *firki*'s wild grasses.

But although the *firki* soils are good for cultivation, clay lands that are flooded each year are not suitable locations for villages. Fortunately, there are also dunes which formed when the area around Lake Chad was much drier than today. These protrude through the later lagoonal clays. For many centuries villages have been built and rebuilt at these places. 'Settle-

ment in the *firki* plains has been concentrated on the sandy islands, or sometimes on other suitable dry spots, and the mixed farming that has been practiced has permitted the continual occupation of nucleated, mud-built settlements over very long periods of time ...' (Connah 1981: 66).

As a result, the landscape around Lake Chad is dotted with distinctive settlement mounds, many of them still with villages on their summits. These mounds have built up from mud and straw houses, which have deteriorated and been demolished, and have had in turn new houses constructed on top of them. Daima is one such mound, located about 5 km from the frontier between Nigeria and Cameroon, and about 45 km from the nearest part of the modern-day Lake Chad shoreline (Figure 99).

FIGURE 99
DAIMA.

Daima was chosen for excavation because it is one of the largest *firki* mounds – more than 10 m deep, and about 250 m long and 170 m across. It therefore offered the possibility of tracking the archaeology of farming settlement over a long period of time – of providing a key archaeological sequence for the region. The excavation was planned accordingly. Test trenches, each a little more than 2 m square, were marked out at 30 m intervals along a transect from the highest point of the mound to its edge. Because the mound was so deep, the sides of the trenches had to be sloped to prevent the deposit collapsing.

'Many practicing field archaeologists dislike having their sections cluttered with walling-boards and cross-beams; it restricts their continual reference to the totality of cross-sectioned deposits which they are striving to understand and it means that they must draw the section in pieces as they excavate instead of being able to treat the whole thing as a unitary problem. Fortunately, there are other solutions to the problem of safety in deep excavation and, in deposits as stable as most of those at Daima, the appropriate one was to batter the sides of the cutting so that they sloped backwards from the bottom upwards and were less likely to collapse' (Connah 1981: 103–5).

Excavation by a team of some 50 local labourers took seven months. About 1500 m³ of deposit was removed; this was still less than one per cent of the total mound volume. The result of the fieldwork was a sequence for the region, starting in about 550 BC and continuing until about AD 1200 when the mound ceased to be used as a village. The trenches had clearly cut through the debris of numerous mud houses that had been built on top of one another (Figure 100). However, it would not have been possible to interpret these features fully without widening the excavation trenches considerably: this was not an option, given the fieldwork resources available. In some parts of the site, the changes in soil texture and colour were so numerous and difficult to follow that the archaeologist abandoned stratigraphic excavation and removed the deposit in horizontal spits, each 40 cm thick (Figure 101).

Daima's excavation history represents the sorts of compromises that are made during every archaeological excavation. Where should test trenches be placed? Should the aim be a full sequence, from the earliest use of the settlement until its abandonment, or else mapping the layout of the camp or village, thereby sacrificing depth for breadth? Should every change in soil colour and texture be followed, which would slow down fieldwork but provide great detail, or should larger amounts of deposit be removed, thus increasing the sizes of samples of cultural and other material from the site?

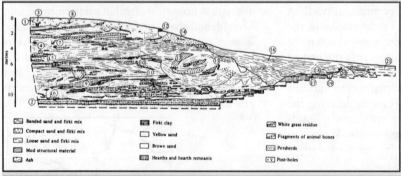

FIGURE 100 DAIMA: EXCAVATION IN STRATIGRAPHIC UNITS. This section drawing (reproduced from the site report) shows the north face of Cutting VIII, and illustrates the extreme depositional complexity that can build up at sites with complex histories.

FIGURE 101 DAIMA: EXCAVATION IN ARBITRARY SPITS. This section drawing is of the same excavation face as that shown in Figure 100, but with arbitrary stratigraphic units.

The excavations described in this chapter have shown that individual fieldwork programmes are tailored both to the specific characteristics of the site, and to the questions that archaeologists bring to the archaeological record – the constant shuttle backwards and forwards between theory and data. There are often many potential ways to dig a given site, and all of them may be technically correct. What unifies them is the central concern that all archaeologists have: to establish accurately the contexts in which they find artefacts and assemblages.

The language of archaeology ...

The survey of the river valley has at last been completed. As a compromise, the team eventually carried out a stratified random sample, as Dr Function had wanted. But Dr Structure and Dr Post paid special attention to the riverine area, looking for a well-preserved village site that would serve their particular purposes. Dr Function felt that this was an unscientific bias in the sample, but eventually agreed to let it pass, for the sake of unity.

They have decided to start their excavation programme at the largest, best-preserved village site. They were able to agree on this quickly, because this focus will serve everyone's aims. Dr Function feels that a detailed knowledge of the artefact assemblages from one site will help in classifying the smaller surface scatters that have been plotted in the outlying ecological zones. Dr Structure and Dr Post, of course, are only interested in a single site.

But now the team must agree on their excavation strategy. Again, they are gathered around the bonnet of Dr Function's battered but reliable Land-Rover, poring over a site plan. The river rolls sluggishly in the background and the birds are silent with expectation. It seems likely that there will be a storm in the afternoon.

Function: 'Well, it's clear enough to me. We must sink a series of test trenches in different parts of the site. Let's see – over here, at the back of the largest hut floor, and in this ash midden, of course. And possibly where we noted pieces of iron slag, just in case there's a smelting area. We must run the water flotation unit for plant remains, and wet sieve if we can – I need the best possible faunal sample.'

Structure: 'I agree with you about the sieving and the flotation samples, of course. But small trenches will be a complete waste of time. We should open up a big area, and take in as many of the hut floors as we can, and the open area in between. We needn't worry too much about the stratigraphy. The whole village was clearly a single phase of occupation.'

Function: 'I really can't see the point of spending time and money excavating an open area.'

Structure: 'I went into this in great detail in my seminar last month – I thought you were there. If we are to understand the structure of the cognitive system, we must also understand the village layout thoroughly. The open areas are particularly revealing, and so I must be sure that they really were open – it's the spaces that make the pattern, you know. And I'd like some good soil samples from the middle of the village, to see if the area was used to kraal cattle.'

Post: 'Really, Dr Structure, years of study just to become an expert on cattle dung. And I really can't endorse your comments about stratigraphy. I'm not prepared to assume that this village was a "single phase", whatever that might mean. If I'm to work out the nuances of the ways in which material culture was used here, we'll need to carry out the most detailed excavation possible. We'll need coordinate plots for each artefact that we find, so that we can work out how everyday items were dispersed between the different family units that made up the community: it's the only way of unravelling symbolic language, you know. And we'll need to pay special attention to animal bones: details of how carcasses were butchered and the body parts distributed around the village are worth their weight in gold. — Damn! My tape-recorder batteries have run out! Hold everything until I've found the spare set!'

chapter 7

Time

How old is it? When did people first live here? How long was the site occupied? When was this kind of artefact first made? Questions such as these have always been fundamental to archaeology. Archaeology in the Western world was born in the realisation that the Old Testament's time-scale was a metaphor rather than a diary. Issues about time and dating have always been at the heart of archaeological practice, and always will be.

Ideas of time

At first glance, dating may seem an uncomplicated matter. We are used to living out our lives within a precisely measured system of years, months, days, hours, minutes and seconds. We have standard, internationally accepted criteria for indicating when events have taken place and will take place. Every part of the world falls into a designated time zone. We know that when it is midday in Lagos it is already 4 p.m. in Nairobi and 10 p.m. in Japan, but only 4 a.m. in California. We can agree that Ghana became independent in 1957 and that President Jomo Kenyatta died on 22 August 1978.

But the concept of time is less straightforward than this. Although a standardised system of time measurement connects airline timetables and electronic communications globally, the majority of the earth's population measures out the passage of days and years in far less precise cycles of seasons, sunrises and sunsets. Some religions hold that death is followed by everlasting life – that there are simultaneously different time dimensions. Other religions, such as Buddhism, believe that the apparently linear flow of time is an illusion, and that people are continually reborn. Many people have a rhythmic notion of time marked, for instance, by the recurrent incarnations of the Hindu god Vishnu, or the alternation between the Chinese principles of yin and yang. Although the Christian calendar, based on the assumed birth of Christ in AD 1, is widely used, so are the Islamic calendar (based on the Prophet's departure for Mecca, in AD 622 in the Christian calendar) and the Jewish calendar (based on the biblical date of creation, or 3761 BC in the Christian calendar).

Standardised time, known as 'Coordinated Universal Time', though now a world-wide convention, was adopted only in 1964.

> 'What, then, is time? If no one asks me, I know what it is. If I wish to explain it to him who asks me, I do not know' (St. Augustine, fifth century AD).

Similarly, the concepts of time that are used in archaeology can be complicated. More often than not, the answer to the question 'When was this artefact made?' will be an estimated span of years, rather than a calendar date.

> Molefi K. Asante, advocating Afrocentric culture in America, has urged African Americans to measure time from when the first slaves arrived: 1619 on the Christian calendar – the year of 'Beginning Again'. In this reckoning, AD 1996 becomes 377 ABA ('After the Beginning Again') (Asante 1991, Olaniyan 1995).

Archaeological date notations and time-scales have to indicate the degrees of such inexactitude. Because archaeologists observe human behaviour indirectly, through material culture, rather than directly, answers to questions such as 'How long did people live here?' can be far from straightforward. Likewise, the manner in which archaeological estimations of time are expressed must reflect the way in which they have been derived. Because of these complications, the discipline of archaeology has developed its own chronological syntax through the years. This can be illustrated by returning to the fictional site of Bobonong and its imaginary

Feature 22a: an oval pit, 1.5 m deep, containing rich artefact assemblages, including a fine collection of decorated ceramics. Once excavations had been concluded, the pit might have had the following stratigraphy:

> BOBONONG FEATURE 22A: STRATIGRAPHY
> Layer One: Surface. Red-brown soil with small ceramic assemblage
> Layer Two: Grey-white ash lens
> Layer Three: Ashy soil with rich faunal remains and assemblage of Bobonong Culture ceramics
> Layer Four: Lowermost layer. Small collection of ceramics and animal bones

In their attempt to understand Feature 22a, our archaeologists may well decide to study some of the things that happen today in a nearby village (an area of study known as 'ethnoarchaeology', and described in greater detail in Chapter 11). They would choose a community that was living in the same sort of grasslands surrounding Bobonong when it was lived in, and that had a similar technology and economy. Then, with the approval and cooperation of the local people, our archaeologists would visit the village periodically, recording in detail where and how pits were dug, what was thrown into them and how long they took to fill up. Essentially, they would be following the principle of uniformitarianism, as old as their discipline itself.

Such an ethnoarchaeological study could result in a wealth of valuable information that would aid the interpretation of the archaeology of Bobonong. But for now we are only concerned with differences in the dimension of time – differences that set the interpretation of the archaeological site apart from the record of the daily lives of the present-day villagers.

At the conclusion of the ethnoarchaeological project, our team would be left with a thick file of data sheets. Each one of these would be a record of observed human activity, logged against a calendar date. Printed out on the project computer, the ethnoarchaeology of a village rubbish pit might look like this:

```
BOBONONG ETHNOARCHAEOLOGICAL PROJECT
RECORD SHEET: RUBBISH PIT
   August 1985   Rubbish pit newly dug – not yet in use
November 1985   Pit contains some food waste
   March 1986   Pit not used since last visit
    July 1986   Nearby house cleaned out; large quan-
                 tity of ceramics dumped in pit
December 1986   Animal bones in pit – informant indi-
                 cates that these were refuse from wed-
                 ding feast
 January 1987   Layer of soil to cover decaying rubbish
   April 1987   Pit not used since last visit
  August 1987   Thick layer of ash from hearth in nearby
                 house
November 1987   Thin scatter of broken pottery
February 1988   Pit apparently no longer in use
    June 1988   Pit filled in and area used as garden
END OF RECORD
```

Clearly, this transcript is a valuable analogue that will aid in the interpretation of Feature 22a. As with all analogues, the strength of the comparison will lie in the combination of similarities and differences.

- The modern rubbish pit and the archaeological feature are similar in size, shape and content, and they have been made by people living in broadly similar circumstances.
- The ethnoarchaeological record is of human activity calibrated against a calendar record that is external to the project. The archaeological record, in contrast, is an indirect impression of human activity calibrated against a ceramic sequence – the 'Bobonong Culture'.
- The ethnoarchaeological record consists of 11 discrete observations, made between one and five months apart, each of equal status. The stratigraphic summary, in contrast, is made up of four phases, with an emphasis on Layer 3, which has a rich and definitive ceramic assemblage.
- The ethnoarchaeological record has a finite beginning and a finite end. The stratigraphic summary, in comparison, begins with the modern land surface and ends at an arbitrary point decided by the excavator.

The point of this hypothetical exercise is to demonstrate not that one source of information is better than the other, but rather that the records are different. Archaeological interpretation tends to operate within a time dimension in which phases of generalised human activity are cross-linked with one another by specific strands of evidence. There is an intimate connection between the delimitation of such phases and the collection of archaeological evidence: we could say that archaeological time is 'subjective time'. On the other hand, contemporary behavioural studies such as ethnography (and historians working with dated manuscripts) tend to place the evidence they work with in the 'objective' framework of Coordinated Universal Time.

Stratigraphy as dating

Because of this subjective nature of archaeological dating, the construction of a site's timescale begins with excavation. When the archaeologist decides what kind of stratigraphic units will be appropriate on a particular site, he or she is also deciding what kind of chronology the site will have. This can be illustrated by going back again to the hypothetical Bobonong example. Feature 22a was formed by a long series of discrete human actions – such as cleaning out a hearth, throwing away a broken pot, dumping the remains of a meal, throwing soil in the rubbish pit to kill the smell, and so on – actions of the sort that are recorded in an ethnoarchaeological study. But (with rare exceptions) the archaeologist cannot discern these discrete activities during excavation. Instead, he or she sees amalgams of many different human actions, grouped together by soil colour and texture as 'layers'.

In a site such as Bobonong, each archaeological layer may span, say, 30 years, and may have been formed by, say, 4000 individual human actions. In an earlier living site, such as a rock shelter used in the Middle Stone Age, a single layer could have ten times this duration and intensity. In a more recent site, such as the midden from a colonial household, a discernible archaeological layer may be formed in a single year. But in each case, the archaeologist is dealing with the consequences of human actions compacted together and then divided into slices.

Seen in this way, the core of the archaeological concept of time is stratigraphy. Indeed, archaeology began as a discipline when researchers first appreciated that, other things

112

FIGURE 102 ARCHAEOLOGICAL TIME. Complex events, which may be lived out over some considerable period (such as the feast in this sixteenth-century engraving), leave behind residues which become single units of time in archaeological reconstructions of the past.

FIGURE 103 ROBERT BROOM EXCAVATING AT STERKFONTEIN. Broom is pointing to the position in the limestone deposits where an important australopithecine fossil has been found. One of the major challenges in the 1930s – as today – was dating such discoveries.

being equal, an assemblage from a stratigraphic layer is older than the assemblage from the layer above it.

As with archaeology in all parts of the world, dating was a major concern in African studies from the earliest years. And until the middle of the twentieth century, establishing a chronology was a matter of linking together the stratigraphic sequences of archaeological sites and, if possible, connecting these sequences to geological and climatological events. The challenge that faced archaeologists working in Africa has been succinctly summarised by Thurstan Shaw:

'The dating problem was crucial, and gave me much anxious thought, of a kind that would seem absurd and unnecessary nowadays. My knowledge of European archaeology had taught me that most of the dating there depended on "cross-cultural" imports: cultures were dated by the presence of objects imported from the civilizations of the Middle East which had their own dating from literary or inscriptional sources. That is putting it crudely, but that was the basis of the system; and on it was erected a whole house of cards, which was ultimately

'Stratigraphy is a chronological ordering of the events and processes responsible for the observed stratification or layering of deposited material. Although the law of superposition plays a central role in stratigraphic analysis, it accounts for cases of deposition only; other principles apply where removal of materials has occurred. In fact, a host of principles and a familiarity with local artifacts and formation processes are needed to practice stratigraphy. Stratigraphic analysis begins with profile drawings on which depositional units and the traces of other processes, such as erosion, are marked. Each unit is described as to sediment color and texture and the nature of clasts, if applicable. These are the basic data for chronological interpretation' (Rathje & Schiffer 1982).

blown down by the winds of radiocarbon dating. Nevertheless, at the time it was the best that could be done. How could this be applied to West Africa? It might work for the last five hundred years, by means of recognizable and dateable European imports after the arrival of Europeans on the West African coast; but what of times earlier than that, which I personally was more interested in than in the last few centuries?' (Shaw 1990: 209–10).

One way of thinking of stratigraphy is as a technique for placing assemblages of artefacts relative to one another in the dimension of time. Thus Layer 3 in Feature 22a, with its rich assemblage of 'Bobonong Culture' ceramics, is above, and younger than, Layer 4 and below, and older than, Layer 2. In the language of archaeology, we say that the stratigraphy of Feature 22a has given us a 'relative date' for the assemblage in Layer 3. If, in the course of excavation, Bobonong's archaeologist had been fortunate enough to find an object of known date associated with the ceramic assemblage, such as a gravestone inscribed with a date in the Christian calendar, we would say that we had an 'absolute date' for Layer 3. The concepts of relative dates and absolute dates are central in understanding the ways in which archaeological chronologies are constructed.

Stratigraphies are the most widespread form of relative dating used in archaeology, and 'reading' a stratigraphy is one of the most important archaeological skills. But there are also a number of other relative techniques for arranging artefacts and assemblages in time series.

'This idea that something is older (or younger) relative to something else is the basis of *relative dating*. The initial steps in most archaeological research today still depend crucially on relative dating, on the ordering of artifacts, deposits, societies, and events into sequences, earlier before later. Ultimately, however, we want to know the full or absolute age in years before the present of the different parts of the sequence – we need methods of *absolute dating* (sometimes called chronometric dating)' (Renfrew & Bahn 1991: 101).

Relative dating

One of the earliest of these techniques to be used was the association of archaeological evidence with independent geological, geomorphological and climatic sequences. The European 'ice ages', first recognised in the nineteenth century, was one such system. To attribute an archaeological site to a position in the series of glacial and interglacial periods was to fit it into a system of relative chronology, however crude. The extension of the concept of glacial phases to Africa, with corresponding pluvials and interpluvials (which has now been shown as unfounded), also served to provide earlier archaeologists working in the continent with a relative chronological framework. This idea that Africa's climate fluctuated between continent-wide wet and dry phases encouraged geomorphologists to look for relic lake levels and now-dry river terraces – scars left on the landscape from those times in the past when rainfall had been greater and water levels correspondingly higher. It followed that, if stone tools could be found on equivalent raised beaches and river terraces from different parts of the continent, they must be of broadly equivalent age. Before the invention of techniques of absolute dating, and their widening application

---

'Interest in past climates was stimulated by the claimed link between northern hemisphere glacials and African pluvials, but it was used more as a relative dating tool than to explain changes in stone tool manufacture or population distributions ... Van Riet Lowe worked with the Geological Survey on the mapping and interpretation of the Vaal River terrace deposits and described them firmly within the pluvial model. The stone artefact assemblages, each showing some technological difference in successive river terraces, were placed in a relative dating framework that was linked with major sea-level changes and the major period of rifting to East Africa. For the next twenty-five years, archaeology students at the University of Cape Town were taught the intricacies of the Vaal River sequence, which now hardly merits mention, and learned to identify terraces and to distinguish between rolled and "fresh" artefacts, and those that were *in situ* or not' (J. Deacon 1990).

after 1960, such geomorphological association was the only method available to archaeologists of pre-colonial Africa for linking together assemblages from widely scattered sites. It is for this reason that much of the earlier writing about Africa's past is strongly geological in tone.

The use of independent sequences to establish relative dates for archaeological sites is still important, particularly when archaeologists are working beyond the range of radiocarbon dating, when other methods of absolute dating are not available, or when cross-checks for absolute dates are important. But climatic change is now recognised as extremely complex and not globally synchronous, and climatic sequences have become correspondingly sophisticated. Most widely used are the results of the long cores that have been drilled through the polar ice-cap and into the sea-bed in various parts of the world.

Ice cores show clearly each year's deposit of compacted ice. Variations in the frequencies of oxygen isotopes in the 'fossil ice' provide plots of changing temperatures. These temperature curves have been shown to correlate well with the evidence from deep-sea cores. The thin columns of sediment found here contain varying frequencies of tiny, single-cell organisms called foraminifera. Foraminifera are sensitive to changes in the temperature of sea water and, like the ice samples from the polar regions, have changing ratios of oxygen isotopes. Together, the study of ice cores and deep-sea cores has

resulted in detailed charts of temperature fluctuations for the past two million years.

Ice cores and deep-sea cores provide invaluable climatic information. But they can also be used for relative dating if global-scale events leave traces on archaeological sites as well as on the polar ice or the sea-beds. Such connections have been made from tracking the ash from volcanic eruptions, and from tracing the phenomenon of geomagnetic reversals (or global changes in the earth's magnetic field).

Other methods of relative dating are far more localised in scope. One technique is to use collections of animal bones from archaeological sites (the 'faunal assemblage'). Animals, particularly micromammals, are sensitive to changes in their environment: if the climate becomes significantly wetter or drier, many species will become locally extinct. Because climatic tolerance varies from species to species, each climatic episode should have a unique faunal profile – its own unique 'fingerprint'. It follows logically that archaeological sites in the same region which have similar faunal profiles should be contemporary. The difficulty, of course, is that people eat animals, and that many faunal assemblages from archaeological sites will reflect food preferences as much as food availability. 'Faunal dating' (as it is termed) has therefore to be based on a close and careful statistical reading of each assemblage. Nevertheless, it has been an important method of inferring chronology, particularly for early hominid sites in southern Africa, where it has not proved possible to use the recent advances in absolute dating (Klein & Cruz-Uribe 1984).

FIGURE 104
PART OF A DEEP-SEA CORE. This section of a core taken from the continental shelf off Cape Town shows light-coloured laminated sands and darker glauconite.

Seriation

Stratigraphies, global climatic sequences and faunal profiles are examples of relative dating techniques that make use of the context of an artefact or an assemblage in establishing a time series. Other methods of relative dating make use of attributes of artefacts themselves, and can be grouped together under the rubric of 'seriation'.

Seriation was first developed as a dating technique for archaeology in an African field study by Flinders Petrie in the late nineteenth century. Petrie had excavated some 2000 burials from an early Egyptian cemetery, and wanted to arrange their associated grave goods in a time sequence. He had very little stratigraphic evidence – few of the burials had been superimposed on earlier interments – so he decided to work with the decorated pots that had been buried with the bodies. By placing the collection from each grave alongside the other assemblages that were most similar to it, Petrie derived a chronological interpretation for the cemetery – a technique which he called 'sequence dating', but which would now be labelled 'seriation'.

Flinders Petrie was working before the age of computers. As a result, his study was crude, intuitive and very time-consuming. If he had been working today, he would have been able to enter the attributes of each grave assemblage into a computer, and then use a technique such as principal components analysis or correspondence analysis to derive the most logical sequence. However, though the methods available for archaeological seriation have changed radically (and develop with every advance in computer technology), the basic assumptions remain the same. Seriation rests on the propositions (often demonstrated to be true) that artefacts made at a particular time will have a number of features in common (their 'style') and that artefact style will change in a consistent way through time. By the use of seriation, a given set of data can be arranged in a logical time series. Once such a time series has been established, additional observations can be placed in their correct positions in the sequence – in other words, they can be given a relative date.

Seriation is used by many other people besides archaeologists, and by all of us in our everyday lives, as part of the set of assumptions that we call 'common sense'. Contemporary fashions, for example, follow clear time trends which can be tracked and manipulated for commercial advantage. In the eighteenth century, elite slave-owners in the wheat and winelands of the Cape built gabled farmhouses in the so-called Cape Dutch tradition. Gable styles have been seriated, and architectural historians use this sequence to date buildings where there is no direct evidence for when they were constructed.

> 'Seriation. A relative dating technique based on the chronological ordering of a group of artifacts or assemblages, where the most similar are placed adjacent to each other in the series' (Renfrew & Bahn 1991).

Seriation has been, and continues to be, a basic tool in archaeological research. But as with all useful methods, it depends on a number of working assumptions, which need to be made quite explicit.

- Firstly, the choice of attributes is always, to some extent, arbitrary. There are many different ways of describing even a simple pot, and some of these characteristics will be appropriate for seriation, and others not. Decoration, for instance, usually fulfils the requirements of seriation. But if pots are undecorated, the archaeologist may decide to use shape attributes. What if the potter had designed some vessels for carrying water, and others for cooking? The archaeologist may erroneously assume that pot shape varied through time, and seriate the assemblages accordingly, while in reality the various pots might have been used for different purposes at the same time.

- Secondly, it is not possible to know, from a seriated sequence alone, which is the beginning and which is the end. We often assume, with little justification, that artefacts 'evolve' from simple to complex forms, or 'degenerate' in the opposite direction. Such interpretations cannot be made from a seriation study itself.

- Thirdly, seriation studies assume that changes in attributes follow a consistent direction. This may often not be the case. People may, for instance, revert to an earlier form of decoration, making artefacts that are more similar to a long-abandoned style than to a recently abandoned style. If this has not been established, an archaeological seriation is likely to end up fatally flawed.

- Finally, the result of a seriation will say nothing in itself about rates of change through time, or whether change has remained at a constant rate through the series. In real life, people may be inspired by a burst of innovation, which may be followed by a long period of conservatism. A seriation study will not in itself identify these different rates of change.

Today, archaeologists have the huge benefit of absolute dating, and many of these inherent difficulties with seriation can be avoided. Absolute dates can be used to pin down the beginning and the end of a seriated sequence. If absolute dates are available for intermediate points in a seriation, rates of change may also be measured. As a result, seriation stands with stratigraphy as one of the pillars of contemporary archaeological method.

'Petrie linked Egypt with the Aegean and determined which end of his seriation was probably most recent. Petrie and other archaeologists went on to test his seriation in stratigraphic excavations and to link it to dated monuments in Egypt. With minor modifications, this seriation, which spans some 2000 years, is still the basic sequence for ancient Egypt' (Rathje & Schiffer 1982: 253).

Clay tobacco pipes from the Cape of Good Hope

The archaeology of Dutch colonial settlement around Table Bay is now well established, and excavation of a number of sites has produced assemblages that bear testimony to the ceramics, glassware, faunal remains and other material that are the debris of everyday life (M. Hall 1993). There is also a rich corpus of documentary sources that permits nuanced interpretations of the archaeological evidence from the early colony. But, important as these documentary correlations and inferences are, they do not provide a chronology that is sufficiently fine-tuned for getting the best out of the archaeological evidence.

Fortunately, almost all eighteenth-century sites have proved to be depositories of large numbers of broken clay tobacco pipes. These were brought to the Cape from the Netherlands, either directly on Dutch East India Company ships outward bound to Indonesia, or via Batavia (modern-day Jakarta), from where the Cape settlement was routinely provisioned. Off-loaded in Table Bay, consignments were warehoused in the Castle, and then sold or issued to free farmers or Company employees. Tobacco pipes were cheap, frequently broken and carelessly discarded, which accounts for their common presence on archaeological sites.

It had long been established that clay tobacco pipes recovered from British and British colonial archaeological sites can be used for dating purposes. Then in 1990, Carmel Schrire, James Deetz, David Lubinsky and Cedric Poggenpoel published a detailed analysis of clay tobacco pipes from Oudepost I, a Dutch East India Company outpost on the southwest Cape coast, which was built in 1669 and abandoned

in 1732 (Schrire et al. 1990). The Oudepost study has demonstrated that the internal bores of Dutch-made pipe stems diminished in diameter with the passage of time, and thus they can be used for the purposes of relative dating.

More recently, this study has been extended, through the use of new statistical techniques and 67 assemblages drawn from 10 archaeo-

105 EIGHTEENTH-CENTURY CLAY TOBACCO PIPES. A set of different pipe bowls, showing shapes and makers' markers that help date examples found in archaeological sites. It has been shown that the internal bore diameters of the stems of pipes such as these show a constant relationship with time in their variation, making them an ideal form of relative dating.

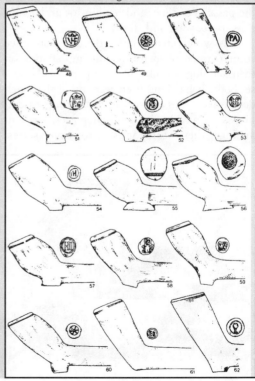

logical sites in and around Cape Town (Yates et al. 1995). Samples ranged from 43 to 2404 stem fragments. In all, 30 174 measurements of the internal bore diameters of pipe stems were taken, using drill bits with even intervals (2 mm in size) in the range 1.4–3.4 mm.

Several statistical techniques were applied in searching for the best way of seriating this large set of measurements; the most successful of these was a method known as correspondence analysis. The relative chronology from the pipe-stem study showed a good fit with the other available chronological evidence. It supported the proposition that the internal bore diameters of clay tobacco pipes used at the Cape of Good Hope did indeed diminish in a consistent way through the eighteenth century. In future, archaeologists will be able to place assemblages of broken pipes from newly excavated sites in their correct relative position in the sequence, and in this way provide a relative date for their associated artefact and faunal assemblages.

Ceramic sequences and the African Iron Age

Potsherds are one of the most common categories of artefact found at the sites of former farming villages in Africa. People made and used pots for a wide variety of purposes – storing food, cooking, eating and drinking, carrying and keeping water – and then often broke the vessels, dumping the sherds on rubbish middens or leaving them scattered over the ground. Unlike artefacts made of organic material such as leather or grass, potsherds usually survive the passage of time, and remain for archaeologists to excavate and study.

Pots were often decorated with distinctive combinations of incisions and impressions on their shoulders, necks or other parts of the vessel body. It has long been recognised that such decorative styles can be used to group assemblages of potsherds into categories, and to arrange these categories into time series.

Ceramic seriation was a foundation stone for the archaeology of Africa before methods of absolute dating became available. Today, these seriations continue to be used, tested and pinned down with radiocarbon dates from excavated sites.

Ceramic seriations for the African Iron Age have been built up in a number of different ways (M. Hall 1987). An older approach, not often used today, characterised assemblages by the presence of a few distinctive vessels – known as 'types' – and then arranged these types in a seriated sequence. This method worked while archaeologists were dealing with a few widely spaced sites. But as the archaeological evidence for the Iron Age began to build up, it was apparent that individual assemblages could show a tremendous amount of variability, and that they were not easily characterised by a few ceramics alone. Archaeologists were being swamped by the increasing amount of evidence available to them.

FIGURE 106 DECORATED POTS FROM EARLY IRON AGE SITES IN SOUTHERN AFRICA. Both the shape of vessels and the style in which they were decorated have been used to classify and seriate ceramic collections from archaeological sites.

More recent studies of Iron Age pottery have used multivariate techniques to characterise assemblages. In his study of central and southern African ceramics, Tom Huffman has isolated a set of basic motifs which were combined by potters to make up composite decorations on clay surfaces, rather like individual words that are combined to form sentences. On this basis, each archaeological assemblage can be characterised by the frequency of different motifs on its vessels, and placed in a time series adjacent to those assemblages with the closest frequency scores (Huffman 1978, 1980).

Once assembled, seriated sequences have been used to suggest the movement of groups of farmers into southern Africa (Figure 107). Huffman has argued that an eastern stream, the 'Matola Phase', spread southwards along the coastlands of Mozambique and KwaZulu–Natal between about AD 200 and AD 300. Several generations later, a western stream (the 'Lydenburg Phase') moved through Zambia and Zimbabwe, replacing the eastern stream along the southeast coastlands. Finally, a central stream, the 'Gokomere Phase', moved southwards into Zimbabwe, filling the space left by the southward-moving Lydenburg Phase (Huffman 1982).

As employed in studies such as Huffman's, terms such as 'phase' (and the more embracing 'tradition') are terminological conventions for seriated ceramic sequences. Archaeologically, the Matola, Lydenburg and Gokomere phases are made up of sets of ceramic assemblages from excavated sites, systematic surface collections and museum holdings. The basis for linking these assemblages together is the consistency of ceramic decoration, quantified by the frequency of decorative motifs. In searching for a historical meaning for such seriation, many archaeologists assume that pottery phases identify socially distinct groups of people. This interpretative device allows them to write history from the dumb potsherds that lie in such quantities on archaeological sites (M. Hall 1987).

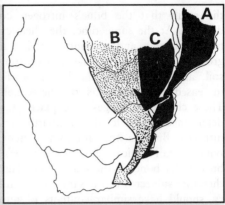

Figure 107 The 'three-stream' interpretation of the spread of Early Iron Age ceramic styles. In this interpretation, an eastern stream (A), known as the Matola Phase, first spread southwards along the coastlands of Mozambique and northern Natal. A second, western stream (the Lydenburg Phase) moved through Zambia and Zimbabwe a few years later, overrunning the eastern stream along the southeast coastlands. Finally, a central stream (C), the Gokomere Phase, moved southwards into Zimbabwe.

Early ceramic seriations for southern Africa have subsequently proved to be wrong. For example, John Schofield, who carried out fieldwork in the first half of the twentieth century, derived a complex, regionally based ceramic sequence. This included the categories NC1, NC2 and NC3, with 'NC' standing for 'Natal Coastal', and NC1 pottery being the oldest and NC3 the most recent. Later research, carried out with the benefit of extensive excavation and radiocarbon dates, has shown that NC2 pottery was the oldest form, NC3 the next in the sequence, and NC1 the most recent (Maggs 1984b). That this should happen is not surprising: seriated sequences are constantly tested against new evidence – both the stratigraphies of excavated sites and new radiocarbon dates, as they become available. Earlier archaeologists had to depend heavily on seriated assemblages alone. Today, seriations can be combined with additional chronological evidence to provide far more secure syntheses of the past.

Stratigraphy and seriation are the most widespread methods of relative dating in archaeology. But there are a number of other more specialised techniques which, in certain circumstances, can be very useful. These include so-called bone dates. When bones are buried in the ground, their chemical composition gradually changes. The collagen in the bone decays, with the result that the bone's nitrogen content declines. At the same time, the chemical elements fluorine and uranium, carried in the ground water that percolates down through the soil, are absorbed by the bones, leading to increased concentrations of these elements. These chemical changes take place at a rate determined by the local soil environment: the nitrogen, fluorine and uranium content of a bone cannot indicate how long it has been buried. But bones in the same assemblage, and therefore subjected to the same chemical history, should have similar contents of nitrogen, uranium and fluorine depending on the length of time they have lain buried. They can therefore be dated relative to one another. 'Bone dates' allow the archaeologist to test whether or not a collection of bones could have come from the same layer in the same site.

The relative dating of bones by assessment of their chemical profiles is widely celebrated in archaeology because this technique was used to show that 'Piltdown Man' was a hoax. In the early years of the twentieth century a human skull, an ape-like jaw and some teeth were found in the south of England and claimed to be the 'missing link' in human evolution. But in 1953 analysis of the nitrogen, fluorine and uranium traces in the various bones showed them to be of widely different ages: 'Piltdown Man' was in fact an elaborate hoax. Interestingly the Piltdown forgery had an indirect, and negative, effect on African archaeology. British physical anthropologists believed for long that the 'missing link' was in their own backyard, and failed to take the early australopithecine finds in Africa seriously for many years (Gowlett 1990).

Absolute dating

There is thus a range of different approaches to relative dating, applicable in different circumstances and in relation to various problems of interpretation. Similarly, there is a range of absolute-dating techniques, and it is important to know when it is appropriate to use them, as well as the constraints that apply in their interpretation. Before looking at these methods in more detail, we need to take a moment to consider what an absolute date is in archaeology, and what is not.

It is sometimes assumed that an absolute date is synonymous with a calendar date – the simple opposite of a relative date. In other words, instead of saying 'This village is older than that village' (relative date), the archaeologist says 'This village was first occupied in AD 453' (absolute date). But in fact, only rarely is it correct to make statements such as the second of these. Specific events are very seldom marked in the archaeological record and, when they are, it is usually the result of a catastrophe. We know, for example, that the Dutch East India Company's *Oosterland* sank in Table Bay in 1697, and that the city of Pompeii in Italy was destroyed by an eruption of Mount Vesuvius in AD 79. More often, even when we have a tight framework of certain calendar years, we cannot relate archaeological assemblages to precise dates. We know, for example, that hearths and food debris left by slaves in Cape Town's Castle must date to between AD 1691 and AD 1703 (Yates et al. 1995). These twelve years are represented by six substantial stratigraphic units, which contain within them individual fireplaces. It is logical to conclude that this part of the Castle's archaeology is a record of clear, individual actions. However, there is no method of teasing these chronological details apart, and the archaeology of slaves at the Castle is written as a twelve-year slice of group history.

Absolute dates, then, are not the same as calendar dates. Rather, they are age estimates which *refer* to a calendrical time-scale. It is for this reason that in order to avoid confusion, some archaeologists prefer to use the term 'chronometric dates'. Absolute or chronometric dating techniques fall into two distinct categories: methods that depend on the principles of radioactive decay (the 'radiometric clocks') and those that are based on other natural processes.

The basis of the radiometric clocks that have now become so important in archaeology is the fairly simple observation that unstable isotopes decay at known exponential rates. Each kind of radioactive isotope is said to have a 'half-life' – the time that it takes for half of the amount of the isotope to decay. In other words, after one half-life, half of the isotope will be left; after two half-lives, one quarter of the original quantity; and so on. By measuring the amount of an isotope and the strength of its residual activity, one can calculate the length of time over which it has been decaying. Some isotopes have half-lives of a fraction of a second, and others have half-lives of many millions of years. Only a few are of any use for archaeological dating.

> **Isotopes** are atoms of the same chemical element (and therefore with the same chemical properties) which have slightly different physical characteristics. Isotopes may be 'stable' – existing in elements in almost unvarying proportions – or 'unstable' – in which case they break down, or 'decay', spontaneously and at known rates. Unstable isotopes are radioactive, emitting alpha, beta and gamma rays. There are about 50 naturally occurring radioactive isotopes.

Radiocarbon dating

The properties of unstable isotopes have been known since the early years of the twentieth century. The principal challenge has lain in measurement. Unstable isotopes exist in very small quantities, which become even smaller as decay progresses. For archaeology, the major breakthrough came in 1949, when Willard Libby first showed that it was possible to measure the beta radiation from the unstable isotope of carbon, ^{14}C, using a Geiger counter. Since then, there has been a series of technical developments that have allowed increasing accuracy with smaller samples. However, the measurement of radioactivity from unstable isotopes, and therefore radiometric dating, remains a specialised task, requiring sophisticated laboratory conditions.

Of the various radiometric techniques available, radiocarbon dating is the most widely used, and the method that has had the greatest impact on archaeological interpretations. Like other unstable isotopes, carbon-14 (written ^{14}C) decays at a steady rate, with a half-life of 5730 years. But the store of ^{14}C in the earth's atmosphere is continually replenished by cosmic radiation. All living organisms absorb ^{14}C from the atmosphere through the food they eat: plants take up carbon dioxide (including ^{14}C) during photosynthesis, herbivores eat the plants, and carnivores eat the herbivores. In other words, we are all very slightly radioactive, and we all have roughly the same proportion of ^{14}C in our bodies as there is in the air we breathe. However, when an organism dies, it stops replenishing ^{14}C, and the ^{14}C in its body at the time of death begins to break down at the known exponential rate of the ^{14}C isotope. By measuring the amount of residual radioactivity emitted from the ^{14}C still in a sample of something that once lived, one can calculate when the organism died.

In view of the principles on which it is based, radiocarbon dating has several constraints.

- It can only be carried out on organic materials – most commonly charcoal from once-used fireplaces, wood, bone or shell. Artefacts made from inorganic materials such as stone or clay can only be dated by association with organic substances.
- It is restricted by the length of the half-life of ^{14}C. In practice, samples older than 50 000 years have too little surviving ^{14}C to be measured.
- It dates the organism which is being dated – but this is not necessarily the same as the age of the archaeological context. For example, when people use well-seasoned wood in a building or timbers that have been salvaged from an earlier structure, the radiocarbon date for such wood will give an estimate of the age when the tree laid down the wood in the sample, not a date for the building.

It was originally assumed that the proportion of ^{14}C in the earth's atmosphere had remained constant, at least for the full range of time over which radiocarbon dating can be used. But this is now known not to have been the case. The amount of cosmic radiation has varied from time to time, affecting various parts of the world in different ways. Consequently, radiocarbon dates are, wherever possible, 'calibrated' by means of a correction curve. This is derived from radiocarbon age estimations of samples from trees, whose annual rings have been counted to determine the true calendar age of the sample ('dendrochronology').

Like all other radiometric methods, radiocarbon dating is a technique for estimating the amount of time that the ^{14}C isotopes in a sample have been in decay, and is therefore distinct

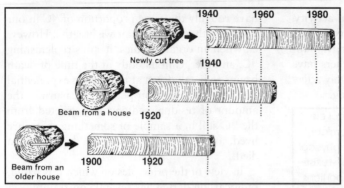

FIGURE 108 DENDROCHRONOLOGY. This method of absolute dating takes advantage of the fact that many tree species lay down a distinct ring of growth each year, and this varies in thickness according to the weather. The result is a pattern of ring widths that is replicated in trees from the same local area. By matching the patterns in newly cut (or cored) trees with wood from archaeological sites, one can build up a chronological sequence.

from a calendar date. In recognition of this difference, a specific notation is used for radiocarbon dates. Firstly, rather than being expressed in terms of a calendar such as the Christian convention of BC and AD, radiocarbon dates are given as 'before the present', or 'BP', where the 'present' is taken as 1950 (when the first radiocarbon dates became available). Secondly, because an age estimate for a specific sample is based on a number of measurements of residual radiation, a radiocarbon date is given as a mean with a standard deviation, thereby expressing the statistical strength of the estimate. Thirdly, as laboratory conditions and techniques are critical in obtaining good age estimates, a laboratory code and sample number are given after the statistical estimate.

For example, the site of Mzonjani, near Durban, has given some of the earliest evidence for farming settlement in southern Africa. A sample of charcoal taken from a pit, and lying next to Early Iron Age potsherds, gave the following radiocarbon age estimation, expressed in conventional notation (Maggs 1980b):

1670 ± 40 BP (Pta-1980)

Interpreted, this indicates that the radiocarbon date was measured by the Pretoria laboratory (Pta), and that it was sample number 1980. There is a 68 per cent probability (a single standard deviation) that the calendar date for the death of the tree from which the firewood came was within the range of 40 years before to 40 years after 1670 years before 1950 – in other words, between ad 240 and 310 (it is part of the convention to use the lower-case 'ad' if the date has not been calibrated). A higher level of probability, 95 per cent, can be obtained by doubling the standard deviation, in this example to ± 80 years, which gives the range for the calendar date as between ad 200 and 350. The charcoal sample from Mzonjani was probably the product of a single evening's cooking, but the closest that the archaeologist can estimate when the meal was consumed is about three human generations. The value of using specific conventions is that they avoid confusion between very different ways of measuring time.

Although radiocarbon dates are age estimates that incorporate wide degrees of latitude, the technique has had a major impact on African archaeology. This impact can be tracked from the regular reviews of new radiocarbon dates for more recent periods of the past, published by the *Journal of African History*. The first dating review appeared in 1961, when there were only six new dates from southern Africa to report (Fagan 1961). By 1970, there were sufficient dates to treat eastern and southern Africa by themselves (Phillipson 1970); by 1980 southern Africa was being treated alone (M. Hall & Vogel 1980).

Country	1961	1970	1980
Botswana	0	0	2
Lesotho	0	0	0
Mozambique	0	0	8
Namibia	0	2	14
South Africa	3	8	104
Swaziland	0	2	0
Zimbabwe	3	16	24

The impact of the technique (as well as some of its potential pitfalls) is equally apparent in the specific history of Great Zimbabwe. Gertrude Caton-Thompson estimated the age of the layers she excavated from the fortunate occurrence of Asian porcelain (of known age) that had been imported on to the site during the course of trading activities. In other words, she was able to cross-date the site by establishing a connection with the Chinese calendar and Emperor lists (Caton-Thompson 1931). With Libby's discovery of radiocarbon dating, it became clear that this technique would conclude the Great Zimbabwe controversy with finality. But when samples from a wooden lintel over a drain in the Great Enclosure were dated, the age estimates were for the fifth and sixth centuries ad – hundreds of years earlier than Caton-Thompson's published conclusions – to the delight of those who were still arguing for non-African origins (Summers 1955).

It now seems probable that these first dates were for seasoned wood that was far older than the buildings themselves. Subsequent series of dates for the Great Enclosure as well as for the Hill ruins have shown that the town was a thriving capital between about ad 1330 (when the first solid plaster houses were built on top of the hill) and the mid-fifteenth century, by which time Great Zimbabwe had been eclipsed by other towns in the region (Huffman & Vogel 1991). Although some recidivists still hold out for the Queen of Sheba or itinerant Phoenicians, the publication of the full suite of radiocarbon dates for this key site has effectively concluded a dating controversy that began more than a century earlier.

Radiocarbon dating and early pastoralism

Domestic sheep and cattle were brought into southern Africa from the north during the last two thousand years, their introduction signalling a change to pastoralist and farming economies. The beginnings of these new ways of life can be traced from the bones of livestock, abandoned as food refuse and preserved in stratigraphical contexts on archaeological sites. Radiocarbon dates from such sites in different parts of the subcontinent can be studied for geographical and chronological patterning, thereby helping archaeologists to deduce both the patterns of spread of early stock-keepers across the landscape, and the period when these happened.

Until recently, almost all radiocarbon dates used in situations such as these were obtained from material (particularly charcoal) that made up the matrix of the stratigraphical layer, rather than from the animal bone itself. This was because large amounts of bone were needed in order to calculate a radiocarbon date: either the bones were not big enough, or else they would be completely destroyed by dating, thus preventing other important studies of these unique specimens.

But now more refined techniques of radiocarbon dating are in use. In particular, the so-called accelerator method yields dates from very small samples of bone. For the first time it has been possible to obtain a direct estimate of the date when an animal was slaughtered, rather than an estimate of the age of other material in an archaeological layer that might have been deposited slowly, over several hundred years.

Judith Sealy and Royden Yates have made use of the accelerator technique of radiocarbon dating to re-evaluate some of the key sites where early sheep bones have been found in the western and southern Cape regions of South Africa and in Namibia. The results of their study show how important context can be in radiocarbon-dating archaeological sites. Sealy and Yates started by reviewing all the radiocarbon dates that archaeologists have obtained from sites with early sheep bones in southern Africa. They found that in all cases, the stratigraphical context was crucial. Because there had been no dates obtained from samples of the sheep bones themselves, these estimates of age depended on associated objects, particularly pieces of charcoal.

In every case, there was the possibility that some unforeseen factor might be distorting the true picture. At some of the archaeological sites, it was clear that the deposits in which the sheep bones had been found had built up very slowly indeed. The remnants of a camp-fire could have lain near the surface in a rock shelter for a hundred years or more before later occupants dropped the remains of a meal into the dust. In this way, a piece of charcoal and a bone, whose true ages were a century or more apart, could be lying next to each other in the ground. At other sites, there was the possibility that sheep bones had been worked down into underlying areas, again setting up a deceptive correlation between the bone and the sample from which the radiocarbon date had been obtained. An archaeological site is an ecological niche in its own right, with a host of insects and other small animals moving the deposits around beneath the modern ground surface. No matter how painstaking and systematic the excavation, there is always the possibility of a false association.

The results obtained by accelerator-dating the sheep bones themselves were startling. In the table below, the earlier dates from a selection of the sites are shown against the new dates obtained by using the accelerator technique. In all cases, the results are significantly different.

Site	Earlier: C14 age estimates: associated samples	New C14 age estimates: bone samples	New C14 dates: calibrated date ranges
Spoegrivier	1920 ± 40 bp	2105 ± 65 bp	165 BC–AD 13
Kasteelberg A	1860 ± 60 bp	1630 ± 60 bp	AD 414–554
De Kelders	1960 ± 85 bp	1325 ± 60 bp	AD 670–790
Byneskranskop	1880 ± 50 bp	1370 ± 60 bp	AD 656–769

For Spoegrivier, a pastoralist campsite in Namaqualand, the new radiocarbon date suggests that pastoralists could have been using the site a century or more earlier than was once believed. In this case, the bone had been left underneath the hearth that had been radiocarbon-dated; clearly it had been there for some time before the later fireplace was used. Only one sheep bone has been recovered from this early layer at Spoegrivier – a right first phalange – which illustrates how tenuous archaeological clues of importance can be.

Kasteelberg is also an open campsite, beneath the shelter of a boulder, further south along the Atlantic coastline. In this case, the new age estimate was some two hundred years

younger than the one suggested by the first radiocarbon sample, which was for a piece of charcoal in the same layer, right at the bottom of the excavation. Here, it seems possible that hunter–gatherers had taken shelter in the same spot, leaving the faintest trace of their presence, to cause confusion almost two thousand years later.

De Kelders is a large cave close to the shoreline on the southern Cape coast. The three centuries' difference between the two radiocarbon age estimates is probably due to the sheep bones being worked down from the overlying stratigraphical level.

Byneskranskop, a shelter in a coastal mountain range within sight of De Kelders, is an example of a different problem. Here the excavators decided to lump together three sub-units into a single layer during the excavation, with the result that charcoal and animal bones from a wide bracket of time were interpreted as if they were part of a far briefer episode.

Sealy and Yates conclude that theirs is only the first stage in an ongoing review of archaeological evidence, made necessary by ever-improving scientific techniques:

'Clearly, much work remains to be done. We need more sites with large assemblages of fauna and pottery, and many more direct radiocarbon dates on the bones of domestic animals. The results reported here demonstrate the limitations of the archaeological record. We cannot trace the beginnings of pastoralism on the basis of dating by association. Direct radiocarbon dates on the objects of enquiry, however, can help us to unravel the complicated interactions associated with the adoption of food production in southern Africa' (Sealy & Yates 1994: 65).

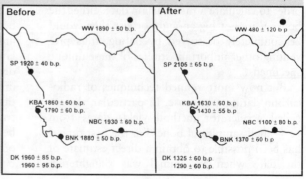

Figure 109 The impact of accelerator dating. These two maps show the original set of radiocarbon dates for sites with early sheep bones (on the left), and the accelerator dates obtained from direct bone samples. Comparison shows significant changes in chronology.

SOME METHODS OF ABSOLUTE DATING		
TECHNIQUE	TIME RANGE	SOURCE MATERIALS
Radiocarbon	back to about 50 000	organic materials, e.g. burnt wood, bone, shell
Thermoluminescence	back to about 80 000	materials with crystalline structure, e.g. pottery
Amino-acid racemisation	back to about 100 000	bone, ostrich egg-shell
Uranium series	back to about 500 000	calcium carbonate (travertine in limestone caves)
Obsidian hydration	back to about 500 000	obsidian
Electron spin resonance	back to about 1m yrs	bone or shell
Potassium–argon	from about 100 000 back	volcanic rock
Fission track	from about 300 000 back	range of rocks and minerals

Radiometric clocks

Although radiocarbon dating is the predominant technique of chronometric dating in use in archaeology today, other methods are important, particularly for older time periods and for specialised circumstances. Some of these methods depend on the behaviour of unstable isotopes other than ^{14}C, while others make use of other natural processes. They are summarised in the table above.

One of the problems of radiocarbon dating is that it is often not possible to date the artefact itself. This makes crucial the association between the assemblage and the sample of organic material that is to be submitted to the laboratory. Sometimes, however meticulous the excavation, apparent associations can be incorrect and result in very misleading chronological conclusions.

Thermoluminescence dating (known as 'TL') has the major advantage of directly dating artefacts, although unfortunately with less precision than is usually possible with radiocarbon dating. TL is applicable to materials with a crystalline structure, notably clay used in potting. Such materials contain small amounts of radioactive material, including uranium, thorium and potassium. Like other radioactive isotopes, these decay at a known rate. As they do so, they emit radiation which bombards the structure of the clay, displacing electrons which become trapped in the crystalline matrix. These electrons are released as thermoluminescent light when the clay is fired to 500°C or more. During firing, the radioactive 'clock' is set back to zero and the process of electron displacement begins again. By heating a sample of pottery to 500°C in the laboratory, and measuring the amount of thermoluminescence emitted, one can calculate the amount of time that has passed since the pottery was fired (or since it

was last heated to the same temperature).

The time range of thermoluminescence dating is much the same as radiocarbon dating. But there is a radiometric technique that can be used for time ranges between about 50 000 years ago and 500 000 years ago: uranium-series dating, which is based on the radioactive decay of uranium isotopes. In this technique, samples of calcium carbonates that have precipitated on cave walls and floors are analysed. These sediments, often known as travertine, contain the radioactive elements thorium and protactinium, which themselves have emerged from the decay of water-soluble, radioactive uranium elements. Because thorium and protactinium are not water soluble, they only form (and begin to decay) when the travertine actually forms over the archaeological deposits. Because, as with other unstable isotopes, the half-lives of thorium and protactinium are known, the age of the travertine can be estimated. The main limitation with this dating method is that it can only be used in sites which satisfy specific geological conditions.

The last example that will be discussed here – potassium–argon dating – is also only suitable if specific geological conditions are met. Fortunately, however, potassium–argon dating can be used at most of the principal hominid fossil sites in East Africa. Since 1961, when the first potassium–argon dates were published for Olduvai Gorge, this radiometric dating method has transformed our understanding of human origins (Gowlett 1990).

The use of potassium–argon dating (abbreviated as 'K–Ar') is restricted to volcanic rocks that formed no less than about 100 000 years ago. The technique is based on the slow decay of the radioactive isotope potassium-40 (^{40}K) to the inert gas argon-40 (^{40}Ar) in volcanic rocks. Because the half-life of ^{40}K is known (1.3 billion years), the amount of ^{40}Ar trapped in a rock sample of given mass will be an indicator of the age of the volcanic eruption in which the volcanic rock was formed.

'Radiocarbon and potassium–argon dating established that successive Palaeolithic cultures were at least as old as similar ones found in Europe, thereby confirming the importance of Africa as a centre of cultural as well as biological development throughout the Stone Age. In textbooks of world archaeology published in the 1960s and 1970s Africa was no longer described as having been a backwater throughout the whole of human history. Instead it was featured as a focal point of progress, especially in early Palaeolithic times' (Trigger 1990).

In many respects, then, time is archaeology's critical dimension. The study of archaeology originated in the recognition that humans have a deep history. Problems of plotting and measuring chronology have always had a special place in archaeological writing. And yet archaeological time can rarely be expressed in simple calendar terms, or in the precise unit measurements that today find expression in the exactitude of Coordinated Universal Time. Sometimes, archaeology's time dimension is rather like a video-tape slowed down until it appears as a series of still-life shots, strung together as jerky animation. In other situations, the action may be faster and smoother, but we only ever see crowd scenes: the details of individual actions are hidden from us and all we have is their rather blurred effects. Frustrating as this may at times seem, archaeology has a major asset that is not shared by any other discipline in the humanities – it can take a very long view of the human condition, plotting our history over a span of more than two million years.

126

chapter 8

People and their environment

In the previous chapter, we looked at time – archaeology's special dimension. Now we turn to the way in which the evidence for human activity can be read from the earth's surface. Ultimately, of course, this distinction between time and space can only be a device to help understand what it is that archaeologists actually do. Time and space in human history are ineluctably linked.

Race and racism

In considering the ways in which humans exist in relation to the world around them, we discover a critical tension running like a tight thread through the history of archaeology. To what extent does the environment shape who people are? To what extent has human history determined the form of the world? This issue has been doubly inscribed in the case of Africa, because of the projections that the 'dark continent' carries for the rest of the world. Like all other anthropological and historical disciplines, archaeology has been entangled with issues of race and racism.

The scientific description of human races has itself a long history. In 1735 Linnaeus drew distinctions between *Homo europaeus*, *Homo asiaticus* and *Homo africanus*, the last being the black-skinned people of Africa. Later writers became interested in assessing the relative superiority of these different groups. By the late nineteenth-century Darwinian theories of evolution had prompted the formation of specialised disciplines such as craniology and eugenics, dedicated to identifying and plotting racial distinctions (Gould 1981). However, Nazi excess in the Second World War put an end to this predilection for racial classification in many parts of the world, with the exception,

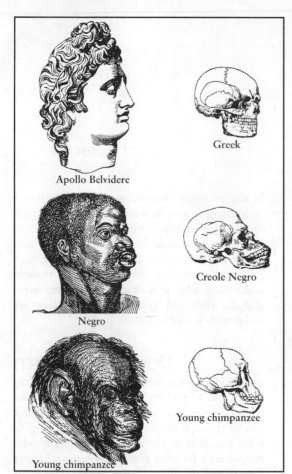

FIGURE 110 NINETEENTH-CENTURY RACIAL EVOLUTIONISM. In this book, published in 1868, it was argued that the 'Negro' was closer to the chimpanzee than to 'Europeans' (Nott & Gliddon 1868).

of course, of places such as the southern United States and southern Africa.

Many archaeologists write as if this were the end of the issue. In their account of the discipline Renfrew and Bahn, for instance, have racism in archaeology stop at the end of the Second World War (with a later lapse in Rhodesia). They even express the hope for 'a more robust methodology', the possibility of 'approaching once again the whole question of racial distinctions, and how these may correlate with ethnic groups: social groups which regard themselves as separate and distinct' (Renfrew & Bahn 1991: 371).

But although craniology and eugenics are obsolete disciplines, there is another level of racism that is widespread, and has a marked

effect on the way in which the past is interpreted. This is the 'soft' racism that makes assumptions about inherited attributes and the effects of the environment on history and society, and colours the way in which Africa's past continues to be understood. A classic embodiment of this set of attitudes is Joseph Conrad's story *Heart of Darkness*, first published at the turn of the century and still influential today. As the Nigerian novelist Chinua Achebe has commented in a lecture:

'Conrad's famous novel, *Heart of Darkness*, first published in 1899, portrays Africa as a place where the wandering European may discover that the dark impulses and unspeakable appetites he has suppressed and forgotten through ages of civilization may spring into life again in answer to Africa's free and triumphant savagery ... Africa is presumed to pursue its dark, mysterious ways and destiny untouched by explorations and expeditions. Sometimes Africa as an anthropomorphic personage steps out of the shadows and physically annihilates the invasion – which of course adds a touch of suspense and even tragedy to Europe's enterprise' (Achebe 1991: 5–6).

In the same year that Achebe delivered this lecture in London, Bernardo Bertolucci's film *The Sheltering Sky* was released – exactly a century after Conrad's voyage down the Congo River. Starring Debra Winger and John Malkovich, *The Sheltering Sky* is the story of Kit and Port, refugees from New York high society, who are drawn southwards, deeper and deeper into Africa. The vast landscape serves as a metaphor for their own drifting, unresolved marriage. Like Kurtz in *Heart of Darkness*, they may satisfy their dark impulses, but at the risk of destruction. Port is stricken by typhoid fever amid a cacophony of flutes, drums and ululating women, and dies in a desert storm. Kit is adopted by a Tuareg camel train and becomes the concubine of its leader. Arriving in a desert village, she surrenders to sensuality, achieving the consummation that was lacking in her marriage, and cuts up her notebooks – the last semblance of civilisation – to decorate the room. But as with Kurtz before her, the price for such indulgence is madness, despite her rescue by the long arm of the American consulate. Africa has taken another victim.

Joseph Conrad, Heart of Darkness (1899) ...

'Going up that river was like travelling back to the earliest beginnings of the world, when vegetation riot-ed on the earth and the big trees were kings. An empty stream, a great silence, an impenetrable forest. The air was warm, thick, heavy, sluggish. There was no joy in the brilliance of sunshine. The long stretches of the waterway ran on, deserted, into the gloom of overshadowed distances ... We penetrated deeper and deeper into the heart of darkness. It was very quiet there. At night sometimes the roll of drums behind the curtain of trees would run up the river and remain sustained faintly, as if hovering in the air high over our heads, till the first break of day. Whether it meant war, peace, or prayer we could not tell ... We were wanderers on a prehistoric earth, on an earth that wore the aspect of an unknown planet. We could have fancied ourselves the first of men taking possession of an accursed inheritance, to be sub-dued at the cost of profound anguish and of excessive toil. But suddenly, as we struggled round a bend, there would be a glimpse of rush walls, of peaked grass-roofs, a burst of yells, a whirl of black limbs, a mass of hands clapping, of feet stamping, of bodies swaying, of eyes rolling, under the droop of heavy and motionless foliage. The steamer toiled along slowly on the edge of a black and incomprehensible frenzy. The prehistoric man was cursing us, praying to us, welcoming us – who could tell? We were cut off from the comprehension of our surroundings; we glided past like phantoms, wondering and secretly appalled, as sane men would be before an enthusiastic outbreak in a madhouse. We could not under-stand because we were too far and could not remember, because we were travelling in the night of first ages, of those ages that are gone, leaving hardly a sign – and no memories' (Conrad 1971: 34–6).

Racism can be defined as the belief that groups of people, sharing common descent and some physical features, have inherent cultural characteristics that make them inevitably inferi-or or superior to other groups. Racial terminol-ogy and assumptions have had a major impact on the writing of Africa's past. For many years, it was standard practice to describe (or have a specialist consultant describe) skeletal material excavated from archaeological sites in racial terms. These reports would assume that a small set of characteristics or measurements, taken from a single human skull, could be used to classify the individual as 'Negro' or 'Boskopoid' or 'Caucasian'. Because nineteenth-century racial theory held that racial origin was the prime determinant of who a person was, it was often assumed that the designations given by physical anthropologists were also ethnic mark-ers. By the middle years of the present century, more than seven races had been claimed as ancestral populations of southern Africa, each associated with a specific 'culture' (Tobias 1974).

Behind its assumptions of racial superiority and inferiority, this anthropological approach to race involved making a huge extrapolation, moving from the physical features of a single skeleton to a set of characteristics that were taken as typical of groups comprising millions of people. Today it is accepted that human physical variability is very complicated indeed, and cannot be examined in this way. In short, race has ceased to be a legitimate biological concept.

'Classifications of man into Mongoloids, Cauca-soids, Negroids, etc. undoubtedly express cer-tain genuine features of human variation but they do so in a crude and potentially mislead-ing way. A mere list of diagnostic characters obscures the important fact that all populations are variable. Within any population individuals differ quite widely in stature and other traits that can be measured on a continuous scale. When we compare two populations we often find that the ranges of variation for such a character overlap, so that some individuals cannot be assigned with certainty to one or other on this criterion alone ...' (Harrison et al. 1977: 184–5).

'In a sense trying to classify people into a few races is like trying to classify books in a library: you may use a single property – size, say – but you will get a useless classification, or you may use a more complex system of interconnected criteria, and then you will get a good deal of arbitrariness. No one – not even the most com-pulsive librarian! – thinks that book classifica-tions reflect deep facts about books. Each of them is more or less useless for various purpos-es; all of them, as we know, have the kind of

Race and ethnicity in Rwanda

Rwanda – a small, densely occupied country – has three ethnic groups: Hutu (traditionally, subsistence farmers who form the majority of the population), Tutsi (in earlier years an aristocratic minority of landowners and pastoralists) and Twa (traditionally, hunters and potmakers). For many years there has been conflict between Hutu and Tutsi, leading to periodic outbreaks of civil war.

Most Rwandans believe that the ethnic distinctions that divide their country are inherent and inherited: an inevitable consequence of one's ancestry. This idea – founded squarely on nineteenth-century racial theory – bedevils attempts to end the endemic warfare.

Recent archaeological and anthropological research in Rwanda and neighbouring areas has been directed at establishing a new understanding of the early history of the interlacustrine region. P. Twagiramutara, J. Ki-zerbo, D. Olderogge and others have argued that ethnicity is the product of multiple factors operating at a local level. They have shown that over the long periods of time which are the special dimension of archaeological work, people have adapted to 'various specific micro-environments, each with its own climate, flora, and fauna', and that 'populations responded in various ways to the conditions created by the diversity of these micro-environments by developing distinctive cultures' (Twagiramutara 1989: 89–90).

In Pancrace Twagiramutara's words: 'Ethnicity is today primarily a historical and cultural phenomenon, rather than, as some authors contend, a biological one. Ethnic affiliation is generally attributed at birth and gradually becomes the source of a prescribed status ... Recent scientific research in Rwanda, Burundi, and neighbouring regions of inter-lacustrine Africa has shown that theories which treat ethnic groups as immutable derive less from indigenous perceptions than from cultural models introduced during the colonial period by European administrators. The idea that ethnic groups are racially distinct became a veritable ideological doctrine, political and cultural, diffuse and mobilizing. With time it has become implanted in the minds of indigenous populations. As a consequence ethnic cleavages are now perceived as facts of nature not to be called into question' (Twagiramutara 1989: 94).

With the escalation of the Rwandan civil war in 1994, many thousands of people died as a result of such racial beliefs.

---

rough edges that take a while to get around. And nobody thinks that a library classification can settle which books we should value; the numbers in the Dewey decimal system do not correspond with qualities of utility or interest or literary merit' (Appiah 1992: 60–1).

But as the Ghanaian writer Kwame Anthony Appiah goes on to stress, to deny the scientific value of the concept of race is not to deny the existence of human physical variability. People *do* look different, some of these differences *are* inherited, and there *has* been a complex relationship between the development of physical traits and the environment. On the other hand, there is no legitimate evidence that such physical differences are linked to intelligence, ability, morality, aesthetics or other aspects of society. Culture is far more important than biological inheritance in shaping human history.

Today, physical anthropologists study human physical variability as a complex network of differently distributed traits, reflecting the complexity of genetic inheritance. In modern research, counting is as important as measuring – ultimately, human biologists are trying to track the effects of individual genes (or groups of genes), and to differentiate these from the effects of the environment during an individual's lifetime. A key concept is the 'Mendelian population', or breeding population (Figure 112) – the group within which most matings will take place for geographical or social reasons, and the group of people statistically likely to have similar genetic make-ups, or 'genotypes' (Weiss & Mann 1985).

Of course, there still abound concepts of race and assertions of racial superiority, inferiority or equality. These, though, are sociological prejudices that have no legitimate connection with modern biology:

'In the human context [race] has been so often misunderstood and abused that some authorities prefer to avoid it. If, for example, we speak of a German or a Jewish race we confuse biological and cultural differences. These are culturally defined groups, and if we call them races we tend to prejudge whether they are also genetically differentiated and, if so, in what ways and to what extent. Such misconceptions easily lead to racist doctrines that assert the purity and superiority of certain groups. No natural populations are pure in the sense of being genetically uniform, though some may have been less affected by recent inflow of genes than others. The question of superiority inevitably involves social and ethical valuations and in practice it is bound up with the desire of one group to dominate and exploit another' (Harrison et al. 1977: 185–6).

FIGURE 111 CEMETERY EXCAVATIONS. Today, physical anthropologists study the statistical variation in collections of human skeletal material, rather than individual bodies. This has shifted attention to graveyards, such as this one in Coburn Street, Cape Town, where more than 70 eighteenth-century graves were exhumed as a result of urban development. Once excavated, human bones must be treated with respect, and the known wishes of any descendants respected.

FIGURE 112 MENDELIAN POPULATIONS. In this simplified example, three villages are separated by geographical features: mountains and a river. Most people marry within their villages of birth, creating 'breeding populations' which coincide with the human geography of the area. But a few, more adventurous individuals find husbands and wives from the other side of the river or mountain pass, and their children will share in the gene pools of two villages. A technological change, such as an easier route across the river, would result in an increase in the frequency of marriage outside each village. Thus it can be seen that genetic make-up is strongly influenced by social and historical factors.

The Mendelian population …

'This revolution in thought has also altered the choice of the basic unit of study in physical anthropology. Few modern workers are prepared to continue to discuss the characteristics of the major races or 'racial constellations' and it is accepted that these extremely large clusters of population have little biological meaning. The approach is now at the level of the breeding or Mendelian population. Not only is this smaller unit easier to define, but it tends to function as a single entity within the ecosystem. A breeding population is a natural grouping which depends on the tendency of people habitually to select breeding partners from within a specific set of potential mates. Although there may be a general resistance to genetic amalgamation between neighbouring populations, there is usually a small amount of gene flow between them, and breeding populations cannot be considered to be closed systems. The boundaries of a breeding population are not maintained by biological factors but depend on cultural or social circumstances that limit or facilitate gene exchange between groups' (Morris 1992: 1–2).

Mendelian populations

An example of the contemporary approach in the study of human physical variability is Alan Morris's work on the Orange River 'contact frontier'. Morris made a biological comparison of four protohistoric populations: Iron Age farmers, herders, hunter–gatherers and European colonists. What he did was to track genetic mixing of these Mendelian populations through the multivariate study of human skeletons (Morris 1992). Many of these collections of human bones had been dug out long ago by amateur grave robbers, and deposited in museum collections. In fact it took a considerable amount of work on Morris's part to re-establish their context as much as possible. In the end, though, he had 341 human skeletons to work from, of which he analysed 297 statistically – in contrast with earlier anthropological studies, in which racial generalisations were routinely made from the assessment of part of a single skeleton.

Morris took measurements from crania and

FIGURE 113 STUDY AREAS ON THE ORANGE RIVER.

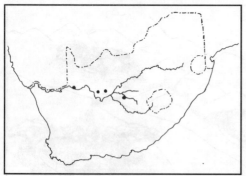

mandibles, combining the results to produce indices that expressed variations in cranial shape. This set of 60 measurements and 20 indices – amounting to more than 20 000 observations altogether – was tested statistically for significant differences. The end result of the study was a statistical plot which arranged the 297 skeletons in a logical relationship with one another, indicating the degree of genetic variability within the samples.

The results of Morris's study showed that the Orange River frontier had been peopled by distinct Mendelian populations, linked by a degree of gene flow. In other words, there were clear cultural preferences in the choice of sexual partners, but these were flexible social traditions. Morris also found that the Mendelian populations did not coincide with the cultural affinities implied by the grave goods or the form of the burials. He interpreted this as 'unidirectional gene flow' – as an unevenness in the choice of sexual partners – and a consequence of differences in status between the groups. In other words, sexual partners were taken by one group from another, but there was little reciprocation. Such complexity is not surprising in modern human biology, since it is accepted as a basic tenet that social practices such as marriage preferences, modulated by status differences, determine the genetic composition of a population. But it is worth remembering that this is precisely the inverse of the tenet held as basic by earlier, racist anthropology. In tumbling into the modern world, physical anthropology has performed a complete theoretical somersault.

Race, genetics and the San

The history of the study of the San (Bushman) hunter–gatherers of southern Africa well illustrates both changing attitudes to human variability and the persistence of popular racial prejudices.

When they were first encountered by European travellers, the San were believed to be either not human, or else the epitome of the lowest form of humanity. Their skulls were prized for measurement, and sometimes their whole bodies were collected for study and display in Europe.

'The Darder Museum is a small museum in Banyoles (Catalonia, Spain) which contains various archaeological and natural history specimens, including stuffed animals, preserved human foetuses and a South American mummy. Its central exhibit is the stuffed, upright body of an almost naked African man holding a spear. The body was obtained in 1829–30 and prepared by the French taxidermist Edouard Verraux and was first displayed in Paris in 1831, as part of an exhibition of stuffed animals. The Catalan naturalist Francis Darder purchased the body from the Verraux collection in 1888

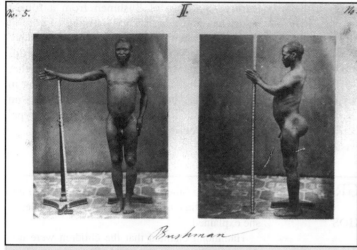

No. 5.

Bushman

FIGURE 114 RACIAL STUDIES. Nine-teenth-century scientists, intent on the classification and study of human races, collected anatomical photographs in which subjects were forced to pose naked in formal positions, usually alongside measuring scales.

and, in 1916, he bequeathed it and his whole collection to the town of Banyoles. Since this time the whole collection has become the Darder Museum, which is managed by a Board of Directors, many of whose members also sit on the Banyoles Town Council' (Jaume et al. 1992: 114).

Even after the demise of scientific racism, San hunter–gatherers continued to be seen as cultural representatives of an early stage in human history – as 'living fossils' that could provide archaeology with analogies for interpreting life in the Stone Age. This approach culminated in detailed studies of San life and beliefs, such as the collection of essays titled *Man the Hunter*, published in 1968 (Lee & DeVore 1968).

More recently, scholars have challenged the view that San hunter–gatherers living in remote areas such as the Kalahari in Botswana have been isolated for centuries. Rather than being pristine survivors from the Stone Age (the 'pure remnant of the unique and almost vanished First People of my native land, the Bushmen', according to Laurens van der Post), it has been shown that the San have had contact with the rest of southern Africa for thousands of years. Their way of life is part of a spectrum of cultural variation, not a relic from an earlier epoch (Wilmsen 1989). Similarly, their physical characteristics are part of the broad sweep of genetic variability rather than an isolated racial remnant. The University of the Witwatersrand's Human Sero-Genetics Unit has tracked the distribution of the physical effects of 14 different

genes across 18 southern African populations, and shown that San populations cluster together, but as part of the genetic profile of the whole subcontinent (Jenkins et al. 1978).

This process of revision has brought the very coherence – and naming – of the San as a group into question. The people themselves do not recognise the term 'San', and define themselves in small, localised communities. Economically, politically and biologically, these people have diverse affiliations. Who are they?

But despite this history of academic questioning and revisionism, the old prejudices about the San have lived on. They have become part of the lexicon of African advertising, conveying qualities of primitiveness or timelessness, or the urban dream of returning to the unspoilt wilderness. Casts of their bodies

'The state of debate about 'San' or 'Bushman' as possible appellations for the general group can be illustrated by the case of two Ju/'hoan brothers, both active in local and national politics in Namibia. At a large community meeting in 1991, each of them argued differently about the word 'Bushman'. One said he never wanted to hear the term used again in post-apartheid Namibia. The other argued that the term could be ennobled by the way in which they themselves now choose to use it. As for 'San', many people at the meeting had heard of it, but knew it has a pejorative connotation in Nama, the language from which it comes. No one advocated its use, or knew of any other overarching term ...' (Biesele 1993: vi).

remain one of the most popular displays in the South African Museum in Cape Town, and living representatives can be observed in the wilds of a Cederberg holiday resort. They evoke the controversies surrounding race as a social and political concept, long after the idea of race has ceased to be part of the daily currency of physical anthropology.

During South Africa's first democratic elections in April 1994, the national television news featured a group of Bushmen from a tourist resort in the Western Cape arriving to vote in the nearby town of Ceres, clad in 'traditional' animal skins. The reporter commented how different from us these people are, and noted that only now, after thousands of years of living in the desert, are they discovering democracy – an irony indeed for anthropology's archetypal egalitarian society.

HUMAN EXHIBIT DISGRACE

NO FUN FOR KHOISAN KIDS

By Shannon Neill

A GROUP of seven Khoisan children were on exhibit at the Holiday and Leisure Expo at the Civic Centre last week and no one at the fair seemed to mind.

In fact the stand with the humiliated, semi-naked children even beat the fluffy rabbits, crocodiles, back-packs, tents and goats to snatch first prize for the best exhibit.

They lay on the ground on a pile of buck-skins, tugging at their inadequate loin cloths as people walked past and waxed lyrical over how cute they were. Eleven-year-old Frieda Kruiper covered her breasts every time a camera appeared.

Occasionally the children were asked to make beads. They did so – reluctantly.

The children were there as part of an exhibit by Kagga Kamma private nature reserve near Ceres – a reserve supposedly devoted to keeping their culture going, according to the woman who brought them to the fair, Ms Bets Hammonn ...

Hammonn explained the exhibit to the fair-goers, and stressed the importance of maintaining the culture of 'Bushmen huts' and bead-making. She said that the children learnt Afrikaans at their farm school so that they could talk to the tourists who came into their craft shop.

'Tourists come to the farm to see them (the Khoisan). They can also see the paintings made by the local Bushmen's ancestors and go tracking with the Bushmen. Tourists stay in luxury chalets,' she explained.

Hammonn claimed that the children were not there simply 'for exhibition'. The trip to Cape Town was also educational, she said. They went to the harbour to see the seals, to Sea Point for an ice cream and to the World of Birds in Hout Bay.

And the big thrill of the trip?

'I'm taking the children to the museum to see their ancestors behind the glass,' said Hammonn.

Ms Farieda Khan, chairperson of Green Coalition – an alliance of environmental, political, labour and developmental organisations – said the exhibition was 'exploitative'.

'These people are being subjected to gross exploitation. They are vulnerable to this sort of exploitation because they have no choice.

'They went to Kagga Kamma because they were landless and homeless and could no longer use their traditional means of survival.'

Khan said the museum was criticised for having people behind glass, but this sort of 'live exhibit' needed even harsher criticism.

'It's like a zoo, and degrading for the family and people gawking at them. This shouldn't be the tourism of the new South Africa.'

Mrs Shereen Parker of the Development Agency for Tourism Advancement said: 'This portrayal of black people is not only racist and objectifying but is also a manifestation of how little control black people have in the tourism industry.'

(South, *11 November, 1994*)

Environmental archaeology

The old idea (known as 'determinism') that people's physical characteristics and culture were entirely shaped by their environments and passed down from generation to generation is no longer acceptable. Although it was taken for granted in the nineteenth century, it has now been discarded by all reputable scientists. But this does not mean that the environment has played no role in the shaping of human history, or that archaeologists are no longer interested in the interplay between environment and culture. On the contrary, environmental archaeology is a well-developed specialism within its wider discipline. And, in recent years, approaches to interpretation have been developed which avoid the pitfalls of determinism.

There is a close relationship between the development of modern approaches to environmental archaeology in the second half of the twentieth century and the steady professionalisation of the discipline. During this time archaeologists were increasingly trained in the application of scientific techniques, and methodologies were developed that enabled human behaviour to be read from an eclectic range of sources. Scientific archaeology filled the vacuum left by the demise of nineteenth-century racial anthropology, and with it came the emphasis on close detail rather than on sweeping generalisations.

'The impression one gets of the organization of archaeology in southern Africa prior to 1960 is that the heart of the subject was seen by both professionals and amateurs alike to rest with the amateurs, or at least with people not employed full-time nor formally educated as archaeologists … It was the injection of scientific method in the 1960s that changed the attitudes of Southern African archaeologists and widened the gulf between the empirical methods used in historically orientated research by amateurs and professionals alike, and the deductive methods based on anthropological and ecological theory used by more recent graduates' (J. Deacon 1990: 50–2).

New approaches were not confined to southern Africa. In West Africa there was increasing professionalisation with the development of the Nigerian Antiquities Service, the creation of a Department of Archaeology in 1957 at Legon in Ghana, and the development of archaeology as a discipline at the University of Ibadan, Nigeria (Kense 1990). In East Africa, the founding of the British Institute in Nairobi led to accelerated research into the Iron Age and attempts to correlate archaeological evidence and language families (Robertshaw 1990). In Desmond Clark's words:

'By the 1960s there had taken place a fundamental change in excavation methods and in the ways in which we looked at our material and tried to understand its behavioural implications. The method of recovery of assemblage distribution patterns and features by "horizontal excavation" of minimally disturbed hominid activity areas was now the normal way to set about investigation of earlier hominid activity areas in the open. The distribution pattern of stones and bones has a story to tell but the problem now is to interpret it correctly. The naive conclusion that concentrations of stone implements and bones were the result of hominid activity soon gave rise to a range of actualistic and experimental studies that were based upon the premise of uniformitarianism. These are experiments to show how fluvial activity can concentrate and disperse materials in a stream; in the ways in which bones become incorporated, broken and dispersed and in ways of distinguishing between the different agents – geological, animal or human – that were responsible: the new science of taphonomy as it is called. There also followed experiments in the manufacture of stone artefacts using different kinds of rocks; in the study of the reduction process giving a more realistic understanding of intention behind the debitage and end products; experiments in using these artefacts and, by the study of the modification present on the edges of utilized pieces, on the manner of use and the material they were used on. These and other such studies are providing the controls that enable the prehistorian to narrow down possible interpretations' (Clark 1990: 202–3).

The reconstruction of the environments in which past communities lived is central to these scientific approaches to archaeology. Appropriately, following the holistic principles of other ecological fields of study, such reconstructions stress the interconnectedness of all aspects of the environment rather than the predominant or determining role of any specific aspect. But solely for the purposes of reviewing the field, it is useful to break down environmental analyses into three areas of study: past climates, the plant environment, and the animal environment.

As we saw in Chapter 2, climate is constantly changing. Some of these changes are global, while other effects are far more regional in nature. In recent years, palaeoclimatology has become a specialised field of study in its own right. Important points of reference are deep-sea cores and cores drilled through polar ice sheets (described in Chapter 7 as part of the discussion of relative dating methods). Together, these have produced long sequences of temperature fluctuations – crucial evidence in reconstructing past plant and animal regimes.

Sea-level changes are closely linked with these fluctuations in climate. The polar ice sheets contain vast quantities of water, and even a slight rise in temperatures causes ice to melt and sea-levels to rise across the globe. Conversely, colder climatic conditions have led to an expansion of the polar ice sheets, and a concomitant lowering of sea-levels. This phenomenon has long been recognised: specific sea-levels were believed to be universal traces of particular ice ages. But it is now known that sea-level fluctuations are far more complex, being the result of a combination of the effects of temperature changes and local shifts in the surface of the earth, known as 'tectonic movements'. Although core sequences have replaced the old scheme of ice ages and interglacials as the primary means of establishing climatic regimes, understanding sea-level changes remains important in environmental reconstructions. Changes in sea-level can flood or expose large expanses of the continental shelf, affecting in turn marine resources, grasslands and the distribution of animal species – the food supplies for human communities.

A recent study carried out along the coastline of the southwestern Cape illustrates the approach that is used in this sort of work (Figure 115). Global climate plots had suggested that the sea-level had been high in the middle of the Holocene, as a consequence of a warm climatic phase. Such a change in sea-level would have dramatically affected the food resources available to hunter–gatherer communities living in the coastal lands. Researchers would have to take it into account in interpreting the archaeological evidence from coastal middens and rock shelters. Consequently, it was important to find out what impact global climate had had in the specific geomorphological setting of the southwestern Cape coast. The method used was to obtain radiocarbon dates from sea shells that had been washed up as part of these old beach levels. Nine sample sites were chosen, accurately surveyed, and dated. The results confirmed that, about 4000 years ago, the sea-level had been about 3 m higher than at present. The effect on coastal morphology would have been considerable: estuarine areas were invaded by the sea, shorelines moved inland by several hundred metres, and new dunefields were formed. As a result of this study, archaeologists now have a much better basis for reconstructing the environment that was used by its Stone Age inhabitants (Miller et al. 1993).

At first glance, changes such as these seem to have little relevance to our modern world. We tend to think of climate as stable – as a repetitive cycle of summers and winters. But in reali-

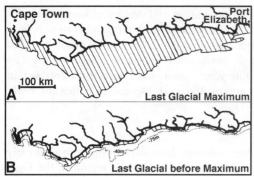

FIGURE 115 SEA-LEVEL CHANGES ON THE CAPE SOUTH COAST. A: The coastal foreland of southern Africa during the height of the last glaciation, when the sea-level was at its lowest. B: Other stages of the last glacial period, when sea-levels were not so low (Van Andel 1989).

ty, climate is changing all the time. Recent studies of Greenland ice cores have shown that in less than 10 years rapid shifts can take place between glacial and interglacial conditions, with concomitant effects on sea-level. This suggests that the earth 'flips' between several stable climatic conditions. Could we experience such a 'flip' in our own lifetime?

'Specifically, environmental scientists have posed the politically charged question: are the catastrophic climate changes measured in this and previous work at the crest of Greenland the result of climate boundary conditions unique to a glaciated North America, or could they recur tomorrow?' (Fairbanks 1993). The answer, it would seem, is yes.

Regional climates

Global climatic shifts interact with local topographical conditions, such as mountain ranges, which may precipitate rainfall or cause rain-shadow effects, and coastlands, which have warming or cooling effects on air-flow. The result is a mosaic of regional climates which are part of global systems, but which are also specific in their characteristics. Understanding such regional climates is particularly important in archaeology, because these were the weather conditions that past communities experienced in their daily lives. Regional climates affected plant growth, the abundance and distribution of animals, and therefore the availability of food resources to people.

There is rich and varied evidence for past climates in southern Africa: sedimentology, fossil pollen grains, lake and river levels, and variations in oxygen isotopes over the past 30 000 years, measured from stalagmites in the Cango Caves. From these sources, it has been possible to build up 'weather charts' for the subcontinent (Tyson 1986).

For example, from about 25 000 to about 20 000 years ago, southern Africa was wetter than today, and also up to 8°C colder. The Drakensberg, much of Lesotho and parts of the highveld had 'periglacial' conditions: cold, arctic-like tundra, and pretty unpleasant places to be. By 12 000 years ago the subcontinent's climate was becoming warmer and drier, although within 2000 years it was again raining more in the central and western regions. This complex, locally varying pattern continued through the Holocene to the present day. For these more recent periods additional sources of evidence are available, including variations in growth rings in long-lived trees ('dendroclimatology') and historical records.

'The climatic history of southern Africa has been characterized by great change and variability. Seldom have there been prolonged intervals without such change. As more evidence becomes available for later periods in the geological time scale, it becomes apparent that climates may have changed abruptly over relatively short time intervals. The same is to be found in the records for climatic changes on the scales of millennia, centuries and decades' (Tyson

Sources of palaeoclimatic evidence in southern Africa ...
• Landforms and sediments. These sources of evidence include sand dunes (which indicate shifts in climatic belts and former wind systems), alluvial sediments (river channel and floodplain deposits), old lake levels, cave deposits and periglacial landforms (which show the influence of frost action).
• Biological and archaeological evidence. These sources of evidence include fossilised pollen grains, charcoal, tree-ring studies, studies of mammals of all sizes, isotopic composition of shell (an indication of temperature change) and stable carbon and nitrogen isotopes in shell (J. Deacon & Lancaster 1988).

As Janette Deacon and Nick Lancaster have summarised the regional situation: 'climatic changes of the Late Quaternary induced significant changes in plant and animal distributions, and in turn these affected human habitats, particularly in the availability of food resources.

The distribution and density of human populations was constrained by the ability of people to cope with changes in the natural productivity of their environments because prior to the last 2000 years, agriculture was not practised in Southern Africa' (J. Deacon & Lancaster 1988: 171).

Ecological interactions

The interplay between human behaviour and climate is subtle and complex. Early racial interpretations offered the view that physical type and culture were determined by climate – that human biology and culture are adaptations to specific climatic conditions. Indeed, extremes of heat and cold have clearly, over long periods, caused adaptations in characteristics such as body shape and skin pigmentation. But it is equally clear that culture – learned behaviour rather than inherited characteristics – has enabled human communities to overcome the constraints of climate. One of the earliest and most striking examples of this phenomenon was the dispersal, over a large part of the earth's surface, of bands of *Homo erectus* more than a million years ago. These people could have coped with the extreme cold of the Pleistocene in the northern hemisphere only because of cultural adaptations: they had already overcome the limitations of their genes.

Today, most archaeologists see climate as a set of possibilities and limitations – rather than a straitjacket that has constrained human history. This is well illustrated by interpretations of the spread of the first farming communities into southern Africa after about AD 200.

Farming demands particular combinations of favourable conditions: soils with adequate nutrients, rainfall during the crop-growing season, and grazing for livestock. These conditions were found in the lower-lying river valleys in southern Africa, in parts of the lowveld, and along the coastal plain. The archaeological traces of these communities show that they were very particular about where they chose to live. At the same time the crop plants characteristic of the Early Iron Age – sorghum and millet – can only grow well with adequate amounts of summer rainfall. Consequently, the western edges of the summer rainfall region were a climatic boundary to the spread of early farming, creating a frontier region in the Eastern Cape that persisted for a thousand years (Maggs 1984b).

After about AD 1000, farmers began to spread to the higher, grassland areas of southern Africa. At the same time they moved towards a greater reliance on cattle-keeping, and built numerous stone villages across the southern highveld. Again, they took advantage of local climatic possibilities, and were ultimately restricted by the westernmost limits of reliable rainfall: the edges of the desert-like Karoo, where different economic strategies of nomadism were needed for human survival (Maggs 1976). Throughout the Iron Age, then, the interaction between people and climate was a subtle balance between possibilities seized and used, and limitations that restricted basic economic parameters and, therefore, further geographical expansion.

At the same time, the spread of farming was also affecting local climatic conditions, sometimes imperceptibly and sometimes more dramatically. Farmers entering the river valleys and coastal lowlands in the first few centuries AD would probably have found a closed forest mosaic. Over the generations that followed, they cut back the vegetation for fields and grazing, creating irreversible changes in the biotic environment (M. Hall 1984a). Because the density of vegetation affects precipitation, farmers were probably changing the climate at the same time as they took advantage of its possibilities. Later, and further north, farming communities in the Toutswe Tradition moved on to the grasslands at the head of the Limpopo River. It has been suggested that the numerous Toutswe sites were abandoned because of drought, probably accentuated by overgrazing (Denbow 1984). Here, farmers probably affected the local climate by reducing grass cover, increasing the intensity of heat reflected from the earth's surface, and reducing rainfall – a well-known cycle on desert margins.

Pollen grains and plant remains

Climate and climatic change, then, are closely integrated with the plant environment. Reconstructing the vegetation around archaeological sites has a central place in environmental archaeology. Sources of evidence range from microscopic remains of plants such as fossilised pollen grains ('microbotanical evidence') to plants preserved in archaeological deposits ('macrobotanical evidence').

The study of fossilised pollen grains is known as palynology. Pollen grains are the very small, male reproductive organs of flowering plants. Different kinds of plants have particular, recognisable shapes of pollen grain. These pollen grains have an outer shell (the 'exine') that is extremely resilient, and can survive in certain sediments for a very long time (Figure 116). In pollen analysis, exines are separated out under a microscope, identified, counted and plotted as a 'pollen diagram'. Like other methods of plant analysis in archaeology, palynology depends on understanding modern plant regimes, both for comparative identification, and for appreciating the different amounts of pollen that each plant produces, and how and how far it can spread. The best conditions for the preservation of fossil pollens are in acidic peat bogs, where there is little bacterial activity. Samples of fossil pollen may be extracted from long cores or from the stratigraphic sections of archaeological excavations.

In comparison with Europe, relatively few pollen profiles have been studied in Africa, largely because of a scarcity of rich, pollen-bearing deposits such as lake beds and peats. Some of the more productive areas in Africa have proved to be swampy lands, for example the sediments near permanent springs. Additional difficulties encountered are the extraordinary richness of many African environments – there are so many tree and grass species that comparative collections are difficult to build up and use – and an as-yet imperfect understanding of pollen abundance and dispersal – the nature of the modern 'pollen rain' (Scott 1984).

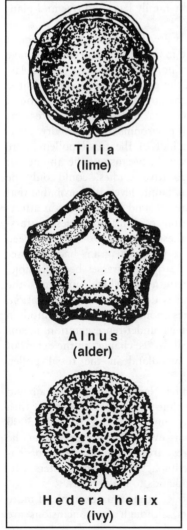

Tilia
(lime)

Alnus
(alder)

Hedera helix
(ivy)

FIGURE 116
POLLEN GRAINS.

Pollen records

Two palynological studies from different parts of Africa well illustrate the problems and the possibilities in using fossil pollen as evidence for past plant environments.

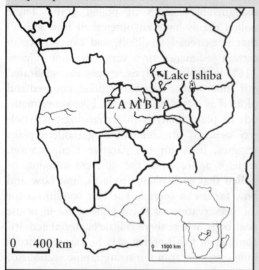

The first of these studies was of the surroundings of Ishiba Ngandu, a lake in northern Zambia (Livingstone 1971). A core taken through the lake bed consisted of about 3.5 m of mud and 1.5 m of sandy soil (from the period before the lake formed). A radiocarbon age estimation from organic material in the lowest lake sediments gave a result of 21,600 ± 400 BP (Y-1415) and microscopic examination of the core samples showed that fossil pollen grains had been preserved throughout the sequence.

Before a pollen diagram could be drawn for Ishiba Ngandu, a study had to be made of the modern vegetation around the lake. Understanding the present-day pollen rain is essential in any palynological study. The lake itself, which is about 5 km² in area, supports a rich growth of aquatic plants. The standing water is surrounded by a roughly equal expanse of marshland, in which papyrus is one of the most common plants. Miombo Woodland, dominated by *Brachystegia*, spreads outwards from the lake and marshlands, and is the dominant kind of vegetation in the region. Further afield is Mopane Woodland (some 60 km to the southeast), as well as a more varied mosaic of woodland, savanna and grassland (about 50 km to the northeast).

In comparison with Europe (where the technique of pollen analysis was developed), Africa has a very diverse vegetation. The laboratory identification of fossil pollens from Ishiba Ngandu required a comparative collection of 16 000 types of pollen. Even so, many plant identifications were possible only to the genus level rather than to that of the individual species.

A pollen diagram is built up from the 'pollen sum' – the full range of pollens that the analyst elects to include in the study. The frequency of each pollen type in the sample is then expressed diagramatically as a percentage of the whole. The pollen sum for Ishiba Ngandu was made up of 47 categories of pollen, including grasses identified to the family level and tree and plant genera.

The results were disappointing. Although it is certain that major changes in climate have taken place in northern Zambia over the last 22 000 years, the pollen diagram showed little evidence for change in the vegetation around the lake. There seem to be two major reasons for this lack of environmental sensitivity. Firstly, more than half of the fossil pollens were from grasses which, because of the absence of detailed comparative studies, could only be classified at the family level. It is probable that climatic changes around Ishiba Ngandu affected the proportions of different species of grasses, and that these changes would have been reflected in the pollen diagram had a closer level of identification of grasses been possible. Secondly, *Brachystegia*, which surrounds the lake today and is dominant in the vegetation, only contributes about 1 per cent to the modern pollen rain. This under-representation means that it is difficult to see changes in the extent of *Brachystegia* woodland in the fossil pollen record.

But the Ishiba Ngandu pollen diagram did show one revealing variation. In the upper fifth of the mud column, spanning the last 3000 years, there was evidence for a decline in the amount of forest around the lake. This probably reflects the impact of Iron Age farmers, cutting back woodlands to make fields.

A second pollen study is an example of more positive results, although the conclusions are

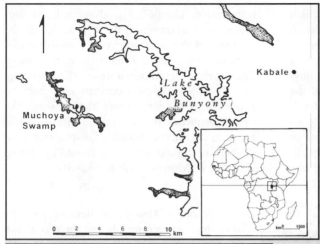

FIGURE 118 MUCHOYA SWAMP, UGANDA.

FIGURE 119 PART OF THE POLLEN DIAGRAM FROM MUCHOYA SWAMP. Pollen diagrams show the varying frequencies of pollen categories, identified to as close a level as is possible, against the depth of the core, which is calibrated with radiocarbon dates (Morrison 1968).

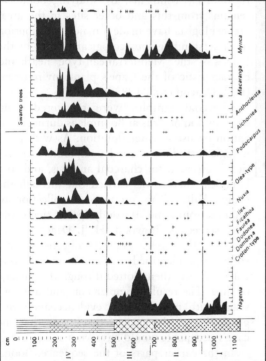

herbs grows in the often-flooded hollows between the sedge tussocks. The margins of the swamp have variable vegetation, probably reflecting different stages in the plant succession. The valley is enclosed by hilly ridges, some of which are covered by dense stands of mountain bamboo (*Arundinaria alpina*), and others of which have been terraced and are used for farming. Dense Montane Rainforest begins about 15 km from Muchoya.

As in the Zambian study, establishing the nature of the pollen rain and comparative pollen samples was extremely challenging. The problem posed at Ishiba Ngandu by *Brachystegia* was paralleled in the interpretation of the Muchoya Swamp core by mountain bamboo, which flowers occasionally and erratically, making an unpredictable contribution to the pollen rain. There were the same difficulties in the Ugandan study in identifying the extremely numerous species that make up the mountain flora.

Nevertheless, the pollen diagram that resulted from the Muchoya Swamp core did show considerable variation through time, allowing the identification of four distinct phases in the vegetation history of the last 25 000 years (Figure 119). These phases have been interpreted as a combination of the effects of volcanic eruptions, human intervention in the environment and climatic change.

'Cores on a transect across the swamp show that it began as a shallow lake created, perhaps, by tectonic uplift. The lower infilling is of lake and swamp sediments and the swamp sedi-

also tentative. This work was carried out in the highlands of southwestern Uganda with the aim of establishing the history of the plant environment over the last 25 000 years (Morrison 1968). Fossil pollen was retrieved from an 11 m core drilled through the Muchoya Swamp, a 600 m wide expanse of sedge marsh high in the Ruchiga Mountains. The core was calibrated with a set of three radiocarbon dates.

Again, the first stage in the study was a plot of the modern-day vegetation. A wide variety of

ments enclose a thick layer of wood peat which was laid down under a swamp forest of *Myrica kantdiana*. This swamp-forest layer is overlain with peat believed to have been laid down by a *Pycreus* sedge swamp of the type which now covers most of the swamp. It is not clear if the breakdown of the swamp forest and the development of the sedge swamp was a normal continuation of the upland swamp succession, or was a return to an earlier stage caused by climatic change giving, perhaps, a rise of the water table. The pollen analyses indicate four periods of vegetation on the hills adjoining the swamp and these are referred to, provisionally, as pollen zones I–IV, Zone I being the oldest. Radiocarbon determinations on the core suggest that these oldest sediments date back to about 25 000 years before the present. The overall sequence of the vegetation zones conforms to the idea of altitudinal displacements of the belts of upland vegetation caused by climatic changes' (Morrison 1968: 382–3).

Macrobotanical remains

FIGURE 120 MACROBOTANICAL EVIDENCE. Surviving fragments of plants – such as this assemblage from a dry cave site in South Africa's Western Cape – give important clues to the environment around a site, as well as to some of the food that people may have eaten in the past.

Macrobotanical remains, as the term suggests, are larger parts of plants surviving in archaeological contexts: seeds, pieces of charcoal and, if preservation conditions are good, other parts of plants (Figure 120). Because it is often reasonable to assume that firewood, bedding, building materials and food were collected within a fairly short distance of the archaeological site, macrobotanical remains can be important indicators of local environmental conditions.

Work carried out in the southern Cape area has clearly shown the value of studying charcoals recovered from archaeological sites. Boomplaas Cave, in the Cango Valley not far from Oudtshoorn, has some 5 m of archaeological deposits spanning the last 80 000 years. Conditions of preservation are good, giving a unique record of human settlement and the relationship between people and their local and regional environments. By studying botanical remains from this and other sites in the area, archaeologists have made a major contribution to understanding the ecological history of the fynbos – the Mediterranean-type heathland characteristic of the Cape's plant environment (H. J. Deacon et al. 1983a).

Charcoal samples were recovered from deposits and hearths at Boomplaas during excavation by using water flotation. As with palynological studies, a good comparative collection is essential for charcoal analysis, and so a botanical survey was carried out through the Cango Valley. This produced a collection of samples from some 70 woody species that could have served as firewood (H. J. Deacon et al. 1983b). The archaeological collections were sorted and identified; variations in firewood collected were then plotted through the passage of time. The results complement (and are consistent with) palaeoclimatic evidence, and give a good idea of the sort of conditions that the cave's occupants would have known.

In the earlier parts of the sequence, Boomplaas Cave was surrounded by woodlands. But between about 25 000 and 16 000 years ago, when conditions were much colder and drier than today, there was a virtual absence of woody plants and shrubs within the cave's collecting range. Steadily, though, the rainfall increased. People began to bring stream-bank species, such as *Silex*, back to their home, perhaps from flood debris along the sides of the river. Other charcoal suggests that there were fairly open *Olea* woodlands and parklands in the vicinity of Boomplaas. After 12,000 BP, a

Water flotation

When archaeologists began to become more interested in environmental evidence, they realised that it is very easy to miss plant remains during excavation. In particular, plant seeds, usually carbonised in cooking fires, are often similar in colour to the soil matrix, and are difficult to collect systematically by means of conventional excavation methods. Some plants produce very small seeds, and these are more readily missed than larger seeds. As a result samples can be biased and a distorted impression of a site's botanical environment can be given.

In order to overcome this problem, a simple technique of water flotation was developed. Compressed air is pumped up through a tank, causing a froth of bubbles. Samples of deposit from the excavation are tipped into the top of the tank. The soil sinks to the bottom, but organic material, being lighter, is caught in the surface turbulence and can be skimmed off. Archaeological flotation units range from sophisticated apparatuses with valves and filters to *ad hoc* adaptations of buckets and dustbins. Whatever method is used, the result can be the recovery of botanical evidence which would otherwise have been lost.

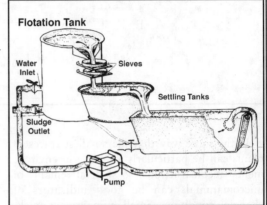

FIGURE 121 WATER FLOTATION. Water flotation is used to aid the recovery of plant remains from archaeological deposits. In this fairly sophisticated example, samples are captured in a range of sieves.

more closed woodland, with patches of thicket, began to develop steadily. This was marked by the gradual increase in the amount of *Acacia karroo*, which was used for firewood – a hardwood that is still favoured for fuel by the local community today. According to the most recent levels that were analysed – dated to about 2000 years ago – *Acacia karroo* was making up some 40 per cent of the wood used for fuel in the cave.

'Fossil charcoals have proved an instructive source of information on aspects of vegetation history in the fynbos region. In particular, the continuous and well-dated sequence in the Boomplaas Cave in the Cango Valley provides an outline of the scale and direction of vegetation change over the periods leading up to and subsequent to the coldest interval of the late Pleistocene, that is relevant in its general trends if not in specific details to the study of the vegetation history of the whole region' (H.J. Deacon et al. 1983b: 179).

Other parts of plants seem to have been remarkably well preserved in a number of sites, particularly where armfuls of vegetation were brought into caves to fill bedding hollows. For example, plant remains from Melkhoutboom Cave in the Eastern Cape indicate the persistence of forest around the site through the full 15 000 years of its occupation, though there were open habitats within range of the cave (H. J. Deacon 1976).

Faunal studies

The animal environment is obviously closely connected with both climatic and plant regimes. For example, at Boomplaas Cave, the change from the cold, dry, open conditions of the Pleistocene to the *Acacia karroo* woodlands of the Holocene had a major impact on the animal populations that could live within the cave's catchment, and therefore on the food options of the human communities. This is reflected in the collections of animal bones excavated from the site. During the cold, dry years, when the lands around the site were far more open than today, quagga, mountain zebra, wildebeest and hartebeest found grazing in the area. But by 6000 years ago, when woodlands were completely established, these herds of large grazers had been replaced by smaller, more solitary browsing animals such as grysbok, steenbok, klipspringer and mountain reedbuck (Klein 1983).

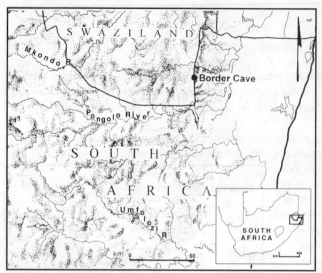

FIGURE 122 BORDER CAVE.

'The study of animal remains from archeological sites is a burgeoning field, commonly known as zooarcheology. The goal of zooarcheology is to reconstruct the environment and behavior of ancient peoples to the extent that animal remains allow. Zooarcheologists are not easy to distinguish from paleontologists whose primary interest is in paleoecology, and some specialists care little whether their samples come from archeological or non-archeological sites. The overlap between zooarcheology and ecological paleontology is likely to grow, since there is so much to be learned by comparing archeological and non-archeological faunal samples' (Klein & Cruz-Uribe 1984: 1).

In the same way that the smallest traces of plants can be particularly valuable in environmental reconstructions, so skeletal remains of micromammals can be good indicators of changing conditions. Small animals react quickly to changes in climate and vegetation, and are often brought to sites by non-human agents, such as birds of prey. They therefore provide independent checks on archaeological conclusions based on human food debris.

An example of the use of microfaunas in archaeological research is Margaret Avery's study of the micromammals from Border Cave, located on the border between South Africa and Swaziland, just below the escarpment of the Lebombo Mountains (Figure 122). Border Cave looks out over the lowveld, and was used intermittently as a living site by human groups for some 200 000 years. By identifying, counting and measuring the mandibles and maxillae of small mammals from the site, Avery was able to reconstruct the vegetation within the hunting range of barn owls – the agents that had brought the bones on to the site. To this end she plotted fluctuations between thick vegetation and fairly damp conditions, and drier, more open grasslands (D. M. Avery 1982).

Faunal assemblages of larger mammals from archaeological sites tend to be more problematic as indicators of environmental conditions because they are invariably food waste. They reflect human cultural preferences and competencies superimposed on the full range of animal species occupying the landscape within a site's catchment. Nevertheless, used carefully, such macrofaunas can also be used for environmental reconstruction. For example, Richard Klein has studied the size variation of black-backed jackals in southern and eastern Africa. Using the observation that the mean body size of animals may be a reflection of temperature regimes (known as Bergmann's Rule), Klein has shown that the length of the first lower molar (an index of body size) of modern black-backed jackals tends to be greater as the climate becomes colder. Since this species is common in fossil assemblages, the technique has considerable potential for tracking changes in the environment.

'Ultimately, it should be possible to use size variation in fossil jackals and other species to construct a detailed curve of climate change in the fynbos zone. This is especially fortunate because local sites rarely preserve paleobotanical remains. The size-change data thus provide a welcome independent supplement and check on schemes of climatic change derived mainly from geomorphic/sedimentological studies' (Klein & Cruz-Uribe 1984: 96).

Integration

Ultimately, the aim of all archaeologists reconstructing the environmental contexts of the places where people lived in the past is to integrate the disparate sources of evidence into a coherent interpretation that allows for the complex interaction of plant and animal life – the ecology of the past. An example is Paul Sinclair's study of the archaeology of Zimbabwe and Mozambique from the earliest years of farming settlement until about AD 1700 (Sinclair 1987). Sinclair was concerned to achieve a balance between the minutiae of individual site studies – the details of faunal assemblages, local soils and vegetations – and the more general sweep of regional history. With this in mind, he used a number of techniques of spatial analysis adapted from geographical and ecological research, including an approach known as site catchment analysis (Higgs 1974).

Sinclair's first task was to assess, in as much detail as possible, the soils, climatic evidence, vegetation and potential for agriculture of the landscape around the sites in his sample. Next, he mapped these environmental factors as site territories – zones of potential land use within a 10 km radius of the site (Figure 123). Because it is reasonable to assume that farmers made practical, sensible choices in their places to live,

such site territories provide a good indication of the way in which the people themselves assessed the environment as a whole. In completing the study, the archaeologist could compare these site territories with the evidence from excavation, allowing an integrated, comprehensive history to be written of the relationship between people and the world around them.

We can see, then, that archaeological approaches to understanding the environment have changed radically. There is little connection between modern research, which stresses the complexity of human culture, the constant interplay between human behaviour and the environment, and the ecological interconnectedness of environmental factors, and nineteenth-century racial determinism, which saw humans as made and constrained by nature and descent.

John Parkington has provided a useful way of conceptualising the manner in which people interact with the world around them. He suggests that archaeologists should think in terms of 'place' – 'not simply the latitude and longitude of an assemblage location but rather the set of opportunities offered by the location and thus the likelihood of particular activities taking place there' (Parkington 1980: 73).

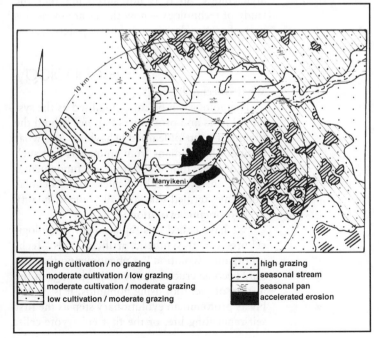

high cultivation / no grazing
moderate cultivation / low grazing
moderate cultivation / moderate grazing
low cultivation / moderate grazing

high grazing
seasonal stream
seasonal pan
accelerated erosion

FIGURE 123 SITE CATCHMENT ANALYSIS AT MANYIKENI, MOZAMBIQUE. In this study, the researcher has placed the site of Manyikeni within its total ecological context by studying the distribution of soil types and modern land use within the range of its economic territory (Sinclair 1987).

chapter 9

Making it

> **technology** the system of rules and procedures that lies behind the manufacture and use of an artefact

Human communities interact with their environments in a wide variety of ways. Some of these are passive and largely subconscious – breathing, for instance. Others involve the use of manual dexterity – picking fruit from a tree, or collecting firewood by hand. But most interactions with our surroundings involve the intercession of technology. The technology can be very simple, such as a roughly fashioned tool used for cracking open nuts; or it can be highly complex, such as the machinery of modern farming. And technology, of course, involves artefacts – the objects shaped by human beings which are the heart and soul of the discipline of archaeology. So it is not surprising that the study of technology – how things are made – is part of archaeology's set of basic practices.

Technology

What is technology?

Technology can be conceptualised as the system of rules and procedures that lies behind the tool itself – sets of learned behaviour. And what distinguishes humans from animals is that such rules of behaviour – culture – are fundamental to our survival. Kathy Schick and Nicholas Toth have termed this specially human quality 'techno-organic evolution':

'We have called this replacement of biological organs with synthetic, artificial tools "Techno-organic Evolution", a phenomenon that has only become crucial in one major lineage in the history of life: tool-using hominids. It is probably as profound an evolutionary step as the first self-replicating life, or the first eukaryote cells, amphibians, reptiles, or mammals. The human lineage is now adapting and evolving not only through the biological transformations it is able to make over time to adjust to its environment, but also through the technological developments and changes we are able to bring about.

And a large part of the environment we are adjusting to is fashioned or shaped by our technology. We cannot escape the biological, organic nature of our existence, but it is now bound up inextricably in the technological realm we have created' (Schick & Toth 1993: 186).

Appreciating the antiquity of technology

Although Charles Darwin, writing in 1871, anticipated that the earliest human ancestry would be traced to Africa, it was a long time before this was recognised and widely accepted. Raymond Dart discovered the 'Taung child' in 1924, but his claim that this was a human ancestor was widely dismissed (Dart 1925). Between 1936 and 1937, Robert Broom found more fossils of *Australopithecus africanus* at Sterkfontein and Kromdraai, limestone caves near Johannesburg, but many anthropologists still refused to believe that these were in the direct line of human descent. A major breakthrough came in 1957, when C. K. Brain, excavating at Sterkfontein, found stone tools in direct association with australopithecine teeth. Two years later, similar discoveries were made at Olduvai Gorge in Tanzania, where it was soon recognised that a new species of hominid discovered there was also associated with artefacts. Called 'Zinjanthropus' at the time, this is now classified as *Homo*, our own genus. The first potassium–argon dates, published in the early 1960s, made it clear that human technology began far earlier than anyone had previously imagined possible, forcing a complete revision of standard notions of humans as tool users and makers (Gowlett 1990).

Charles Darwin wrote:
'It is therefore probable that Africa was formerly inhabited by extinct apes closely allied to the gorilla and chimpanzee; and as these two species are now man's nearest allies, it is somewhat more probable that our early progenitors lived on the African continent than elsewhere. But it is useless to speculate on this subject' (Darwin 1871: 240).

The earliest artefacts

The earliest stone tools were very simple – one or two flakes struck from a chunk of rock. So what criteria are used, at this crucial threshold, for distinguishing human-made artefacts from accidents of nature – for recognising the beginning of humanity? This question has been complicated by recent research, which has shown that the boundaries between humans and animals are less well marked than had been thought. There are a number of well-documented cases of animals both using and making tools. For example, the Californian Sea Otter breaks open the hard shells of clams by floating on its back, placing the shellfish on its chest and hammering at it with a rock held in its paws.

FIGURE 124 THE CALIFORNIAN SEA OTTER AT WORK WITH A HAMMERSTONE. In this illustration, the otter floats on its back with a stone on its chest and cracks open the shellfish. This constitutes deliberate tool use.

The skill of the Californian Sea Otter may be inherited, rather than learned, and may not satisfy the criterion for culture. But a second example stretches the bounds of our definitions even further. Kathy Schick and Nicholas Toth taught a chimpanzee called Kanzi – an inmate of the Language Research Laboratory in Atlanta, Georgia – first how to use stone flakes, and then how to make them. There is no doubt that Kanzi had *acquired* technological skills (Schick & Toth 1993).

'This level of culture or shared learned behavior in chimpanzee tool use is unique in the non-human world and gives us a glimpse of what the primeval stages of culture may have been like in our own evolutionary past. We do not know how far back in time chimpanzee tool making and tool use goes; it could predate the chimp–human evolutionary split, or it could be quite recent. It is interesting to speculate whether, if left alone without human interference for several million more years, chimpanzees or other primates would have taken a similar evolutionary course of tool use and brain expansion to what occurred in human evolution' (Schick & Toth 1993: 58).

It is useful to think of the difference between, on the one hand, sea otters, chimpanzees and other tool-using and -making animals and, on the other hand, early hominids as one of degree. For human communities, tool use became central in adaptation: early people could not have survived without technology. But for chimpanzees like Kanzi, tool-making is little more than a diversion, inspired by the promise of an unusual morsel of food.

Identifying stone tools

What distinguishes a stone tool from a piece of naturally broken rock? Identifying artefacts involves following the same logic that lay behind the making of the stone tool in the first place.

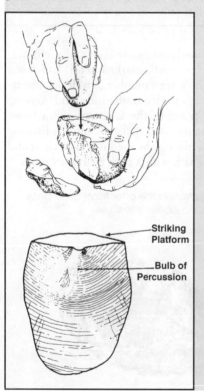

Picking up a river boulder and hitting near its edge with another stone will detach a 'flake'. Often, quite a few flakes can be struck from a single piece of stone (which is then known as a 'core').

Each flake has a number of distinctive features (Figure 125). The surface where the hammer stone hit the core should be clear: this is known as the 'striking platform'. Shock waves of the blow, travelling through the core, create a distinctive bulge on the inner side of the flake beneath the striking platform: this is known as the 'bulb of percussion'.

Some flakes will have been used without further working. But others will have been elaborated further as 'formal tools' by systematic, secondary flaking, or 'retouch', to make a working edge or to shape the tool. Similarly, the core will have its own distinctive features. These include 'flake scars', the negative images of the flakes that have been removed from the core.

Although these features are quite clear, they can also be produced by a number of natural agencies, such as rocks bashed together in a river during a flood. To be certain of correct identification, one must assess flakes and cores in the full context in which they have been found.

FIGURE 125 MAKING A FLAKE. A: striking platform. B: bulb of percussion.

Experimental archaeology

One of the difficulties in researching the threshold of humanity (and in understanding many other parts of the archaeological record as well) is interpreting the patterns of behaviour that resulted in the ephemeral scatters of chipped and flaked stone constituting the sum of our evidence. Analogies with the behaviour of non-human animals have only a limited value, simply because such animals are not human. Moreover, the concept that modern hunter–gatherers are 'fossil' communities – windows into the distant past – is now no longer accepted. And perhaps most dangerous of all is our 'common sense', that largely subconscious storehouse of our own experiences in life. Despite the fantasy of the 1966 British film *One Million Years BC*, with Raquel Welch lost in the past in a fur bikini, our earliest ancestors were very different from us, both physically and intellectually, and lived in a way that would be a horrifying nightmare to the average city-dweller of today.

This problem – the inadequacy of our imagination – can best be tackled by systematically re-creating as many of the factors as possible that could have contributed to the archaeological record. For example, Kathy Schick and Nicholas Toth have worked as members of the Koobi Fora project in Kenya. While their colleagues have been excavating the small scatters of very early stone tools that make this part of the world an archaeological treasure house, Schick and Toth have been making sites of their own. They started by designing a series of systematic experiments, of increasing sophistication, that replicated the full range of stone tools that were known from the Koobi Fora area. Every chip and flake of waste material was marked and plotted, and the effects of environmental agencies such as wind action and flash floods monitored. Replica stone tools were used in butchering a variety of animal carcasses, and in tasks such as cleaning skins and working bone and wood. The result of this work was a set of highly detailed analogues which could be set against the sparse evidence of the early archaeological record.

Experimental archaeology

'Experimental archaeology is an attempt to re-create aspects of ancient life-styles by using the same materials, techniques, and strategies believed to have been employed by ancient peoples. In this way we can explore in detail how early peoples made their tools, how difficult this task was and how much time it took, what by-products were generated, how they used their tools, which types were useful for which tasks, how well they worked, how they became damaged in use, and, overall, how their technologies fit into their lives' (Schick & Toth 1993: 20).

FIGURE 126 REPLICATING THE USES OF STONE TOOLS. By using freshly made stone tools for some of the purposes that they may have served in the past, archaeologists can study early technology under experimental conditions. Here, a stone blade is being used to skin an antelope carcass.

Typologies

Even the earliest archaeological sites, such as those in the Koobi Fora area, can contain many hundreds of artefacts. If archaeologists are to study these effectively, and offer interpretations of the rules and procedures that defined systems of technology in the past, they need ways of ordering the evidence. Such classifications are known as typologies, and are as basic to archaeology as stratigraphies, site plans and dating techniques.

> **typology** 'The systematic organization of artifacts into types on the basis of shared attributes.'
> **attribute** 'A minimal characteristic of an artifact such that it cannot be further subdivided.'
> (Renfrew & Bahn 1991)

One of the most extensively used typologies in archaeology is based on Thomsen's Three Age System of 1836; this took the general raw material attributes of stone, bronze and iron, and ordered archaeological assemblages accordingly. When archaeologists working in southern Africa needed a way of systematically ordering for the first time the archaeological evidence for early farming, they used exactly the same approach that Thomsen had adopted more than a century earlier. They proposed an Iron Age, which would be defined by the presence of evidence for iron smelting and particular forms of pottery (M. Hall 1987). In subsequent research, these initial broad groupings have been broken down into ever more refined typological categories. As a general rule, the longer the history of research and the larger the quantity of excavated material, the more complex the typological systems in use. Typologies are essential research tools, developed to deal with the problems in hand.

Devising typologies overlaps with dating. In addition many typologies are systems of relative dating because they order artefacts according to the proposition that attributes have changed with the passage of time (Chapter 7). However, it is important to realise that typologies are not *inevitably* dating systems. It is quite often the case, for example, that artefacts are ordered in functional categories, such as scraping tools, cutting tools or polishing tools. Variations between sites may well, in this case, reflect differing environments rather than temporal change. Alternatively, some archaeologists have used computer-based, multivariate classification techniques, such as various forms of cluster analysis, to produce statistical typologies that make clear assumptions about neither artefact function nor time change.

The important point is that typologies are closely connected with the questions that archaeologists ask about the technology they are studying. There is no such thing as an 'objective' or 'correct' typological system, although it is certainly important that typologies are systematic, that all the assumptions that lie behind them are clearly set out, and that they are capable of dealing with the full range of variation to be found in the assemblages for which they have been designed. It is also important that new typological systems are not invented with every new research project: writing history from archaeological evidence involves synthesising the results of many different field studies, and this can become impossible if each one presents a different way of ordering the evidence. For these reasons, contemporary studies carried out across fairly wide regions often tend to use common classificatory languages.

A typological system which is now used extensively in Stone Age research in southern Africa was developed by Janette Deacon, initially in her analysis of stone-tool assemblages from three excavated cave sites in the southern Cape: Kangkara, Nelson Bay Cave and Boomplaas Cave (J. Deacon 1984). Deacon's typology is an adaptation of an approach used in Japan, and is based on what is termed a 'reduction sequence' – the stages by which the raw material is changed (or 'reduced') to a finished tool. Sets of classes and sub-classes have been defined by tracking these various stages in arte-

> 'Archaeologists start out with a question they are attempting to answer and a basic understanding of the cultural and environmental causes of variability in the artifacts they are analyzing. Drawing upon this knowledge, they select a set of relevant attributes and define their states. These attribute states are combined into types, which in turn form typologies' (Rathje & Schiffer 1982: 208).

fact manufacture.

Each class and sub-class is identified by a numerical code. Within the category 'Stone' (coded '0') are five primary categories: manuports (00 – unused lumps of raw material brought to a site), waste (01 – the by-products of stone-tool manufacture), utilised pieces (02 – artefacts showing damage which has resulted from their use), formal tools with retouch (03 – artefacts with deliberate flaking in a repeated pattern to make a working edge), and formal tools shaped by grinding or polishing (04).

These primary categories are further subdivided into sub-categories. So, for example, formal tools with retouch (03) are divided into tools that are assumed to have been used for scraping (03–100), small blades known as microliths (03–200), tools with retouch that has been step-flaked (03–300), tools with blunt ends (03–400), points (03–500) and tools known as 'burins', which were probably used for working bone (03–600). Further division allows individual types to be identified. Therefore 'adzes' are coded 03–310, and are traced through the typological system as follows:

```
0   stone
        03        formal tool with retouch
              03-3     step-flaked retouch
                    03-310   adze
```

As with all typological systems, Janette Deacon's scheme is based on a set of assumptions about the nature of variation in artefacts – about the underlying technological processes. In this case, the basic approach is functionalist: Deacon assumed that the primary reason for making a stone tool is practical. This is clear in her choice of names for finished artefacts. Subclass 03-310 is labelled an 'adze', by definition an implement for working wood. This designation is not based on observation – we are not able to see human behaviour directly through archaeological sources alone. It is rather an assumption, in this instance a good one, because it has proved consistent with a range of other, indirect sources of information about how Stone Age people used artefacts. Assumptions like these are the grist of archaeological

Type no.	Type name
03–310	ADZE

Definition

Adzes may be made on flakes or on pebbles, the latter often retaining cortex on the ventral surface. They have one or more straight or slightly convex working edges which have been shaped by one set of flake scars and also show secondary step-flaking resulting from use at a steep angle and in a chopping motion. They are generally larger than scrapers, the mean length from southern Cape samples being between 25 and 40 mm, but show less variability in size through time than do the scrapers. Hornfels is the preferred raw material when available, but silcrete and chalcedony are also used. Quartz and quartzite are rarely selected for adze manufacture. Mastic traces on adzes from Melkhoutboom show that they were hafted and a few specimens still in hafts suggest they were end-mounted. Retouch on opposing sides suggests that they were sometimes reversed in the mount.

Adzes are found in small numbers in most LSA assemblages, but are better represented in late Holocene sites where they sometimes outnumber scrapers (J. Deacon 1984: 391).

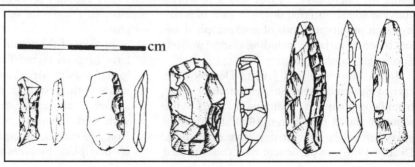

FIGURE 127 STONE ADZES. Conventional drawings of stone tools, showing plan and side views, and details of retouch.

151

research. Without them, there would be very little indeed that we could say about the past which would be of any interest.

The assumptions that lie behind systems of classification – and the implications that often come from ordering evidence – can be tested and explored further by experimental archaeology: by the approach which, in an earlier example, we illustrated by means of the Koobi Fora project. There may be a constant interplay between the sorting and classifying of artefacts, new fieldwork and experiments to establish the viability of new ideas.

FIGURE 128
MICROWEAR DAMAGE. This can be seen on the working edge of this small stone tool, known as an adze. By studying the pattern of microwear damage under a microscope, we can deduce some of the purposes to which the implement was put.

Again, the place of stone tools labelled 'adzes' in southern African Stone Age studies may serve as an example. Microwear studies are a branch of experimental archaeology. By first making replicas of implements, using the same raw materials, and then subjecting these modern tools to different sorts of use, such as cutting and scraping, one can replicate the sort of wear that would have resulted when stone tools were used for everyday activities in the distant past. Such microwear is clearly visible under the microscope. In this way it has been convincingly shown that different sorts of activity result in various kinds of microscopic damage to stone surfaces, including distinctive striations and polishing (Keeley 1980).

Johan Binneman and Janette Deacon have carried out microwear studies on stone tools from Boomplaas Cave spanning that part of the sequence dated to between 14 000 and 1500 years before the present day (Binneman & J. Deacon 1986). In particular, they concentrated

on adzes, seeking to test the long-held belief that these implements were used for woodworking. Binneman and Deacon first made adzes of their own, and then carried out a variety of tasks using them. Microscopic wear was identified and recorded, and then compared with archaeological examples of similar implements. They found that working with fresh wood and charred wood produced distinctly different kinds of polish, such as also found on the Boomplaas specimens. Clearly, their intuitive typological identification had been justified in this case.

A second example comes from the other end of the continent. Wadi Tushka, near the border between Egypt and Sudan, was flooded by the reservoir behind the Aswan Dam (the focus of the massive Cultural Resource Management project described in Chapter 3). But before the waters rose, archaeologists were able to rescue information from a wide range of sites. One of these – Site 8905 – consisted of scatters of stone tools discarded between 12 000 and 15 000 years ago. What had these stone tools been used for?

Almost 4000 artefacts were recovered from the excavation – too many for a complete microwear analysis. The first stage in the analysis was to take a 5 per cent stratified random sample of the assemblage. Each stone tool in the sample was then examined under the microscope, and polish, edge damage and striations were noted. From this, it was deduced that Site 8905 comprised two different campsites. One of the camps had been a place where people worked wood, scraped animal skins and cut meat – activities consistent with a hunting camp. The second camp had probably been a place where people fished, taking advantage of the seasonal Nile floods (Becker & Wendorf 1993). Again, microwear studies provided vital clues to the nature of human activities in the past.

In view of the abundance of stone tools that have been recovered from Stone Age archaeological sites in Africa, and their potential to tell us about the past, lithic typologies dominate the specialist archaeological literature concerned with early hunter–gatherer communities. In Iron Age studies, the equivalent place of honour is occupied by ceramic typologies, again because of the abundance and potential of these assemblages.

Most ceramic typological systems that have been used in Africa have taken account of functional variations within assemblages, differentiating between particular shapes of pots and bowls, and allowing for the obvious fact that they were made for a variety of purposes. However, Iron Age pottery was often richly decorated with a plethora of motifs that are known to have varied from area to area and through time. Iron Age archaeologists have thus tended to concentrate far more than their Stone Age colleagues on artefact style, and have developed typological systems accordingly.

Style and function

'The scene is familiar. A lonely scout outside a circle of covered wagons hears a rustle, then an arrow pierces the side of a covered wagon. He pulls it out and with a quick professional glance identifies the tribe of the man who shot it. This banal Hollywood scene is the envy of archaeologists – to be able to pick up an artifact, identify it at a glance, and interpret its meaning' (Wiessner 1983: 253).

One of the ongoing theoretical issues in archaeology is the nature of, and relation between, 'style' and 'function' in artefacts. It is often assumed that these are discrete categories of attributes. A knife, for instance, may have functional attributes (the length and width of its blade) as well as stylistic attributes (the decoration on its handle). Many archaeologists have assumed that style is what is left over after function is accounted for: the features of an artefact that have no apparent use. Others have attributed style to 'ethnicity', but without examining what, in turn, ethnicity actually is. In James Sackett's words:

'In comparison to the artifacts many archaeologists have at their disposal, stone tools seem particularly modest, silent, and alien. For more than a century we have known that they can be grouped as if they were fossils into types and assemblages, and that such groupings tend to vary in significant and fairly consistent ways according to the time period and geographic region from which they derive. Indeed, when viewed as an exercise in natural history, classification of the lithic archaeological record has become a fairly refined enterprise. Yet the actual cultural significance of our classifications remains obscure' (Sackett 1982: 59).

Sackett suggests that it is rather more useful to think in terms of dual domains: artefact attributes may be both stylistic *and* functional, depending on how the artefact is used in a particular time and place. Some of this complexity has been demonstrated by Polly Wiessner in a study of the material culture of San hunter–gatherers living in the Kalahari.

Wiessner defined style as 'formal variation in material culture that transmits information about personal and social identity'. Further, she broke this broad definition down into two additional categories. Wiessner sees 'emblemic style' as transmitting a clear message to a defined target population. Emblemic style is about conscious identity, and carries information about groups and boundaries. Secondly, Wiessner writes about 'assertive style'. This is personally based, and carries information about individual identity – the personality of the person who made a specific set of artefacts.

Wiessner concentrated in particular on San projectile points – the equivalents of the kinds of artefacts that often dominate the archaeological record, and that have usually been seen in no-nonsense, functional terms. She found that arrows are widely exchanged as part of a San

FIGURE 129 VARIATION IN !XO SAN PROJECTILE POINTS. Polly Wiessner's study of material culture in the Kalahari has shown that variation in the form of artefacts such as these arrowheads carries considerable social meaning.

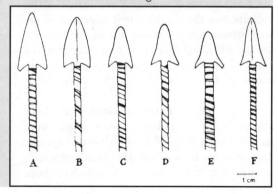

A   B   C   D   E   F

1 cm

custom known as *hxaro*. They are reciprocal gifts that establish partnerships between people who often live a long way apart, underwriting relationships of mutual sharing, assistance and extended visiting.

Wiessner recorded the attributes of arrows, following what the San themselves considered distinguishing features. She showed that the arrows had both emblemic and assertive style, in that they mark the identity of language groups as well as the 'signature' of individual arrow-makers. And, of course, arrows were simultaneously functional, being crucial in hunting activities.

'Style was contained in a wide range of attributes on projectile points including those of shape as well as others that might have important functional properties, such as size and tip thickness. The choice of attributes in which to invest style appeared to be the result of historical events, rather than following coherent principles' (Wiessner 1983: 273).

Archaeologists will never be able to read the social meaning of artefacts at a glance. Such instant analysis will remain a Hollywood fantasy. But studies such as Wiessner's Kalahari work have shown that it is possible to appreciate the complex meaning of material culture. Typological systems, as a stage in the process of interpretation, must take this complexity into account. Artefact categories should stimulate sets of questions. Rather than just assuming a 'common sense' notion of style, archaeologists need to come to grips with constant interplay between the way evidence is ordered, and its interpretation: 'Precisely where does style reside? Are things which happen to be stylistic anything else but stylistic? How does style relate to function and other such notions with which it is so often paired and even contrasted?' (Sackett 1982: 67).

Ceramic typologies

There is less consensus about ceramic typologies for the African Iron Age than for Stone Age lithic collections. At one extreme archaeologists have developed syntheses that look at the broad sweep of the last two thousand years, making connections without specifying detail. For example, David Phillipson's influential survey of the African Iron Age concentrates on the big picture, offering this definition of the 'Chifumbaze complex' (known by most other archaeologists as the 'Early Iron Age'):

'The earliest iron-using communities over an enormous area of eastern and southern Africa show a very remarkable degree of homogeneity, to the extent that archaeologists generally attribute them to a single complex, here named the Chifumbaze complex. Radiocarbon dates indicate that the complex first appeared in the area around Lake Victoria during the last few centuries BC, and that in the first three hundred years of the Christian era it expanded southwards as far as Natal ...' (Phillipson 1985: 171).

At the other extreme there are those approaches to typology which work from records of the detailed combination of specific decorative attributes. Tom Huffman's approach to ceramic classification which has been described in Chapter 7, has been to identify 'core concepts' – the 'underlying rules' that directed the potters in their work. Huffman argues that core concepts are expressed in vessel shape, decoration, the combination of motifs to form layout, and the placement of decoration on the vessel. In his research he has evaluated similarities of assemblages numerically across these sets of attributes, producing measures of connectedness that can be read as social relations.

'Iron Age archaeological cultures are largely defined by ceramics because no other artifact category occurs in such profusion, exhibits as much variability and is influenced to the same degree by idiosyncratic behaviour. Therefore, it is axiomatic that Iron Age cultures can be identified solely on the basis of their ceramic assemblages, and that relationships between ceramic units represent relationships between groups of people, even though the nature of the relationship may need further interpretation' (Huffman 1978: 2).

Tim Maggs, working with ceramics from early farming sites in KwaZulu–Natal, has produced a different approach to the making of classifications. For example, in his study of Msuluzi Confluence, the seventh-century farming village discussed in Chapter 4, Maggs

MSULUZI CONFLUENCE: CHARACTERISTICS OF THE POTS (after Maggs 1980a)

CHARACTERISTIC

CODE   DESCRIPTION

SHAPE
2   Pot with curved, everted neck
3   Lip profile rounded
4   Lip profile flattened
5   Lip profile tapered
7   Groove on lip
31   Notches on lip

POSITION OF DECORATION
8   Whole of neck
9   Upper neck
32   Lower neck
33   Plain band between decorated band on neck, sometimes divided by a horizontal groove
10   Body–neck junction
11   Just below (attached to) body–neck junction
12   On body (not attached to body–neck junction)

DECORATION MOTIFS – CONTINUOUS
14   Band of several horizontal grooves
15   Band of oblique hatching
16   Two or more bands of oblique hatching
34   Band or bands of even cross-hatching
35   Band or bands of uneven cross-hatching, where the one series of lines is more than twice the distance apart compared with the other
17   Band of horizontal and oblique or vertical cross-hatching
23   Band of interlocking parallelograms, hatched
36   Band of interlocking parallelograms, alternately hatched
21   Band of interlocking rectangles, hatched
19   Band of interlocking triangles, hatched
20   Band of alternate (pendant) triangles, hatched
37   Bands of opposed hatching without intervening groove. Two or more horizontal bands of oblique hatching where the direction of the hatching alternates from band to band. Two such bones form a herringbone pattern
38   Bands of opposed hatching with intervening groove
39   Cord effect, where a band is thickened to stand out in relief

DECORATION MOTIFS – DISCONTINUOUS
25   Horizontal quadrilaterals, hatched
26   Oblique quadrilaterals, hatched
40   Vertical quadrilaterals (ladder), hatched or cross-hatched
27   Short horizontal row or rows of impressions
29   Curvilinear motifs
41   Applied decoration, bosses or strips
30   Miscellaneous decoration

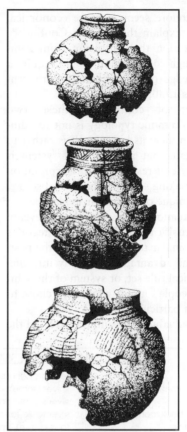

FIGURE 130 POTTERY FROM MSULUZI CONFLUENCE.

restricted his analysis of pots to the 45 vessels that were relatively complete, reasoning that a typology that included single sherds (such as Huffman's system) could be misleading. A set of 34 characteristics was used to describe each pot, and a simple matrix used to identify those combinations of characteristics that occurred most frequently. On this basis, the Msuluzi Confluence assemblage could be compared with similarly described assemblages from the nearby third-century site of Mzonjani and the ninth-century site of Ntshekane. It is notable that this typological analysis picked up strong evidence for continuity through the Kwa-Zulu–Natal sequence, and in this way specifically countered Huffman's suggestion that there had been more than one migration into the region:

'The new evidence from Msuluzi Confluence and Mzonjani ... shows that many characteristics of the seventh-century pottery from Natal were already present in the third century. Local evolution therefore seems a more economical hypothesis to explain the Msuluzi Confluence ceramic expression than diffusion from Zimbabwe, although confirmation would require a better knowledge of the fifth and sixth centuries' (Maggs 1980a: 139).

The point of contrasting these two approaches to ceramic typology is not to adjudicate between them as histories. It is rather to emphasise again that a typological system is part of the cycle of research and interpretation – of history-making – rather than an absolute, objective technique of describing evidence.

In some situations, it is possible to develop typological classifications that follow categories known to be similar to those in use in the past. These have the advantage of directly inferring the technological rule set, or system of thought, that was in people's minds when they chose to make or use a particular sort of vessel.

Anselm Maduabuchi Ibeanu has stressed the importance of taking such factors into account in ceramic analysis: 'if the main focus of archaeology is human behaviour instead of artefacts … archaeologists would need to step out and demonstrate (rather than assume) observed relationships between pottery types and social institutions' (Ibeanu 1992: 159). To illustrate his argument, Ibeanu turns to Nigeria's Igboland, where potters classify their pots according to the function that the vessels will perform. For example, in northern parts of the country, where conserving water for the dry season is of vital importance, a part of each settlement is set aside as the *owoko*, where rainwater is collected and stored. Potters make distinctive long-necked, globular vessels for the *owoko*, and these are known as *ite owoko* or *ite odo*. *Owoko* ceramics also carry social meaning:

'These pots, apart from serving as water storage, constitute part of the bridal wealth …

SOME HOUSEHOLD POSSESSIONS OF PHILIP ANHUYZER IN 1827

FURNISHINGS
cupboards (4): front, back, upper rooms, kitchen
wardrobes (3): back room, upstairs
chests (4): upstairs
racks (2): upstairs
pipe rack (1): upstairs
dumbwaiters (6): front room, upstairs
bureau (1): front room
writing desk (1): upstairs
tables (11): front room, hall, back room, upstairs, kitchen
chairs (39): front room, hall, upstairs
easy chair (1): upstairs
sofa (1): hall
beds (3): upstairs
washstand (1): hall
close stool (1): back room
periwig stand (1): back room
looking glasses (6): front room, hall, upstairs
pictures (18): passage, front room, hall, upstairs
window curtains (4): front room, hall
window sashes (2): front room

TABLEWARE
crockeryware (some): back room, upstairs
cups (21): hall
saucers (21): hall
coffee cups (12): hall

teapots (2): hall
knives (some): upstairs
silver sweetmeat forks (3): upstairs
silver table forks (9): upstairs
forks (some): upstairs
silver tablespoons (9): upstairs
silver teaspoons (4): upstairs
silver soup ladle (1): upstairs
silver salt cellars (4): upstairs
silver mustard pot (1): upstairs
silver sugar pot (1): upstairs
silver jugs (2): upstairs
silver cooler (1): upstairs
glass decanters (9): upstairs
wineglasses (some): upstairs
tumblers (some): upstairs

HOUSEHOLD UTENSILS
letter press (1): upstairs
clock (1): hall
lamps (2): passage, upstairs
shade (1): front room
candlesticks (10): back room, upstairs, kitchen
snuffers (2): kitchen
spittoons (3): front room
basin (1): hall
copper pail (1): upstairs
chamber pots (3): upstairs
buckets (3): kitchen
coffee urn (1): back room
tea urns (2): upstairs
tea kettles (3): upstairs, kitchen

tea canisters (2): hall
jugs (2): hall
brass jug (1): kitchen
basins (4): hall
flasks (some): back room
bottles (some): back room
tin canisters (3): upstairs
tobacco boxes (2): upstairs
china pots (set): back room
large pots (4): upstairs
iron pots (4): kitchen
stew pot (1): back room
sweetmeat pots (2): hall
stewing pan (1): upstairs
chafing dishes (2): upstairs, kitchen
baskets (2): kitchen
smoothing irons (4): back room, upstairs, kitchen
grindstone (1): upstairs
sieves (3): upstairs
choppers (2): upstairs
hatchet (1): kitchen
copper pestle (1): upstairs
copper mortar (1): upstairs
sausage spout (1): upstairs
funnel (1): upstairs
coffee mills (2): upstairs
brass cock (1): upstairs
waiters (5): upstairs, kitchen
silver waiter (1): upstairs
iron ladle (1): kitchen
chimney chains (5): kitchen

Mothers buy many *owoko* pots for their well-behaved daughters on marriage. And this is the pride of daughter-in-laws in their matrimonial homes. The new wife buries her pots in the *owoko* of her mother-in-law. *Owoko* is therefore exclusive property of women. With the influx of modern water containers and galvanized water tanks one would have expected a decline in the production/use of *owoko* pots and *ipso facto* the *owoko* itself. However ... according to the women, none of the modern containers could give them the pleasant and body-cooling effect of drinking water from the *owoko*. Moreover, *owoko* is the pride of women and represents the value systems of the society which have shown resilience through time' (Ibeanu 1992: 161).

Ibeanu's Igboland study shows that, to be fully effective, ceramic classifications used by archaeologists need to take into account the intentions of the potters if these can be ascertained, as well as the social relations of the people using the pots (particularly, in this case, gender relations). Such intentions and social relations can often be established where there are oral or documentary sources of information to supplement the ceramic evidence.

An example of a ceramic classification system that takes advantage of such sources is the Potomac Typological System – POTS for short – that has been used in studies of early colonial settlement in the Chesapeake region of Maryland and Virginia, North America (Beaudry et al. 1983). POTS uses terms found in inventories and other documents left by the people themselves, and therefore probably reflects function more accurately than many other systems.

'If pots are to be used for more than dating sites and the features on them, some attention needs to be paid to function. Given the primitive state of research in this area, what is needed is a scheme which will allow the systematic description and comparison of assemblages and which, by assessing function in even a crude way, will allow a preliminary appreciation of just what sort of functional variation exists between assemblages in time and space' (Beaudry et al. 1983: 19).

Inventories and other forms of lists are often part of the documentary evidence that historical archaeology can use in interpreting artefactual evidence. Even in their crude form, without the sort of sophisticated unpicking that lay behind the development of the Potomac Typological System, they can usefully be seen as classificatory systems for past technologies, reminding us both of the diversity of material culture, and of the fact that only a small portion of this material culture survives to become part of the archaeological record. For example, Philip Anhuyzer, resident in Barrack Street, Cape Town at the close of the eighteenth century and in the early nineteenth century, had his household inventoried after he died – a standard procedure at the time. Comparison of the list of Anhuyzer's possessions with archaeological assemblages from a contemporary site next door has illuminated the rather sparse impression of material culture that came from excavation (M. Hall et al. 1990).

Pottery

Potsherds can be very common on archaeological sites. People often used, and broke, large numbers of pots, and fragments generally survive the passage of time well. The craft of potting played an important part in village life, and there are several ways of finding out more about it.

One approach is to try to trace the clays that were used. Leon Jacobson has analysed sherd samples from a number of different sites in southern Africa, using Induced X-ray Emission Spectroscopy (known as PIXE). In this method, a small part of each potsherd's surface is bombarded with a beam of protons produced by a Van de Graaff accelerator. The beam excites the electrons on the potsherd's surface until it is turned off, at which point the electrons revert to their original states. But in doing so, the electrons send out X-rays which have energies and wavelengths characteristic of the chemical elements in the potsherd. These X-rays are measured and plotted as a graph, which can be compared with graphs from the PIXE analysis of other potsherds, or from samples of clay drawn from the places where potters may have gathered their raw materials.

Although the equipment used in such studies is extremely sophisticated (and expensive), the basic principle is simple. Clays contain a common range of chemical elements, but in differing proportions. These proportions remain constant after the clay has been collected, moulded into a pot, fired, used, broken, and eventually collected by the archaeologist. In other words, the chemical 'fingerprint' of the clay from the source of raw material is the same as the chemical 'fingerprint' of the potsherd. By matching the two, the archaeologist can make inferences about the geographical relation between villages and sources of raw materials, the degree of specialisation by potters, and the extent to which pottery was bartered or exchanged across the countryside.

In one of his case studies, Jacobson looked at a set of potsherds from archaeological sites scattered across South Africa's Northern Province, dated to the last thousand years, and from villages occupied by the ancestors of the modern-day Venda (Jacobson et al. 1991). The study area was dissected by the Soutpansberg, which has clay sources both to the north and the south, although they come from distinct rock formations. In view of these different 'geochemical signatures' it was possible to use PIXE to distinguish pottery on the basis of the clay, which came from separate sides of the mountains. Jacobson and his colleagues found that

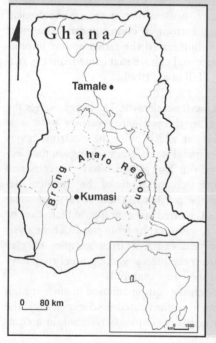

FIGURE 131 THE BRONG-AHAFO REGION OF GHANA.

most of the pots were broken and abandoned close to the sources of their raw materials, which suggested that, in this case, potting was largely a local village industry. However, a small but significant number of sherds were made in the south and then carried over the mountains to the northern area. This result is consistent with oral traditions recorded in the area, which indicate that people in the north tended to marry women from the south, and that a bride would often take pots with her to her new husband's home.

Another, complementary approach in studying the technology of pot making is to work with contemporary craftsmen and women. At Krobo, in Ghana's Brong-Ahafo region (Figure 131), people claim descent from the pottery makers for the Bono State: dated to between the thirteenth and eighteenth centuries AD, this was one of the early Akan states of the West African forest regions (Effah-Gyamfi 1980). Although the old skills are fast being forgotten, people still know enough to help archaeologists document the full cycle of manufacture.

Pottery makers (in this case, exclusively women) are very particular about the sources of clay they use, and will go to some trouble to keep them secret from rival craftswomen. There are strict taboos around digging the clay, including a prohibition against menstruating women and women who have had sexual intercourse the previous night. Often the clay is dug by young girls and old women. Before the clay is taken out, a chicken may be sacrificed to Nsuta, the river god. People believe that bad luck will follow if the taboos are broken: the pots might break, or the potter's hands might swell.

Pot making usually takes place in the dry harmattan season when there is little agricultural work to do, no rain to damage the unfired pots, and plenty of dry bark for firing. The clay is first pounded in an old wooden mortar, and unwanted inclusions are removed to ensure that the raw material has an even plasticity. No tempering material is added because the local clays have adequate quartz and mica inclusions in them. Once the clay has been thoroughly mixed, it is transferred to a wooden bowl.

The potter next takes a large lump of clay and begins to mould it into the desired shape, mostly using her hands; she also smooths the surfaces with a corn cob or palm nut, and uses a wet rag to shape the rim. Once roughly formed, the vessel is left to dry for up to two days. Then the leather-hard vessels are further scraped and smoothed into shape, and burnished smooth with a pebble. Decoration is added; the Krobo potters prefer grooves in most cases.

Finally, the vessel is fired in a bonfire kiln. This is made by collecting slow-burning wood bark into a heap and setting it on fire. The pots are carefully stacked in the smouldering embers, placed upside down in a dome formation. More bark is stacked around and over them, and the kiln is left for about an hour. The pots are taken out of the bonfire and cleaned: now they are ready for use.

Philip Anhuyzer's inventory serves to remind us that there are important technological categories other than stone tools and the fragmented sherds of ceramic vessels. These particular artefacts have attracted tremendous emphasis in the archaeological literature because they are very numerous on archaeological sites, and because they usually show a considerable amount of variability in their form, thus facilitating typological analysis.

Other materials that have been important in the creation of human technologies over wide spans of time and space include bone, shell, leather and wood. Under suitable conditions, all of these may survive for considerable periods of time. For example, at the twelfth-century site of Mapungubwe, on the border between

South Africa and Zimbabwe, evidence has been found for a sophisticated bone-working technology. Ivory was sawn, trimmed and polished to make bracelets, and the points of bone were worked into a variety of designs. In one part of the site a cache of more than 100 rough blanks was excavated. As Elizabeth Voigt, who has examined the collections, has noted:

'It is difficult to visualize a group being able to utilize the amount of bone produced in what was probably a relatively short period of occupation. The evidence suggests that the bone tools were being made in sufficient quantities to produce a surplus, and that at Mapungubwe we have a group of skilled bone-working craftsmen who were manufacturing well-finished tools for trade' (Voigt 1983: 77).

Further to the north, and many years earlier, people living by hunting, gathering and fishing along the banks of the lakes and rivers that were once to be found in the Sahara fashioned a variety of bone harpoon points with intricate designs. These have been classified in typological systems by archaeologists, following the approaches more commonly used for lithic and ceramic technology (Sutton 1974).

Other organic materials, such as leather and wood, are less frequently preserved on archaeological sites: only under special conditions will such artefacts survive the passage of time. For example, wells dug into the courtyards of Cape Town's Castle in the seventeenth century have excellent micro-environments for organic preservation. Abandoned leatherwork includes a collection of shoe soles and bits and pieces of clothing. Woodwork

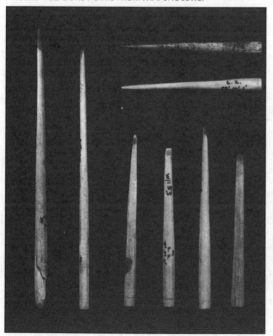

FIGURE 132 BONE POINTS FROM MAPUNGUBWE.

FIGURE 133 BARBED BONE HARPOON FROM ESH SHAHEINAB, NILE VALLEY.

may survive in very dry environments, such as the deposits in some rock shelters, or in water-logged conditions, such as on fully submerged shipwrecks.

Artefacts made from materials like these may require specialised laboratory techniques to ensure their preservation once they have been removed from their archaeological contexts. Laboratory conservation plays an important role in ensuring that maximum information is gained from organic artefacts, and that they survive in archaeological collections for study by future research workers.

Metal working

The study of metal working has a particularly important place in the archaeology of technology. The chronology of the origins of iron working in the continent is still controversial, with dates as early as the sixth century BC claimed but not universally accepted. It would seem certain, though, that iron technology was closely linked with the development and spread of agriculture, as metal implements would have been essential for clearing and hoeing fields (M. Hall 1987).

The method of iron working used in Africa was the 'bloomery' process. Iron smiths would prepare a cylindrically shaped clay furnace and fired-clay air pipes, known as *tuyères* (the French term for a pipe). The furnace was loaded with iron ore and charcoal, and fired. The required smelting temperature of about 1200°C was achieved by pumping air with bellows through the *tuyères*. When the heart of the furnace was hot enough, a cake of iron particles

(the 'bloom') was separated from the waste material (the 'slag'). Later, the bloom was re-heated and hammered in a forge; in this way the required iron implements were fashioned.

Our understanding of iron technology has been considerably aided by experimental archaeology. Initially, this was slow to get off the ground.

'One of the anomalies of archaeology in Africa has been the lack of adequate information about the technological attributes of iron production. Scholars of stone technologies have devoted extensive efforts, both descriptive and experimental, to the elucidation of the mechanical processes that lead to certain types of form. Experimental study of stone technologies, though, has not been matched by comparable work in iron technology. This is paradoxical, for iron technology represents a significant change towards technological complexity and thus would seem to ask for corresponding effort to understand the behavioral and technical complexities associated with the wide variety of technological variants in Africa' (Childs & Schmidt 1985: 121).

Early experiments attempted to replicate furnace conditions in laboratory conditions. For example, Terry Childs and Peter Schmidt built a furnace at Brown University in the United States, using as far as possible raw materials described ethnographically from Ethiopia. They then plotted furnace temperatures during the course of their simulated smelt. Later experimental studies were carried out in Africa, taking full advantage of the skills of smelting still remembered by village communities. (Iron is rarely smelted today in most parts of the conti-

FIGURE 134 AN IRON-SMELTING FURNACE. This reconstruction of the smelting process shows the clay-walled furnace with *tuyères* in place. Bellows would be used to pump air into the furnace through the *tuyères*, raising the temperature inside the furnace to the level required for smelting to take place.

nent.) For example, in a reconstruction of traditional methods in the Nyika area of northern Malawi, a furnace was built and fired by local villagers, and nearby mines were surveyed and sampled, chemical analysis being made of the ores used during the Iron Age (Wenner & Van der Merwe 1987). The result of this work has been a good understanding of the properties of raw materials and furnace fuels, the temperatures required in smelting and the ways in which these can be achieved, and the chemical processes that take place inside the furnace.

Experiments such as these have a direct application in the interpretation of the archaeological residues of iron working: the bases of furnaces, broken *tuyères* and heaps of slag which mark old industrial sites. For example, there is extensive archaeological evidence for early iron working in the Phalaborwa region of the Northern Province, South Africa, where similar activity is to be found in the present day (Van der Merwe & Scully 1971). Detailed analysis of one iron-smelting complex, about 25 km from Phalaborwa, has allowed estimates to be made of the amounts of both raw material and labour involved in the technology. At this site, a group of seven furnaces was surrounded by slag heaps estimated at 180 tons. From the results of experimental archaeology, it could be deduced that this amount of waste emanated from the production of about 48 tons of iron. This would have required about 800 tons of charcoal, or the wood from about 7000 trees (Van der Merwe & Killick 1979). The effect that such pre-colonial iron working had on the environment is apparent.

Early iron working at KwaGandaganda

Despite the long-used distinction between the Stone Ages and Iron Ages in African archaeology, iron objects are found comparatively rarely on early village sites. This is partly due to the selective processes of preservation: iron corrodes rapidly under most conditions. But it is also because iron implements were rare, probably considerably valued, and reluctantly discarded.

In addition to iron artefacts, there may be evidence for smelting and forging, both of which leave durable archaeological traces in the form of furnace bases (baked hard by the intense heat of the smith's fire), broken *tuyères* and considerable quantities of 'slag' (abandoned waste products).

One very effective way to learn more about iron-working technology is through detailed examination of the physical structure and chemistry of small samples cut from excavated artefacts and of waste products. An example is provided by KwaGandaganda, an Early Iron Age village that was occupied continuously for about three hundred years from the seventh century AD. KwaGandaganda has now been flooded by the Inanda Dam on the Mngeni River near Durban. But before it was destroyed, archaeologists were able to learn a considerable amount about the lives of its occupants more than a thousand years ago.

Petrographic, metallographic and chemical analyses of metal artefacts from Kwa-Gandaganda were carried out by the Archaeology Materials Laboratory at the University of Cape Town (Miller & Whitelaw 1994). Specimens were either sectioned with a diamond saw and then mounted in acrylic resin and ground and polished, or else thin-sectioned for petrographic examination. The prepared samples were then examined through both a conventional

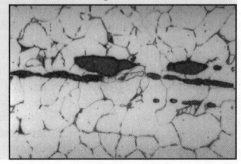

FIGURE 135 IRON FROM KWAGANDAGANDA. This micrograph (magnified 140 times) shows a polished section through an iron bead. The dark inclusion is slag, elongated when the metal was hammered out while hot. The lighter crystals are 'ferrite', or low-carbon iron. The rounded shape of the ferrite crystals shows that they were heated to about 900°C after the bead had been completed, and then cooled slowly. This may have happened in an accidental hut fire, which gives a clue to the way in which this particular artefact entered the archaeological record.

microscope and a Scanning Electron Microscope. The result was a set of detailed profiles of both the physical structure of each specimen and its chemical composition. From this information, deductions could be drawn about sources of raw material, the technology used by the iron smiths, and the relation between finished items and waste products.

The study showed that smelting and forging technology at KwaGandaganda had been similar to that at sites in Botswana's Tsodilo Hills, where collections from Early Iron Age contexts had also been the subject of detailed metallographic analysis. The KwaGandaganda smiths had obtained their iron ore as haematite, which occurs as outcropping bands in shale formations inland from the coast, and from consolidated iron-rich sand that had formed under waterlogged conditions nearer to the Indian Ocean. 'The technology used was simple, and characterised by the production of inhomogeneous bloomery iron, a lack of any systematic heat treatment other than cyclical annealing during hot working, the absence of casting and of wire drawing, and the fabrication of items of jewellery from sheet metal or from strips chisel-cut from sheet' (Miller & Whitelaw 1994).

But the metallographic study also had wider implications for understanding both village life in KwaGandaganda and the way in which Early Iron Age society was organised. As the Iron Age in southern Africa spans almost two thousand years, and continued into the colonial period (during which ethnographers and travellers left records of the societies they encountered), archaeologists have often extrapolated back from the recent to the more distant past. One of the general features of ethnographic accounts is the observation that smiths smelted iron in seclusion, away from villages, and that there were complex rituals and beliefs that reinforced this separation. In contrast, the unfashioned bloom of iron would often be brought back to the village and forged into implements in full public view.

The practices of iron working, then, reflect fundamental principles about the nature of the world. If there were evidence that the recently observed segregation of iron smelting also occurred in the earliest years of farming settlement, then there would be sound basis for arguing that wider aspects of belief had remained unchanged through the full two thousand years of the Iron Age. But if, on the other hand, there were to be evidence that people in the Early Iron Age had not shared these recent prohibitions, then this would suggest that considerable changes had also taken place in the society's larger cosmology.

The archaeology of KwaGandaganda was used to address this wider question. Fragmentary metal artefacts had been found in a midden which also contained food refuse, broken pottery and other objects, and which had built up over a layer of cattle dung. It is probable that this midden was near the centre of the village. There was also direct evidence for iron forging: forge bases, surviving as small, hardened hollows in the ground and filled with dark soil and slag, as well as slag-encrusted *tuyère* nozzles. But was there any evidence for iron smelting as well – an activity that would, in recent times, be prohibited in such a public place?

Metallographic examination of the slag samples showed that they were the waste products of both forging and smelting. It is possible that this debris from smelting was deliberately brought into the village from a secluded smelting site some distance away, but this seems unlikely, particularly as there is evidence from other archaeological sites in the region suggesting in-village smelting. A more logical explanation is that people in the Early Iron Age had systems of belief significantly different from their descendants in the Late Iron Age.

'It is notoriously difficult to distinguish between iron smelting and iron forging slag … yet the identification of the small nodules in the KwaGandaganda sample as forging slag is clear, based on their morphology and the distinctive microstructure and chemical composition of the analysed specimen … the evidence from Kwa-Gandaganda, while not conclusive because of the absence of a furnace, supports the evidence of smelting within the settlement at Ndondondwane and Magogo … suggesting that either Early Iron Age people dealt with the anti-social qualities of smelting in ways other than seclusion, or that smelting was not yet considered dangerous to the well-being of society and did not require seclusion' (Miller & Whitelaw 1994).

Buildings

The range and complexity of technology are, of course, immense, and archaeologists often find themselves dealing with artefacts that are far more complex than stone tools, pottery, bone work and iron implements. Indeed, because archaeological research can continue into the present, the full range of human technical ability falls within the ambit of the discipline.

For example, providing shelter has often led to the creation of complex artefacts. On the southern highveld – the vast grasslands that cover much of South Africa's interior plateau – one finds the remains of thousands of stone-built villages that were first constructed in about the fourteenth century AD. These follow complicated sets of rules in their design – combinations of circular 'primary enclosures', linked to create complexes by stretches of 'secondary walling' (Figure 136). In his study of these architectural traditions, Tim Maggs used exactly the same principles that are applied in designing a typological system for ceramics or stone tools (Maggs 1976).

Scanning the aerial photographs, he first identified specific morphological types, defined according to their structural details. These were then plotted across the landscape. Representa-

tive sites were excavated to provide a chronology of radiocarbon dates. Each stone-walled village – the basic unit of study in Maggs's project – was the consequence of hundreds of different design decisions by the farmers who built the walls. Regularity was given by tradition – by the regularity in the sets of decisions characteristic of human learned behaviour. Although the southern highveld in the fourteenth century AD is very far removed from the circumstances in which our first ancestors fashioned simple stone implements more than two million years ago, the basic principles of archaeological analysis are the same.

To the west, in the sandveld of the Cape west coast, colonial expansion produced a distinctive form of architecture which is still to be found in areas such as the hinterland of Verlorenvlei. These 'longhouses' began as basic rectangular thatched cottages, and were expanded with additions as family units grew in size (Figure 137). Again, it is possible to study them as artefacts constructed according to specific sets of rules which conferred the regularity of a tradition. By measuring a large sample of standing buildings, John Gribble has suggested what this rule set could have been: the subconscious 'competence' that directed colonial subsistence farmers in their choices of the 'proper' way of building a house (Gribble 1989). Again, our understanding of the basis of these technological processes is the same as in situations widely separated by time and space.

FIGURE 136 ARCHITECTURE OF THE SOUTHERN HIGHVELD. Complex architectural plans such as these are typical of Iron Age farming villages on the South African southern highveld.

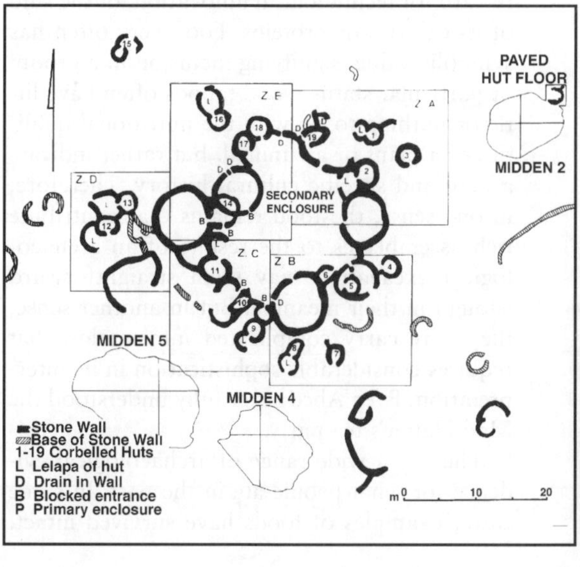

FIGURE 137 LONGHOUSES AT VERLORENVLEI. These Cape west coast buildings expanded with the needs of the families which occupied them.

Food

chapter **10**

One way of thinking about food is to see it as a consequence of the interaction between technology and the environment. Thus, for instance, the minds of our early ancestors were focused by the problem of survival: the ubiquitous handaxe, found in many parts of the world, was probably a general purpose tool that served equally well in cutting up an animal carcass and digging up edible tubers. Then again, Africa's first farmers worked to improve the yield of the land, and iron implements were far more efficient in clearing fields for cultivation than were stone tools. Finally, the stone villages built across southern Africa's highveld more than five hundred years ago served to contain and protect domestic cattle, the backbone of the economy.

Thinking about food

Food can be complicated: it is more than a reward for technological innovation, or the sum of its calories or proteins. Food very often has symbolic value, signifying inclusion in a group, or particular status. Food taboos often have little or nothing to do with the nutritional qualities of a plant or an animal, but rather indicate a long and specific cultural history. Therefore, in one sense, the food remains that contribute rich assemblages to the results of an archaeological excavation may seem straightforward enough in their meaning. But in another sense, they may carry complicated information that requires considerable sophistication in its interpretation. Even Alice never fully understood the Mad Hatter's tea party.

There is a wide range of archaeological evidence for what people ate in the past. In some cases, examples of foods have survived intact.

FIGURE 138 THE COMPLEX MEANING OF FOOD. This nineteenth-century engraving of London's barbaric Union Club shows how a meal can be an opportunity for a range of social exchanges that have little to do with eating.

More often, the evidence is made up of the more durable parts of food waste: carbonised seeds or the bones of animals, birds and fish. Technology found on a site, of course, indicates how food was prepared and stored, while pictures on the walls of rock shelters may show the tasks involved in procuring food. With all these sources of information, though, archaeologists face the challenging task of discerning between the functional daily routines of using available foodstuffs for survival and the symbolic daily tasks of using food to express social meaning. Were plants used as food or for ritual purposes? Do faunal assemblages reflect the range of species available in the local environment, or did a set of cultural preferences modulate what was eaten? Do rock paintings show mundane activities, or are they complex metaphors for astract belief systems?

Like technology, then, food procurement must be seen as more than the collection and cultivation of provisions. Nowadays archaeologists find it useful to think in terms of 'foodways' – systems of procedures that ensure nutritional needs are met, and express cultural connections between people.

FIGURE 139 SORTING FOOD RESIDUES. The remains of meals once eaten on an archaeological site are important evidence for what people were doing in the past. Here, food residues are being sorted into different categories in the field, prior to being taken back to the laboratory for more detailed study.

Evidence for food production in West Africa

One of the most important areas of archaeological study is the origins of food production – the domestication of wild plants and animals.

. It used to be believed that the origins of the farming way of life could be traced to a single 'Neolithic Revolution' that took place in the Near East. In this earlier interpretation, farming was seen as spreading outwards from here, reaching 'backward' regions such as Africa comparatively late in human history. Now, however, farming is known to have developed independently in different parts of the world, including Africa. Once they were introduced into new areas, domesticated plants and animals developed extremely complex histories and underwent subsequent genetic changes.

Finding archaeological evidence for early farming can be particularly challenging. Domestication involves human intervention in the processes of natural selection: people notice favourable characteristics in wild animals and plants (such as tractable behaviour or nutritious fruits) and then try to ensure that these charac-

FIGURE 140 EARLY MAIZE COBS FROM ARCHAEOLOGICAL SITES IN MIDDLE AMERICA. As hunter–gatherers concentrated more and more on wild forms of maize, they began to affect the genetic make-up of the plant species, encouraging plants with larger cobs. Such genetic changes in plant and animal species are the basis of domestication and therefore of the farming way of life.

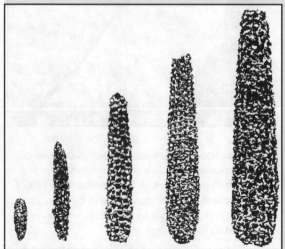

teristics become more frequent. They may do this in a wide variety of ways, such as gathering and sowing seeds, protecting plants from wild competitors, or culling a herd in such a way that those animals most suitable for human use have a better chance of surviving. The problem for archaeologists is that, in most cases, these patterns of behaviour affect the morphology of plants and animals only over a long period of time. For example, differences between the bones of domestic cattle and their wild ancestors may remain imperceptible for many centuries. Maize, one of the best known of the early plant domesticates, was gradually brought from a wild to a cultivated state in South America. Although the difference in size between the wild progenitor and modern domestic maize is startling (Figure 140), this change took place over many centuries. Archaeologists working with botanical remains from sites left by the earliest farmers find it difficult to tell initially domesticated maize cobs apart from wild ones.

A further difficulty is that in many cases there may not be any surviving direct evidence for farming. Animal bones are often well preserved in archaeological sites, but in some conditions, particularly on exposed open sites, they may not survive the passage of time. Botanical remains are usually more fragile and subject to decay and complete destruction. Pollen grains last well, but only in suitable soils and deposits. Often, then, archaeologists have to infer the presence of a farming way of life from indirect evidence such as pottery, stone tools used for food preparation, or the remains of houses, which indicate a settled way of life and by implication the cultivation of crop plants.

The archaeology of early farming in West Africa illustrates many of these challenges and difficulties. However, work here in recent years is revealing a picture that is consistent with the rest of the world. There is now clear evidence for the indigenous development of farming in the savanna and forest regions, and for a long period of adaptation to local ecological conditions. As Bassey Andah has stressed, 'to talk about the "Neolithic Revolution" along the same old lines, even if in new garb, is to continue to claim that there were no equivalent agricultural revolutions in Africa'. What this amounts to is a 'refusal to recognize several centuries, and in some cases thousands of years, of solid progress towards improved agriculture adjusted to African ecological conditions' (Andah 1993: 254).

Ann Stahl suggests that the best term to describe the changes that led from hunting and gathering to farming in West Africa is 'intensification' (Stahl 1993). In central Ghana, where Stahl has excavated at the important Kintampo rock shelters, there were well-established hunter–gatherer groups which moved around the forests and savannas, possibly following seasonal cycles, and returned frequently to favoured living places (Figure 141). A good example of this way of life is provided by the 'Punpun phase' – a collection of assemblages of artefacts and food debris left in central Ghanaian sites between about 1750 and 1350 BC. The people who lived here had a few pots and few definite stone tools (although they fashioned large numbers of rough quartz flakes), probably because the need for mobility discouraged possessions. They ate a variety of wild foods, in particular giant land snails (*Achatina achatina*),

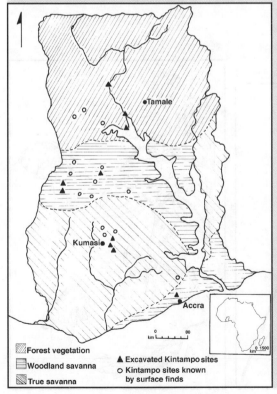

FIGURE 141 KINTAMPO SITES IN GHANA.

Forest vegetation
Woodland savanna
True savanna

▲ Excavated Kintampo sites
○ Kintampo sites known by surface finds

the shells of which are found in large quantities at their living sites. Other foods included monkeys, tortoises, monitor lizards and freshwater turtles, species that inhabit the forest edge of the savanna as well as the dense woodlands along the courses of rivers. Excavators also found abundant seed husks from wild hackberries (*Celtis* sp.), from the oil palm (*Elaeis guineensis*), and from *Canarium schweinfurthii*, a plant known as the incense tree, which has edible fruits. Today, the oil palm is a domestic plant species second in economic importance only to the yam.

The archaeological evidence suggests that these hunter–gatherers experimented with plant species that were to become important cultigens, and were beginning to concentrate on particular animal foods (even if today the giant land snail seems an unlikely candidate for domestication). These initial attempts at domesticating plants and animals are examples of Andah's trajectories towards farming that operated within local ecological frameworks.

The Punpun phase overlaps, and may be completely contemporary, with what has become known as the Kintampo Complex. This is a group of assemblages, from both Ghana and neighbouring Ivory Coast, which, although still clearly connected with the long hunting and gathering traditions of West Africa, provides unequivocal evidence for the use of domestic species. James Anquandah, reviewing the evidence for the Kintampo Complex after some 25 years of research, was able to list almost 30 sites, some excavated and some known only from surface materials, located in both savanna and forest zones. Of the 20 radiocarbon age estimations that have been obtained for Kintampo Complex sites, 17 range between the nineteenth and twelfth centuries BC (Anquandah 1993).

Although the number of bones excavated from dated sites is still small, there is now no doubt that the people of the Kintampo Complex kept domestic sheep or goats or perhaps both – it is impossible to tell sheep and goat apart from small samples such as these. Stahl points out that even small numbers of domestic animals would have had a marked effect on their owners' lifeways, reducing mobility and encouraging people to settle more permanently

167

in one place. Not surprisingly, then, some Kintampo Complex sites consist of small villages of mud houses, several with stone foundations, although people also continued to make use of rock shelters, and hunting and gathering continued to make a major contribution to diet.

There is no unequivocal, direct evidence for plant cultivation, despite some very suggestive clues. The cultivation of tree crops can be inferred from the dramatic increase in oil-palm pollen grains, preserved in a core taken from the site of Bosumpra, Ghana, and dated to between 1550 and 1050 BC. Because oil-palm and yam cultivation are closely connected in West Africa today, this has been taken as suggesting that yam cultivation began at the same time as well. The inference is strengthened by the observation that many Kintampo Complex sites are found near the modern woodland–savanna margins – areas particularly suited to yam and oil-palm cultivation. Kintampo Complex sites have numbers of small grindstones indicating an increase in plant-food processing. Large numbers of ceramics (in contrast with assemblages from the Punpun phase) indicate cooking and storage, which are characteristic of the farming way of life. Moreover, the presence

of raw materials not found in the area of the site – particularly the stone used to make polished implements – shows that there were wide-reaching trade networks; these again are often a feature of the farming way of life.

All in all, the emerging history of the Kintampo Complex well illustrates the ways in which local communities made increasingly sophisticated use of the resources available to them, in this way creating the basis for modern farming ways of life. It also demonstrates the importance of archaeozoological and palaeobotanical studies in archaeological research.

In James Anquandah's words, 'the Kintampo complex is a "neolithic" tradition combining characteristics of sedentism and building technology; a mixed subsistence economy, including hunting, fishing, gathering of wild crops and animal domestication; cottage industries and crafts such as potting, various ground and flaked stone implements, milling equipment and stone beads; and the rudiments of terracotta art … What is now urgently required to prove a fully tropical "neolithic" is macro- or micro-botanical evidence for yam cultivation' (Anquandah 1993: 259–60).

FIGURE 143 YAMS, A WEST AFRICAN STAPLE.

FIGURE 142 OIL-PALM CULTIVATION.

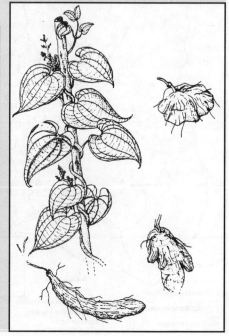

Plants

As we have seen in Chapter 8, plant remains from archaeological sites are important for researchers in establishing the nature of the local environment. The same assemblages will almost always provide vital information about the contribution that plants made to people's diets. For example, in his continuing study of the palaeoecology of hunter–gatherers in the Eastern Cape, South Africa, Hilary Deacon decided to re-excavate Melkhoutboom Cave, which had first been dug more than thirty years earlier. By using recovery techniques designed for fragile and often indistinct organic material, including water flotation, Deacon excavated a rich and diverse floral assemblage, and hereby established in some detail the role that plant collecting had played in the foodways of these hunter–gatherer communities (H.J. Deacon 1976).

Melkhoutboom is located in a sheltered kloof in the Cape Fold Belt Mountains, about 60 km from the coast, and about 650 m above sea-level. The deposits were well stratified, and consisted of a series of alternating ash layers and organically rich horizons. Radiocarbon dates showed that the sequence spanned 15 000 years. Artefacts recovered included stone tools, pieces of leather (some with sewing), cordage, netting and matting, reeds, wooden artefacts, bone artefacts, shell and pottery.

The plant remains were well preserved because of the dry micro-environment of the cave. Corms were the most frequent category, in particular the genus *Watsonia*. Because plants only become available at particular times of the year, Deacon was able to deduce the seasonal collecting strategies of the shelter's one-time occupants.

'The kind of adaptation to the Holocene environment evidenced at Melkhoutboom would seem to have been general in the Eastern Cape, and at Melkhoutboom specifically the geophytes Watsonia, Hypoxis and Moraea appear to have been the main plant foodstuffs and denote occupation through spring and summer. Watsonia ... is the most common plant food represented in the remains and on this basis it is suggested as a staple food in the economy. It has been suggested that the importance of plants such as Watsonia and Hypoxis rests on their being widely distributed and seasonally widely available' (H.J. Deacon 1976: 120).

A remarkably wide range of plants has been used for food and medicinal or ritual purposes at one time or another in the past. As with other aspects of archaeological interpretation, it is important to acquire a systematic understanding of these applications, rather than one dependent on the siren song of 'common sense'. Ethnobotanical studies can help us in this way, for they open an illuminating window on to the

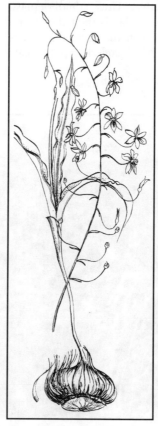

FIGURE 145 AN EDIBLE CORM. *Cyanella hyacinthoides* (known locally as *raaptol*): the corm (the swollen base of the stem) has a nutty flavour and is usually roasted before being eaten. The flowers are white or mauve (Metelerkamp & Sealy 1983).

FIGURE 144 MELKHOUTBOOM CAVE.

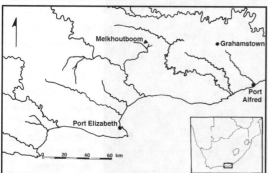

past, as well as providing comparative collections for identifying floral assemblages from excavations. For example, Fiona Archer has surveyed the edible plants that can be collected in the Kamiesberg, northwestern Cape, recording their indigenous names and nutritional qualities (Archer 1982). Wendy Metelerkamp and Judy Sealy have published a similar study for the Doorn Karoo, inland of the Cape west coast, an area rich in archaeological sites with favourable conditions for plant preservation (Metelerkamp & Sealy 1983). They collected information on plant use from Klaas Mouton, a shepherd living in the area, who had learned as a child the skills of using veld plants for food and medicinal purposes.

'Prehistoric people must have developed an intimate knowledge of edible and medicinal plants and the seasons in which they are available. Farmers and farm labourers in remote areas today still know about some of these plants, but the information is not being passed on to the next generation, because commercially prepared foods and medicines are becoming more readily available. Thus ethnobotanical information collected today is the tail end of a long tradition, of which the greater part has already gone forever' (Metelerkamp & Sealy 1983: 4–5).

It is now widely recognised that plant and animal remains are among the most useful and important categories of evidence that come from archaeological excavations. But this was not always acknowledged. In many earlier excavations, food refuse was not studied or retained, and a considerable amount of evidence was thus lost. At Great Zimbabwe, for example, R. N. Hall simply dumped all the animal bones he had found over the crest of the Hill, forming his own secondary midden at the base of the slope. Much later, it was possible to recover some of this lost evidence (Brain 1974), but there is still a large hole in our knowledge of the economy of the early Zimbabwe state as a result of misguided depredations.

The mistakes of previous fieldworkers are a salutary warning against complacency. Just as we view some past excavations with horror, so will future archaeologists have much to say in criticism of our own standards of analysis. Techniques of analysis in areas such as faunal studies are being improved all the time, and for this reason the amount and quality of evidence available about past foodways are constantly increasing.

A specific set of procedures has been developed to study animal bones from archaeological sites in a systematic manner. These have been described cogently by Richard Klein and

FIGURE 146
DOMESTIC ANIMALS. Domestic animals such as cattle and sheep were of central importance in villages in the past, as they still are in rural communities today. Faunal collections from archaeological sites provide important evidence for the nature of past economies.

Kathryn Cruz-Uribe, who have based their approach on their work with collections from Spain and southern Africa (Klein & Cruz-Uribe 1984). Formally referred to as 'zooarchaeology', this specialism is more commonly known as faunal analysis.

As with other aspects of archaeological research, faunal analysis begins long before the first animal bone is found. The design of the excavation, decisions about where to excavate, the method of stratigraphic control, and recovery techniques will all affect the nature of the faunal assemblage and the quality of information that it can provide about the food people ate. It is now usual to sieve all deposit from an excavation, as archaeologists recognise that a range of smaller objects may be lost if one relies solely on the eyesight of the person wielding a trowel in a trench. The choice of mesh size will also have a major effect on the faunal sample. If the mesh is too small, excavation will be slow and the faunal assemblage small; but if the mesh is too big, the bones of complete categories of food, such as small birds and fish, may be completely lost, fatally biasing the interpretation. Over-enthusiastic sieving and inappropriate packaging in the field can cause damage to crucial specimens. For these reasons, archaeologists often work from the earliest stages in a project with faunal specialists.

Klein and Cruz-Uribe describe the initial

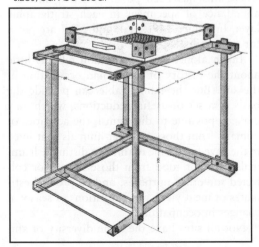

steps in faunal analysis as sorting bones into size categories and body parts, identification, sexing, ageing and measurement. These processes depend on a close knowledge of animal skeletons and the use of comparative collections.

'All bone identifications are ultimately based on comparisons with the skeletal parts of known taxa. An "identification" is made when the analyst believes there is a satisfactory match between a fossil bone of unknown taxon and a skeletal part whose taxon has been previously established. Most analyses thus depend upon the availability of a "comparative collection", comprising skeletons of those taxa that are likely to be represented in a fossil assemblage. Of course, an experienced analyst can make many identifications from memory, by comparison with mental images of often-seen parts. Gaining sufficient experience to do this is vital if an analyst wants to process large bone samples in a reasonable amount of time' (Klein & Cruz-Uribe 1984: 21).

After these initial stages in faunal analysis, researchers proceed to estimate the relative abundance of the various species – an essential step if one is to draw comparisons between different assemblages in order to learn about the use of past food resources. There are two standard measures of abundance that are in common use in faunal analyses:

- NISP: the Number of Identified Specimens. The advantage of the NISP statistic is that it is easy to calculate. But there are several disadvantages in using this measure. NISP does not take into account the fact that the skeletons of some species have more parts than skeletons of others. NISP will also overemphasise the importance of animals that reached the archaeological site intact: for example, small mammals that were brought home whole, in comparison with larger animals which were butchered away from a living site and whose bones failed sometimes to make the archaeological record. NISP counts are, in addition, very sensitive to bone fragmentation; this will often not have affected all species in the faunal assemblage equally.
- MNI: the Minimum Number of Individuals. The MNI count is the smallest number of individual animals that could have accounted for

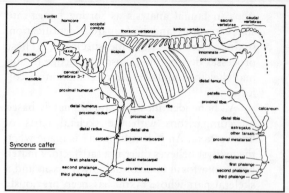

FIGURE 148 THE SKELETON OF THE CAPE BUFFALO. Faunal identification depends on the use of comparative collections, made up of labelled skeletal parts from complete specimens.

all the identified bones in an assemblage. It follows that the MNI count can never be larger than the NISP, and is usually a lot smaller. The Minimum Number of Individuals is calculated by first attributing all the identifiable bones to their species. Next, the MNI is calculated for each body part within the species; the largest count is then taken as the MNI for the species as a whole.

Klein and Cruz-Uribe suggest that, in assessing species abundance in a faunal assemblage, the best approach is to take into account both NISP and MNI estimates.

The language of archaeology ...

Site name: BOBONONG
Species: DOMESTIC CATTLE

Skeletal element	NISP	MNI
Scapula	27	14
Ribs	116	5
Humerus	30	15
Radius	32	16
Ulna	10	5
Femur	23	12
Patella	22	11
Fibula	2	1
TOTALS	262	16

(Part of an imaginary faunal report)

The next stage in a faunal analysis is the conversion of these statistical profiles into usable archaeological information. To this end the researcher may convert MNI summary figures into Meat Weight Estimates by multiplying

MNI or NISP figures by an estimate of the meat yield of each animal. This will allow for the relative contribution of different-sized animals in the diet. But Meat Weight Estimates may also be misleading because they cannot allow for size variations in individual animals or for situations where carcasses were not completely consumed. As with the analysis of all archaeological evidence, interpretative assumptions come into play at an early stage.

There are numerous examples of the ways in which faunal analysis can be used in archaeology. Some of these studies follow the methodology which has been described here, while others apply variant approaches which individual archaeologists feel may be more appropriate to the specific circumstances of their research.

Rose Cottage Cave, in the Ladybrand area of the eastern Free State, South Africa, was probably an 'aggregation site', a place where hunter–gatherers came together in relatively large numbers as part of their annual cycle of movement across the landscape (Wadley 1991). There are large faunal assemblages from the site, culled from a wide variety of animal species that included fish and frogs, birds, equids and antelope. The people who lived here probably hunted, collected, trapped and snared animals. In fact, more than 50 species are represented in the excavated collection of bones (Plug & Engela 1992).

The results of the faunal study from Rose Cottage Cave were presented in a form which has become standard in archaeological reports: a table of identified animals (to species level, where this has been possible) set against the abundance of specimens in each stratigraphic layer. In Figure 149, NISP and MNI are given for each animal.

Taken alone, this information tells us little about the history of the human occupation of the site. But the faunal table can provide the basis of a set of useful deductions, which may make it possible to distinguish the activities of humans from those of other animals that lived in the cave from time to time, to distinguish animals used for food from those hunted or collected for other purposes, and to provide estimates of meat yield and indications of seasonal changes in occupation.

Not all sites have the same diversity of animal species as Rose Cottage Cave. The sites of farming villages, for instance, will often produce species lists that are dominated by a narrow range of domestic animals. This proved the case with excavations carried out by Innocent Pikirayi near the town of Mt. Darwin in northern Zimbabwe. Pikirayi's aim was to trace the archaeology of the Mutapa state, the polity that succeeded Great Zimbabwe on its demise as a regional capital in the late fifteenth century (Pikirayi 1993). Pikirayi carried out sample excavations at three sites: the Great Zimbabwe Tradition site of Baranda, a later loopholed structure at Muchekayawa Hill, and Chengu-ruve Hill, which was possibly the Portuguese trading site of Massap.

Pikirayi found that Baranda and Chenguruve Hill both showed a considerable dependence on domestic stock – cattle, sheep and goat. The Muchekayawa Hill assemblage, however, did not include any domestic animals, which may reflect the economy of the people living here, or alternatively may be a comment on the inadequate size of the faunal sample (Pikirayi 1993). In sum, faunal studies are not in themselves the end of archaeological interpretation, but need to be read in conjunction with the full range of archaeological evidence.

SPECIES	LEVELS					
	Mn-A2 a	b	P	Ja-Ha	DCM-DB	G-Ru
Papio ursinus	17/5		4/1	6/3	1/1	
Cercopithecus aethiops			2/2			
Vulpes chama	2/2					
Canis mesomelas	10/2	1/1	1/1	12/2		
Canis cf. mesomelas	1/1					
Canis sp.	5/1		1/1	2/1		
Aonyx capensis			1/1			
Suricata suricatta			2/2			
Cynictis penicillata	1/1					
Atilax paludinosus	2/2			5/2		
Viverridae sp. indet.	17/4	1/1	2/1	3/1		
Hyaena brunnea	2/1					
Hyaena sp.	1/1					
Panthera pardus	10/3		2/2			
Felis caracal			1/1			
Felis cf. caracal			1/1			
Felis lybica	8/3		4/3			
Carnivora gen. et sp. indet.	10/5		2/1	12/3		
Equus burchelli/quagga	6/4			5/3	6/1	
Equus capensis					2/2	
Equus sp.	1/1			1/*	5/2	
Procavia capensis	253/1	29/2	53/6	95/16		
Phacochoerus aethiopicus	47/5	3/1	22/1	66/8	6/1	
Suidae sp. indet.	4/1	4/*	1/*			
Bos primigenius f. taurus	21/6					
Capra hircus	28/2					
Ovis aries	16/4					
Ovis/Capra	19/5					
Connochaetes cf. taurinus				3/1		
Connochaetes gnou	65/15	3/1	9/2	28/9	7/3	1/1
Alcelaphus buselaphus	16/7	3/1	2/1	28/10	8/3	
Damaliscus dorcas	66/9	5/1	11/4	39/9	7/2	
Connochaetes/Alcelaphus	35/1	4/*	9/2	3/2	22/1	1/*
Megalotragus priscus					5/1	
Alcelaphinae sp. indet.	9/*			15/1		
Sylvicapra grimmia	7/2			14/6		
Antidorcas marsupialis	290/22	26/3	18/4	106/19	17/4	
Antidorcas bondi				8/3	3/2	
Antidorcas sp.				4/*		
Oreotragus oreotragus	1/1		1/1	14/5		
Raphicerus campestris	13/3	2/1		13/4		
Raphicerus sp.			1/1			
Oreotragus/Raphicerus				3/1		
Pelea capreolus	30/6	1/1	3/1	24/6		
Hippotragus cf. equinus			2/1			
Hippotragus cf. leucophaeus				4/3	1/1	
Tragelaphus strepsiceros				2/1		
Taurotragus oryx	30/7	2/2	8/3	53/10	3/2	
Redunca fulvorufula	14/4	8/1	5/1	3/1	2/1	
Pelea/Redunca	2/*					
Bovidae sp. indet. (small)	72/4	10/1	40/1	81/2		
Bovidae sp. indet. (medium)	452/3	53/*	78/*	208/3	17/1	2/1
Bovidae sp. indet. (large)	343/2	31/*	29/*	111/3	27/1	
Bovidae sp. indet. (very large)	13/*			5/*	2/*	
Xerus inauris	14/4					
Pedetes capensis	11/4			8/6	1/1	
Hystrix africaeaustralis	11/4		2/1	9/4		
Rodentia gen. et sp. indet.	1/1		1/1			
Lepus saxatilis	11/2					
Lepus cf. saxatilis	14/2			1/1		
Lepus sp.	39/1		1/1	4/2		

FIGURE 149 FAUNAL SPECIES LIST FOR ROSE COTTAGE CAVE. Species lists for archaeological sites follow particular conventions. In this example, the formal taxonomic name for each animal is given, followed by the NISP and MNI estimates for the assemblage from each archaeological unit.

Coastlines

Faunal studies in archaeology can take a wide variety of forms, depending on local contexts and on the categories of animal species found in local habitats. One of the more specialised sub-fields is to be found in the archaeology of coast-lines. In the words of Geoff Bailey and John Parkington,

'[coastlines] are a classic illustration of the ecological concept of an ecotone: a boundary zone at the junction of two major ecosystems, which combines some of the characteristics of each, as well as developing unique characteristics of its own which are a product of the zone of overlap. Some of the advantages of the coastal ecotone for human subsistence are: variety of marine and terrestrial resources within a limited geographical area; a suite of organisms unique to the intertidal zone of the coast edge, including molluscs, crustaceans and edible sea-weeds; potential abundance and concentration of food supplies in the case of some of the marine resources; and more productive conditions for terrestrial plants and animals because of high water tables, more equable climatic conditions or forest-edge effects. To these may be added the natural bounties of the sea shore, such as stranded sea mammals and sea birds beached by storms, breeding activity or other

Figure 150 COLLECTING SHELLFISH. Coastlines are often rich resource areas which have been used by human communities for many thousands of years.

factors' (Bailey & Parkington 1988).

Archaeological sites excavated in such areas usually have a diversity of faunal evidence, including fish bones, bird bones and shellfish. Each category of food animal requires specialist study, although the general principles are the same. This is well illustrated by sites in the Eland's Bay area of the Cape west coast, a region which has become something of a laboratory for detailed ecological studies of coastal habitats.

The most conspicuous sites in the Eland's Bay landscape are shell middens – large heaps of food waste that have often built up over many centuries (Figure 151). Some of these middens are in rock shelters, while others are in the open, close to the shoreline. Because shell-fish tend to be clustered on reefs, people came back to the same places over and over again. As a result accumulations of shell developed, some of them spectacularly large. In common with much of southern Africa's coastline, Eland's Bay has many middens, although increasingly these important sites are being damaged or destroyed by modern coastal development.

Shellfish vary in their distribution across the intertidal zone, which affects the returns gained by shellfish collectors in relation to effort. Shell-fish also vary in their nutritional value. By identifying and measuring samples of shell waste from middens, faunal specialists can reconstruct this aspect of early diets.

At Eland's Bay, analysis of shell-midden samples has revealed changes in diet that came about through time and changes that depended on the precise location of the midden site. Changes in diet that came about through time have been interpreted as a consequence of the shifting position of the shoreline, which moved as the sea-level altered. Naturally, intertidal food resources are very sensitive to such changes. On the other hand, differences between samples from middens on the coastline and in rock shelters have been interpreted as reflecting the food-collecting strategies of hunter–gatherer communities. When people intended to eat shellfish close to the point of collection, they gathered whatever food they could. But when they intended to carry food back to an inland rock shelter, they were more selective, collecting mostly mussels, which have

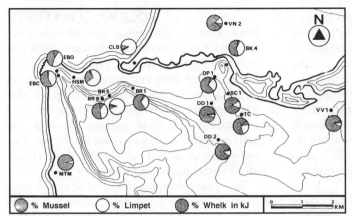

FIGURE 151 SPECIES COMPOSITION OF SHELL MIDDENS AT ELAND'S BAY. Each midden is made up of a variety of shellfish species. Proportions of the dominant species vary according to site location.

a higher yield of edible meat. The result of these temporal and spatial variations is seen in the complexity and variability in shell-midden composition.

'The locations and sizes of coastal camps have changed substantially through the Holocene. We can show that between about 4400 and 3000 years ago people chose to occupy rock-shelters such as Eland's Bay Cave and Tortoise Cave, where they left moderate-sized volumes of shell debris ... Soon after 3000 years ago both of these caves show minimal occupation and preferred sites were open situations located right next to productive intertidal rocks ... After 1800 years ago the large open middens were apparently abandoned as living sites and settlement shifted back into caves and rock-shelters, although many very small open middens accumulated at this time ... Almost certainly related to this is a notable change in midden contents. Deposits between 4400 and 3000 bp in the caves and those at the large sites dated between 3000 and 1800 bp ... consist almost entirely of mussels, with very few limpets and small numbers of other marine resources. By contrast, sites which post-date 1800 may be limpet-dominated if they lie near to sheltered shorelines, or have about equal proportions of limpets and mussels. The numbers of marine birds, fish and rock lobster remains in these later sites are also much higher. We have the distinct impression that the later populations were far more extensively exploiting the range of marine foods than were their immediate predecessors' (Parkington et al. 1988: 27).

Not surprisingly, coastal assemblages may also include large numbers of fish bones. Cedric Poggenpoel has worked with a number of such collections from the Eland's Bay sites, and again there is evidence for variability in diet both through time and as a consequence of the position of a particular site in the landscape (Poggenpoel 1987). For example, at Eland's Bay Cave (which has the most substantial of the rock-shelter deposits in the area), Poggenpoel found that 13 species of fish had been eaten consistently over the last 15 000 years. Tortoise Cave, a smaller shelter looking out over the Verlorenvlei lagoon, had a fish assemblage of more than 45 000 fish bones, some 800 of which were identifiable. Here, 9 marine species of fish were important. Diepkloof Cave, which is further up Verlorenvlei and some 18 km from the present-day shoreline, yielded a far smaller collection of fish bones, with only 2 species predominating. As with the shellfish fauna, the consumption of fish clearly reflects the position of the site. The changing environment also critically affected the food that was available. But in this case there may have been the additional complication of changing techniques in catching fish, as people moved from lines to a greater reliance on tidal fish-traps. As with all forms of faunal analysis, the interpretation of patterning in assemblage diversity and abundance needs to be highly nuanced.

'Fish bones can probably tell us much about changing techniques of catching fish, about the kinds of places in which people chose to fish and about the changing conditions of the water bodies in which people caught fish ... Several characteristics of the faunal assemblages are used. Initial sorting of the bone establishes the range of species present from level to level as well as the body parts represented. The kinds of fish as well as the number of species inform us about the conditions in the lower reaches of the river. Measurements of certain body parts, particularly ... help to identify the size of the fish caught, and in some cases to differentiate between similar species. These data, along with modern observations of the distribution, behaviour and habitat preferences of fish, allow us to reconstruct the history of the Verlorenvlei' (Poggenpoel 1987: 212).

Bird bones also form part of coastal faunal assemblages. Again, the baseline for interpreting these collections is a detailed knowledge of species ecology, including information about habitat preferences, diet and breeding behaviour. Graham Avery has added to this ornithological information by building up a database of birds regularly beached along the Cape west coast. Each month, a team walked sample stretches of beach, recording carcasses that would have been available as food resources to Late Stone Age communities.

Avery's research has shown that the mortality of various common bird species varies according to season. For example, at Eland's Bay 84 per cent of all beached sea birds recorded during the sample year were found between October and April. During this part of the spring and summer, sea birds would have provided a regular source of food.

The results of Avery's beach survey, supplemented by the conventional use of comparative collections in museums, have helped us to interpret the bird faunas from archaeological sites. Avery found that at Eland's Bay Cave the assemblage was dominated by Cape cormorants, with Jackass penguins, Whitebreasted cormorants and Cape gannets next in importance. Most of the birds were probably scavenged along the coast, although some of the cormorants (which can roost on the shore in large flocks) may have been stalked and killed with sticks or clubs. In all respects the Eland's Bay collections show the complex ways in which humans interacted with the changing coastal environment (G. Avery 1987).

Bone chemistry

Bones from archaeological sites give information about past foodways, indicating which animals were eaten, revealing preferences for different cuts of meat and providing estimates of meat yields. Recently it has been shown that past diets can also be indicated by the chemical composition of bone samples, through the archaeometric analysis of isotope ratios. This technique, described in Chapter 4, is closely allied to techniques of radiometric dating.

In a paper mapping out ways of establishing diets through isotopic analysis, Stanley Ambrose and Michael DeNiro have noted that several major classes of food can be distinguished by their isotopic composition (Ambrose & DeNiro 1986). This is because characteristic ratios between carbon isotopes are established during plant photosynthesis – the so-called C_3, C_4 and CAM pathways. Domestic crops grown in Africa by Iron Age farmers – maize, sorghum and different species of millet – have C_4 pathways, but other common foods – such as rice, nuts and most vegetables and fruits – are C_3 plants. On the same principle, terrestrial and marine plants can be distinguished from one another by their nitrogen isotope ratios. The isotopic composition of animal tissue reflects

FIGURE 152 C_3 AND C_4 PLANT FOODS.

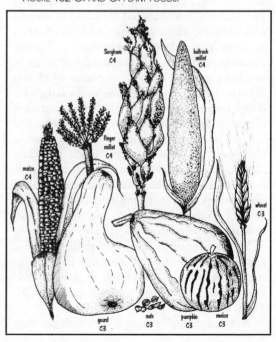

the carbon and nitrogen isotopic ratios of the plants at the base of their food chains. 'Given these basic differences in the isotopic composition of food resources, it should be possible to use $\delta^{13}C$ and $\delta^{15}N$ values to distinguish between human populations relying mainly on animal products as opposed to plant foods, the meat of grazing animals as opposed to that of browsing animals, or C_3 as opposed to C_4 plants' (Ambrose & DeNiro 1986).

Ambrose and DeNiro analysed tissue samples from 10 species of carnivores, 13 species of grazing animals and 18 species of browsing animals in Kenya and Tanzania, and found that the isotopic 'signature' of food was indeed evident in the tissue. They then went on to analyse human bone samples from museum collections in eastern and southern Africa, comparing $\delta^{13}C$ and $\delta^{15}N$ values with ethnographic information about diet. The results were encouraging:

'The agreement between the isotopic composition of bone collagen from the populations analysed and their diets as inferred from ethnographic and archaeological evidence is remarkably close in almost every case. Those groups depending largely on the milk, meat and blood of domestic animals have the highest $\delta^{15}N$ values, while those that subsist mainly on plants have the lowest ones. Groups subsisting mainly on C_4 plants or the protein of grazing herbivores have higher $\delta^{13}C$ values than those depending on a mix of C_3 and C_4 plants and grazing and browsing animals' (Ambrose & DeNiro 1986: 322).

The results of this study suggested that it is possible to use stable isotope ratios to deduce diets from archaeological samples where no ethnographic evidence is available to aid the interpretation. Subsequent research has shown that this is indeed the case.

The old slave woman of Vergelegen

Despite the numbers of slaves who lived and worked at the Cape – at the end of Dutch rule the majority of Cape Town's population was enslaved – we know relatively little about their everyday lives. In particular, information about slave diets would help in understanding this central aspect of the Cape's history. Through study of the skeleton found at the eighteenth-century site of Vergelegen (see Chapter 4) we can make inferences about some aspects of slave diet and about this particular slave's state of health.

'The general long-term health of the woman from Vergelegen appears to have been good. Her teeth are remarkable in that there is no tooth decay at all. All teeth are present in their sockets and the wear is moderate but not yet heavy ... The general good health of the skeleton is negated by the presence of extensive osteoarthritis throughout the body and particularly in the vertebral column ... This woman, therefore, suffered severely from arthritis, especially in her hands and her back. The damage to the vertebral column is so severe as to indicate a substantial degree of disability towards the end of her life' (Sealy et al. 1993: 85–6).

Additional information has come from the chemical analysis of bone samples taken from the skeleton:

'Body tissues, including bones, are manufactured from the foods that people eat. Complex metabolic reactions ensure that the chemical composition of bone, muscle etc. remains approximately constant, in order for these tissues to fulfil their functions. There may be minor variations in the elemental constituents of tissues, or in their isotopic composition, which are of no functional consequence. Such variations can sometimes be attributed to particular foods or categories of foods in the diet. Thus the chemical composition of bone reflects the composition of foods eaten in life, providing a valuable means of reconstructing aspects of the lifestyles even of long-dead individuals' (Sealy et al. 1993: 86).

Bone is living tissue which continues to be replaced: a person's skeleton contains at any one time a mix of bone laid down at particular stages in life, and different bones have various rates of tissue replacement. Of the parts of the skeleton, ribs have a high rate of tissue turnover. In contrast, teeth form in childhood, and tooth enamel is not renewed once it has formed. Therefore, however old people may be, the composition of their tooth enamel reflects the conditions of their childhood.

This difference between the ways in which bones and teeth are formed can be used to compare the childhood diet of a person with the sort of foods they ate as an adult, even if the person has long been dead and all that remain are the fragments of a skeleton.

The basis of this sort of study is the isotopic analysis of bone samples; in particular the proportions of carbon-13 (written $\delta^{13}C$) and nitrogen-15 (written $\delta^{15}N$) in a bone's protein residue (known as 'collagen'). It has been established that people who eat a lot of seafood, such as Alaskan Eskimos (or Inuit), have bone collagen with enriched $\delta^{13}C$ and very high $\delta^{15}N$. In contrast, farmers who for the most part eat cereals, such as maize, have bone collagen with very enriched $\delta^{13}C$ and low $\delta^{15}N$.

The results of the Vergelegen study were particularly interesting because the chemistry of the tooth samples (formed in childhood) was different from the chemistry of the rib samples (formed in the last few years of the woman's life). The nitrogen isotope readings for the tooth samples were much lower than the estimates for the bone samples:

'The Vergelegen woman's teeth have relatively positive $\delta^{13}C$ and low $\delta^{15}N$. This pattern is likely to result from childhood consumption of foods derived from tropical C_4 plants, rather than seafood. By contrast, her femur and rib show slightly more positive $\delta^{13}C$ values, but markedly increased $\delta^{15}N$. She ate much more food of marine origin in adulthood than she had done as a child' (Sealy et al. 1993: 88).

The results of the chemical analysis of the bone samples fit in well with the documentary sources that are available. These indicate that slaves received substantial quantities of fish. But the chemistry of the woman's teeth suggests that captivity on a Western Cape farm had not always been her life, and that as a child she had lived in a tropical or semitropical area where she had had a very different diet, probably dominated by maize.

Foodways of the Fish River

Understanding past foodways is more than the sum of individual specialist analyses, however sophisticated these may be. The most challenging task, as in all other aspects of archaeology, remains that of writing history – of putting together all the various fragments of evidence into a coherent interpretation of the way in which people lived in the past.

This art of synthesis is well illustrated by the example of research in the catchment of the Fish River – a rugged and mountainous area east of Grahamstown – and on the coastal plateau to the south (Figure 153). This part of southern Africa has long been a frontier region, firstly between pastoralists, hunter–gatherers and mixed farmers cultivating fields at the margins of the summer rainfall region, and later between indigenous communities and burgeoning European colonial expansion. A rich archaeology extends the history provided by documentary sources and oral traditions (S. Hall 1990).

In designing a research project to investigate the archaeology of the Fish River and its hin-

FIGURE 153 THE FISH RIVER AREA IN THE EASTERN CAPE, SOUTH AFRICA.

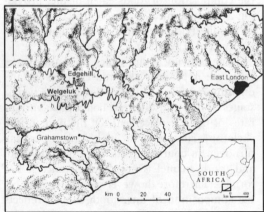

FIGURE 154 THE KOONAP RIVER VALLEY.

terland, Simon Hall started by collecting together all the available ecological evidence. He established that there are a number of different ways in which the land could have been used by human communities, but that these were all likely to have been structured by the varying quality of pasturage – the veld conditions which decisively affect the quality of graze and browse for wild animals, as well as the manner in which pastoralists can keep domestic livestock. The higher land, lying above 1000 m in the Winterberg range, is cloaked by sourveld. Here the main pasture grass for wild animals and livestock alike – *Themeda triandra* – is palatable in the spring but of little or no value to animals at other times of the year. 'The high carrying capacity of the Winterberg sourveld is limited only to the summer growing season, and any traditional free-range pastoralist groups would have had to move elsewhere once the growing season ended because, no matter what bulk of graze is available, stock will lose condition rapidly and die' (S. Hall 1986: 42).

In late summer, wild animals would have migrated down to the lower-lying Koonap and Fish River valleys. Such a pattern of land use was probably adopted by some pastoralists as well. In these sweetveld regions grasses retain their nutritional qualities for longer periods of time. The carrying capacity of the sweetveld is less, however, than that of the sourveld in spring months. Alternatively, some pastoralists may have kept livestock in the sweetveld areas for the whole year, although this would have required careful management of grassland resources.

Away from the mountains, the higher rainfall of the coastal plateau has resulted in leached soils and, as in the high Winterberg, grasses are good only in the spring months. But these coastlands are also cut by deep river valleys which shelter better patches of grazing. Here too, with good veld management, pastoralists could have taken good advantage of the varied possibilities for using the land.

Thorough ecological assessment such as this allows the researcher to assess the possibilities of different archaeological sites before the time-consuming processes of excavation and analysis begin. Because Hall was interested in the past economy of his study area, and the way this had changed through time, he used his ecological model of possible land use to choose where to dig. He reasoned that sites close to the borders of separate ecological zones – living sites where people could have taken advantage of the maximum range of possibilities in getting food – would have the most informative assemblages preserved within them. Thus he focused his attention on the Koonap valley and the two rock shelters of Edgehill and Welgeluk.

Both sites proved to have rich stratified deposits, and provided a good record of the human communities who lived here through the past 5000 years. The key theme in Hall's interpretation of the evidence from his excavations was economic intensification: the tendency of hunter–gatherers to move from wide-ranging social and economic systems to more restricted networks, making use of smaller regions. Hall has argued that this transition – essentially the same pathway that led to plant and animal domestication in other parts of Africa – was marked by an increasing reliance on resources available all the year round in the immediate river valley, rather than on animals that migrate across the full range of the veld seasonally or on plants that are only seasonally available. In all this, people were coming to identify more with 'place' – a change in attitude that was marked out in artefact use as well as food debris (S. Hall 1990).

Edgehill is an east-facing rock shelter about 600 m above the Koonap River. Hall laid out a four-metre-square grid against the back wall of the shelter, and in from the drip line, reasoning that this was the part of the overhang where people would most probably have chosen to live. Excavation was in 5 cm spits through the first metre of undifferentiated, grey ashy soil. Beneath this, and down to a depth of about 1.7 m, the excavators were able to follow natural layers – ashy soils varying between grey and red coloration. Later, the assemblages from these spits and layers were aggregated into eight units on the basis of the overall stratigraphy of the site. Radiocarbon dates ranged from 5500 ± 70 BP (Pta-3581) for the lowermost Unit 8 to 1830 ± 60 BP (Pta-3564) for Unit 1.

Welgeluk is on the northern bank of the Koonap River, about 7 km downstream from Edgehill. This shelter faces southeast, and is

FIGURE 155 EXCAVATIONS AT WELGELUK. At this stage in the excavations, the deposits in the pit had been removed, and the burial cairn had just begun to be visible as a dark stain at the base of the trench.

only about 10 m above the level of the river. Excavations were in the southern part of the shelter, so placed to avoid large blocks of sandstone that had fallen from the roof. Some 3 m² of deposit were excavated to a maximum depth of 2.2 m. In contrast with Edgehill Shelter, excavation could follow a natural stratigraphy, and a total of 128 separate horizons were eventually grouped into four major units for interpretation. The lowermost unit was a burial of at least six people under a cairn of river slabs (Figures 156 and 157). The radiocarbon date for the first available charcoal sample, a little above the burial complex, was 4560 ± 70 BP (Pta-3947), and the date for Unit 1 was 510 ± 50 BP (Pta-3934).

Hall supplemented his excavations at Edgehill and Welgeluk with a close survey of their

hinterland, mapping all archaeological traces. 'Eleven other rock shelters in the region of Edgehill and Welgeluk show some traces of occupation either in the form of deposit or rock paintings. These all cluster along the riverine fringe. While geologically the immediate river banks are the most likely places at which shelters will form and survive, three other shelters located up to 5 km from a perennial water course showed no evidence of LSA occupation. The conclusion is obvious. When LSA hunter–gatherers scheduled visits to the area the main settlement focus was orientated along the river bank. Specialist trips away from the banks would have been undertaken, but predictable water and riverine resources would have focused "permanent" camps close to the river' (S. Hall 1990: 79).

Both excavated sites had rich faunal assemblages. These provide the key to connecting the history of human use of the land with modern-day ecological evidence. The people who had lived at Edgehill and Welgeluk hunted browsing antelope such as grysbok and steenbok, and also ate bushpig and buffalo. They collected ostrich eggs and relatively large numbers of tortoises and freshwater turtles, as well as freshwater mussels, fish and crabs. The frequency of these riverine species increased from the oldest to the younger archaeological horizons, which shows that, from about 4000 years ago, hunter–gatherers began to concentrate more on the resources of the Koonap valley than on those of the wider region in which they were living.

The remains of plant foods were poorly preserved at Edgehill. But luckily, the excavators were able to recover a good assemblage from

FIGURE 156 THE BURIAL COMPLEX AT WELGELUK.

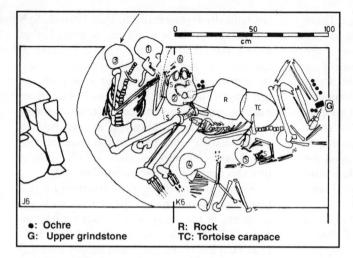

FIGURE 157 PLAN OF THE WELGELUK BURIALS. A series of interments have been super-imposed on one another, creating a complex problem for excavation. The flexed position of the skeleton is characteristic of the Late Stone Age.

●: Ochre
G: Upper grindstone
R: Rock
TC: Tortoise carapace

Welgeluk. This included parts of the corms from a geophyte, possibly *Moraea polystachya.* Commonly known as *bloutulp,* this species has toxic leaves but a corm that may be edible. There were also remains of storage plants belonging to the Dioscoreaceae family – tubers that could be cut into strips and roasted. Seeds and fruits included *Pappea capensis,* which is a rich source of oil, possibly serving medicinal or ritual purposes.

In interpreting foodways in a study such as this, Hall found it necessary to integrate the artefactual evidence with the information gained from food residues. To this end he used Janette Deacon's typological system for the southern African Late Stone Age (described in Chapter 9). Both sites had substantial lithic assemblages – more than 43 000 stone tools were excavated from Edgehill. At both sites, over 95 per cent of the stone was classified as waste, the remainder being formally retouched tools. Other artefacts included worked bone (mostly points), shell ornaments, pottery, and one or two pieces of leather and iron in the uppermost layers.

An important aspect of the stone-tool technology used in the valley was the raw material. Quartz and sandstone were readily available in the area, as was the dense, highly metamorphosed shale known as hornfels. But one important raw material – silcrete – could only be obtained 40 km to the south of the sites. Therefore the frequency of the use of silcrete in making stone tools could be taken as a measure of the range of interaction of hunter–gatherer

groups in the past.

Study of the artefact assemblages showed that between about 5000 and 6000 years ago people living at Edgehill and Welgeluk changed from using hornfels for most of their implements to a greater reliance on silcrete (a pattern that has been noted at other sites in the Eastern Cape as well). Why did this happen? Hall rules out purely functional reasons, suggesting instead that hunter–gatherer groups were establishing more tight spheres of social interaction. This was part of the same process of closing in that saw them concentrate on locally available riverine sources of food:

'The active manipulation of raw material as an expression of social identity is a symptom of an ever-spiralling relationship between population, space and competition for that space, and the resources it contains. Clear and unambiguous methods of signalling identity and, therefore, rights of access and rights of denial, were required' (S. Hall 1990: 179).

This social and economic change is reflected in other aspects of the archaeological record. In particular, burials can be seen as symbolic activities which relate people to places in special ways: they are ritual ways of passing on rights from generation to generation. 'Burial and its associated ritual is not a self-contained and isolated sub-system of hunter–gatherer life. It reflects, relates to and is inseparably linked with social and economic process' (S. Hall 1990: 233).

The Welgeluk burials were of at least six people covered by a stone cairn and dated to between about 6000 and 4500 years ago. There had been two or three burial episodes, and care had been taken in the selection of slabs for the cairn. The graves contained the remains of an adult male, probably about 65 years old; a second, similarly aged man, buried with lumps of ochre and a cache of silcrete flakes and cores; a 30-year-old of indeterminate sex, with no grave goods; two infant burials, one with a string of ochre-stained ostrich-eggshell beads around the waist, and the other with a shell necklace; and part of the skeleton of a juvenile, buried with some marine shells and a warthog tusk.

Similar burials have often been found in other rock shelters in the southern and eastern Cape. For example, at Matjes River Shelter (on the coast), more than 100 burials are known to have been exhumed by grave robbers (S. Hall & Binneman 1987). The association of one of the Welgeluk burials with silcrete underlines the importance of raw material as a stylistic marker of territory (S. Hall 1990). Comparison with burial practices in other parts of the world, including Australia, the Near East and California, has suggested that cave burial indicates 'exclusive' social identity – part of the way in which social identity is maintained and established in the face of competition. Hall argues that the ritual elaboration of infant burials was perhaps part of 'an idealized future picture, in which a range of denied social obligations is symbolically represented' (S. Hall 1990: 238).

Apart from the wild species of animals that were hunted and collected by people living in the Koonap, the uppermost layers of the two rock shelters have evidence for a new way of life: pastoralism. The faunal assemblage from Edgehill included bones from at least one sheep; the collection from Welgeluk, at least two. In common with other parts of the wider region, pastoralist communities were clearly moving into this area in the first millennium AD.

An additional source of information for this crucial economic change comes from rock art. Paintings in the study area include representations of both cattle and fat-tailed sheep. However, Hall has noted that these images have differing patterns of distribution: images of sheep are found predominantly in rock shelters in the coastal area, while paintings of cattle are found only in the mountainous areas of the Winterberg.

'It is proposed that the discrete distributions of cattle and sheep images represent progressive stages in the geographical displacement and/or assimilation of foragers from the coastal regions by pastoralists and agropastoralists. The occurrence of sheep paintings in the coastal areas may represent a first stage in this process and suggests that at this early time of contact, the landscape was still being shared by pastoralists and foragers ... The second, later

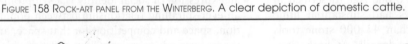

FIGURE 158 ROCK-ART PANEL FROM THE WINTERBERG. A clear depiction of domestic cattle.

182

phase in this progression is represented by the discrete distributions of cattle paintings within the pastorally more inaccessible escarpment area, and this may demonstrate regional displacement and confinement of foragers to this area' (S. Hall 1986: 44).

Both excavated sites, particularly Welgeluk, have pottery assemblages that span the possible period of interaction between hunter–gatherers and pastoralists. Because they lie within the sweetveld and have water available throughout the year, it is likely that these places were visited regularly by pastoralist groups. There would have been a sustained, complex history of interaction (S. Hall 1986). This 'frontier pattern' continued into the period recorded in historical documents. From the late seventeenth century onwards, European travellers described a complicated economic and social situation: pastoralists (called Gonaqua), Xhosa farmers, colonial settlers and Bushman hunter–gatherers all lived in the region. In time, hunter–gatherers were pushed out into the more rugged parts of the landscape, areas that were of little use for farming or livestock herding. European colonial contact thus came towards the end of a long period of assimilation during which, though there had been conflict, there had also been the merger of pastoralists, farmers and hunter–gatherers (Peires 1981). There are records of the exchange of cattle, corn and dagga for the rain-making prowess of the Bushmen. 'These historical records of barter transactions, especially between foragers and agropastoralists, provide a basis for the interpretation of some of the changes visible in the archaeological record of the contact period, and may also have influenced the incorporation of cattle into Bushman rock art' (S. Hall 1986: 42).

Simon Hall's work in this part of the Fish River catchment demonstrates the full complexity of economic interpretation. In his study he has woven together diverse sources of information that include

• site sampling (inferring the history of a large study area from site surveys)
• the use of ecological and environmental evidence from climate, grassland productivity and the distribution of raw material resources
• the evidence of rock paintings
• ethnographic and historical sources
• stratigraphic excavation and radiocarbon dating
• faunal analysis, plant studies and human skeletal material.

Networks

Archaeological 'places', then, are locations where regular patterns of human behaviour have resulted in assemblages of artefacts and food debris. This, the archaeological record, is partly the consequence of the everyday quest for the basic necessities of life such as food and shelter. But it has also been formed from social interactions – for example – by the long-term interplay of herders, farmers and hunter–gatherers in the Fish River frontier zone (Chapter 10), or by the interaction of different communities in the Orange River area (Chapter 8) of South Africa.

Social archaeology

An area of study sometimes labelled 'social archaeology', and regarded as a separate specialism, investigates these social interactions. Certainly, looking for the evidence of social relationships in archaeology may involve char-

FIGURE 159 MAKING ARTEFACTS SPEAK: STONE TOOLS. One of the challenges for social archaeology is deducing the forms of interaction between early people from the sparse traces they have left behind.

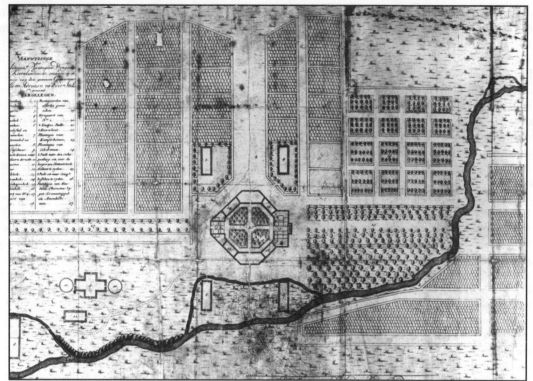

FIGURE 160 MAKING ARTEFACTS SPEAK: VERGELEGEN. Complex human landscapes are artefacts that have the potential to tell us about the relationships between people who lived there, supplementing documentary evidence in important ways. This early-eighteenth-century plan of a slave estate in the Cape countryside reveals the strong sense of order in the mind of the man who conceived the layout, and the emphasis on difference between slave and master. The slave lodge where 'Flora' was buried (Chapters 4 and 10) is the rectangular outbuilding above and to the right of the octagonal manor-house garden.

acteristic methods and arguments. But to separate 'social' archaeology from 'functional' studies of technology, foodways or the environment is to set up a false dichotomy. It is a part of the definition of humanity that people learn social behaviour. Therefore all archaeology is social archaeology in one way or another.

One of the problems in studying the relations between people in the past is obvious, quite simply stated, but nevertheless fundamental: we cannot see such relationships. Just as the set of rules that defines a technological process, or the preferences and decisions that give shape to foodways, cannot be known from direct observation, so social relationships cannot be seen directly in the archaeological record. What we have are rather the consequences of these relationships – the material culture, varying in scale from a single artefact to a whole landscape, that has resulted from people forming networks.

Whereas a social anthropologist or sociologist would carry out fieldwork with a tape recorder and a camera, interviewing people and building up an understanding from their own testimony of the network that interconnects them, the archaeologist must rely on the implications of those artefacts left behind: 'making silent stones speak', to use the felicitous title of Kathy Schick and Nicholas Toth's book (Schick & Toth 1993).

Because of this basic characteristic of most of their evidence, it is particularly important that archaeologists fully understand the relationship between material culture and social behaviour in present-day circumstances (or from situations where the perspectives and intentions of artefact makers and users themselves are well recorded). Studies of these relationships are described as 'ethnoarchaeology'. Ethnoarchaeology is really another variant of uniformitarianism – the founding principle of archaeology as a discipline – advancing the proposition that the formation processes of the past are to be found in the formation processes of the present day. Ethnoarchaeology is closely linked to experimental archaeology. And ethnoarchaeology shares with uniformitarianism and experimental archaeology the danger of imposing sophisticated, contemporary interpretations on an archaeological record which is often fragmentary and malleable: making silent stones say only what it is we want to hear.

> One of the most difficult tasks in archaeology is the interpretation of material culture in terms of human behaviour. How were pots used in the past? Why are houses and other buildings constructed to different designs? Here, archaeology has a lot to gain from the methods of ethnography. Archaeologists have developed a specialised field of study known as *ethnoarchaeology*. Like ethnographers, they may live among contemporary communities. Such studies have the particular purpose of understanding how material culture is used.

In reviewing ethnoarchaeology in Africa, Kofi Agorsah has highlighted some of its problems. He has pointed out that ethnoarchaeological research has tended to concentrate heavily on hunter–gatherer communities, and that many interpretations have assumed that a simple analogy between the better-known present and the imperfectly known past is an appropriate path to explaining the archaeological record. 'Many scholars who do ethnographic research and are able to make even the most tenuous link between their material and archaeology have enjoyed the liberty of claiming that they are doing ethnoarchaeology' (Agorsah 1990: 192). Agorsah suggests that more sophisticated approaches need to be developed, and that ethnoarchaeology has to move away from its obsession with 'traditional' societies and look at a far wider range of modern-day circumstances in which the dynamics of interactions involving material culture can be directly observed.

> 'Ethnoarchaeology is carried out in industrial societies like our own and in non-industrial communities such as those of !Kung Bushmen and Kalinga villagers. Archaeologists who excavate can record events only in terms of their material traces. Ethnoarchaeologists document events from two perspectives: the artifacts involved, and associated behaviors and beliefs. These two perspectives are essential, in that they are the source of many of the principles used by archaeologists, who dig to infer past behaviors and beliefs from material traces' (Rathje & Schiffer 1982).

Ethnoarchaeology: unravelling culture

One of the most common working assumptions that archaeologists make is that 'cultures' or 'traditions' – geographical areas with recurring associations of similar artefacts – are somehow equivalent to social units such as 'tribes' or 'chiefdoms' (M. Hall 1984b). This concept became popular in European and North American archaeology in the first part of the nineteenth century. It was a useful way of building up interpretations beyond the bare frameworks of assemblages of potsherds or stone tools. Spread out across a laboratory table, a collection of broken pottery does not seem to say much about the lives of the people who once made or used the clay vessels. But by thinking of their makers as people having unambiguous social connections with other people who made similar pottery, an archaeologist can get some sense of history.

All good research is based on assumptions such as these. Without them, it would be impossible to develop stimulating ideas for future study. But assumptions must also be teased apart, shaken up and continually tested: after all, they are useful guesses rather than established sets of facts.

The assumption that an archaeological culture is the equivalent of a 'people' has often gone unchallenged in African archaeology. Authors of general studies of the continent like to offer maps with broad, sweeping arrows indicating the movement of pottery styles, writing as if pots had legs and made their own way through the countryside. There have been relatively few studies of what people meant to do when they made something similar to, or different from, other people.

Ethnoarchaeology is the key to testing assumptions such as these. It is only by questioning craftsmen and women working today that the archaeologist can offer new viewpoints about what assemblages from the past may mean.

One important ethnoarchaeological study, which has wide-ranging implications for archaeological interpretations, was carried out by Ian Hodder in the late 1970s (Hodder 1982). Hodder visited communities in the Nuba Mountains of Sudan, in the Baringo District of north-central Kenya, on Kenya's Leroghi Plateau and on Zambia's Zambezi floodplain. He was interested in testing two common assumptions.

The first is that archaeological collections – 'material cultures' – are simple indicators of the degrees of interaction between groups of people in the past. In other words, when artefacts such as decorated pottery are similar in an identifiable geographic region through a specific period of time, it is assumed this shows that groups of people had a lot to do with one another. Likewise, differences between contemporary and geographically adjacent 'material cultures' are taken as indicating that their makers lived separate lives.

Hodder's second question was whether the form of artefacts (what is commonly referred to as 'style') simply 'reflects' some sort of ethnicity. Many archaeologists write as if people made things in traditional ways almost without thinking – as part of their subconscious identification with their group. Hodder wanted to find out if this really is the case.

The results from one of Hodder's study areas can serve to illustrate the complex and stimulating conclusions that he drew. The area south of Kenya's Lake Baringo is home to three tribes: the Tugen (who have a mixed pastoral and agricultural economy), the Pokot (who are pastoralists) and the Njemps (pastoralists who practise some agriculture). All three tribes are characterised by a lack of central authority, by dispersed clans and a system of age sets that identifies people over wide areas as social equals (Figure 161).

Hodder visited more than 400 compounds in the Njemps area and on the fringes of the Tugen and Pokot tribes. He recorded the outlines of the life histories of more than 500 adults and also measured pots, basket work, wooden containers, stools, spears and shields, recording who made them and where they were acquired. He also recorded details of personal adornment. The result was a comprehensive ethnography for the region, collected in such a way that it could be used to address archaeologists' questions about the meanings and uses of 'material culture'.

The results were unambiguous. Tribal borders were clearly marked by changes in styles of dress and household possessions. For example, the boundary between the Tugen and the Njemps was demarcated by differences in ear

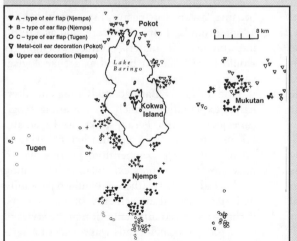

Legend:
▼ A – type of ear flap (Njemps)
+ B – type of ear flap (Njemps)
○ C – type of ear flap (Tugen)
▽ Metal-coil ear decoration (Pokot)
● Upper ear decoration (Njemps)

Pokot
Lake Baringo
Kokwa Island
Mukutan
Tugen
Njemps

0 8 km

FIGURE 161 KENYA'S LAKE BARINGO AREA. The map shows the distribution of different styles of ear ornamentation, and their clear coincidence with different ethnic groups.

FIGURE 162 NJEMPS EAR DECORATION. This woman's distinctive clothing marks her ethnic identity.

decoration, basket drinking-cups, wooden eating-bowls and shield types.

However, Hodder found that this did not confirm the standard archaeological assumption that differences in material culture reflect a lack of contact between separate social units. As marked as the differences between the possessions of the Tugen and the Njemps was the frequency of movement between these tribes. Cross-border marriages were common, and most people living near the boundaries of their tribal areas had relatives by marriage in the neighbouring tribe. Also, most men had 'cattle friends' in other tribes – a system of spreading the usual risk to herds and flocks by leaving cattle and goats in the care of allies. Hodder also learnt that whole families could change tribes after negotiations with the elders. Such families usually changed their dress and possessions completely, becoming indistinguishable from other members of their new community. In other words, the Lake Baringo ethnography proved to follow patterns precisely inverse to those predicted by the standard archaeological model.

Hodder found that the reason for this situation was the intense and long-standing economic competition between tribes. For years, there had been extensive raiding of cattle and goats. Protection and retaliation were in the hands of the *moran*, the young, unmarried men of the tribe. As a member of a tribe, a person qualified for the protection of his or her *moran*. Consequently, clear tribal identity was crucial in everyday life. One woman explained that she could be attacked as a foreigner in Njemps land if she were travelling there dressed as a Pokot. A Tugen woman said she had been told by an elder to dress distinctively so that she could be identified as a friend in times of fighting. In other words, material culture was far from being a passive 'reflection' of identity: people used and manipulated objects according to their needs and circumstances.

Of course, it is to be expected that ethnoarchaeological studies such as these will show up many purely archaeological assumptions as simplistic and naive. Most archaeologists do not have the benefit of living informants, oral histories or documents to test and flesh out their working assumptions. Ethnoarchaeologi-

cal studies can seem like discouraging 'cautionary tales' – conclusions that demonstrate how difficult archaeological interpretations can be, without offering solutions. Ethnoarchaeological work is more worthwhile if insights can be applied with benefit in various situations, leading to a more sophisticated understanding of the past.

Hodder's demonstration that a high level of economic interaction can make differences in material culture significant and essential has implications for interpretations in a wide range of archaeological contexts. Two examples illustrate the point.

Pastoralism was first adopted as a way of life in the Western Cape region of South Africa between 1800 and 1500 years ago. For many centuries, stock-keepers and hunter–gatherers lived in the same areas, sometimes in alliance and sometimes in conflict. Archaeologists studying assemblages from both rock-shelter and open sites in the region have noticed that well-established ways of making stone tools and shell beads were retained for longer, and changed more slowly, among hunter–gatherer groups living in the more mountainous regions. They have suggested that this is evidence for the retention, and intensification, of ways of making things that dated back to a time before the beginnings of pastoralism (Parkington & Manhire 1996).

This line of reasoning is clearly at variance with the old assumption that material culture passively reflects the degree of interaction between people. If this had been the case in the Western Cape, then hunter–gatherers, as they became aware of pastoralists, would have adopted similar material culture, and as a result indistinguishable material-culture assemblages would have been left behind as archaeological sites.

Hodder's Lake Baringo study offers an alternative explanation, which fits the archaeological evidence better. Perhaps, like the Tugen and Njemps, hunter–gatherers and herders were in intense economic competition: grazing would have upset the ecological balance in hunting lands, and hunter–gatherers would have inhibited the seasonal movements of pastoralists. Perhaps increased differentiation in the styles of stone tools and shell beads was a way of asserting identity at a time when identity had become significant.

A thousand or so years later, Dutch colonists arrived in the Western Cape, also with an intense interest in domestic livestock, which they needed to obtain by barter from indigenous pastoralists so that they could provision their ships. Hodder's Lake Baringo study sheds light on an event recorded with puzzlement in the official journal of the Dutch settlement at the Cape in September 1658. Krotoa was a pastoralist woman who had lived with the Dutch as an interpreter and been renamed by them as 'Eva':

'Towards evening they thanked us politely and gratefully in good Dutch words for the presents they had received. They then left. When Eva reached the matted hut of Doman, also known as Anthonij, outside the fort, she at once dressed herself in hides again and sent her clothes home. She intended to put them on again when she returned to the Commander's wife, promising, however, that she would in the meantime not forget the Lord God, whom she had come to know in the Commander's house ...' (Thom 1954: 343).

A second example is from Zululand. In the high grasslands above the Mfolozi River, the probable boundaries of chiefdoms in the late eighteenth century can be reconstructed from recorded oral traditions by means of Thiessen Polygons, a geographic method of working out the most logical use of the landscape. This study suggests that the territory of the chiefdom of kwaKhumalo coincided with the distribution of a distinctive group of archaeological sites. These, classified archaeologically as 'Type B'

settlements, had distinctive stone-built stock enclosures arranged in circular plans and clusters of mud and thatch houses around the perimeter of the village. They have been dated to the last few hundred years (too close to the present for accurate radiocarbon dates). It is a reasonable conclusion that they were built by the Khumalo. As there is no apparent environmental reason for the particular distribution of Type B stone enclosures, their use probably served to distinguish members of the Khumalo from the neighbouring Buthelezi chiefdom.

Archaeological excavations were carried out in middens attached to villages in both kwaKhumalo and kwaButhelezi. Nqabeni is a large Type B settlement with characteristic circular stone stockpens, and is one of the larger kwaKhumalo villages. Elangeni, like other villages in kwaButhelezi, had timber stockpens which have not survived the village's abandonment. Oral traditions indicate that this was one of the residences of Phungashe, a Buthelezi chief in the late eighteenth century. Both excavations produced the usual archaeological assemblages comprising fauna and artefact collections. What is notable, though, is that the pottery from one site was identical to that from the other: open-mouth bowls, and U-shaped and incurved bowls and pots without necks, all clearly part of a common tradition.

Here, too, the traditional archaeological concept of a 'culture' is inappropriate for this set of circumstances because it demands that different aspects of archaeological assemblages vary in harmony. In other words, differences in architecture between kwaKhumalo and kwaButhelezi should be matched by equivalent dif-

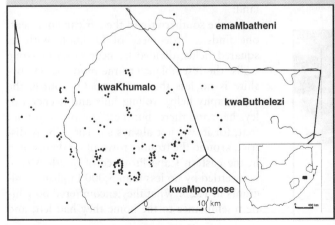

FIGURE 163 DISTRIBUTION OF KWAKHUMALO SETTLEMENTS. Thiessen Polygons, drawn from two principal sites on the Babanango Plateau, show that the distribution of stone-built Type B settlements corresponds with the projected boundaries for the two chiefdoms.

ferences in pottery. Again, the Lake Baringo model of economic competition and the active use of material culture suggests a better explanation.

People living in Zululand had an exogamous system of marriage: they chose wives from other clans, and their brides moved to live in their husbands' villages. The new alliances made through marriages were marked by the payment of bridewealth to the wife's family. Chiefdoms such as the Khumalo and Buthelezi were interlinked by complex webs of such relationships. In the early nineteenth century these alliances were consolidated as the Zulu Kingdom. Nevertheless, there was intense economic competition between the chiefs: oral traditions record that Phungashe fought with some of his immediate neighbours throughout his reign. Women, on the other hand, retained strong links with their own families. Just as they had learnt pot-making from their mothers, so they taught pot-making to their daughters in their new homes.

'The borders of the chiefdoms were political-ly important, incursions were contested by the chiefs, and the forms of male-dominated activities, such as settlement design, were passed down through lineages within the boundaries of chiefdoms. Women, in contrast, moved freely between chiefdoms as marriages were arranged across borders. The women took with them traditional concepts of pottery design, with the result that similar ceramic assemblages are found over a broad region' (M. Hall & Mack 1983: 192).

The point is not that Lake Baringo tribes such as the Tugen and Njemps were historically or ethnically linked with the Khumalo or with the pastoralists and hunter–gatherers of the Western Cape. It is rather that the Kenyan ethnoarchaeological study has presented a provocative and stimulating model of the relation between everyday household items and dress and the ways in which people organised alliances and handled competition. It allows in this way a deeper understanding of the archaeology of two distant and different regions.

Spatial analysis

Understanding the social relationships between people in the past requires us to think in spatial terms, by expanding the concept of 'place' and looking for the ways in which communities used material culture to map out their position in the landscape. James Deetz has referred to this as the study of the 'cultural landscape': 'the entire range of terrain from the house lot, the smallest and the most frequently studied, through gardens and field systems to truly large units of analysis, entire regions that bear the imprint of a shared set of values' (Deetz 1990: 2). Deetz has used this idea of the cultural landscape to paint a sweeping impression of the way in which colonial settlers in South Africa's Eastern Cape marked their appropriation of the land:

'At the southern tip of the African continent, one finds a little piece of England. With its squared fields, divided by hedgerows or stone walls, the resemblance to the moors of Derbyshire is no less than startling. Of course, the topography helps, rolling hills and deeper valleys here and there, but there is more to it than that, for it was not always so. The Albany district, around the frontier town of Grahamstown in the eastern Cape Province of South Africa, was settled by no less than 5,000 English immigrants in 1820. What they encountered bore little resemblance to the home they had left, and

FIGURE 164 STUDYING BEADS. Ostrich-eggshell beads, often found in considerable quantities at Late Stone Age sites, were markers of identity. By measuring variations in their sizes, Royden Yates (Department of Archaeology, University of Cape Town) is able to identify the distribution of different ethnic groups.

high expectations gave way to deep disillusionment. Where fifty acres might have sufficed to run a certain number of sheep in England, five times that amount was needed in this new home. Arid, hot, and covered with thick bushes and thorns, aloe, spekboom, and euphorbia, it must have seemed terribly intimidating. Yet through perseverance they prevailed and recreated the landscape they had left with remarkable precision in many parts of the district. This was not the case for all parts, however, and even now, when one moves from the cooked landscape of the 1820 settlers to the remnants of the raw bush, the contrast is spectacular. The previous landscape served well as browsing ground for the cattle of the indigenous Xhosa herders, as it does even today, but for the English settlers it could in no way suffice for the needs of their agricultural pursuits. So, in creating a landscape through making it useful to them, the settlers at the same time were making a powerful cultural statement, latently symbolic, that impresses to this day' (Deetz 1990: 1).

Archaeologists have made use of a number of approaches in analysing this spatial dimension of the past. Sometimes straightforward description has sufficed. But in other cases archaeologists have productively used systematic techniques of spatial analysis to isolate and study patterning in archaeological evidence. Such methods have a similar status to typological systems or statistical analysis in archaeology: they are ways of asking questions more clearly and consistently, rather than providing answers in themselves. A wide range of approaches has been used, chosen according to particular archaeological circumstances. Some methods have been developed specially, while others have been adopted from the allied discipline of locational geography. Three examples, suitable for different scales of spatial evidence, illustrate the approaches.

The method of Site Catchment Analysis has already been described in Chapter 8 through the example of the reconstruction of the economy of the Mozambican site of Manyikeni. Unlike many other spatial techniques, Site Catchment Analysis can be used in the study of a single site of any scale – whether hunting camp, farming village or city. Site Catchment Analysis is based on the observation that distance can have an economic cost. The further a resource is from a living site, the greater the price in human labour in procuring it, and the less the net return in economic terms. Consequently, people will tend to make sensible choices about where to live, placing themselves closest to their most important food resources:

'... prehistoric economies can be classified as to whether they were mobile, sedentary, or mobile-cum-sedentary. The concept of economic territoriality allows us to delimit the habitually exploited area around a site from which any of the above types of economy was practiced. Through the use of the technique of site catchment analysis and an assessment of past and present economic potential of the site territory, we may make a start in the study of man's changing relationship with his environment through time' (Higgs & Vita-Finzi 1972: 36).

Apart from helping to establish the economic territory of a single site, Site Catchment Analysis has also been used to build up interpretations of land use across regions.

Unlike Site Catchment Analysis, most other techniques of spatial analysis start with the relations between sites, rather than with the single site, using the region as the basic unit of study. An example of such an approach is the use of Thiessen Polygons, mentioned earlier in this chapter in the context of farming villages on the high grasslands of KwaZulu–Natal. Thiessen Polygons are simple geometrical shapes that divide the landscape up in the most logical

Site Catchment Analysis in the Niger Delta
Nwanna Nzewunwa has used Site Catchment Analysis in his study of prehistoric economies in the Niger Delta region (Nzewunwa 1980). By looking at the spatial relationship between the positions of archaeological sites and places where food resources were to be found (shellfish beds, fishing grounds, mangrove swamps, plant foods and places where animals could be hunted or trapped), he was able to supplement the sparse results of archaeological excavation with a reconstruction of the ways in which past communities had made use of the possibilities of the environments within a viable 'economic distance' of the places where they lived.

manner, starting from a given distribution of settlements. As with Site Catchment Analysis, Thiessen Polygons assume that distance is always significant. The polygons are mapped out by first drawing straight lines between each pair of neighbouring sites. At the mid-point of each of these lines, perpendiculars are drawn. This second set of lines makes up the polygon boundaries.

Thiessen Polygons are particularly useful for inferring what went on in people's minds when they decided where to build their settlements. Quite often, polygon boundaries will coincide with natural features of the landscape, such as rivers, the implication being that these were used to delimit local territories. Thiessen Polygons are best used at an early stage in a spatial study to sort out visually confusing site distrib-

FIGURE 165 CENTRAL PLACE THEORY. This hypothetical survey region shows the sort of settlement hierarchy which Central Place Theory has been designed to analyse.

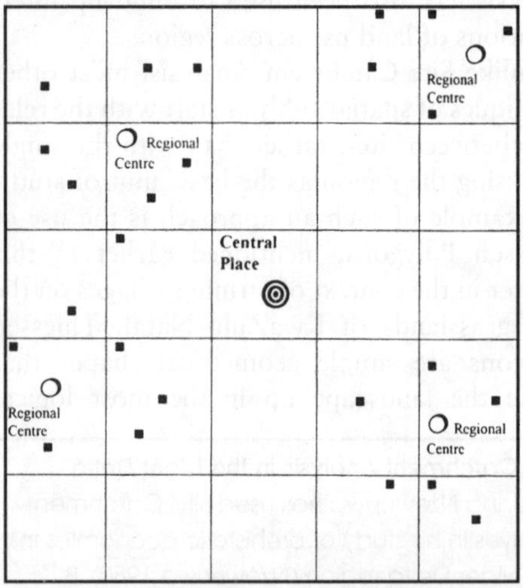

utions into patterns that are strong enough to warrant further study.

To use Thiessen Polygons in a spatial study is to concentrate on the landscape rather than on the nature of the settlement: hunting camps, villages and cities all have equal status, being undifferentiated dots on the map. Our third example of spatial technique was designed with the opposite emphasis. Central Place Theory was developed by German geographers in the 1930s in order to explain the spacing and functioning of cities in industrial Europe. The founding proposition of Central Place Theory is that sites will fall into regular size categories, and that smaller sites will tend to be placed in a regular manner in relation to the single, largest 'central place'. A study using Central Place Theory starts with the assumption of a uniform, featureless environment, and then seeks to account for the ways in which particular circumstances have distorted the predicted underlying pattern.

It is important to remember that Site Catchment Analysis, Thiessen Polygons, Central Place Theory and other techniques of spatial analysis are theoretical models that predict the relationships between some settlements and their environments, or between some settlements and others. They are not analogies that can, in themselves, explain any specific archaeological settlement pattern. Techniques such as these are properly used to refine interpretative ideas, and to analyse specific study regions systematically. Methods of spatial analysis rest on particular assumptions about human behaviour, such as rationality in the assessment of distance costs or the primacy of economic decisions. But these assumptions may not be applicable to a particular case study.

Town and village in early Egypt

Its field is full of all good things, and it hath provisions and sustenance every day. Its ponds are full of fishes, and its lakes of birds. Its plots verdant with herbage, and its banks bear dates. Its granaries are full of barley and wheat, and they reach into the sky.

— Poem from the Egyptian New Kingdom (1550–1070 BC), in praise of a new city (Hassan 1993: 568).

The beginnings of town life in Egypt can be traced back to the upper layers of the site of Merimde Beni-Salama, dated to about 4000 BC. This large settlement had rows of houses and workshop areas, and a population that has been estimated at between 1300 and 2000 people. This new way of living heralded major social changes in the Nile Valley. By 3000 BC most of Egypt was united as a single nation-state (with the city of Memphis as its capital) stretching some 1300 km along the

FIGURE 166 THE UPPER NILE VALLEY.

banks of the river. The pharaohs – the kings of Egypt – ruled over a land divided into administrative districts, known by the Greek name *nome*. Each *nome* had its own capital, and was part of a network of smaller administrative centres and villages.

Archaeologists have been carrying out excavations in Egypt for more than a century, making spectacular discoveries. The best known of these are the grave goods from the tomb of Tutankhamun, who ruled the New Kingdom between 1339 and 1329 BC. But despite such finds, and the prominence of early Egyptian architecture in the modern landscape, remarkably little is known about early social geography – the details of towns and villages in the different districts, and the ways in which they were connected with one another.

Fekri Hassan has tackled this research problem by developing a model – an interpretation based on informed speculation – that predicts the size, distribution and relations between cities, towns and villages in early Egypt. He has studied ancient textual sources and the available archaeological evidence, and integrated these with historical and present-day analogies with modern Egypt and other parts of the world.

This sort of approach has a long tradition in archaeological research. Geographical techniques such as Central Place Theory and Nearest Neighbour Analysis have often been used in the study of early societies. But Hassan's study of Egypt stands apart from many other examples of 'archaeo-geography'. He argues that the organising principles of early Egyptian cities, towns and villages were different from those of more recent urban centres. Important factors were the extent of local resources, the amount of food and tribute that could be transported, and the effectiveness of the king's or chief's ideological or military control over the districts in a domain. Early Egyptian towns were never exclusively urban, and had significant numbers of farmers living within their limits. Hassan contrasts this situation with states in which craft production, trade and economic competition were major factors – the examples around which standard approaches in locational geography have been developed.

Records of early Egyptian settlement are textual and archaeological; nevertheless both sources are clearly incomplete. Inscriptions giving lists of towns have survived on temple walls, although small villages and hamlets, not considered important by the priests, are rarely mentioned. Mounds (known as *tells* or *koms*) indicate where towns and larger villages once stood, as long as they had been occupied for a sufficient length of time for substantial archaeological deposits to accumulate. Even so, many are believed to lie buried beneath the mud deposited by periodic fluctuations in the Nile's course. Smaller villages had far less impact on the landscape, and were often washed away in seasonal floods. Therefore, both textual and archaeological evidence for town and village life are incomplete.

Hassan has tackled this problem of incomplete evidence by taking into account historical data from medieval Egypt as well as studies of

POSSIBLE SETTLEMENT HIERARCHY FOR A *NOME* IN UPPER EGYPT DURING THE NEW KINGDOM (1550–1070 BC)				
SETTLEMENT	No.	POPULATION SIZE	TOTAL POPULATION	PERCENTAGE
City/town	1	2 000	2 000	5%
Large village	5	800	4 000	10%
Medium village	24	550	13 200	35%
Small village	65	300	19 500	50%
Total population for each *nome*			38 700	100%

Source: After Hassan 1993.

modern land use along the Nile floodplain. This has allowed him to estimate the number of villages that could have been supported by the agricultural productivity of the floodplain and Delta regions, the possible populations of such villages, and the likely ratio of the number of villages associated with each regional town. Instead of taking for granted that economic rationality and the needs of trade were determinant forces – the approach taken by many urban geographers – Hassan has assumed that urban and rural networks in early Egypt would reflect a political organisation in which a divine king owned the land and mediated between the gods and the people; a system of taxation that supported the towns at the expense of the countryside; agricultural productivity that was heavily dependent on human labour; and transport networks that relied on donkeys and Nile transport boats.

In order to strengthen this interpretation, Hassan has checked his calculations against other sources of evidence and against comparable situations elsewhere in the world. Estimates of population for towns were compared with estimates of the areas covered by archaeological sites and the possible densities of living areas. The sizes and networks of villages predicted for early Egypt were compared with circumstances today in rural India.

By combining these different sources, Hassan has been able to sketch out a demographic structure for early Egypt. He estimates that capital cities such as Memphis or Thebes would have had populations of between 20 000 and 40 000 people. Beyond these city limits were the administrative districts – the *nomes*. Although the number of *nomes* in the kingdom varied from time to time, Hassan believes that there were usually 22 in all, averaging 350 km^2 in area. A typical *nome* extended up to 10 km on either side of the river, and stretched up to 43 km along the floodplain.

Within each *nome* there was a city or town that served as its capital, and a hierarchy of large and small villages that made up its hinterland. These are illustrated in the accompanying table, which has been based on the estimates that Hassan derived in his study.

It can be objected that Hassan's model for early Egypt is too speculative – that the empirical foundation derived from field research is too flimsy to support predictions of this nature. On the other hand, studies such as these serve both to integrate existing knowledge and to suggest directions that future fieldwork might take. Certainly, one should evaluate the assumptions on which interpretative approaches are based before applying them in archaeological situations.

'An awareness of the structural differences between towns and cities in early state society and commercial urban centres of later times is necessary for an understanding of early urbanization. The relations between incipient agriculture, a pre-industrial mode of transportation, divine kingship and centralized government form the basic structure shaping the size, location and hierarchy of towns in ancient Egypt and similar societies' (Hassan 1993: 568).

Polities

Identifying spatial patterning in the archaeological record does not, in itself, tell us what such patterning may mean. To interpret these networks requires us to use some concept of social organisation. Like the very first stone tools, networks of archaeological sites are silent until the archaeologist brings some model of human behaviour to bear on them. And as with other forms of archaeological explanation, there is the danger of assuming too much, of bringing inappropriate and poorly formulated analogies to the bare skeleton of a past settlement system, to the slight traces of where people once lived that survive today.

A fairly neutral concept that may be useful in interpreting past settlement patterns is the idea of the 'polity'.

'This term does not in itself imply any particular scale or complexity of organization. It can apply as well to a city state, a hunter–gatherer band, a farming village, or a great empire. A polity is a politically independent or autonomous social unit, which may in the case of a complex society, such as a state society, comprise many lesser components. Thus, in the modern world, the autonomous nation state may be subdivided into districts or counties, each one of which may contain many towns and villages. The state as a whole is the polity. At the other end of the scale, a small group of hunter–gatherers may make its own decisions and recognize no higher authority: that group also constitutes a polity' (Renfrew & Bahn 1991: 154).

But despite this and similar attempts to avoid value-laden concepts, it is a commonly held assumption that polities can be arranged in a hierarchical order, starting with the most simple forms of networks and ending with the most complex, and that this hierarchy reflects different stages in the evolution of human society. The modern form of the idea was crystallised in the nineteenth century, in the work of ethnographers, such as Lewis Henry Morgan, who were profoundly influenced by the developing concepts of biological evolution. Morgan and his contemporaries thought of human history as a series of stages, progressing from 'savagery', through 'barbarism', and ending with 'civilisation' – the pinnacle of human achievement. Those people then falling under European colonial control – Australian Aborigines, hunter–gatherers of the Kalahari, African 'tribesmen' – were seen as occupying fossil stages in cultural evolution, and therefore as representative of Europe's own distant, dark-shrouded history (Gould 1981).

Today, it is generally recognised that such theories of social evolution are untenable, and are also closely linked with assumptions of racial superiority and inferiority. But many of the nineteenth-century concepts that formed part of social evolution are still in circulation, sliding around like unstowed cargo, and causing a good deal of damage. As Kofi Agorsah has pointed out, Africa has been widely seen as a laboratory where hunter–gatherers can be studied in life, and their behaviour taken as analogous to behaviour in the depths of the Stone Age (Agorsah 1990). 'Civilisation' is widely assumed to be the opposite of the hunter–gatherer way of life, and is an appellation reserved for societies with fine arts and writing. In popular culture, the contrast is epitomised in the 1981 film, *The Gods Must be Crazy*, by the encounter between N!xan the Bushman and a Coca-Cola bottle. The film itself was the biggest foreign-made box-office hit in US history.

One way of correcting such bias is to take account of the complexity of many hunter–gatherer belief systems. San metaphors that involve the eland, for instance, have a complexity that is difficult to express within the conceptual limitations of English as a language – a complexity which spills over into oral performance. In Megan Biesele's words:

'I advance the possibility that certain social tasks may be accomplished exclusively in the special world of expressive forms. It seems, to begin with, that this world is a realm of play whose rules not only allow but demand a heightened manipulation of reality for social ends. It has the capacity to involve individuals at a deeper level than their mere participation in a shared cognitive system. There is a kind of cultural rumination endlessly going on there, a milling process that brings the unseen into harmony with the seen, the old with the new; all aspects of the ongoing life of society are its grist ... Such a view should allow us to understand the place in culture of what seems on the surface to be supererogatory artistic behaviour, which is actually integral to the life of traditional societies. Individuals and social groups act through expressive forms to articulate meanings that must be shared in order to perpetuate society as an entity of shared understandings. The forms work by containing, exploring, commenting on, turning inside out, and in a myriad ways reinforcing the cognised models ... which keep cultural systems continuing in their environments' (Biesele 1993: 192–3).

Nevertheless, there are clear differences in the ways in which people organise themselves in space. The San of the Kalahari do seem more similar to the Aborigines of Australia than, say, the people of the Zulu Kingdom in the nineteenth century. How can we conceptualise the broad sweep of the variability of polities without using the flawed notion of social evolution?

One way is to think in terms of the degree of fixity of social networks in space – the ease with which groups of people move or relocate across the landscape, and the effect that this has on archaeological settlement patterns. What makes Australian Aborigines and Kalahari hunter–gatherers intrinsically similar is their fluidity in community organisation and settlement pat-

FIGURE 167 BAMBOO HOL-
LOW, GIANT'S CASTLE,
DRAKENSBERG. This panel
of rock art well demon-
strates the complexity
of San thought. Early,
simplistic explanations
saw just a group of
men hunting an ani-
mal, probably a cow.
But it has been shown
that the picture
depicts San medicine
men in a state of
trance, leading a rain
animal across the veld.

terns, which involve frequent fission and relocation. Another way of looking at this is to see
space as a resource rather than a dimension.
Instead of merely existing in space, human communities could be said to consume it, incorporating perceptions of position and distance in
the material culture of their settlement patterns.

For example, the stone-built enclosures
which have been recorded across the vast grasslands of the southern African plateau (and
which have been described in Chapters 5 and 9)
form loose clusters along the ridges above river
valleys (Maggs 1976). There was clearly a considerable investment of labour in building these
settlements but, at the same time, we also know
that they were used only for a limited period.
The archaeological evidence reveals a continual
pattern of building and rebuilding: the
stonework from abandoned settlements was
stripped down to the foundations and used in
new structures near by. The same pattern of
past behaviour is evident further south on the
high grasslands of the Babanango Plateau,
where at any one time a network of stone-built
villages lay across the foundation traces of earlier, similar networks (M. Hall 1981). The
result is a landscape rather analogous to an
archaeological site, with 'layers' of earlier
building traces superimposed on one another.

These stone buildings vary in size and shape,
probably depending on the sizes of the herds
and flocks kraaled in each. There is a weakly
developed tendency for clusters of villages to
incorporate a somewhat larger stone enclosure.
Tim Maggs has called these bigger kraals 'elongated Type V' settlements (Maggs 1976). But
there is no unambiguous hierarchy in settlement
size – no places that are the equivalent of the
few major centres like Toutswemogala on the
northern edge of the grassveld in present-day
Botswana.

The highveld settlement pattern implies a
balance between, on the one hand, an identification with place strong enough to produce a
strong architectural tradition and a considerable investment of labour in building and, on
the other hand, a continual process of abandonment, movement and rebuilding. Although
individual villages had varying numbers of
domestic animals (implied by variations in
kraal sizes), no regional or central capitals
emerged. This suggests that there were social
and practical constraints on the accumulation
of village wealth beyond a certain level. Such an
archaeological pattern conforms to a 'chief-
domship'. One of the characteristics of this
form of social and political organisation is a
tension between the forces of centralisation,
which allow individuals to build up political
and economic power, and competition for
authority between rivals. Through time, chiefdoms are constantly fragmenting and re-form-
ing as factions gain power, build up strength
and subsequently lose control to other groups

(Cohen & Service 1978).

In contrast, the archaeological traces of Late Stone Age hunter–gatherer communities are far more ephemeral than the Iron Age villages of the southern highveld. Often, sites consist of nothing more than a small scatter of worked stone, a few formal tools and some chips and flakes – the traces of a temporary camp, occupied for a few days. John Parkington's painstaking reconstruction of Dunefield Midden on the Cape's west coast has shown that this site was formed from a nucleus of several cooking hearths, around which people camped for a few days while they took advantage of seasonally available foods (Parkington et al. 1992). According to Lyn Wadley and Aron Mazel, it is useful to think of these communities in terms of aggregation and dispersal: people come together in larger groups at some times of the year, and then split up into smaller communities again (Mazel 1989; Wadley 1987).

But it would be a mistake to read the ephemeral nature of archaeological sites as evidence for an ephemeral society. Late Stone Age hunter–gatherer groups clearly had a marked sense of place, and would have known the details and possibilities of the landscape in inti-

FIGURE 168 SUPERIMPOSED ROCK PAINTINGS. 'The meaning of these patterns is not yet clear. All we can say at present is that this superimpositioning is consistent with shamanistic art. In trance vision, images are often superimposed on others' (Lewis-Williams & Dowson 1989:148).

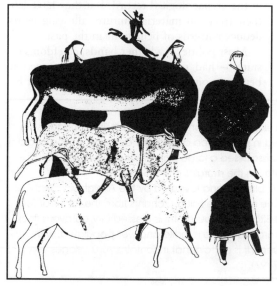

mate detail. Painted rock shelters were visited repeatedly; here new images were placed over earlier pictures, producing sites rich in ritual meaning (Lewis-Williams & Dowson 1989). The reciprocal exchange of gifts served to place people relative to one another in space. Rather than seeing Late Stone Age communities as impermanent, we should rather say that the landscape was used as a whole, without fixity.

Cultural anthropologists have developed the idea of the 'band' to describe situations in which people lack formal leaders, show few marked disparities in status between themselves, and usually have complex mechanisms of sharing to prevent the accumulation of wealth by individuals.

'Bands ... are small scale societies of hunters and gatherers, generally of less than 100 people, who move seasonally to exploit wild (undomesticated) food resources. Most surviving hunter–gatherer groups today are of this kind, such as the Hadza of Tanzania or the San of southern Africa. Band members are generally kinsfolk, related by descent or marriage. Bands lack formal leaders, so that there are no marked economic differences or disparities in status among their members' (Renfrew & Bahn 1991: 154).

In contrast with both the stone villages of the southern highveld and short-term camps such as Dunefield Midden, sites like Great Zimbabwe show a considerable degree of fixity: the radiocarbon chronology establishes that this place was occupied continually, and as a major centre, for about 200 years. Great Zimbabwe was the nexus of a three-tier settlement system and also a capital where considerable amounts of wealth had accumulated. Stone walls, representing a massive investment of labour, marked out considerable differences in status, and these differences were maintained through time. Although there was probably fission, with groups of people moving away to settle elsewhere, we have little difficulty in recognising in Great Zimbabwe a capital city (Sinclair et al. 1993b).

Archaeological sites such as Great Zimbabwe, and the network of architecturally similar settlements that are spread across and beyond the high Zimbabwe Plateau, are clear evidence for a different sort of polity from the chief-

197

FIGURE 169 BUILDING FOR STATUS. The intricate herringbone and chevron patterns built into the walling at the centre of the Zimbabwean site of Nalatale emphasise the status of the rulers of this fifteenth- to seventeenth-century state, which followed the demise of Great Zimbabwe.

domships of the southern grasslands. Instead of representing patterns of fission, which prevented the development of particular centres of power, Zimbabwe-type stone buildings (*madzimbahwe*) mark out lines of control through which individuals maintained their authority. Such forms of society are usefully referred to as 'states'. States are represented in the archaeological record by particular patterns of artefact disposal and of residential architecture, stratified settlements, and evidence for specialised military groups, as well as authority signified through the use of material culture (Haas 1982).

'The ultimate sanction of power in early Zimbabwe must have been force: the possibility of coercion that encouraged peasant communities to acknowledge the authority of regional administrators at their *madzimbahwe*, and that led this local nobility, in turn, to respect the dominance of Great Zimbabwe ... But if force was the ultimate sanction, there were nevertheless more direct ways in which the rulers of

Zimbabwe underlined their authority and worked for the cooperation of their subjects. Archaeologically the most obvious of these was the monumental architecture of the capital and the *madzimbahwe*' (M. Hall 1987: 94).

Networks do not only consist of sites – the hunter–gatherer camps, farming villages and towns considered so far in this chapter. Networks also comprise the interconnections between these nodal points – spatial relations that range from the *hxaro* gift exchanges studied by Polly Wiessner (Wiessner 1983) to the systems of trade that connected towns such as Jenne or Great Zimbabwe with places hundreds of kilometres distant. These interconnections are social relations and, like the rule sets that lie behind technology, they cannot be seen directly in the archaeological record. But they have left their traces in material culture, allowing us to deduce patterns of behaviour in the past.

Most polities – whether bands, chiefdoms or states – had regular forms of interconnection between communities that were marked out by

Great Zimbabwe was the capital of one of a number of early African states. These complex polities either pre-dated European colonial expansion or developed in response to the possibilities of trade with new markets. For example, complex polities developed in West Africa at an early date, becoming nodal points in networks of trade that, directly or indirectly, crisscrossed a large part of Africa. Here is a description of the Kingdom of Jenne by the Inland Niger Delta, on the margins of the Sahel:

'This city is large, flourishing and prosperous; it is rich, blessed and favoured by the Almighty ... Jenne is one of the great markets of the Muslim world. There one meets the salt merchants from the mines of Teghaza and merchants carrying gold from the mines of Bitou ... Because of this blessed city, caravans flock to Timbuktu from all points of the horizon ... The area around Jenne is fertile and well populated; with numerous markets held there on all the days of the week. It is certain that it contains 7007 villages very near to one another (al-Sa'di, *c.* 1655 in Connah 1987: 97).

artefacts. Ian Hodder's ethnoarchaeological work in Kenya demonstrates this well (Hodder 1982). The styles of ear decoration, basket drinking-cups, wooden eating-bowls and shield types that define what it is to be Njemps or Tugen can be seen as markers of social networks that run like fine veins across the landscape in the Lake Baringo region. One of the reasons for the wide-ranging conformity in ceramic decoration produced by southern Africa's first farmers might be that common pottery decoration signified for people living in separate villages connections of mutual dependence – an equivalent of Njemps or Tugen women claiming the protection of young warriors through the form of their ear decoration.

'Early farmers in southern Africa still made extensive use of hunted and gathered resources and probably had few domestic animals. In addition, cultivation of small stands of crop plants was probably fraught with difficulties in the early first millennium: soils, particularly in the south-eastern coastal areas, were often inherently low in fertility, the climate variable and crops at risk from disease, insect damage, wild fauna and a host of other factors. Thus I would suggest that, after crop plants were introduced into southern Africa some two thousand years ago, the modified forces of production demanded relations of production in which reciprocity and sanctions against accumulation were, if anything, more greatly stressed than they had been earlier. Ceramic decoration, with its widely distributed set of commonly recognized motifs, was, I would argue, part of a set of active symbols which served to signify these relations of production in precisely the same way that rock art and gift exchanges signified relations of production within and between hunter–gatherer camps' (M. Hall 1991: 143).

Trade and barter

Apart from establishing identity, networks were also conduits for economic transactions, ranging from exchanges of everyday commodities to formal trade in rare and exotic goods. For example, there is evidence for the manufacture of salt in the lowveld of South Africa, probably in excess of local needs and for barter and exchange in other areas. Similarly, in some areas where iron ore and timber for charcoal manufacture were readily available, there are concentrations of iron-smelting furnaces which would have produced much more processed iron than could have been used locally. This suggests that iron was traded from the lower-lying river valleys to the high grasslands of southern Africa, where a lack of raw materials would have precluded local smelting. Evidence for such patterns of localised trade and barter is preserved in recorded oral traditions (Maggs 1982b).

Salt and iron for making agricultural and hunting implements are everyday necessities that have left a visible trace in the archaeological record. There can be little doubt that other items, such as leatherwork and woodwork, were also bartered and that evidence for their trade has slipped from sight because of selective preservation with the passage of time. An ordinary resident of an African village a thousand years ago would have had a keen sense of where essential commodities could be obtained and of what needed to be bartered for them. It is also probable that the regional exchange of these goods would have been bundled together with other forms of social interaction such as marriages, tributary payments and gift exchanges, even though we can now see only part of the bare framework of this social landscape.

But trade connections were also important beyond the local region, in more exotic items,

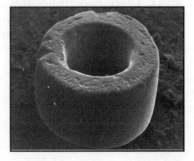

FIGURE 170 TRADE BEADS, MAPUNGUBWE. This photograph, taken with a scanning electron microscope, shows a soapstone bead from the twelfth-century site of Mapungubwe on the Limpopo River. Trade connections between this African polity and the Indian Ocean world were important. The bead, which is only 2.56 mm across, has a slight groove, probably as a result of being strung on a cord. Detailed studies such as these help to track trade goods and therefore the networks of early trade.

ARCHEOLOGY — O

and for the benefit of a small segment of the community living in village or town. Because the development of trade networks was closely connected with the formation of early states, tracking the distribution of trade goods is an important part of writing the past.

Some trade goods can be identified from their attributes. Imported Asian porcelains, for example, were the key to Gertrude Caton-Thompson's Great Zimbabwe chronology (Caton-Thompson 1931), and they are found in large numbers at early colonial sites. The well excavated in Cape Town's Barrack Street contained an assemblage of Chinese-made porcelain for which it was possible to attribute a date of manufacture (M. Hall et al. 1990). Trade goods such as these almost speak for themselves, and are invaluable in tracing trade networks. Other trade items are less tractable. Glass beads, for instance, are sometimes excavated in large quantities. There are substantial assemblages both from twelfth-century Mapun-gubwe and from Great Zimbabwe, as well as from later sites such as the nineteenth-century Zulu Kingdom towns of Mgungundlovu and Ondini (M. Hall 1993). Glass trade beads were not made in Africa, and they were consequently prized here as rare and valuable commodities. They were the linchpin in many early trade contacts, but they are frustratingly difficult to trace to their source. New advances in studying their chemical composition are helping to source these important markers of early trade routes (Saitowitz 1990).

In linking together settlements, then, trade networks range from the local to the global. From the trade in iron artefacts between high grasslands and wooded valleys, to the movement of fine Chinese export porcelain from one end of the known colonial world to the other, people have left behind traces of complex economic and social connections. George Beste, who wrote with wonder about the New World in 1578, gives us a sense of the possibilities that sixteenth-century Europeans saw in trade:

'Whatsoever sundry sorte of corne, grayne, and meates former yeares have had, we not only have all the same in farre greater abundance, but thereunto are added thousandes of new things simple and compound, never heretofore seene or heard of. And as for coverture to defend the bodye, the matter is growen to such excellencie of architecture and building, to such finenesse of cloth and silkes of all sortes and colours; that man studieth no more to multiplye the encrease thereof; so much as to devise fashions, to make it serve more for ornament, than for necessarie uses. And the chiefest cause of all these effects (next after ye divine Providence) is the searching wit of man ... One of the excellentest artes that ever hath bin devised is the arte of navigation ...' (Collinson 1867).

Beste's experience must have been shared by now-unknown Africans, centuries earlier, contemplating the opening trade southwards along the Nile, by caravan across the Sahara, or along the shores of the East Coast.

FIGURE 171 TRADE BEADS. *Two of King Panda's Dancing Girls*, painted by George French Angas. Angas's paintings were stylised, but he captured well the importance of glass trade beads in the nineteenth-century Zulu Kingdom.

Tracking trade routes in the Sahel

One of the most important questions in the archaeology of West Africa is the nature and extent of trade networks that existed before documentary history. (This issue will be discussed again in Chapter 13.) Abubakar Garba has analysed the physical properties of stone materials from the sites of Daima and Gajiganna to ascertain where they came from (Figure 172). Garba found that stone used for artefacts at both sites had been imported, sometimes from 250 km away, and he was able to identify particular geographical areas which supplied these early Sahel towns: the Mandar Mountains and Biu Plateau to the south, and Hadje el Hamis to the north of Lake Chad (Garba 1994). Studies such as these build up an imprint of early trade routes, invaluable in establishing the extent of social networks.

FIGURE 172 TRADE ROUTES IN THE SAHEL.

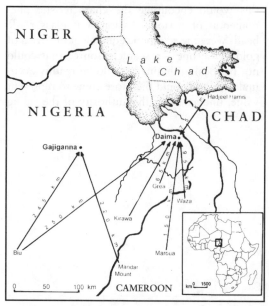

Early trade networks and East Africa

The earliest evidence for trade contacts between communities on the East African coast and other continents comes from accounts of explorers and geographers. For example, the *Periplus of the Erythraean Sea* was probably written in about 100 AD as a guide to the ports of Arabia, East Africa and India. The *Periplus* refers to the port of Rhapta, possibly on the coast of modern Tanzania: 'the last mainland market town of Azania, which is called Rhapta, a name derived from the small sewn boats … Here there is much ivory and tortoiseshell. Men of the greatest stature, who are pirates, inhabit the whole coast and at each place have set up chiefs.'

Rhapta and other market towns were subordinate to a kingdom in Arabia, from where

201

Arab captains sailed with 'hatchets, swords, awls, and many kinds of small glass vessels; and at some places wine and not a little wheat, not for trade but to gain the goodwill of the barbarians'. In return, the merchants received ivory, rhinoceros horn, tortoiseshell and coconut oil (Freeman-Grenville 1962).

For many years, there are no further known accounts. But early in the twelfth century al-Idrisi compiled a book of travels that was based on what he had heard of the adventures of traders and travellers. He wrote that the Arabs knew of a number of landing points along the coast known as 'Sofala', suggesting trade near the estuary of the Zambezi River, and possibly further to the south as well.

Although it is difficult to make precise connections, the archaeological evidence confirms these documentary sources. Kilwa – later a thriving Islamic city-state on the Tanzanian coast – was first occupied in the eighth or ninth century AD. People lived by fishing, gathering shellfish and growing crops. But they also spun cotton and made large quantities of shell beads, probably for trade into the African interior. The major export from Africa was probably ivory (Chittick 1974). A second early point of contact was at Chibuene on the Mozambican coast between the mouths of the Zambezi and Limpopo rivers. Here, Paul Sinclair has excavated imported Persian ceramics and glass beads, radiocarbon-dated by association to the eighth century AD (Sinclair 1982).

The persistence of these early traders in making landfalls on the dangerous and difficult East African coast attests to the value of the commodities that could be obtained through trade.

Similarly, people living in the interior – in areas such as the dry Limpopo River valley – also realised the potential of the new trading contacts. At Schroda, a ninth-century village site high up the valley, trade contacts were sufficiently regular to result in a significant assemblage of glass trade beads and cowry shells. In return, the villagers traded animal skins and elephant ivory (Hanisch 1981). As this trade enriched the local population, villages grew larger, and the possibilities for the accumulation of wealth increased. It is likely that these new economic circumstances enabled a small class of people to gain economic and political power, leading directly to the development of Mapungubwe, one of southern Africa's first state systems. Later, Indian Ocean traders became more interested in gold than in ivory and animal skins, and the centre of economic power shifted from the Limpopo Valley to the Zimbabwe Plateau, laying the economic foundation of the rise of Great Zimbabwe (M. Hall 1987).

Why were apparently useless trade goods such as glass beads and cowry shells the key to such major economic changes in pre-colonial southern Africa? Those polities that have been loosely grouped as 'chiefdoms' held much of their wealth in cattle, and livestock herds can only be built to a certain size before they are too large to protect or graze in the neighbourhood: this would encourage the characteristic phenomenon of periodic fission. But glass trade beads were the economic equivalent in Africa of gold in Europe – a scarce resource that could not be locally obtained, could be readily accumulated, and could therefore come to represent value, underwriting the authority of the ruling

chapter 12

In the mind

Many histories that have been written by archaeologists are what we could call an 'outsider's view': they are presented as if the archaeologist is looking down on the broad sweep of human experience from a high vantage point, mapping out the economy or the settlement pattern, for example, from a detached point of view. Until quite recently, this approach was accepted without question. But as we saw in Chapter 4, challenges have come from the panoply of new approaches that hang together rather uneasily as 'post-modernism'. These newer ways of looking at the past insist that archaeology must be about the 'insider view' – about what the people that we study had to say for themselves.

Making artefacts speak

The problem, of course, is that it has always been difficult to get artefacts to 'say' anything at all. Whereas aspects of the past such as diet or the social relationships between towns and villages have been convincingly inferred from patterns in material culture (and strongly supported by ethnoarchaeological research), what people in the past actually thought about their world still seems to many archaeologists to be completely inaccessible – way beyond the possibilities of archaeological evidence except in unusual circumstances. Consequently, what Colin Renfrew has called 'the Archaeology of Mind' (Renfrew 1982) is still a frontier zone – a wild land where competing theories fight on, and where there are no maps and few signposts. Many have turned back to the safe, civilised world of more traditional archaeology.

Edith Wharton's novel *The Age of Innocence* (first published in 1920) caught the essence of another safe, civilised world: the New York drawing-room society of her own childhood in the 1870s. Comparison of Wharton's verbal portrayal of a dinner party with Martin Scorsese's visual treatment of the same event in his 1993 film of the novel illustrates the central dilemmas for an archaeology of mind.

The dinner party is given for their cousin the Duke of St. Austrey by Mr and Mrs van der Luyden – direct descendants of the first Dutch governor of New Amsterdam, the pinnacle of New York aristocracy, 'the arbiters of fashion, the Court of Last Appeal'. Wharton uses her considerable ability to describe the setting:

'The dinner was a somewhat formidable business. Dining with the van der Luydens was at best no light matter, and dining there with a Duke who was their cousin was almost a religious solemnity ... The van der Luydens had done their best to emphasize the importance of the occasion. The du Lac Sèvres and the Trevenna George II plate were out; so was the van der Luyden 'Lowestoft' (East India Company) and the Dagonet Crown Derby. Mrs van der Luyden looked more than ever like a Cabanel, and Mrs Archer, in her grandmother's seed-pearls and emeralds, reminded her son of an Isabey miniature. All the ladies had on their handsomest jewels, but it was characteristic of the house and the occasion that these were mostly in rather heavy old-fashioned settings; and old Miss Lanning, who had been persuaded to come, actually wore her mother's cameos and a Spanish blonde shawl' (Wharton 1974: 55).

Scorsese, in contrast, chooses to capture the dinner party visually. The screenplay has the off-camera commentary fall silent ('The van der Luydens knew how to give a lesson ...'). In a sequence of four shots, the camera first closes in on the opulent table setting, cuts to a close-up of a single porcelain plate with a perfectly presented hors-d'oeuvre, moves to a position directly above the table, showing the symmetry of the full table setting and the twelve people around the table, and then pans behind the shoulders of the diners with the light playing on the table glass, the silks of the dresses and the jewellery. The power of film used in this way is to imply an insider's view – the way that Mr and Mrs van der Luyden, their guest the Duke, Miss Lanning and the Archers would have

'read' the table setting without putting the meaning into words.

Mark Leone, writing about the archaeology of merchant capitalists a century earlier and to the south, in Annapolis, sees clocks, watches, scientific instruments, table settings, landscaping and garden design as part of the creation of a similar 'natural' order, something that gains its power through being taken for granted, through *not* being verbalised:

'The impression was created by wealthy people, who were increasingly threatened, that in order to demonstrate understanding of the laws of nature, particularly those involving sight, natural laws could be made to operate in concrete, sometimes experimental, settings. The rules of perspective in architecture and in landscape gardening, when expressed as the great city houses, the classic Georgian homes with their inevitable formal landscapes, were intended as witnesses to an ability to observe and copy nature accurately. Second, the implications of these homes and landscapes were to convince people that a rational social order based on nature was possible and that those with such access to its laws were its natural leaders' (Leone 1988: 250).

Such an archaeology of mind – also known as 'cognitive archaeology' – raises some formidable questions:

• What is the nature of the relation between words and objects? Can objects be considered part of language, and 'read' as testimony of what people thought in the past, or do they have other, non-verbal qualities?

• Can material culture be 'read' to uncover the thoughts of its makers and users when we have no ethnography, no words to aid our interpretations?

These and other methodological and theoretical issues remain far from resolved.

Brain power

The mind starts with the brain (Figure 173). In primates, the brain is tightly encased by the skull, or 'cranium'. With care, one can make an internal cast, or 'endocast', of the inside of the cranium, reproducing the outline of the brain's outer membrane. Although there is little detail presented, the study of these casts has allowed

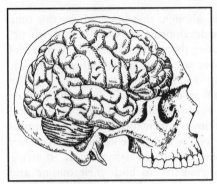

FIGURE 173 THE HUMAN BRAIN.

physical anthropologists to infer the evolution of the brain from the australopithecines onwards through the early hominids to modern humans.

During this long road of evolution, the human brain has changed in both size and shape. Brain capacity is conventionally measured in cubic centimetres. Chimpanzees have brains between 400 cm^3 and 500 cm^3 in size. Our australopithecine ancestors had brains larger than this, while modern brains vary between 1300 and 1500 cm^3 in size. Clearly, human cultural and social abilities were enabled by this aspect of physical evolution.

But it has also been shown that there is little direct relation between brain size and intelligence: people with big heads are not necessarily brighter than people with small heads. This is because brain shape and structure are also important. During the course of evolution, our brains have become more wrinkled, increasing their surface area and the amount and complexity of information that they can process. The human brain has also become 'lateralised' – divided into sides with (for a right-handed person) the left side of the brain usually controlling language skills. Particular parts of the brain have developed as specialised centres.

It is believed that these changes in structure are closely linked to the ability to carry out complex tasks. Endocasts do not show a great deal of detail of the brain membrane, but there is indirect evidence, in the internal morphology of the cranium, for lateralisation in the brain structure of *Homo erectus*. It is now widely accepted that the essential structural elements of the modern human brain had evolved by two million years ago (Gowlett 1984).

The evolution of the brain, as well as developments in the anatomy of the larynx and the dexterity of tongue and lips, is indirect evidence for the emergence of language. And because the use of words is so important in transmitting knowledge from person to person, generation to generation, language is usually considered an essential part of the notion of humanity.

What is language? When we speak or write, we use a series of symbols to stand for what we mean. The way in which this comes about is complex, and understanding of the fundamentals of language is still a contentious area of study.

In its simplest form, a symbol is something that represents something else. We can see this most clearly when we attempt to learn a new language ourselves. The teacher might hold up an object, and have the class recite its name – the sound symbol that stands for it. When we know a vocabulary of such names, and a set of rules for ordering the words, we can talk about the object to somebody else without having it in front of us any more.

FIGURE 174 THE COMPLEX WORLD OF SYMBOLS. Everyday streetscapes are assemblages of symbols which we have learned to 'read' without a second thought.

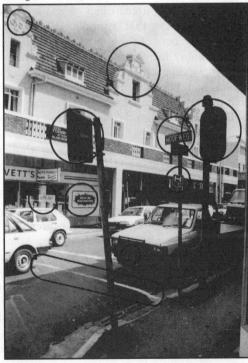

But the more proficient we become in a language, the more we string together sentences without thinking of the form of the object that lies behind the word. We also introduce a whole range of abstract concepts, things that we cannot see and may not be able to define: air, health, love, god. Our system of symbols has taken over: it has become an autonomous mechanism, an encyclopaedia of categories, memories and knowledge about knowledge (Sperber 1975).

> **language** 'the patterned use of sound as symbols, is mirrored in other means of human communication – music, art, writing – and indicates the fundamental basis of human behaviour. The ability to construct symbols in the head and in the material world that model past experience, present predicaments and future decisions, provides the foundations for modern human behaviour and culture. It must, too, have played an important part in the survival strategies of the early hominids' (Foley 1987: 45).

Symbolic communication, then, is far more than verbal language. Words are accompanied by facial expression, body language, spatial positioning and a wide range of material objects. Cognitive archaeology begins with the acknowledgement that symbolic communication is at the core of the human condition.

Our ability to recognise the earliest symbol systems is, not surprisingly, tentative. Kathy Schick and Nicholas Toth, though, consider that there is good cause to be able to read symbolic behaviour from the material traces left by *Homo erectus*.

'A rudimentary definition of a symbol is something used to stand for or signify something else. Do we have any evidence for the use of symbols during this time period? Various claims have been made for use of different objects as ornaments or the use of ochre (a natural iron oxide pigment, often red but sometimes yellow or brown), which develops an apparent symbolic importance in later prehistory that was maintained among many recent and modern cultures. This evidence is, however, again quite inconclusive during this period of our prehistory.

'The handaxes themselves might give some indication, though, that hominids by this time may have developed some sense of an aesthetic, of something that was pleasing and meaningful to them because of its shape and form. This is especially so in the later stages of the Acheulean, from about 500,000 to 200,000 or 100,000 years ago. Bifaces in this time period are sometimes undeniably, strikingly beautiful (whether you're an archaeologist or not). They can be extraordinarily symmetrical (showing bilateral symmetry in both their outline and their cross section) and show very even, regular edges – all the while maintaining a sharp, cutting efficiency' (Schick & Toth 1993: 282).

Schick and Toth's argument, as with so many interpretations of archaeological evidence, has to be inferential. We have no way of opening a window on to a scene in the daily life of *Homo erectus* and studying early people's use of symbolism in communicating with one another. But there are other sources of inferential evidence as well, and together they make a convincing case for complex symbolic behaviour at different times in the distant past. Glyn Isaac, for instance, has suggested that stone tools can be thought of as the products of a 'cognitive map' (Isaac 1976). From the very beginning of toolmaking, people began to think in regular shapes, not simply reducible to functional necessity, and these shapes became increasingly standardised. We cannot know what these

FIGURE 175 STONE AGE AESTHETICS? Does the symmetry of many early stone tools indicate an aesthetic sense?

forms meant to people, but we can see them as evidence for symbolic communication. A great virtue of Isaac's cognitive map is its concordance with the construction of archaeological typology: we can see our stone-tool classifications as reflections of the increasing ability of our earliest ancestors to think like us.

The idea of time

Another line of evidence for symbolic thought is the idea of time. Time is an abstract concept, with considerable philosophical implications, as we saw in Chapter 7. Thinking about time stretches our minds:

'The vastness of geological time can be disconcerting, and can cause conceptual problems. Most people, used to time marked out in hours and days and years, stretched to a generation on either side of them, can easily understand past events when related to those markers. Much of history, measurable in terms of months and years, is comprehensible in this way. To move, though, beyond written history is to move to a new scale, to one where individual years and individual generations are invisible, and the observable units of time – thousands and millions of years – bear no relationship to those we live in today' (Foley 1987: 15).

Similarly, concepts of time must have stretched the symbolic capacities of our ancestors. Again, we cannot know this aspect of past thoughts and beliefs directly, but we can read the archaeological record for evidence that early people thought in abstract terms about the past and the future.

The most important line of evidence in this regard is deliberate burial of the dead. Careful burial, in particular the provision of 'grave goods' such as personal ornamentation or provisions, has been taken as indicating that people had some sort of spiritual life. This in turn implies the ability to think in symbolic terms.

There is extensive evidence for deliberate burial from European and Asian archaeological sites. These seem to have extended back into the Middle Palaeolithic, and as much as 100 000 years ago.

'From the Upper Palaeolithic period there are many well-established cases of human burial, where the body or bodies have been deliberately laid to rest within a dug grave, sometimes accompanied by ornaments of personal adornment. The act of burial itself implies some kind of respect or feeling for the deceased individual, and perhaps some notion of an afterlife (although that point is less easy to demonstrate)' (Renfrew & Bahn 1991: 343).

Perhaps the earliest evidence for deliberate burial in Africa comes from Border Cave, on the frontier between South Africa and Swaziland. Here an infant skeleton was excavated in 1942. This four- to six-month-old child, known as 'Border Cave 3', was found in a shallow grave; the body had been buried with a *Conus* shell ornament. Some of the bones were stained reddish-brown, which suggests the use of haematite for ritual purposes. Nitrogen values (a technique of relative dating described in

FIGURE 176 GRAVEYARDS. Burial practices often reveal concepts of time.

Chapter 7) established that the bones were not intrusive to their stratigraphic layer, which has a radiocarbon date of greater than 49,000 years before the present, and a date inferred from the site stratigraphy and an oxygen isotope chronology of about 100,000 years before the present (Beaumont et al. 1978). If it is indeed this old (and if the skeleton was excavated from a true grave), then Border Cave 3 is one of the earliest examples of deliberate human burial in the world.

For the more recent end of the long Stone Age in southern Africa – the last 1000 years – there is widespread evidence for deliberate burial. In the Eastern and Southern Cape there were many cave interments, implying both a sense of space and a sense of time, and a sophisticated set of symbolic perceptions about the world and the passage of time (S. Hall & Binneman 1987). In other parts of the subcontinent there have been finds of burials both from living sites and from the open landscape. Many of these have been disturbed or accidental finds, and have not been properly excavated with the care necessary to establish their full context. An exception is the burial excavated from the rock shelter of Klipfonteinrand in the Clanwilliam area of the Western Cape (Figure 177). This was the body of a young adult man, buried with his knees drawn up to his chest – a characteristic burial position. There were no grave goods that have survived the passage of time, but three ochre-stained grindstones lying on top of the burial show that care was invested in the interment (Parkington & Poggenpoel 1971).

We cannot know the detail of Late Stone Age symbolic concepts of time and space. All we can do is to read the evidence that implies the existence of such perceptions. But in other, more unusual circumstances there is considerably more information available. One context is early Egypt, where the careful study of inscriptions has revealed details of a complex set of calendars and an abstract sense of history and the future.

The first Egyptian calendar was based on the annual helical rising of the dog-star Sirius, which was regarded as the goddess Sopdet. This coincided approximately with the annual inundation of the Nile – the critical event in Egypt's ecological cycle and the economic basis for the

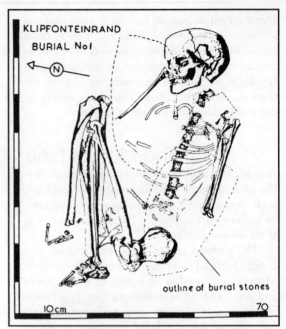

FIGURE 177 BURIAL AT KLIPFONTEINRAND. The burial of a young adult man, interred in a typical flexed position, with knees drawn up to his chest. The skeleton was excavated from a rock-shelter deposit, and the body had been deliberately buried within a living site.

Egyptian state. Sopdet's ascent fixed the beginning of the first month, which was followed by eleven more lunar months, averaging 354 days in all. Every two or three years, an additional month of 29 or 30 days would be added to the year. Later, between about 3000 and 2700 BC, a schematic lunar calendar of 365 days was devised. This consisted of 12 months, each of 30 days, with 5 extra days after the twelfth month to celebrate the birthdays of the gods. Each month consisted of three 10-day weeks. The Egyptians recognised that this calendar would get out of phase, but also that it would correct itself on a cycle of 1460 years (Aldred 1984). Apart from the astronomical skill and mathematical ingenuity needed to devise such a system, the Egyptian calendar reveals a complex, abstract, symbolic notion of time long beyond the individual human lifespan.

This wider view of human symbolic expression helps put the development of writing into its historical context. Certainly, the invention of systems of writing has been one of the most important processes in human development:

'The very existence of writing implies a major extension of the cognitive map. Written symbols have proved the most effective system ever devised by human beings not only to describe the world around them, but to communicate with and control people, to organize society as a whole, and to pass on to posterity the accumulated knowledge of a society' (Renfrew & Bahn 1991: 347).

But at the same time, writing is only one, late form of that human symbolic expression which began with the first spoken words and shape ideas for stone tools more than two million years ago.

Symbolic behaviour, then, has a deep antiquity, and embraces a far wider sphere of communication than verbal expression. Although archaeologists can rarely be palaeo-sociologists, and observe this behaviour directly, they are able to interpret the material remnants of past symbolic worlds. Pursuing the 'archaeology of mind' is viable, exciting and richly rewarding in terms of what it can tell us about ourselves and our past.

Bassey Andah has commented:

'Oral cultures taxed the observation/memory aspect of the brain more than do written cultures. They were generally more independent than written forms of secondary and tertiary devices. Put differently they were more dependent on the primary living natural faculties rather than on secondary man-made devices. Orally literate people are more faithful to everything seen, heard and smelt than those of written cultures – who often lose the ability to use these by default. They tend to seek what is thought to be significant in their quest to be graphic. Meaning is reduced to the essence and often the essence is not comprehended because of this desire …

'Writing, despite its several advantages, among which are the provision of recording facilities (storage as an aid to human memory) and language shift from aural to visual domain, has disadvantages also. It invariably simplifies and thus distorts speech … By systematising, fixing and making available more permanent forms of storage, writing did not necessarily improve on man's understanding of cultural and natural phenomena' (Andah 1990: 25–6).

The origins of writing in Africa

The development of early Egypt as a powerful economic and political entity was facilitated by writing. We know that papyrus writing-paper had been invented by the beginning of the First Dynasty (about 3000 BC) because two rolls of blank papyrus have been found in the store chamber attached to a tomb at Saqqâra.

'Writing, as elsewhere, was developed in Egypt not for the purpose of enshrining great thoughts in a memorable literary form, but for the utilitarian purpose of recording the minutiae of state business in a portable and durable form, and not entrusting it to fallible human memory. Precise instructions could be issued at a distance and reports received from afar' (Aldred 1984: 89).

Writing was the responsibility of a small group of skilled professional scribes who served the interests of the state's ruling elite. For example, the explorer Harkhuf, returning to Aswan from a trading expedition southwards into the Sudan in about 2350 BC, wrote to King Phiops II reporting that he had captured a dancing pygmy, which the king then instructed him to bring to Memphis. Less exotic uses of writing included records of the fluctuating heights of the Nile and census reports on numbers of men and sizes of livestock herds.

A system of calculation was developed in parallel with writing. This was based on a decimal system, and was used for such tasks as taxation and estimates of building requirements. By 2000 BC Egyptian mathematicians were able to solve complex fractions.

Egyptian writing was based on a set of symbols known as hieroglyphs. Hieroglyphic symbols may represent the objects that they depict, or stand for sounds or groups of sounds. Egyptian writing consisted entirely of these pictures, although the object that serves as the symbol cannot always be identified today.

Hieroglyphic writing was developed independently in Egypt, although there was contact with Mesopotamia, where writing also developed. The system was regularised to a set of

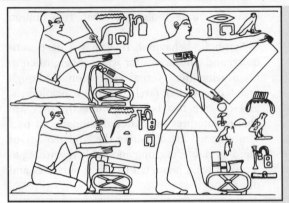

FIGURE 178 EGYPTIAN SCRIBES WRITING AND READING. In this relief from the tomb of Mereruka at Saqqâra, dated to around 2390 BC, the steward Khai reads an inventory on papyrus which the scribes have prepared.

some 700 images in the Third Dynasty (about 2650–2575 BC), and from then onwards was used largely unchanged for some three thousand years.

There are four basic principles in hieroglyphic writing:
• A hieroglyph can be used in a pictorial way. For example, the sign of a man with his hand to his mouth might stand for the word 'eat'.
• A hieroglyph might represent or imply another word suggested by the picture. For example, the sign for 'sun' could stand for the word 'day'.
• Hieroglyphs serve as representatives of words that share consonants in the same order. For example, the Egyptian words for 'man' and 'be bright' are both spelled with the same consonants, and therefore can be represented by the same hieroglyph.
• Hieroglyphs can stand for individual consonants, or combinations of consonants.

There were other early systems of writing in Africa as well. Further south, along the middle reaches of the Nile, cities and states developed in Nubia. Once seen as outliers of Egypt, these are now recognised as indigenous developments with strong connections to the north. As in early Egypt, the development and use of writing facilitated the centralisation of economic power and authority (Connah 1987).

The Sudanese Nile has long served as a trade corridor between the African interior and the Mediterranean. Various forms of written documentation span some 5000 years of this history. State formation in Nubia began with the rise of the kingdom of Kerma, with its large fortified city and houses of wood and clay (Figure 180). Kerma was wiped out by Egyptian colonisation of the Middle Nile during its New Kingdom in the second half of the second millennium BC. It was at this time that the temples at Abu Simbel, described in Chapter 3, were built. Once Egyptian colonial power began to wane, a second Nubian kingdom developed in the ninth century BC. This was called Napata, but was widely known as the Kingdom of Kush. Napata dominated the Middle Nile until the fourth century BC (Connah 1987). The range of archaeological information from Napata is limited, although some hieroglyphic inscriptions are known.

A new centre of power developed in the Sudan after the fourth century BC. This was based on the city of Meroë, about 200 km south of modern-day Khartoum. Meroë was particularly important in the first century AD, although the city continued to thrive for another three hundred years in all, and became the focus of a number of subsidiary towns. Meroë has evidence for an elite central area, a wider residential district, temples and extensive iron working.

'With such an extreme environment, Nubia would seem to have been an unlikely place for the development of states and the appearance of cities. Yet not only did these things happen, they happened here earlier than anywhere else in tropical Africa. It is little wonder that a common historical explanation has been to regard such developments as 'secondary' in character, resulting directly from contact with Egypt and

FIGURE 179 HIEROGLYPHIC WRITING.

| set | uta | set | xui | maki er | sad | heh |

They are safe, they are protected (and) guarded until eternity

210

FIGURE 180 THE MIDDLE NILE VALLEY.

Peter Shinnie has written:
'Meroë was an African civilization, firmly based on African soil, and developed by an African population. That an urban, civilized, and literate state existed deep in the African continent and lasted nearly a thousand years in itself constitutes an achievement of outstanding importance' (Shinnie 1967).

South-West Asia. An examination of the archaeological evidence reveals a very much more complex situation, in which exotic influences undoubtedly played a continuing although fluctuating role but where important contributions came from within, so that the resultant social complexity had its own quite distinctive Nubian characteristics' (Connah 1987: 64).

Like other cities on the Nile, the rulers of Meroë made use of writing. This was the Nubian 'Meroitic alphabet', used from about the second century BC until about the fourth century AD. Meroitic is still not understood, even though the first inscriptions were recorded in 1909, and phonetic values for most of the signs worked out by 1919. This is because the language in which the documents are written bears no relation to any known language: 'Meroitic has, with Etruscan, the distinction of being one of the two ancient languages the phonetic values of whose signs can be read with reasonable certainty, but the meaning of whose words cannot be understood. Its inscriptions are of two kinds: those in hieroglyphs, based on Egyptian prototypes, and those in the distinctive Meroitic writing' (Shinnie 1967: 133–4).

Cognitive maps

Recognising the antiquity and importance of symbol systems is one thing: studying them is another. Cognitive archaeology tests the limits of current archaeological theory and methodology with problems analogous to the interpretation of Meroitic script. The central issue is this: can all human symbolic behaviour be studied as if it were language? Were the shape systems of the first stone tools, or concepts of time and history, consequences of the same physical development of the brain and larynx that enabled language? Are verbal and non-verbal symbolism part of the same system of communication? Or is the material world somehow different?

One reason why questions such as these are particularly difficult to answer is that the nature of the material world that we live in today is itself remarkably under-theorised. Arguably, the last major theoretical contribution was Marx's

study of fetishism made over a century ago. Theoretical work in the social sciences has concentrated on production and representation rather than on consumption and the nature of materiality itself (Miller 1987).

'Our lives today are dominated by the material objects that proliferate all around us, and by the prospects and problems they afford. It is peculiar that the history of this 'world of goods' has, at least till very recently, been so little addressed by historians. Economic history has long been entrenched; social and cultural history have vastly expanded their domains in recent years. Yet none of these disciplines has set the history of consumer societies high on its agenda; and, though the opportunities are present, the three have rarely joined forces to tackle what ought to be a fruitful and unifying mutual concern' (Brewer & Porter 1993: 1).

The language of archaeology ...

Dr Structure, Dr Function and Dr Post have finished their excavation and returned back to their university in Dr Function's Land-Rover. All the finds from the excavation have been sorted, marked and catalogued. Now the process of study and interpretation must be continued in the laboratory.

It is tea-time. The three sit in their customary places, drinking from their usual mugs. Before long, the conversation turns to their interpretation of their site ...

Function: 'Well, the first things to think about are the village layout and the pottery collection. I think we have a fair idea of what the plan of the settlement was, don't you?'

Structure: 'Yes – but only because Post and I insisted on extensive excavation. If we'd done what you wanted, we'd just have a lot of little pinpricks across the site, and no idea where the houses had been, or the livestock kraal and grain stores.'

Function: 'Yes, yes! But let's just forget about that, shall we, and get back to the point. How are we going to *interpret* this village plan? What does it *mean*?'

Structure: 'Well, it's clearly symbolic, and an expression of the cognitive map – the way in which people conceptualised their world. I use the example of traffic lights in my lectures – I find it helps people to understand what structuralism is all about. You know; we all recognise red as "stop" and green as "go". And we make a whole set of other associations as well. Red is danger, fire, destruction, while green is safety, growth, renewal. Red and green can be said to be *oppositions* in our cognitive map – they go together as pairs, and each defines its inverse. The concept of oppositions is really useful for archaeology, because it means we can read what people were thinking from their material culture.'

Function: 'But how does this help us with our Early Iron Age village plan?'

Structure: 'Well, we know from ethnoarchaeological studies that rural subsistence farmers think of their village architecture as sets of oppositions. Men live to one side of the village, and women to the other. Important people live up the slope, and subservient people at the bottom end of the settlement. In other words, their settle-ment pattern is a direct expression of their cognitive map. These people are direct descendants of the Early Iron Age farmers that we're interested in. So it follows that we can read off the same set of oppositions from our archaeological evidence. We should be able to work out where the men lived, and where the women lived, and which houses were used by the most important people in the village.'

Function: 'Well, that all sounds rather naive to me. And terribly deterministic – the idea that how we see things and express them is fixed by a "cognitive map" that we have no control over. You spend a lot of time accusing *me* of determinism, because I'm interested in the environment and what people had to eat. But your interpretation seems much more deterministic than mine!'

Post: 'For once, I agree with Dr Function – it *is* a very deterministic way of looking at things.'

Structure: 'Well – let's hear your interpretation, Dr Post. You're very quick to criticise everyone else. How about writing a bit of history yourself? What do you think was going on in the Early Iron Age?'

Post: 'The first thing to do is to forget about all these universal principles like "cognitive maps". We should see our site like a book – a text that we can read if we know how. Of course there's a great deal of significance in the way the village is laid out – I quite agree with you about that, Dr Structure. But the plan is the result of the particular dynamics between the people who lived here, and the way that we write its history is going to be largely determined by us – by the decisions we've made in the field, and by our arguments and agreements – which is why I've been taking so much trouble to get everything on my tape recorder.'

Function: 'What about the ceramics, Post? What about the way people were decorating their pots – all these motifs, and the way in which they are so often arranged in similar ways?'

Post: 'Pottery decoration illustrates my approach very well. We should start thinking of it as a language – of the motifs as words that string together to make sentences. All material culture is another form of language. Our task is to *read* the past as closely as we can.'

Function: 'Well, you sound very convincing, Post – you always do. But I don't know that you

The complexity of the relation between language and other symbol systems is well demonstrated by recent interpretations of southern African rock art – the paintings and engravings that are to be found in many parts of the subcontinent, particularly in the higher, mountainous regions.

An old view of the meaning of the art, one which is still widely held today, is that the paintings can be read in a simple, literal manner: as the rather naive views of the world that Bushmen painted for pleasure and leisure. In this view, the pictures represent the world around the shelters where Bushmen lived, and the scenes depicted are of everyday life, such as hunting, dancing and warfare. Many years of detailed research have resulted in this 'art-for-art's-sake' interpretation being comprehensively discredited. Instead, it is now known that the paintings are part of an extremely complex form of symbolic communication. The challenge in rock-art research is to get an 'insider's view', to see the art 'through Bushman eyes'.

'What did the artists themselves believe about the cavalcade of animals that traverses the rocks of southern Africa? What strange actions, perhaps rituals, are the animated human figures performing? When we adopt this approach, we find that all the "simplicity" and "primitiveness" is a mirage. The haze of prejudice lifts, and we see, by means of the art, into the heart of Bushman religious experience. The great theme of Bushman art is the power of the animals to sustain and transform human life by affording access to otherwise unattainable spiritual dimensions' (Lewis-Williams & Dowson 1989).

But how can such an 'insider view' be achieved? The key to recent research has been the use of relevant ethnographic sources. These include modern anthropological studies of people living in areas such as the Kalahari who share the belief systems of earlier Bushman communities. They also include the invaluable records of Bushman beliefs made by Wilhelm Bleek and his sister-in-law Lucy Lloyd in the late nineteenth century. Bleek started by interviewing /Xam Bushman convicts who had been brought to Cape Town to work on the breakwater. Later, some of these men brought their families to the Bleeks' Mowbray home, where Bleek and Lloyd took down nearly 12 000 pages of verbatim accounts.

It is now accepted that both paintings and engravings were closely associated with Bushman medicine people, or shamans. Shamanism in Bushman communities was practised principally at trance dances, during which altered states of consciousness were achieved by hyperventilation, intense concentration and rhythmic dancing (Figure 181). During trance, medicine men could perform a number of tasks, including healing, rainmaking, visiting distant camps in out-of-body travel, and the control of animals. All these shamanistic activities were depicted in the rock paintings, which were probably made as remembered trance experiences – as part of the process of communicating these vital experiences.

The advances that have been made in the interpretation of rock paintings have massively expanded our knowledge of this part of history. What we now have is a range of various specific interpretations that all rest on the shared recognition of the complexity of the art's meaning (Dowson & Lewis-Williams 1994a). Writing about these modern approaches, Thomas Dowson and David Lewis-Williams have noted:

'As the decade of the '70s went by, an emphasis on both nineteenth- and twentieth-century Bushman ethnography at the expense of purely Western aesthetics produced unexpectedly rich results. Up until that time, the opacity of the ethnography had seemed to rival that of the art it was expected to explain. Eventually it was recognized that the key to understanding the ethnography lay, somewhat paradoxically, in the realization that it does not "explain" the art. Rather, both the art and the ethnography are expressions of Bushman beliefs, couched in Bushman languages, terms, categories, metaphors, symbols and cosmology:

FIGURE 181 THE TRANCE DANCE.

both have to be "unpacked". Once that process of "unpacking" had started, it became clear that both the art and the Bushman belief system out of which it came were far more subtle, complex and, to Westerners, elusive than had ever been supposed' (Dowson & Lewis-Williams 1994b: 3).

In appreciating the possibilities and difficulties of an "archaeology of mind", we need to bear in mind that in this case there has been an ethnography to "unlock". In other words, the non-verbal symbolism of southern African rock art has been explicated only because it has been read alongside verbal sources – in particular the Bushmen's own accounts of their beliefs, as dictated to Wilhelm Bleek and Lucy Lloyd. This is the reason why rock-art research in Africa is now far more sophisticated than readings of Upper Palaeolithic art in Europe, where there are no parallel ethnographies to serve as the paintings' Rosetta Stone.

Rock painting and engraving

Southern African rock art was made with a variety of paints and techniques.

Red pigments – the most durable of the colours – were mostly ochre or ferric oxide ground to a fine powder. White colouring, which lasted less well, included silica, clay and gypsum, while black was made from charcoal, soot and minerals such as manganese oxides. It has been less easy to identify the liquid medium in which the pigments were mixed. Chemical tests have shown that paints include traces of amino acids, and these were probably derived from blood – a possibility which is supported by some ethnographic accounts of the use of antelope blood in painting. Other possible media include fat, urine, egg white and plant sap (Lewis-Williams & Dowson 1989). Paint was sometimes applied with the finger, and also with quills, feathers or very thin bones. Engravings were made by pecking, incising and scraping the rock surface.

Southern African rock art is still difficult to date directly, although new techniques of radiocarbon dating, using very small samples of paint, open the possibility of an absolute chronology. In the meanwhile, the firmest evidence comes from paintings on loose stones and pieces of the rock face excavated from dated stratigraphic layers in rock-shelter sites. The oldest of these dates is from a rock shelter in Namibia – Apollo II Shelter – and is about 26,000 years before the present. Engraved stones from Wonderwerk Cave near Kimberley have been similarly dated to more than 10,000 before the present day. Much of the surviving art is, however, much younger than this (many of the very old paintings will have long weathered away). Pictures of ships and European colonial settlers indicate that the artists were

FIGURE 182 THE 'WHITE LADY OF THE BRANDBERG'.This painting, from the Brandberg range of Namibia, is of a man with body decoration carrying a bow and arrows. The image has long, and erroneously, been described as the representation of a white woman.

still very active in many areas in the seventeenth, eighteenth and nineteenth centuries. This chronological span makes the southern African art fully contemporary with Europe's Upper Palaeolithic art, but far more long-lived as a tradition of representation (Lewis-Williams & Dowson 1989).

Through the years, there have been various claims for the authorship of the paintings, including a variety of alien colonists from the north and (in one argument) from outer space. Such claims have usually derived from a reluctance to attribute anything made with skill or aesthetic judgement to Africans – an equivalent of the racist interpretations that have been offered for Great Zimbabwe. One of the more bizarre interpretations has been that of a painting of a man, carrying a bow and arrows, preserved in the Brandberg in Namibia (Figure 182). Long known as the 'White Lady of the Brandberg', this image has attracted more than ordinary misrepresentation. For example, Henri Breuil, one of the foremost authorities on European cave art in the first half of the twen-

FIGURE 183 PAINTING OF THE TRANCE DANCE. This panel is one of the clearest representations of the trance dance. A person lies supine in the centre, with a shaman kneeling next to the patient. People dance around the central figures, clapping their hands. The arrows probably are 'arrows of sickness, expelled from the patient by the shaman during curing'. Compare this example of a rock painting with the ethnographically recorded trance dance portrayed in Figure 181.

tieth century, wrote to the South African prime minister, General Smuts: 'I send you the portrait of a charming girl, who has been waiting for us on a rock in the Brandberg range for perhaps three thousand years; do you think it well to keep her waiting much longer?' To which Smuts replied: 'You have upset all my history ... When you publish these paintings, you will set the world on fire and nobody will believe you.'

At this time, neither man had seen the painting. As David Lewis-Williams and Thomas Dowson have pointed out, 'the famous White Lady of the Brandberg is neither white nor a lady'. 'The White Lady and accompanying figures are clearly Bushman rock paintings, striking but no different from many paintings throughout southern Africa. Only someone unfamiliar with the broad sweep of Bushman rock art would wish to single out the White Lady for special treatment' (Lewis-Williams & Dowson 1989: 7).

It is now widely accepted that most rock art was the work of Bushman painters, although there is still the possibility that Khoikhoi artists made more of a contribution than is currently believed (Dowson & Lewis-Williams 1994b).

What do the paintings mean? Many now accept that they were the work of Bushman medicine people, and that they represent states of altered consciousness. But there is a range of viewpoints within this broad consensus (Dowson & Lewis-Williams 1994a).

One example of the interpretation of a set of images is given by Lewis-Williams and Dowson's exegesis of a circular group of human figures (Figure 183). This would be widely accepted as the representation of a dance scene, but Lewis-Williams and Dowson argue that it is the important 'trance dance'. Described in the historical ethnography, and still carried out today by Bushman groups in the Kalahari, this dance provided the route for a medicine person to the other world of altered consciousness (Figure 181).

In the centre of the painting in Figure 183, a person lies in a supine position, and is tended by a kneeling medicine man. What this represents is the process of healing, which was a key function of medicine people in trance. The dancers perform the trance dance around this central group, while the arrows stand for the

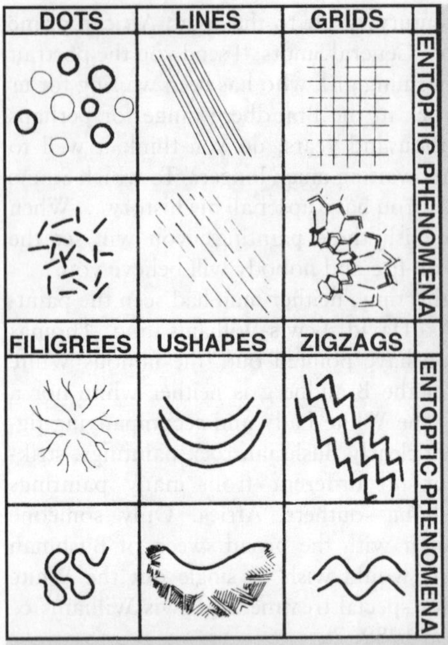

DOTS	LINES	GRIDS	
			ENTOPTIC PHENOMENA
FILIGREES	USHAPES	ZIGZAGS	
			ENTOPTIC PHENOMENA

FIGURE 184 ENTOPTIC PHENOMENA. These geometric forms are experienced at an early stage of an altered state of consciousness.

(Figure 184). It has been suggested that these are paintings of 'entoptic phenomena' – the luminous geometric shapes, including zigzags, chevrons, dots and grids, that are an early stage in the trance experience, and are derived from the structure of the human nervous system. Similar entoptics are experienced by some people entering altered consciousness by other means, including hallucinogenic drugs.

'The relevance of this neuro-psychological research to Bushman rock art is clear. We already know that the artists were, at least in many instances, shamans who entered an altered state of consciousness and would therefore, like all other people in similar circumstances, have experienced entoptic phenomena. When we turn to the art, we find these very forms – grids, dots, zigzags and so on. For reasons not yet fully understood, it seems that there are more entoptics in their pure forms among the engravings than the paintings, but they certainly occur in both art forms' (Lewis-Williams & Dowson 1989: 61).

sickness drawn out of the patient's body during the healing process (Lewis-Williams & Dowson 1989: 38–9).

Not all the images that make up this rich artistic tradition are of people or animals. Some are abstract, executed in a variety of shapes

Systems of opposition

But what of situations where there are no ethnographic sources to provide the key in interpreting non-verbal symbolic representation – where there is no equivalent of the Bleek and Lloyd archive or the testimony of Bushmen living in the Kalahari today? In one sense, all cognitive interpretations depend on studies that have used verbal sources, either as generalisations about the way in which the human mind works, or as analogies which identify the processes of symbolic expression and extend these to the partial evidence of the archaeological record.

The most widely used of the generalising approaches is structuralism, already described in Chapter 4. Structuralist theory was derived from linguistic research, and so it is hardly surprising that it has been influential in the interpretation of symbolic communication other than language. Structuralist interpretations of archaeological patterns such as regularities in

the layout of Iron Age villages (the 'Southern Bantu Cattle Pattern') and the architecture of the central part of Great Zimbabwe rest on the argument that all human actions are guided by cognitive templates, by structures of thought of which we are rarely specifically aware. For example, Margot Winer and James Deetz have looked at the way in which the colonial landscape and architecture of the Eastern Cape were created in the nineteenth century (Winer & Deetz 1990). In a carefully nuanced argument, they have suggested that the founders of the village of Salem – established in 1820 by a party of immigrant Methodists from the Great Queen Street Chapel in London – marked out an idealised 'cognitive map', which was their 'memory' of rural England before extensive industrialisation. This structural model determined how a landscape could be visually pleasing – how big fields should be, and how they should be bounded, and how vistas should be set up by the positioning of houses.

FIGURE 185 HOUSE FAÇADES: STRUCTURALISM. In a structuralist interpretation of house architecture in the nineteenth-century Eastern Cape, it has been argued that houses conformed to cognitive rules, in which the symmetry of the house's exterior was set in opposition to the irregularity of the interior room plan.

Because such cognitive maps are comprehensive views of the world, Winer and Deetz expected to find the same symbolic architecture in the design of the houses. What they noted was a contrast between the interiors and exteriors of buildings. Regular Georgian façades recalled the contemporary fashions of England, while asymmetrical 'hall and parlour' floor plans referred to a far older form of house organisation. Winer and Deetz explain this unexpected juxtaposition as a consequence of disruption and relocation. In their view, English settlers were evoking both contemporary fashion and a memory of rural life in order to cope with the experience of Africa.

The emphasis in structuralist interpretations of material culture is on the comprehensive effect of cognitive maps. 'It is terribly important that the "small things forgotten" be remembered. For in the seemingly little and insignificant things that accumulate to create a lifetime, the essence of our existence is captured. We must remember these bits and pieces, and we must use them in new and imaginative ways so that a different appreciation of what life is today, and was in the past, can be achieved' (Deetz 1977: 161).

Consequently, we should expect that the symbolic system of Eastern Cape settlers would have structured the acquisition and use of possessions within the household, and that these patterns would be reflected in the rubbish discarded at archaeological sites.

The structuralist interpretation of the colonial settlement of the Eastern Cape has provided a vivid image of the manner in which non-verbal symbols were used to assert domination and establish identity. It has also integrated the full range of archaeological evidence – from the broad sweep of the landscape to the details of house layout and table settings – in a single interpretative scheme. Critics of this form of explanation would point out, however, that structuralist interpretations tend to work 'against history'. Although the ways in which the Salem settlers created and arranged their landscape emerge vividly, the sense of the constant historical movement of the area fades into the background. Other, more historically tuned explanations seem possible. Rather than being part of a general cognitive process, could the opposition between house plans and façades not be a result of the reconciliation of the ideals of domestic unity (the hall and parlour combination) and a 'public sphere' (Georgian façades placed carefully in vistas)? (M. Hall 1993)

Post-structuralism

The call for a form of narrative (or 'discourse') is characteristic of alternative approaches in the quest for an archaeology of mind. These approaches can be grouped together under the loosely defined rubric of 'post-structuralism' (Chapter 4). Post-structuralism is often set up in opposition to studies such as Winer and Deetz's research in the Eastern Cape, inasmuch as it resists the application of universal principles of conceptual organisation and the apparent timelessness of structuralism. But post-structuralism is as much founded in language theory as structuralism, and represents the further development of the proposition that material culture can be 'read' like a book. There is much greater theoretical and methodological continuity between structuralism and post-structuralism than is often acknowledged.

One influential school of post-structuralist interpretation has become known as 'contextual archaeology'. Contextual archaeologists reject the notion of 'objective truth', or the idea that the archaeologist can stand apart from the past and weigh and assess past human behaviour in a detached, definitive manner. Rather, they insist, the meaning of material culture must emerge from the totality of its context,

FIGURE 186 HOUSE FAÇADES: POST-STRUCTURALISM. A post-structuralist interpretation of house design insists that the specific history of the building be taken into account. Houses such as these, in the nineteenth-century Cape village of Zuurbraak, were constructed by a community made up of English immigrants and emancipated slaves. The design shows the amalgamation of British and indigenous Cape ideas.

and this context must include the background and objectives of the archaeologist as well. The past and present are inevitably bound together. In Ian Hodder's words, 'It is … by looking for significant patterning along dimensions of variation that the relevant dimensions are defined. The symbolic meaning of an object is an abstraction from the totality of these cross-references. The meaning of an object is derived from the totality of its similarities and differences, associations and contrasts' (Hodder 1991: 138).

Christopher Tilley has amplified this approach further. Tilley asserts that the material world is part of language. Building on the same theoretical foundations that have supported structuralist interpretations, Tilley sees the meaning of objects as lying in the system of relations between signs, and not in the signs themselves (Tilley 1989). In the terminology of linguistics, meaning is displaced along a chain of signifiers. Material culture can have no 'absolute' meaning nor can the process of analysis ever be complete. The task of the archaeologist is thus to write – and to write and write.

This post-modernist approach leads to the concepts of the 'text' and of 'reading'. In archaeology, or so post-modernists claim, there are many 'readings', none of them 'right' or 'wrong' (Hodder 1989). Some archaeologists have taken this relativity to its extreme. Bjørnar Olsen, for example, sees an infinite chain of possible meanings (Olsen 1990). He regards the

Oromo ornament

The complexity of meaning in material culture, and the need for a fully contextual reading of artefacts, are demonstrated in Aneesa Kassam and Gemetchu Megersa's study of the ways in which ornaments are used by the Oromo in Ethiopia, Kenya and Somalia (Kassam & Megersa 1989). Traditional Oromo society is composed of two institutions, *Qaalluu* (spiritual authority) and *Gada* (temporal power), and members of both wear distinctive insignia.

'The most important *Qaalluu*, or *Abbaa Muda*, is distinguished by the *laddu*, three iron bracelets worn on the wrist of the left arm. According to myth, iron was of meteorite origin and "fell from heaven". It is significant that the first *Qaalluu* is also said to have "come down from heaven". In Oromo there are a great number of ornaments made out of iron and its substitutes – copper, brass and, more recently, aluminium – collectively known as *sibbilla*. Iron has various connotations, including that of protecting the wearer from evil forces, but in the present context it represents strength, divine power and resistance' (Kassam & Megersa 1989: 25–6).

tradition of interpretation which seeks to recover the inherent meaning of an object, as impossible and nostalgic. Instead, material culture should be read as 'open' and 'plural'. Objects (European megaliths in Olsen's example) are 'empty sites', 'eternally open to signification'.

Olsen believes that these plural meanings cannot be ranked in order of veracity because they are all in some sense 'true'. Hodder, in contrast, still seeks to establish veracity by 'fixing' meaning – by establishing context – for 'it is the context which allows us to fix meanings. It is the context in which a signifier is used (written) which screens out the polysemy and limits the interpretation' (Hodder 1989: 69). But in turn, this argument is circular, as Hodder himself recognises, for the definition of the attributes of an object depends on the definition of context, while the definition of context depends on the definition of attributes (Hodder 1991: 141).

These post-modernist confusions and uncertainties – in particular the way in which this approach tends to lead inexorably to the impossibility of writing any history at all – has stimulated a reaction. It is now argued that archaeologists need to go back to the object itself and question whether material culture can be reduced to a mere analogue of verbal language, or whether its symbolism is somehow different. Chris Chippindale, for instance, has argued:

'Insofar … as artifacts and texts are the same thing, the study of artifacts as if they were texts produces the same insights. Insofar as artifacts and texts are different, the study of artifacts as if they were texts ignores their artifactual character. Under the definition of archaeology as concerned specifically with the *artifactual* aspects of history and of anthropology, the artifact is fundamental, especially in prehistory, where other direct evidence is lacking' (Chippindale 1992: 254).

Chippindale advocates the study of the shapes of artifacts as a way of getting to their fundamental character – a character that lies beyond what people thought they were doing:

'The great regularities of prehistory take place over so many human generations that one can be sure that larger regularities are involved than anything people were aware of, or consciously chose to do at the time. No *Homo erectus* ever said, "We've had the Acheulean for quite long enough now; it's really time we went on to the Middle Palaeolithic." The real questions, the real issues of "meaning" in artifacts, are in the means by which consistency in design was maintained, and not maintained, over *la longue durée*: there is much more to these things than what people thought they were doing: there is much more to their study than guessing at what people thought they were doing' (Chippindale 1992: 274–5).

This approach takes us back to the fundamentals of archaeology – to typological systems as classifications of form, and to the special qualities of archaeological time, discussed in Chapter 7.

Another 'post-postmodernist' approach has been to return to the fundamentals of semiotics – the study of symbols. For example, Jean Molino has applied the principles of semiotics to the question of the meaning of artefacts (Molino 1992). Molino takes the material world as comprising sets of signs. The central point about signs is that they have material existence, both as production (because language cannot encode a meaning prior to the existence of the sign) and as reception (because it offers access to knowledge): 'having been produced, the sign exists materially as an object of the world among the other objects of the world: image, word, rite, work of art, or scientific theory.' The sign is thus 'irreducibly new', a combination of form. Its fundamental structure is not purely formal, since it is a consequence of the 'symbolic function', which is an autonomous function, alongside nutritive and reproductive functions. In other words, the symbolic function must be seen as prior to language.

'Any social practice is symbolic through and through, and there is no tool, no activity, no product that is truly empty of meaning. But this material existence is only one aspect of the sign – in addition, the sign has an "aesthetic" existence, in that it is received by someone. Thus the sign is reference, as well as object, and the object is only a trace of the full sign. This partiality denies the possibility of "objective", positivist study, since all archaeology has are the traces of meaning' (Molino 1992: 17, 22).

As the 'symbolic function' exists prior to language, the material world – as a set of signs – is distinct from verbal communication. But at the same time the linguistic distinction between signifier and signified ensures that objects divorced and isolated from the original context in which they were produced can only be partial traces of the full system of signs that once existed. By distinguishing between the objective reality of these traces and the necessary indeterminacy of later analysis, Molino draws a distinction between objects as constituted in past symbolic systems (in the Early Iron Age, for example) and objects as transcribed in successive texts (for instance, in archaeological papers written about the Early Iron Age).

These approaches are confusing and sometimes confused, as is always the case on the theoretical frontier of any discipline. It is still apt to conclude with Marx's comment on material culture and its meaning: 'A commodity appears, at first sight, a very trivial thing, and easily understood. Its analysis shows that it is, in reality, a very queer thing, abounding in metaphysical subtleties and theological niceties' (Marx 1974: 76).

Writing the past

chapter **13**

In the preceding chapters, I have tried to expose archaeology's inner structure, its own 'cognitive system', the skeleton of the discipline, the way in which the longer history of Africa has been written, and the history, disagreements, success and excitement of this enterprise. I have put forward the view that archaeology, as a set of practices, hangs together around a cluster of key concepts. These include the notion of 'material culture', the recognition of the importance of context, ideas about time, place and the relationships between people and their environments, studies of subsistence, technology and social networks and, emerging more recently, the most difficult quest of all – an 'archaeology of mind'.

Now, in this final section, I want to show how these different aspects of the discipline can come together in specific research projects, and demonstrate what archaeologists *do*. Many case studies could serve this purpose. I have chosen two examples that seem to me illustrative of Africa's place in the wider world. Both research projects have clearly shown Africa's part in global history, disproving the colonial caricature of the 'dark continent' where nothing of significance ever happened.

The first case study is of urban origins in West Africa. It makes clear the role archaeology has played in demonstrating that the cultural richness of town life in the Sahel was an indigenous development, and not merely a by-product of the spread of civilisation from the Mediterranean. The second example, set some 6000 km to the south and 100 000 years earlier, is central to the ongoing debate about the origins of modern humans – about our common ancestry.

West Africa: the archaeology of Jenne-jeno

Historians have long acknowledged the importance of complex societies, of states, in West Africa. But they have also understood the Sahel's early cities, with their crowded streets and busy markets full of exotic commodities, as originating in stimuli from far away – the consequence of trade from across the Sahara, and ultimately the offshoot of the earlier civilisations of the Mediterranean littoral. In his book *Ancient Ghana and Mali*, for example, Levtzion wrote:

'*Sahil* is the Arabic word for "shore", which is well understood if the desert is compared to a sea of sand, and the camel to a ship. Hence, the towns which developed in the Sahel ... may be regarded as ports. These towns became both commercial entrepôts and political centres. Those who held authority in these strategic centres endeavored to extend it in order to achieve effective control over the trade. Thus trade stimulated a higher level of political organization, while the emergence of extensive states accorded more security to trade. Political developments in the Western Sudan, throughout its history, are related to the changing patterns of intercontinental and trans-Saharan trade routes' (Levtzion 1973, cited in Connah 1987: 102).

Earlier archaeological research in West Africa tended to go along with this view, adhering to what Susan Keech McIntosh and Roderick McIntosh (1984) have termed the 'historical school'. In this writing about early cities, archaeologists framed and limited their questions in terms of the documentary evidence, 'documenting the town site as it was during the time period covered by the historical sources that describe it. It is in this sense that much of West African early town research conducted to date is particularistic; it describes a particular site at a particular time in reference to particular historical documents' (McIntosh & McIntosh 1984: 76).

In contrast, in their own research McIntosh and McIntosh advocated an explicitly processual approach. Rather than concentrating on indi-vidual towns, they set their sights on the region, examining human settlement within its environmental setting. 'In West Africa, this means that the research focus has shifted radically, from historical correlation at individual towns, to documenting development processes of entire urban systems, beginning at a period predating the emergence of fully recognizable urban centres (McIntosh & McIntosh 1984: 78).

The result of this reorientation of archaeological objectives has been an effective challenge to the old historical synthesis. Contrary to the established wisdom, it has been clearly demonstrated that West African towns – and the states they served – had indigenous origins many centuries before the development of trans-Saharan trade. Understanding the archaeology of these towns is in fact an important contribution to understanding urbanism as a process in human history on the global stage.

McIntosh and McIntosh's major fieldwork comprised a regional site survey and trial excavations in Mali over a seven-month period in

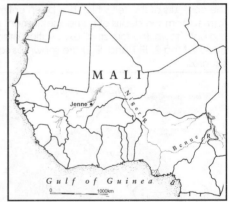

FIGURE 187 WEST AFRICA AND THE CITY OF JENNE.

FIGURE 188 THE INLAND NIGER DELTA.

1977 (McIntosh and McIntosh 1980). Starting at the historic city of Jenne (Figure 187), alongside the Inland Niger Delta, they set out to discover what was happening in the western Sudan during the 'silent millennia' before the rise of the great empires of Ghana, Mali and Songhai. They also wanted to discover what material culture and settlement patterns looked like in the region's historical period, from approximately AD 800 to the present day.

The focal point for the survey and trial excavations was the site of Jenne-jeno, a large mound some three kilometres from the bustling modern city. Although historians had discounted local oral traditions, present-day occupants of Jenne had long identified the mound – or *tell* – as their ancestral city (McIntosh & McIntosh 1981). Jenne-jeno was a marked feature in the local landscape, some 800 m in length, and covered by a thick blanket of broken potsherds. Mud-brick house foundations were still visible on the mound's surface, and the foundations of

FIGURE 189 SITE PLAN OF JENNE-JENO. This plan shows the contours of the *tell*, which has been entirely formed from the debris of human settlement in the early town. The four small excavation areas (Mnd 1, Mnd 2, JF 1 and JF 2) are shown as solid squares.

the city wall could still be traced around part of the site (Figure 189). It was clearly an abandoned town of importance, a place that would repay sample excavations.

Tells such as Jenne-jeno (and Daima, also near the Inland Niger Delta, which was described in Chapter 6) have complex formation processes: these affected McIntosh and McIntosh's excavation strategy. *Tells* are in essence artificial hills, formed entirely from the debris of human occupation. Over time the mud-brick houses of the town aged, weathered and were abandoned – flattened to form the foundations for subsequent buildings constructed over them. Collections of rubbish accumulated in backyards and corners; they were in their turn sealed beneath subsequent buildings. As the Jenne-jeno mound accumulated, some parts were dug out again for human burials within the town's cemetery. Later, a number of artefacts were collected by treasure hunters. More recently, modern farmers have ploughed the surface of the mound for dry-ground crops. In addition to these cultural formation processes, natural formation processes have operated, including rain gullying, sheetwater erosion and wind deflation (McIntosh & McIntosh 1980).

Because of this complex site taphonomy, and the limited resources available in their first field season, McIntosh and McIntosh could not hope to study the spatial layout of the early town itself. Although there was clearly a lot that could (and still can) be learnt from the excavation of house plans and their positions relative to one another, this would have demanded a very time-consuming and expensive strategy of horizontal excavation. In addition, the McIntoshes' Mali project had been designed to tackle problems that were more temporal in nature: how old were towns such as Jenne-jeno, and did they pre-date the inception of the trans-Saharan trade? Consequently, they decided to concentrate on questions for which there was a reasonable possibility of obtaining answers.

'The goals of these exploratory excavations were four-fold: to determine the depth and nature of the deposits; to establish a gross chronology of the site by means of both radiocarbon dating and ceramic analysis; to investigate the specific economic issue of possible local domestication of African rice, millet and

FIGURE 190 EXCAVATIONS AT JENNE-JENO.

sorghum; and to examine the possible early emergence of urbanism in the Inland Niger Delta' (McIntosh & McIntosh 1979: 230).

Four trenches were marked out, each 3 m by 3 m, and designated Mnd 1, Mnd 2, JF 1 and JF 2 (Figure 189). These trenches revealed some 5 m of well-stratified continuous deposits resting on sterile floodplain alluvium (Figures 189, 190; McIntosh & McIntosh 1979).

The second part of the Mali fieldwork in 1977 was the site survey: this would allow the McIntoshes to interpret Jenne-jeno within its regional context, and uncover the processes of urbanisation in action. The McIntoshes chose the area for this site survey because it is representative of the rural hinterland of the modern town of Jenne, and because it includes a wide diversity of land forms and vegetation types. Before the survey began, a programme of stratified random sampling was devised, following the principles described in Chapter 5.

• All upland areas not subject to seasonal flooding (and therefore not able to sustain permanent settlement) were mapped from aerial photographs and gridded into numbered transects, each 2 km long and 0.5 km wide.

• Mounds on the floodplain were identified on aerial photographs, and each assigned a reference number.

• A table of random numbers was used to select a 20 per cent sample of both the transects and the mounds.

• Each selected transect was searched on foot; and each mound selected was visited to ascertain whether it was an archaeological site.

• Every site discovered was mapped and information regarding its topography, vegetation,

dimensions and surface features was recorded. Surface collections of pottery were made (McIntosh & McIntosh 1979).

It was this combined information – the assemblages from the four excavated trenches at Jenne-jeno and the 42 sites from the stratified random sample – that formed the basis for McIntosh and McIntosh's interpretation of the urban history of this part of the Inland Niger Delta.

The first question asked – particularly important in this case, where the research strategy had been largely designed to address an issue of dating – concerned chronology. During excavation of the Jenne-jeno trenches, great care was taken to establish tight stratigraphic control. The effort was rewarded by a clear stratigraphic sequence. When samples of charcoal were radiocarbon-dated and calibrated, they proved to be consistent with the relative dating inferred from the stratigraphy (Figure 191).

The lowest absolute and uncalibrated age estimate (from layer 30 in Mnd 1) was 210 ± 180 bc, indicating a 68 per cent probability of a calendar date lying between 390 and 30 BC, although the sample did not come from the very bottom of the lowermost occupation level. In the process of 'rounding off', which is characteristic of archaeological chronologies, McIntosh and McIntosh placed the beginning of the Jenne-jeno sequence at about 250 BC.

The uppermost radiocarbon dates were more ambiguous, since it seems likely that some deposits continued to form well after Jenne-jeno had ceased to function as a town of any importance. However, a slightly lower sample (from the bottom of layer 2 in Mnd 2) belonged unambiguously to the period of the town's occupation, and gave an age estimate of 1120 ± 140 ad, or a 68 per cent probability of a calendar date lying between AD 980 and AD 1260. McIntosh and McIntosh interpreted the age estimate in the light of the documentary evidence: this suggested a gradual decline of the town, until its final abandonment around AD 1400.

The quality of Jenne-jeno's stratigraphic sequence has allowed a detailed interpretation of changes in the composition of assemblages through time: more than 30 distinct natural depositional units have been identified in some of the excavation sections. Nevertheless, McIntosh and McIntosh found it convenient to synthesise the evidence for the site's history by devising a set of composite 'phases' – the generalised 'time slices' discussed in Chapter 7.

- Phase I. This first phase lasted from about 250 BC to AD 50 and is defined by the absence of permanent mud buildings and the predominance of finely made sand-tempered pottery.
- Phase II. This is defined by permanent mud-brick architecture, and dated to between AD 50 and AD 400.
- Phase III. Dated to between about AD 400 and about AD 900, this phase provides evidence of increasing population density, with more houses and crowded cemeteries.
- Phase IV. Starting in about AD 900, this phase was characterised by the steady decline of the town, until its eventual abandonment in about AD 1400, according to documentary sources (McIntosh & McIntosh 1980).

As is often the case, the relative chronology of the Jenne-jeno sequence has proved to be as important as the set of absolute radiocarbon dates. McIntosh and McIntosh (1980) carried out an attribute seriation of ceramics from the excavated units. This showed that there was a consistent pattern of change in the frequency of decoration and pottery shape, which supported the interpretation of the stratigraphic sequence and the radiocarbon age estimations. What is important was that the ceramic seriation, calibrated by the radiocarbon dates, could provide a basis for the relative dating of the surface collections of ceramics acquired during the stratified random sample of the survey area. In other words, the relative frequency of attributes from an undated surface collection could be matched with the relative frequencies of attributes in the dated assemblages of ceramics from Jenne-jeno.

This framework of relative dates proved to be the key to interpreting the pattern of regional settlement in Jenne-jeno's hinterland. However, before an interpretation could be developed, it was necessary to present a full profile of the region's environment and principal ecological relationships.

The West African savanna consists of grasslands, with varying densities of trees and shrubs, and is bordered by tropical rainforest in the south and by the Sahara Desert to the north. These savanna grasslands comprise a parallel series of environmental zones, running roughly from west to east (Figure 192).

'A hypothetical traveller, journeying due north from the Nigerian coast, could traverse in less than 1500 kilometres a whole range of environments, from coastal mangrove swamp to true desert. On the way he or she would pass through tropical rainforest, forest–savanna mosaic, relatively moist woodlands and savanna, wooded steppe, and subdesert steppe' (Connah 1987: 99–100). One consequence of this environmental zonation is the range of ecotones and ecozones in close proximity to one another. Such proximity would allow and encourage the exchange of raw materials and products (Connah 1987).

However, there are also environmental constraints in the savanna lands, foremost of which

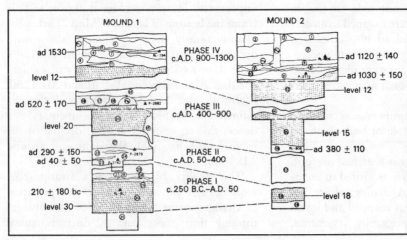

FIGURE 191 JENNE-JENO: PHASES OF OCCUPATION AND RADIOCARBON DATES. This is a diagrammatic presentation of Jenne-jeno's four stratigraphic phases and the radiocarbon age estimations.

is water availability. Rainfall is markedly seasonal, and the wet season becomes shorter from south to north. In consequence, the margins of perennial rivers and lakes are particularly important for human life. The Inland Niger Delta is one such water body – a vast interior region of swamps and standing water which cuts across the Sahel's environmental zonation (Figure 193). The Delta is fed by the Niger and Bani rivers, and for six months of each year an area of some 30 000 km² can be covered by flood waters (McIntosh & McIntosh 1980, Connah 1987).

Seasonal flooding of the type characteristic of the Inland Niger Delta makes agriculture possible in an arid environment without the need for irrigation technology. It seems certain that the key to the economy of this area was the cultivation of the damp delta sediments in the early summer rains, and the propagation of a second harvest after the wet season, once the flood waters had receded (Connah 1987). However, other aspects of technology were vitally important in the area. Iron and slag were found in the lowermost excavated levels at Jenne-jeno and at all the sites recorded in the regional site survey. In contrast, no evidence for Stone Age settlement was found at all, despite the confident prediction that early experiments with intensive wild-plant gathering – an early stage in experimental domestication – had taken place at the delta margins (McIntosh &

McIntosh 1980). This seems to imply that iron implements were essential for exploiting this difficult land, and that iron working was a key aspect of the technology of the first farming settlement.

Other aspects of technology must have been well developed at Jenne-jeno. The town was an urban centre that probably supported a range of specialist craftspeople. However, one of the consequences of a limited sampling strategy in the mound excavations – with its emphasis on establishing the vertical sequence and the site's chronology – was a comparative dearth of information about the way the town functioned. But McIntosh and McIntosh did find evidence for a number of crafts, including pottery production and textile manufacture. On the basis of the documentary sources they argued that early Jenne-jeno was as important in the wider networks of production and trade of the Sahel as Jenne was shown to have been in the documentary records of the last five hundred years.

Information about foodways was also limited, but for rather different reasons. The site's taphonomy – the layer upon layer of hard compacted clays from abandoned mud-brick houses – made sieving impracticable. Water flotation at the site was also not possible, as excavations had to be carried out during the dry season. However, the excavators were able to take some bulk samples back to the modern town for

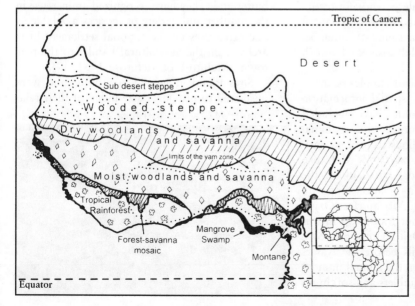

FIGURE 192 WEST AFRICAN ENVIRONMENTAL ZONES. West Africa's ecological zonation has created a wide range of environmental variations between the extremes of the tropical rainforest along the Atlantic coast, and the Sahara Desert.

FIGURE 193 THE FLOODPLAIN OF THE INLAND NIGER DELTA.
The Inland Niger Delta is a vast seasonal floodplain that supports intensive agriculture without
the need for mechanical irrigation.

detailed examination. As McIntosh and McIntosh (1980) insist, the reconstructed economy
of the town has to be read against these
methodological constraints.

Cultivated plant foods must have been important from Jenne-jeno's first days as a settlement, for firmly identified botanical remains of
African rice (*Oryza glaberrima*) were found in
the lower levels of Phase II. Further up the
sequence, there was evidence for the use of a
variety of wild plant foods as well (McIntosh &
McIntosh 1979). Faunal samples were small,
but bones from domestic cattle have been tentatively identified from Phase I deposits, and
there were clay figurines that are probably
models of domestic livestock from Phase II levels. Hunting, fishing and collecting wild animals were in evidence from the earliest days:
bones from catfish and Nile perch were recovered from Phase I onwards, as well as faunal
collections that included a range of antelope,
crocodiles and tortoises (McIntosh & McIntosh
1980).

How can these rather small samples be interpreted? In the absence of spatial information
from the site (which could have included
domestic hearths and storage areas, animal
pens and specialised buildings to process agricultural produce), McIntosh and McIntosh
have turned to the ethnoarchaeology of the
modern city of Jenne and its relationships with
its rural hinterland. Today, African rice (*Oryza
glaberrima*) is the dominant food crop in this
part of the Inland Niger Delta. Crops are sown
on the low floodplain soils before the waters
rise. Later in the year, when the annual inundation has subsided, various millets and sorghums

are cultivated in the moist soils as the flood
waters recede. This natural hydrological regime
has permitted the production of vast surpluses
of staple commodities and these have been mar-
keted at Jenne, supplying Saharan towns 500 to
1000 km away (McIntosh & McIntosh 1979).
The McIntoshes argue that the presence of
African rice in the botanical samples from the
Phase II layers, coupled with the building of
mud-brick houses at this time, signals the beginning of the 'rice–fish–cattle subsistence complex', which was the basis of Jenne-jeno's
importance in the Sahel.

The argument that Jenne-jeno was the focus
of the highly productive cultivation of the delta
floodplain is also the key to interpreting social
networks, and understanding the relations
between the town and the hinterland settlements plotted during the regional survey. This
aspect of the research was specifically designed
to establish whether there had been a hierarchy
of settlements in the region.

'A large site like Jenne-jeno does not evolve
in isolation. Although archaeologists tried for
years to devise a list of traits by which urbanism could be positively identified at an archaeological site, no set of criteria was ever recognized as totally satisfactory or universally
applicable. A more productive approach has
been borrowed from geographers, who have
found it useful to investigate the relationship
between the urban centre and its surrounding
hinterland. They have recognized an increase in
the number and variety of services available as
one progresses up the regional settlement hierarchy from the agricultural hamlet to the true
town' (McIntosh & McIntosh 1981: 17).

Sites found in Jenne-jeno's hinterland were
measured to provide a size index of their rela-

FIGURE 194 CERAMICS FROM JENNE-JENO.

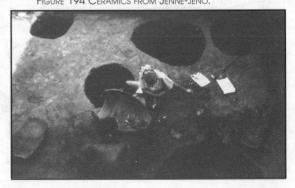

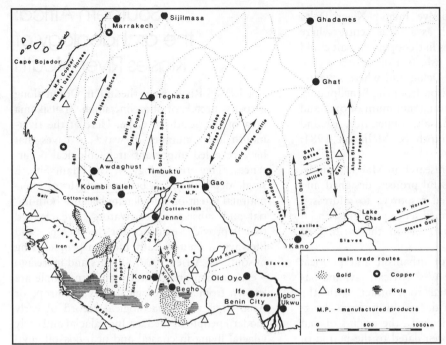

Figure 195 Pre-colonial trade routes in West Africa. It has been argued that a wide variety of commodities were traded across West Africa's ecological zones long before the trans-Saharan trade-routes were opened up.

tive importance, and then tied to Jenne-jeno's sequence of radiocarbon dates by means of the relative dating sequence established for ceramics. When the survey had been completed, McIntosh and McIntosh found that all the archaeological sites in the region were *tells* standing at least 2 m above the floodplain. This implied that each settlement had been in use for at least a few centuries. Most of the sites were quite small in their spatial extent, with about a quarter of the sample smaller than the smallest villages of the present day. Clearly, there *was* a hierarchy of settlement. But were the sites contemporary with one another? If they were, this would indicate there had been the sort of complex networks that one would expect around an urban centre.

Here the role of relative chronology proved crucial in the interpretation. When the surface collections of ceramics made at the hinterland sites were subjected to the same attribute analysis carried out for the excavated assemblages from Jenne-jeno, it became clear that, at least in their earlier phases, an overwhelming majority of the recorded settlements had been contemporary with one another and with Jenne-jeno. Interestingly, though, this settlement pattern had changed through time: the surface collections (representing the last pottery in use at a

particular site) showed that many sites had been abandoned before Jenne-jeno's own final decline and abandonment. McIntosh and McIntosh have interpreted their evidence as suggesting a peak of settlement in the hinterland coinciding with the end of Phase III and the beginning of Phase IV at Jenne-jeno, when the population density of the delta floodplain could have been ten times that of the present day. This is indeed strong indication of a complex urban polity – a state system – with Jenne-jeno at the centre of the network (McIntosh & McIntosh 1981).

It is unlikely, though, that Jenne-jeno's importance and prosperity were due solely to its status as a local agricultural market. Early documentary sources show that Sahel towns were important centres for regional as well as long-distance trade. Both McIntosh and McIntosh (1981) and Connah (1987) have argued that towns such as Jenne-jeno fulfilled this role before the rise of the trans-Saharan trade. For example, iron and copper were worked from Jenne-jeno's earliest years, but there are no ore supplies near by, and copper for smelting must have been obtained from deep in the Sahara. This implies networks of trade and barter.

'We suggest that Jenne-jeno's location at the southwestern extreme of the navigable and agriculturally productive Inland Niger Delta promoted its growth as a trade centre where Saharan commodities like copper and salt could be traded for dried fish, fish oil and rice produced in the Inland Delta, and where savanna products, including iron from the Benedougou, could be obtained with a minimum of overland travel in exchange for salt, copper, rice, fish and other staples' (McIntosh & McIntosh 1981: 20–1).

The McIntoshes' research in Mali is a model example of a successful project, designed and executed with limited resources to address a specific and well-defined set of problems, and it has had a major impact on the writing of Africa's past.

'The emergence of urbanism and political centralization in the West African savanna has long been attributed to contact with the Mediterranean world, resulting from long-distance trade. Suspiciously, the origins of that trade have usually been dated to the period of the earliest historical sources that touch on the subject. Archaeology has until recently played a confirmatory, some might even say a sub-servient, role in the stock historical interpretation. It has been a case of so much historical information being available that archaeologists have failed to ask the sort of questions that they might have asked otherwise. As a result, the quality of archaeological data available to shed light on the origins of cities and states in the West African savanna is poor. Fortunately there have in recent years been some exceptions to this general rule. The work at Jenne is a notable example. Reviewing such new evidence, along with the older evidence obtained over the last eighty years or so, leads to questioning the long-accepted external-stimulus explanation' (Connah 1987: 120).

FIGURE 196 ARCHAEOLOGICAL SITES NEAR THE MOUTH OF THE KLASIES RIVER.

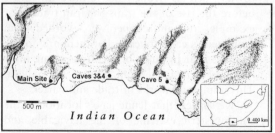

Southern Africa: the archaeology of Klasies River Mouth

The Klasies River meets the Indian Ocean along a rocky stretch of shoreline in the Tsitsikama area of the Southern Cape. Here at the river-mouth are a number of wave-cut caves that have revealed important archaeological occurrences. The archaeology of the Main Site, a single depository, has become a focus of international attention and debate because both initial and subsequent excavators have claimed that it provides evidence for the presence and lifeways of anatomically modern people living in southern Africa 100 000 years and more ago – earlier than anatomically modern people are known from archaeological sites in Europe or Asia. 'It is an archaeological record of early modern people of the Last Interglacial and early Glacial living in coastal and near-coastal environments and is almost unique in its fullness' (H.J. Deacon & Geleijnse 1988: 5–6).

The first excavations at the Klasies River Mouth shelters were carried out by John Wymer between 1967 and 1968 (Singer & Wymer 1982). The full sequence of the deposits was explored in large stratigraphical units, which resulted in massive, though selective, assemblages of stone tools and faunal remains. Singer and Wymer's report included a palaeo-climatic interpretation and a dating sequence that placed the fragmentary human skeletal remains from the site in context. The kernel of their interpretation was that Klasies River Mouth was a living site used by people who were anatomically more similar to us than to earlier hominids, and that this living site was more than 100 000 years old (Singer & Wymer 1982).

The assemblages of mammalian fauna from Wymer's excavation were important indicators both of the changing environment and of the foodways of the people who had lived in the shelters. These were studied by Richard Klein as part of his wider study of the palaeoecology of the Southern Cape. Klein concluded that the Klasies River Mouth people had hunted both small and large animals, butchering larger carcasses away from their 'home base' and bringing choice cuts of meat back to the shelters (Klein 1976). In turn, this interpretation attracted the interest of Lewis Binford, a father figure of New Archaeology (see Chapter 4). Binford had been studying the ethnoarchaeology of Alaskan Eskimos, and had concluded that the prevalent interpretation of early hominid sites, which stressed organised hunting and the use of home bases, was erroneous. On the basis of his study of the ways in which Eskimo hunters butchered animal carcasses (and the nature of butchering damage on animal bones), Binford argued instead that hominids had behaved differently. They were opportunistic scavengers who collected what they could from the carcasses of large animals already ravaged by carnivores.

'Ideally, I would like to go out and study a group of people who are obtaining a large proportion of their diet by scavenging. In that situation I could quite directly study the relationships between the dynamics and the static by-products remaining from various scavenging tactics. Unfortunately, I know of no opportunities for doing this. I face a situation quite common for archaeologists: I cannot gain a first-hand knowledge of many behavioral and dynamic conditions that characterized the human past by studying contemporary homologies or analogies. I must fall back, then, on a different approach. I must use what knowledge I have to tease out new knowledge and understanding. I have previously suggested that hominid scavengers might well be expected to exploit heavily the marrow bones and perhaps the heads remaining on the sites of ravaged carcasses. I start here by seeking out an archaeological case characterized by the properties I suspect as indicative of scavenging. If such a case can be found, then I can study the fauna in detail, searching for patterning previously unsuspected' (Binford 1984).

The Klasies River Mouth cave sites fulfilled this requirement.

In the same year that Binford's faunal study was published, Hilary Deacon began a new programme of excavation at Klasies River 'Main Site' – the combined sequences of Caves 1 and 2. The aim of this interdisciplinary project, based at Stellenbosch University, was to study changes in the productivity of the South-

FIGURE 197 MAIN SITE, KLASIES RIVER MOUTH.

ern Cape environment, and the effects of such changes on human populations over a long period of time (H.J. Deacon & Geleijnse 1988). An important part of these wider aims was to explore further Singer and Wymer's claims for a very early modern human population at Klasies River Mouth. If their interpretation was correct, then it was likely that the environment

FIGURE 198 PLAN OF MAIN SITE, KLASIES RIVER. This plan shows the different caverns that comprise Main Site at Klasies River. Cave 1, the lower shelter, has three parts: Cave 1B, which is separated by a rock spur, and Caves 1 and 1A, which are stratigraphically linked. Cave 2 (shown by a dotted line in this plan) lies above Cave 1, forming a second 'storey'.

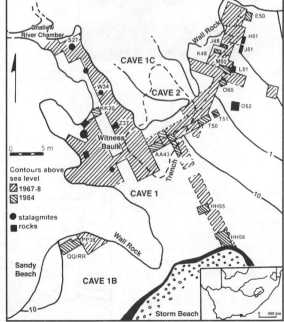

229

would have been used in a modern way for a very long period of time, with significant ecological implications.

The Stellenbosch project was also designed to correct the rough-grained sampling strategy followed in Wymer's excavations, and to gain further information about the sites' contentious chronology. Hilary Deacon thus proceeded by positioning a series of grid squares, normally a square metre in size, to give a complete section through Wymer's sequence in the Main Site (Figure 198). Excavation followed the natural

stratigraphy, the aim being to identify the finest division possible: such 'units' could be as thin as 5 mm. Similar units were grouped together for the purposes of interpretation and called 'members'. Wherever possible, these members were correlated with Singer and Wymer's earlier stratigraphy.

Singer and Wymer had sieved selectively, and through a coarse mesh. As a result, many of the smaller stone artefacts and bones had not been collected. Larger bones not considered identifiable had been thrown away. For its part the excavation strategy of the Stellenbosch team sought to correct the sample biases in the earlier assemblages by recovering the maximum amount of material possible. Sediments from each unit were sieved through a 3 mm mesh and the residue was washed with sea water. Additional bulk samples, each between 2 kg and 8 kg, were collected for detailed study in laboratory conditions (H.J. Deacon & Geleijnse 1988).

Because interpretations of both the chronology and the patterns of human behaviour at Klasies River Mouth depend crucially on how the stratigraphic sequence is read, one must understand both cultural and natural formation processes.

The deposits in Main Site accumulated on a 6 m rock bench against a cliff face, and behind a protecting dune that has since been removed by rising sea-levels. Side chambers or caves in the cliff face became blocked off as a large cone of debris from human occupation and natural

FIGURE 199 FINE-GRAINED STRATIGRAPHY AT KLASIES RIVER MAIN SITE.

FIGURE 200 DIAGRAMMATIC SECTION THROUGH MAIN SITE. The stratigraphies of Caves 1, 1A and 2 can be linked as a continuous sequence of finely stratified deposits. Cave 1B is disconnected, and its association with the Cave 1–1A–2 sequence depends on relative dating.

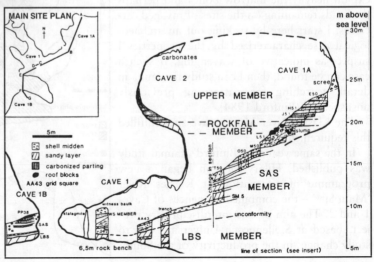

230

deposits built up. The lowermost openings – caves 1, 1B and 1C – became inaccessible in the early stages of accumulation; and in the later stages, with its opening perched high in the cliff, Cave 2 became habitable and then filled up with deposit. By the time people finally stopped visiting the sites, more than 20 metres of sediments had built up through the stacked caverns. Subsequent natural formation processes included water saturation and shifts in the underlying layers, which caused episodes of slumping. The consequence of all this has been a stratigraphy that is extremely challenging to interpret (H.J. Deacon & Geleijnse 1988).

Singer and Wymer's excavations, which used large stratigraphic units, lumped together episodes of natural deposit accumulation and the debris from human occupation: this gave the impression that the Klasies River Mouth shelters were used continually as a living site. 'Broadly, the sequence can be regarded as a continuous one, from top to bottom, and it remains as a monument to the adaptive resourcefulness of Upper Pleistocene people, who appear to have come to terms with their environment in a manner far more successful than is usually imagined' (Singer & Wymer 1982: 107).

But the Stellenbosch excavations, with their emphasis on the fine detail of the stratigraphy, have shown that Singer and Wymer's conclusion was not justified (Figure 199). In fact the Klasies River Mouth shelters were visited sporadically; and sometimes there were long periods of absence. During their visits, the early hunter–gatherers left behind them different sorts of material traces. These included small hearths, shell middens and plant material, some of which was probably the inedible residue from meals; this subsequently formed carbonised horizons in the site (H.J. Deacon 1993).

Establishing a chronology for the Klasies River Mouth sequence has been difficult because many of the deposits date to beyond the limits of the radiocarbon technique (Chapter 7). For this reason, the interpretation of the stratigraphy is crucial. In addition it has been possible to use absolute dating techniques other than radiocarbon. Although there has been debate about the site's chronology in the past (notably by Binford 1984), there is now general consensus about the overall age of the Main Site column of deposits.

The stratigraphy of the Main Site falls into two parts: the major depositional pile which accumulated through Caves 1, 1A and 2, and which can be read as a continuous sequence; and the much shorter sequence in Cave 1B, which is separated to the south by a substantial rock spur. Indeed the Cave 1B sequence would probably have been disregarded, had it not contained one of the most important human fossils from Main Site, known as 'Mandible 41815'. In view of the importance of relating Mandible 41815 – the jaw-bone of an anatomically modern person – to the main sequence, a complicat-

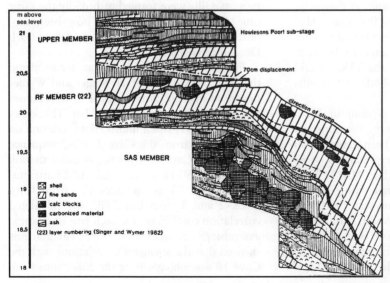

FIGURE 201 DETAILED SECTION THROUGH THE TOP THREE MEMBERS OF KLASIES RIVER MAIN SITE. This section drawing clearly shows the complexity of the Klasies River Mouth stratigraphy. Note in particular the slump of sands from the RF Member, which has in turn distorted the way in which the underlying SAS Member deposits lie.

ed interpretation of both absolute and relative chronologies has been developed for Main Site.

It is easiest to start with the sequence through Caves 1, 1A and 2. Singer and Wymer's lowermost excavation horizons were labelled Layer 38 and Layer 39, but together they represent probably tens of thousands of years of time. Indeed, the Stellenbosch excavations have shown that there were many thin units within this lowermost part of the site. These have been grouped together as the 'LBS Member', named after the light-brown sands that are a feature of this part of the sequence (H.J. Deacon & Geleijnse 1988). Shell samples from the LBS Member, correlated with deep-sea cores on the basis of oxygen isotope variations, suggest a date of about 120 000 years (Singer & Wymer 1982). This is supported by amino acid racemisation dates for the same member, which give an age estimate in excess of 100 000 years (Bada & Deems 1975).

The LBS Member is overlain by three more major depositional units. The SAS Member includes numerous rich shell lenses, while the RF Member has distinctive sands and rock falls from the cave roof and a considerable amount of slumping in the deposits: this makes the stratigraphy complicated to interpret. The top of the main sequence has been labelled the Upper Member; its deposits accumulated to the point where they almost filled Cave 2. Attempts to radiocarbon-date the Upper Member have shown that it is too old to be within the range of the technique. An upper limit to the entire sequence can thus be set of 50 000 years (H.J. Deacon & Geleijnse 1988). Amino acid racemisation dates have given a range of between 90 000 and 65 000 years for the SAS, RF and Upper members together (Bada & Deems 1975).

The second stratigraphic column in Main Site – the shorter sequence in the disconnected Cave 1B – has only recently been dated by an absolute technique. Most interpretations of its age, and the age of Mandible 41815, have depended on methods of relative dating. Singer and Wymer's initial argument was that their Layer 10 in Cave 1B (which contained Mandible 41815) must be more than 100 000 years old because the stone tools matched those in the lowermost part of the Cave 1–1A–2

sequence. In essence, this was a crude form of dating by artefact seriation. Binford (1984) rejected Wymer and Singer's relative chronology and substituted one of his own, arguing on the basis of 'faunal seriation' that the Cave 1B sequence was far younger than Singer and Wymer had claimed. However, a closer look at Binford's argument reveals a classic tautology. His dating follows his interpretation of the Cave 1B fauna as having been hunted rather than scavenged. Because he believes that hunting could have occurred only in the more recent history of Klasies River Mouth, he 'seriates' the Cave 1B deposits as comparatively recent. But at the same time, he uses the 'late' date of the Cave 1B deposits as part of his argument that hunting developed as a mode of behaviour only in more recent times. And, as Deacon and Geleijnse point out, Cave 1B could not have been occupied late in the Klasies River Mouth sequence for the simple reason that, by this time, it was packed full of natural sand accumulations and debris from much earlier human occupations.

The next technique of relative dating used for the problematic Cave 1B was a comparison of the lithology of its sands with that of the sands from the Cave 1–1A–2 sequence. Deacon and Geleijnse (1988) have shown that the nature of the grains of sand that make up the matrix of Cave 1B is similar to those that form the matrix of the base of the SAS Member in the main stratigraphic pile. This suggests that the two cave fills were formed at broadly the same time. Their interpretation has now been supported by electron spin resonance dating (H.J. Deacon & Geleijnse 1988).

Finally, Anne Thackeray has reconsidered the class of evidence which Singer and Wymer first used in their chronological interpretation: the stone-tool assemblages. What Thackeray did was to carry out a multivariate seriation on the artefacts from the Cave 1–1A–2 sequence and also the Cave 1B sequence in order to look for a match. Working from a list of 12 attributes and with 28 assemblages (20 from Cave 1–1A–2 and 8 from Cave 1B), she calculated correlation coefficients for each pair of possible assemblage associations. Her calculations showed that the strongest correlations with the Cave 1B assemblages were the collections from the lower part of the SAS Member, and thus further supported the argument that Mandible 41815 is about 100 000 years old (A. Thackeray 1989).

Mandible 41815 belongs to a rather fragmentary collection of human bones from the Klasies River Main Site – parts of the skeletons of at least ten people. There is no evidence for deliberate burial, and no possibility of linking cranial bones with other parts of the skeletons that are represented in the collection. The physical anthropology of the Klasies River people would tax even the most astute jigsaw fanatic: what remain are parts of upper and lower jaws, isolated teeth, a frontal bone and other cranial pieces, an ulna, a vertebra and a clavicle. Two maxillary fragments (the upper jaw) were found in the lowermost levels of the LBS Member. Most of the rest of Singer and Wymer's fragmented finds, as well as a human ulna from the Stellenbosch excavations, came from the lower part of the overlying SAS Member, and were dated to about 90 000 years ago. It has been suggested that these people may have met their end as a result of cannibalism (White 1987). Although this is a controversial suggestion, it does convey a good impression of the fragmentary condition of the collection.

The conclusion drawn from the measured study of the human bones is that the Klasies River people differed physically from earlier hominids and had bodies similar to our own. But their build tended to be heavy and there were more marked physical differences between men and women than in human populations today. It has been argued that a direct line of descent can be traced from the Klasies River community to Holocene and modern African populations, in particular the San of the Kalahari (Rightmire & H.J. Deacon 1991).

What was the nature of the environment over the long period during which early people visited and revisited this part of the Tsitsikama coastline? We have shown in Chapter 8 that the regional climates of southern Africa were continually fluctuating at these times. Not surprisingly, therefore, both the macrofauna and the microfauna from Klasies River Mouth reveal changes that reflect in turn changes in the vegetation of the caves' hinterland. For example, Richard Klein's study of the larger animals has established that there were changes in the relative proportions of species that live in open grasslands and those that prefer more closed habitats. But the picture for the smaller species is different. Environmental conditions at the time of the earliest occupation seem to have been much the same as those at the time of the most recent use of the site. However, in the middle period of the sequence the vegetation around Klasies River Mouth was more closed (Klein 1976). Analysis of the microfauna supports this view. The small animal bones come mostly from the natural deposits, when humans were not living at the site, and were deposited in the shelters by birds and small carnivores. Margaret Avery has demonstrated that conditions around the caves were most similar to the present day during the central part of the sequence, rather than at the beginning or end of the occupation (D.M. Avery 1987).

Despite these environmental changes, there is remarkable continuity in stone-tool technology throughout the four stratigraphic members of the Cave 1–1A–2 sequence. These assemblages show remarkable uniformity, being characterised by the production of standardised flake-blades from cobbles that had been carefully shaped into appropriate cores before the blank flake-blades were struck off. Overall they are grouped as belonging to the Middle Stone Age (H.J. Deacon 1989).

One exception is the 'Howieson's Poort' substage, which occurs quite high up in the sequence, sandwiched between other Middle Stone Age assemblages. The name is confusing: it comes from a site in the Eastern Cape where stone tools like these were first described. In the assemblages from the Howieson's Poort substage, the basic technology of the Middle Stone Age is supplemented by extensive retouching of small flake-blades into a variety of specialised tools. 'It is an industry based on the production of small flake-blades and the delicate trimming of many of them into a series of specialized forms' (Singer & Wymer 1982: 87). Silcrete, which has better flaking qualities, was preferred as a raw material, even though this probably had to be brought to Klasies River Mouth from some distance away. Hilary Deacon has suggested that this technological change – and the subsequent switch back to the highly uniform

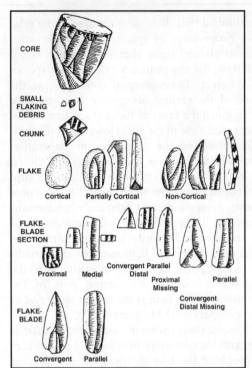

FIGURE 202 TERMINOLOGY FOR PRODUCTS OF THE FLAKING PROCESS AT KLASIES RIVER MOUTH. In their study of stone artefacts from the University of Stellenbosch excavations, Thackeray and Kelly made use of a typology which reflected the 'reduction sequence' of the Middle Stone Age flake-blade technology.

from the SAS Member (dated to between about 100 000 and 80 000 years ago) have been studied in detail by Anne Thackeray and Alison Kelly (A. Thackeray & Kelly 1988, A. Thackeray 1989).

Thackeray and Kelly applied a typological system that took into account the flaking process and other technological attributes. It was also close enough to Singer and Wymer's typological scheme to allow comparisons to be made with the earlier study (Figure 202). Their detailed research led to a number of conclusions:

• The object of stone-tool working was the production of long flake-blades. These are either parallel-sided or convergent, forming a point.

• The proportions of the different products of flaking were remarkably consistent throughout the 20 000 year sequence, indicating a single 'technological tradition'.

• Most raw materials used were locally available, but some stone might have been brought to Klasies River from up to 20 km away.

• Cores were for the most part worked into rough form away from the site, probably on the beach, from where most of the raw material came. But subsequent stages in stone-tool manufacture took place in the rock shelters.

• Subtle changes in stone-tool style took place through time: flake-blades tended to become shorter and more uniform as time passed.

• Less than 3 per cent of the artefacts making up the stone-tool assemblage were retouched. Retouch generally consisted of shallow notching, and retouched artefacts were often damaged, probably from their use as implements (A. Thackeray & Kelly 1988).

The purpose to which these stone tools were put is still not entirely clear, although many of them must have been utilised in processing food. For the Klasies River excavations have produced large assemblages of animal bones, shellfish and evidence for plant foods. The interpretation of this evidence has been the subject of considerable debate. The various argu-

Middle Stone Age tool-making tradition that had been the norm at Klasies River Mouth before the Howieson's Poort interlude – may reflect responses to the environment:

'The coincidence of the Howieson's Poort horizon with a period of variable and deteriorating environmental conditions suggests that this archaeological phenomenon may be linked to the problems of coping with increasing environmentally-related stress. Such stress may have more to do with the maintenance of populations and their social structures under conditions of lowered habitat productivity, than simply coping with colder and drier climates' (H.J. Deacon 1989: 560).

Deacon has been careful to point out that environmental stress of this kind was probably not a simple, deterministic response to the environment. On the contrary, the increase in carefully worked points might reflect social factors such as an increased consciousness of territorial boundaries.

The 1967–8 excavations at Klasies River Mouth produced huge collections of stone artefacts. Smaller assemblages, recovered with finer-meshed sieves, resulted from the University of Stellenbosch's excavations, and collections

ments are closely connected with the larger question of whether the archaeology of Klasies River Mouth is a very early example of the modern human way of life.

The first detailed interpretation of foodways at Klasies River was put forward by Richard Klein on the basis of his detailed study of the faunal assemblages. Klein found that the frequency of body parts in the assemblages varied according to the size of animal: the bigger the carcass, the more likely it was to be represented in the cave assemblages by cranial or foot bones. By analogy with patterning in faunal assemblages from sites in other parts of the world, Klein argued that this patterning was a consequence of the 'schlep effect'. Hunters often brought home smaller animals intact, but butchered larger animals at the site of the kill, discarding less useful parts away from the 'home base'. Klein suggested that animal feet may have been brought back as 'handles' on skins, or because feet were particularly valued, perhaps as a source of sinews for sewing. He argued that larger animal heads may have provided bone that could be utilised in making artefacts (Klein 1976).

Klein's reading of the faunal evidence was challenged by Binford as part of his wider interest in the archaeology of scavenging. Klein had analysed the fauna by following the widespread archaeological practice of tabulating Minimum Numbers of Individuals (see Chapter 10). But Binford rejected this approach because 'the bones recovered from human sites do not represent complete individuals that were once there (as MNI methods assume), but instead represent the biased introduction of already selected and sometimes processed anatomical segments to a site for further processing and/or storage, or for consumption' (Binford 1984: 49). In other words, Binford argued that when an animal is killed and butchered, parts of little use are discarded off the archaeological site, while other parts may be processed for easy transport. Meat is not consumed or brought to archaeological sites in anatomically complete units, as MNI counts assume.

On the basis of his re-analysis of the Klasies River fauna housed in the South African Museum in Cape Town, Binford came to a number of conclusions:

- A substantial group of body parts from both small and large animals was poorly represented in the faunal assemblage. These body parts represent the entire axial skeleton except the head – the parts that commonly remain at predator kills unless there is intense competition among feeders.
- Heads and lower legs were frequent for larger animals; these were perhaps the scavenged remnants of predator kills brought back to the caves.
- Heads and lower legs were poorly to moderately represented for smaller animals; this indicates that the smaller animals were butchered and partly consumed away from the site (Binford 1984).

Binford's argument, then, was that the Klasies River Mouth people killed some small bovids, but consumed choice parts of these carcasses at the kill and returned with small parcels of less favoured meat. Large animals, in contrast, were scavenged, and marrow-yielding bones and remnants of meat left by carnivores at their kill sites – body parts such as the lower leg, head and neck – were brought back to the shelters (Binford 1984).

We should note here that Richard Klein's and Lewis Binford's interpretations of the same faunal collections are diametrically opposed. Perhaps the issue will be resolved by the eventual publication of the full faunal assemblages from the later University of Stellenbosch excavations. But, as has been pointed out, the wide-ranging debate about the interpretation of the larger animal faunas has tended to divert attention from the fact that other sources of food were important too at Klasies River Mouth. Indeed, animals, whether hunted or scavenged, may have been of little importance to the people who lived in these caves.

One of these sources of food was shellfish. Klasies River Mouth has the oldest known evidence for the systematic exploitation of shellfish in the world. Collections of shell from the University of Stellenbosch excavations have been studied in detail by Francis Thackeray. Thackeray identified each specimen to species level wherever possible and calculated Minimum Numbers of Individuals in order to derive indices for the changing abundance of different species. He found that the brown mussel (*Perna*

perna) was the dominant species in the SAS Member, and occurred in the assemblages with other rocky-shore species. But higher up the deposits *Perna perna* declined in importance, conceding pride of place in the overlying RF Member to the sand mussel *Donax serra*, which continued to be common in the Upper Member. Thackeray also noticed that there was a general decline in the abundance of shell through time. He suggested that this patterning marked a changing environment: declining sea-levels took the shoreline further from the site and resulted in sandy shorelines replacing a rocky intertidal zone (A. Thackeray 1988).

Apart from marine resources (which also included seals and penguins), another major source of subsistence was edible plants. Hilary Deacon (1989) has pointed out that, in contrast to the Early Stone Age (when sites were concentrated in river valleys or close to the coast), Middle Stone Age people lived on the coast and in rock shelters high in the mountains. Deacon believes that this settlement pattern, which was to continue into the Late Stone Age, signals the use of the fynbos geophyte flora.

'Natural fields of geophytes form resource-rich patches along the mountains and in acid soils along the coastal margin. It is the distribution of these resources that explains the wide range of Middle and Later Stone Age locations. The conclusion is that Middle Stone Age people did not differ from Later Stone Age people in their basic subsistence ecology' (H. J. Deacon 1989: 557).

Deacon also believes that this developing reliance on plant foods can be plotted through the Main Site sequence at Klasies River. Although the conditions of preservation in the caverns have been such that it is difficult or impossible to make specific plant identifications, the steady increase in carbonised residues around hearths probably represents the increased use of geophyte residues, and matches the decline in the abundance of shellfish. In other words, Middle Stone Age people were moving from a predominantly coastal way of life to more terrestrial foodways (H. J. Deacon 1989: 1993).

A regular settlement, involving seasonal movement between the coastal region and the mountain areas in response to the seasonal availability of plant foods, implies some sort of 'cognitive map' of the landscape and a social organisation that allowed people to make planned, forward-looking decisions about the use of resources. Many of the thin occupation levels that contribute to the Klasies River Mouth sequence – which were discerned during the fine-tuned excavations carried out by the University of Stellenbosch – consisted of small hearths with food debris and stone tools scattered around them. It has been suggested that these were the traces left by nuclear families. 'The discreteness of the hearths and their size suggests each represents the domestic focus of a nuclear family, and ethnography would point to this being the domain of a particular woman' (H. J. Deacon 1993: 89).

These hearth features have been studied in detail by Zoë Henderson (1992). Henderson concentrated on an excavated area of 2 m by 1.5 m in Cave 1B, about a metre above the place where Mandible 41815 had been found, and in a part of the sequence that has been correlated with the SAS Member in Cave 1 (Figure

FIGURE 203 PLOT OF ANIMAL BONES IN KLASIES RIVER CAVE 1B. The plan shows bone fragments and a hearth (AF1).

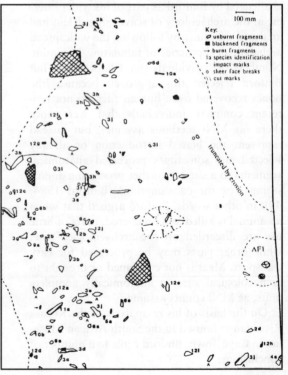

236

203). She found three identifiable 'occupation horizons' and evidence for at least five hearths, each up to 0.5 m in diameter. She has interpreted this as indicating that food was prepared by individuals or small families, and that each hearth was used for a few weeks or months. All the hearths were associated with rich concentrations of stone artefacts and food waste, some of which could be conjoined. The animal bones were very fragmented, but there were signs of impact damage and cut marks. It is clear that shellfish had been cooked on the open fires (Henderson 1992).

Further social implications have been drawn from the long-term trends in stone-tool form. Thackeray and Kelly have pointed out that changes in artefacts over the period they studied, between about 100 000 and 80 000 years ago, are not obviously functional. 'The changes in flake-blade attributes ... are of the kind often labelled "stylistic" by archaeologists ... and can be considered to be a reflection not of social reality, but rather the structuring principles of the society – the way things might be ideally, rather than the way they are in practice.' Interpreting these patterns is not straightforward:

'Without knowing the social and historical circumstances in which the MSA II convergent flake-blades were used, one can only speculate on why they become more standardized and shorter relative to width through time. In order to understand why the attributes take the form they do and what they meant in a culture–historical context, we need to study the collections in terms of the contexts in which they were produced, used, discarded and incorporated into the archaeological deposit. A great deal more experimental, replication and contextual studies need to be done to obtain this information for Late Pleistocene contexts for which ethnographic analogues may not be available' (A. Thackeray & Kelly 1988: 23).

However, the conservatism of the people who made these implements is marked. It takes a persistent and definite set of design decisions to keep things the same through episodic visits to the same site over a very long period of time.

Do these cognitive indicators, coupled with the fragmentary physical remains, amount to evidence for modern behaviour? There are two schools of thought on this issue. In the one

camp are those who believe that the Klasies River people were like ourselves. They argue:

- The Klasies River Mouth hearths and middens imply modern organisation of domestic space and rules of cleanliness. 'It is evidence of this kind that may be cited in support of an argument that the early anatomically modern people in the Late Pleistocene had modern cognitive abilities' (H.J. Deacon 1993: 89).
- Artefact patterns through time indicate 'style' in artefact design. 'There can be no question that there is evidence for planning, symmetry and a sense of aesthetics in the Klasies River Main Site Middle Stone Age assemblages' (A. Thackeray 1989: 53).
- It is possible that people living at Klasies River Mouth practised personal adornment, which is often taken as an indication of modern behaviour. Small pieces of red ochre were found throughout the SAS and Upper members, as well as pieces of soft yellow sandstone, which may also have served as pigment (Singer & Wymer 1982).
- There is evidence for food sharing. 'Klasies has been facetiously described as the oldest seafood restaurant in the world and shellfish collecting was carried out on the same scale as in the Holocene. Why collect hundreds of thousands of shellfish and accumulate them at a specific locality if not to share? Food sharing at the Klasies River Mouth site is not a subject for debate. It is self-evident' (H. J. Deacon 1985: 60).
- The presence of Middle Stone Age sites high in the mountains, as well as on the coast, coupled with the extensive carbonised horizons revealed in the Klasies River Mouth excavations, shows that people had a structured, planned way of making a living that incorporated a close knowledge of the ways in which plant foods could be used. Such a use of the environment was essentially the same as the subsistence strategies followed in the Holocene and by San hunter–gatherers today (H. J. Deacon 1989).

Contrary to this 'essentially modern' interpretation are the arguments that Middle Stone Age people did not exploit their environments as efficiently as Holocene hunter–gatherers, and that they were not capable of doing so because of inferior intelligence. 'Some possible limitations on the hunting capabilities of the Klasies people may be implied by the fact that, in contrast to later peoples, they concentrated their attention on the most docile of the available large bovids (eland) and largely ignored the (?too dangerous) suids, one or both species of which were probably abundant in the vicinity' (Klein 1976: 83).

Scavenging (if indeed it was as much in evidence as has been claimed) was part of this 'catch-as-catch-can' existence, indicating an absence of planning and systematic sharing. In this interpretation, the conservative stone-tool traditions were not a consequence of carefully maintained 'stylistic markers' but rather of mere expediency.

'Almost all the tools are most consistent with a variety of cutting and scraping tasks. If one views collections of stone artefacts with substantial retouch and secondary and tertiary modification as giving clues about the *use life* of tools (that is, how long tools were actually either planned for use or were actually employed as tools), then the MSA assemblages must rank as very expedient, because tools had very short use-lives. One obtains the picture of

a very regularly produced and expeditiously used toolkit, most generally employed in cutting tasks of moderate-to-light duty' (Binford 1984: 36).

In conclusion, some aspects of the interpretation of Klasies River Mouth remain open, and are likely to do so until further fieldwork projects at this and other Middle Stone Age sites have produced more evidence that can used to address unresolved issues. But there can be no doubt that the site is one of the most important in the world.

'Main site is one of the most important Late Pleistocene archaeological sequences available for study. This claim can be made on a number of grounds: as a laboratory for studying site formation processes in a cave environment, as a test of dating methods that are alternatives to radiocarbon, as a source of information on changes in a terrestrial ecosystem in the first half of the Late Pleistocene, as a record of sea-level changes and as an archaeological record of the behaviour of early anatomically modern people and the occurrence of their physical remains' (H. J. Deacon & Geleijnse 1988: 12).

chapter 14

Past tense

Klasies River Mouth and Jenne-jeno are places very far apart in space and in time. They epitomise the diversity of archaeological practice in Africa, the range of ways in which people lived in the past, and some of the major transitions in human history that are central both to Africa's past and to humanity as a whole.

FIGURE 204 EARLY STEPS: THE AUSTRALOPITHECINE TRACKWAY AT LAETOLI, TANZANIA.

Issues such as the origins of modern people and the beginnings of urban life are far from resolved, and will be the focus of exciting and revealing research projects for years to come. Archaeology is central to their exploration, as well as to a host of other concerns, some of which have been mentioned in this book: hominid evolution, the origins of plant and animal domestication, the effects of environmental change, early art and artistic expression, the history of technology, gender relations, colonial settlement, the political and social uses of the past, the management of cultural resources, and ways in which our early history can be communicated to a wide range of people.

Modern archaeology can line up an impressive battery of analytical techniques in the assault on such questions. Some of these are based on ingenuity and have been applied to an extensive range of circumstances: reconstructing foodways from the now-fragmentary residues of meals, for instance, requires methods of faunal and floral analysis that have been refined into a set of highly specialised techniques. Others, such as statistical tests and the use of computers, are now standard in a wide range of natural sciences and social sciences. Others again are in the forefront of new research methods: light isotope mass spectrometry, for instance, is becoming widely recognised as a way of tracing chemical indicators and will have important applications in a range of environmental studies.

But while the modern archaeologist is as likely to be encountered in a laboratory or at a computer screen as in a hole in the ground, fieldwork still has a central role in the discipline. Although few will live out popular expectations of adventures in hostile jungles or discoveries of fabulous treasure, most archaeologists will spend some time digging. And although methods of excavation are as varied as the world in which archaeological sites are to be found, they all rest on techniques of horizontal and vertical control which have been practised through the full history of the discipline.

Whether working in a rock shelter like

FIGURE 205 THE COMPLEXITY OF EVERYDAY OBJECTS. The artist Willie Bester uses everyday objects (tin cans, wire, bits of sacking, car tyres, plastic bags) to build complex montages and thereby create images of life in Cape Town's townships. His work celebrates 'the lives and achievements of their principal subjects. But the artist makes clear that these lives have been led in the most dehumanizing circumstances: apartheid South Africa systematically degraded its oppressed people and eliminated their leaders ... in choosing to communicate this vision in society's waste matter, Bester is demanding that even this material be looked at again and revalued' (Godby & Klopper 1996). This work is titled *Challenges Facing the New South Africa* (1990).

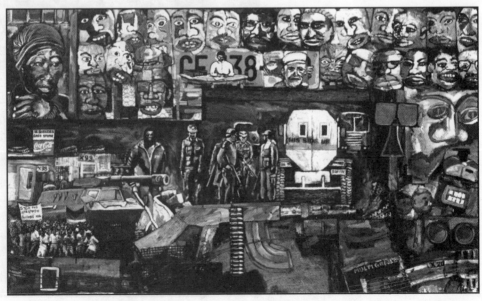

Klasies River Mouth, where food debris and natural deposits have accumulated over tens of thousands of years, or at a settlement mound like Jenne-jeno, where clay houses have been built one on top of the other as the town expanded into a trading emporium, context is everything. The ability of archaeologists to reconstruct what happened in the past is based on their close attention to the associations between different artefacts, and between artefacts and the places where they are found.

Such artefacts – whether buried beneath the ground, lying on the sea-bed or visible in the world around us – are incredibly varied in their size, form and function. This variation is reflected in the different specialisms within archaeology as a discipline. As we have seen, some archaeologists concentrate on evidence which cannot be seen with the naked eye, such as microscopic wear marks on stone and bone tools. Others study landforms – cities or landscapes – which are too large for us to comprehend as a whole without the aid of aerial photographs. But despite such variation, all artefacts have in common their human authorship. They are all products of the human mind, and they all have the potential to inform us about the human minds that visualised them and brought them into being in the past.

The centrality of everyday objects gives archaeology as a discipline an excitingly varied nature. On the one hand, evidence for the past – such as food waste and simple technology – invites commonplace explanation. But on the other hand, the very familiarity of everyday objects often disguises the complex meanings that they can carry – meanings that are often the more powerful for not being made explicit.

One of the defining characteristics of humanity is the way in which people create a material world, whether this be an assemblage of stone tools or a modern city. Such collections of objects are arranged and used in ways that are often taken for granted by the people who make or use them. Their meaning is habitually unstated or understated. This gives artefacts a great potential for revealing the nature of the past, but also presents archaeologists with a considerable challenge: how to put into words meanings that were not put into words in the past.

Function: 'Now, just come and look over here, Post. I've managed to reconstruct several of the pots from our excavation. If you look closely, you can see the impressions of seeds that were pressed into the clay before it was fired. Be careful! It took me hours to put this together, and I don't want a clumsy idiot like you breaking it into tiny pieces again.

'What do you mean? You can't understand what this can tell us about the past? I would have thought it was obvious! If we can identify the seeds from their shape, then we know some of the plant foods that these early farmers were using. It's just a matter of common sense.'

Post: 'But don't you see my point of view, Dr Structure? I know you think all this talk about the complex meanings of artefacts is just hot air. But bear with me – let's try a simple experiment. Think of everyday objects that become threatening for no other reason than they're out of place.

'Let me start you off. Littering – sweet papers and cold drink cans tossed on the ground rather than in the bin. Safety pins used as earrings, or cross-dressing, or accountants wearing bright ties. Or cornflakes for supper and horse-meat in hamburgers …

'Get the idea? We're all used to thousands of artefacts in our everyday lives. But if some of them get out of place, they can become very disturbing, and then all of a sudden we can see just how much meaning they really do carry …'

Archaeology, then, is a mixed set of practices; a hands-on philosophy; the ability both to excavate a trench with straight sides and to appreciate the complex meanings of things.

And what of archaeology in Africa?

As many of the examples of archaeological work in the continent have shown, African archaeology is fully cosmopolitan. Studies of micro-wear damage to stone tools, for instance, are part of an international specialism that has common assumptions and methodology. Other fields of inquiry are not restricted by geographical boundaries: the origins of anatomically modern humans, or of the farming way of life, or the archaeology of colonial settlement are all global research domains.

But at the same time, Africa has long carried a specific set of meanings for the rest of the world: the 'dark continent'; the epitome of savagery or of pristine nature; a timeless place where hunter–gatherers of the Stone Age still live and play. As this book has shown, Africa, like Europe or Asia or North America, is many places with many histories. But because of the history of prejudgement and prejudice about

FIGURE 206 AFRICA: THE 'DARK CONTINENT'. This Rhodesian publicity poster shows a subservient black slave at the feet of a faint, ghost-like Queen of Sheba. It sought to perpetuate the myth that Great Zimbabwe was the product of a European, rather than an African, civilisation. The original caption to the poster read: 'Palace and Temple, stronghold and a source of legends, this is Zimbabwe. Its builders vanished from the earth, but in their high, silent walls they left the stuff that dreams are made of. For information, apply to the Publicity Association, Fort Victoria' (Frederikse 1982).

Africa, to 'write back' from the continent is still to make a claim from the margins of world history.

This combination – a fully cosmopolitan discipline practised in a continent that has always attracted particular prejudices – has ensured that a thread of tension has run through the study of Africa's past. Whether assemblages from early Egyptian tombs, medieval bronzes from West Africa, terracotta sculptures from the south or collections of artefacts assembled by missionaries and adventurers, Africa's material culture attracts mixed responses. For some people, Africa's artefacts display all the qualities of artefacts from other parts of the world, including in their range utilitarian objects, fine craftwork and pieces that have a universal aesthetic quality. But for others, anything African is inherently primitive and timeless, always ethnographic, never 'art'.

This tension has characterised the West's representation of Africa and its artefacts throughout the twentieth century. Albeit a simplification of a complex cultural history, the modern response to Africa can be caught in three archetypal moments.

The first of these is purely fictional: the appearance in 1899 of Joseph Conrad's novel *Heart of Darkness* (discussed in Chapter 8), in which his narrator encounters 'the earliest beginnings of the world', the 'impenetrable forest', the 'heart of darkness'.

The second occurs eight years later with Pablo Picasso's 1907 visit to the Musée d'Ethnographie in the Palais de Trocadero, Paris, and his discovery of the primitive force of African art. 'Who knows what chords were sounded upon the strings of the instrument which is Picasso, after he discovered the moldering masks and dust-coated ceremonial idols of Black Africa heaped in long-neglected tangles in the ethnological department of the Museum of Man in Paris – yet a few of these notes would vibrate within his own artistic language throughout his life' (Duncan 1968: 46).

The third moment occurred in 1920, when Carl Jung journeyed in the Sahara and discovered in Africa an outside vantage point from which he could look back on Europe's civilised psyche:

'At last I was where I had longed to be: in a

non-European country where no European language was spoken and no Christian conceptions prevailed, where a different race lived and a different historical tradition and philosophy had set a stamp upon the face of the crowd. I had often wished to be able for once to see the European from outside, his image reflected back at him by an altogether foreign milieu ... I felt cast back many centuries to an infinitely more naive world of adolescents who were preparing, with the aid of slender knowledge of the Koran, to emerge from their original state of twilight consciousness, in which they had existed from time immemorial, and to become aware of their own existence, in self-defence against the forces threatening them from the North.

'While I was still caught up in this dream of a static, age-old existence, I suddenly thought of my pocket watch, the symbol of the European's accelerated tempo ... The deeper we penetrated into the Sahara, the more time slowed down for me; it even threatened to move backwards. The shimmering heat waves rising up contributed a good deal to my dreamy state, and when we reached the first palms and dwelling of the oasis, it seemed to me that everything here was exactly the way it should be and the way it had always been' (Jung 1973: 266–8).

For Jung and many after him, Africa was an archetypal image of the dark subconsciousness, the 'black under the skin', 'a potentiality of life which has been overgrown by civilisation' (Jung 1973: 274).

These three encounters, and a mass of less momentous experiences, have ensured that images of Africa have been woven into the patterns of Western culture. More recently, in 1995, this ambiguous relationship between Africa and the rest of the world was exposed again in the writing and reaction evoked by the Royal Academy's exhibition in London, *Africa: The Art of a Continent*. This collection of more than 800 objects ranged from southern Africa to the Mediterranean and from five thousand years ago to the present. In the words of the curator, Tom Phillips, 'it is a privilege to celebrate for the first time, in these rooms, the fertile contribution to the visual culture of the world from the whole of this vast and infinitely various continent; and to make here a praise song for Africa' (Phillips 1995: 20). For the

African American writer Cornel West, 'this monumental exhibition is unprecedented in the history of the art world. Never before has there been gathered such a rich and vast array of African art-objects and artefacts from such a broad timespan. And rarely has any exhibition embraced the artistic treasures of the whole of Africa, from Egypt to Ife to Great Zimbabwe' (West 1995: 9).

Yet despite the reasonable expectation that the Royal Academy show would be received with, at least, a benign lack of interest, *Africa: The Art of a Continent* provoked some hoary old prejudices. Simon Jenkins of *The Times* played to the same gallery that Rider Haggard had found so receptive a century earlier:

'On Monday night I put on my best suit and attacked the African art show, talk of the town at the Royal Academy. I was immediately stumped. Outside were a dozen prancing Zulu war drummers, skimpily clad in raffia briefs,

FIGURE 207 COLONIALISM IN AFRICAN ART: MALAWI WOOD CARVING.

243

beaming and whooping at the passing guests. The guests had no idea how to react. Were these renegade militants, satirising the white man's image of Africa? Or were they one of the exhibits, "performance art" courtesy of the Bank of Ulundi. Should we throw coloured beads, or raise a fist in salute? Ambassadorial limousines cruised the forecourt menacingly, as if about to spew AK47s and mow us all down ...' (Jenkins 1995).

Jenkins was no happier inside the Royal Academy. 'I can appreciate a well-crafted meat platter from KwaZulu or an intricate Nigerian Igbo-Ukwu bowl. The decoration is pretty. I can see that the ubiquitous masks may have served their purpose in amusing or horrifying the communities for whose religious beliefs they had meaning. But put them on a pedestal, light them and declare them to be something quite different – art – and my eye judges them as

such, and judges the selector. The daubs and rock paintings and carvings are awesome echoes of the past. But most of the exhibits are "found objects" of the past century. They are crude and – a word detested by the politically correct – primitive' (Jenkins 1995).

In short, Africa was just not up to standard.

Jenkins's compatriot, Richard Dowden of *The Spectator*, came to the same conclusion: 'Is there any art in the continent? You may pronounce a Zulu platter beautiful but it is only a meat dish. Can it therefore be art? You may say Kente cloth from Ghana is magnificent but it is only Asante proverbs woven into cloth through signs and symbols' (Dowden 1995). Dowden then went on to offer his readers a paragraph of potted history which let them off the legacy of four centuries of invasion, pillage and plunder. For him, 'the greatest problem of all' is, again, 'political correctness'.

'The PC line on Africa is that it was the Garden of Eden before the Europeans pitched up and ruined it. Since then everything wrong with Africa, from genocide in Rwanda to drought in Sudan, is blamed on outsiders ... If it were true that African culture had been wiped out by imperialism, Africans would simply be copying European art, building neo-classical houses, painting like Rembrandt and writing like Jane

FIGURE 208 *BUTISI TART?* Chickenman Mkize's sign takes René Magritte's playful challenge to Western art ('This is not a pipe') and gives it a slight ethnographic edge. Mkize was aided by KwaZulu–Natal's Tatham Art Gallery, where he sold his work from a grass verge outside the front door until his death in 1995. The Gallery sells numbered-edition T-shirts of similar signs, and Mkize's work is to be found in art collections in North America and Europe.

Function: 'So what do you think about this review by Simon Jenkins in *The Times*, Post?'

Post: 'An old mistake, I'm afraid. Jenkins thinks that "art" is the same the world over, and that the best art has to be European: Rembrandt, Titian and all those other "old masters" hanging in his National Gallery. It's the arrogance of the coloniser.'

Function: 'But how can you say that! *The Times* is one of the world's leading newspapers – they wouldn't make such a mistake in what they publish!'

Post: 'Come, come, Dr Function – what happened to that "critical voice" you're always telling your students they have to learn? Of course *The Times* can be prejudiced; we can all be prejudiced – even you. Look at the language Jenkins uses. He writes about "attacking" the art show, about dancers who "prance" and limousines that "cruise menacingly". Paintings are "daubs". The whole review is a concoction that belittles and denigrates Africa.'

Function: 'Well, I'll look at it again. But I wish you weren't so strident, Post; even reading the newspaper's no pleasure when you're around?'

Austen. But Africans are not doing this. The fact is that Africa survived imperialism rather well. Its spirit was not crushed. Its culture and society, especially the family, remain as strong as ever. Faced with imperialism, war or drought, Africa falls back on its greatest strength: survival. Conservative but adaptable, Africa absorbed the impact of European intervention and did well out of it. The Europeans, so full of plans and dreams for Africa, were finally defeated, their plans and dreams swallowed up in Africa's mysterious maw and transformed into something quite different' (Dowden 1995).

Politically, it is not really surprising that in 1995 the British press should shrug off Africa and its sculptures and textiles, genocides and famines. Rather than a continent of endless possibilities, Africa is now perceived as a liability, with little left to offer the West. As previous chapters in this book have shown, the study of the past is always a political process. It can be added that the study of contemporary art and

FIGURE 209 AN AFRICAN IMAGE OF EUROPE. San painting from the Koue Bokkeveld in South Africa's Western Cape. Colonial settlers systematically obliterated hunter–gatherer communities on the northern frontier, killing men and often enslaving women. This obviously male figure wears a wide-brimmed hat and heeled shoes, and is smoking a pipe (Yates et al. 1993).

artefacts is equally political. Archaeology 'came of age' at a time when the rest of the world discovered that the continent had a history. Now, at the end of the millennium, this interest has been played out for some people, and Africa is back on the margins of Western consciousness.

The commentaries by Jenkins, Dowden and others on Africa's history and culture reduce the continent to an amusing side-show, a vast colourful craft market, a mass of people whose purpose is merely to survive. These, of course, were exactly the attitudes of those droves of Europeans who set off to civilise Africa with the benefits of European enlightenment. In their writing, Jenkins and Dowden reveal a London still enveloped in the dense fog of its own dark past.

But perhaps the vehemence of Jenkins's and Dowden's opposition reveals the underlying point of their commentary: that their reactions were not so much about Africa as about Europe at the end of the century. Kwame Anthony Appiah caught this point in his essay for the exhibition's catalogue:

'We might as well face up to the obvious problem: neither *Africa* nor *art* – the two animating principles of this exhibition – played a role *as ideas* in the creation of the objects in this spectacular show.

'Take, first, "Africa": through the long ages of human cultural life in the continent, and, more particularly, in the half dozen or so millennia since the construction of the first great architectural monuments of the Nile Valley, most people in the continent have lived in societies that defined both self and other by ties of blood or power. It would never have occurred to most of the Africans in this long history to think that they belonged to a larger human group defined by a shared relationship to the African continent ... Only recently has the idea of Africa come to figure importantly in the thinking of many Africans, and those that took up this idea got it, by and large, from European culture ...

'There is no old word in most of the thousand or so languages still spoken in Africa that well translates the word "art" ... We have received ideas about art and about artists: and my point is that most of these ideas were not part of the cultural baggage of the people who

FIGURE 210 WEST AFRICAN CARVED STOOL. This was part of the 'ethnographic' collection that Irma Stern made in the Belgian Congo in 1942.

made the objects in this exhibition ...

'If African art was not made by people who thought of themselves as Africans; if it was not made as art; if it reflects, collectively, no unitary African aesthetic vision; can we still not profit from this assemblage of remarkable objects? What, after all, does it matter that this pair of concepts – *Africa, art* – was not used by those who made these objects? They are still African; they are still works of art. Maybe what unites them as African is our decision to see them together, as the products of a single continent; maybe it is we, and not their makers, who have chosen to treat these diverse objects as art. But it is also *our* show – it has been constructed for us now, in the Western world' (Appiah 1995).

From early in the twentieth century, Western artists, writers and philosophers had discovered and appropriated the shapes, colours, textures and essences of Africa and used them to con-struct a vantage point from which to appraise and celebrate Western modernity, civilisation and achievement. In this, they had continued the discoveries and appropriations of earlier centuries: the depredations of merchant traders and, later, the territorial expansions and claims of high colonialism. But in 1995, with the certainties of colonialism and modernism no longer secure, it was time to discard Africa again as 'mysterious' and 'primitive', and to discount its rich and varied material culture as an inconsequential collection of 'found objects'.

Despite the celebratory intention of *Africa: The Art of a Continent* – to reverse the long-standing appropriation of Africa by the West and establish the rights of African art in the international cultural arena – a certain ambiguity on the part of the Royal Academy itself seeped through in the way the exhibition was mounted. The catalogue – a massive 600 pages – presented its artefacts against bland and featureless backgrounds: white, dove-grey and black. Similarly, in the exhibition itself, the objects were displayed in darkened rooms, spot-lit: 'when you leave these galleries, gloomy beyond the call of conservation, the lingering feeling is that in 1995, as in 1895, Africa is the dark continent' (J. Hall 1995). The essays in the catalogue, surveying the collections region by region, are by professional museum curators and art historians. In the gallery, labelling was minimal and context understated: 'mystifyingly minimalist' (J. Hall 1995). Overwhelmingly absent are the voices and lives of the people who made and used these things.

Such ambiguity, and the shallow fatigue of *fin de siècle* critics, can best be shown in perspective by travelling back half a century to the time when the South African artist Irma Stern visited the Belgian Congo. Stern's response to Africa – taking its inspiration for an art that merged the images of the continents – was characteristic of the whole century. And finding Africa 'endless, like a green dream of Creation Day', her writing was untrammelled by post-colonial dyspepsia.

'Here I was in the region of the Bakuba, the most artistically creative native race in the Congo, who only one generation back had been man-eaters. It was strange to plunge right among so savage a tribe, and yet only to be aware of a rare artistic taste which had for years been exciting and stimulating the art world of Europe. Here were the creators of magnificent pieces of sculpture, carved out of wood, of fetishes and masks, grotesque and beautiful, revealing primitive Africa in all its fear-ridden phantasy, with its witch-craft and taboos, with its ancestral worship and its world alive with spirits ...

'Now the palace of the King of the Bakubas was before me. High walls made of bamboo formed a kind of court. The King was being advised of my arrival. There he comes, a huge man in the prime of life, his broad bare breast stained with red ochre. Enormous white copper rings were around his wrists and ankles. From his hips down he wore a brilliant Pompeian-red closely-woven raffia garment. His brow was decorated with the royal sign of the horns on a band of thin gold. A golden hatpin adorned with a heavy piece of turquoise was stuck in his bushy hair.

'"I am a painter, and I am going to show all the pictures I paint in the Congo in my country, and after the war in Europe, so that people may learn to love the natives of the Congo as much as I do." This was being translated to the King by his clerk, who spoke French fluently. "Now I have come here," I continued, "to try and collect from you some of the lovely work your tribe is known to produce." The King smiled. "And then I shall also show your people's work with my pictures, so that the white people in my country may learn what beautiful things the black man in the Congo creates."...

'The "town crier" had announced my visit to the King, and what I was wanting to buy, and now the people were bringing me their things – masks and figures, mats of all kinds, and paint and medicine boxes all covered with angular designs and with two or three horns as a kind of crest, cut out of the red wood of the N'gula tree. They came with swords, the handles of which were worked in a fine silver filigree, and with the swastika engraved on each.

'On leaving, the clerk asked me: "The King of the Bakubas wants a favour from you. We hear that you are going to Johannesburg. Will you please send him a small portable Remington."

'I was breathless with astonishment. This king, only one generation removed from man-eating, the King of the Bakubas with six hundred and eight wives – a typewriter!!

'It does look as though centuries are easily leaped over' (Stern 1943: 23–5).

Irma Stern gives her 'Bakubas' a voice, and her enthusiasm is boundless. But in her response to Africa – and in her story of the Remington typewriter – she captures precisely the tension that is at the core of Europe's response to Africa. The Congo and its people were inspirational, and their artefacts were forms that could be transported with ease from the ethnographic cabinet to the painter's easel. But at the same time the European response was patronising and assumptive of superiority: how strange and wonderful that a man with more than six hundred wives and a cannibal father could value an artefact as sophisticated and complex as a typewriter.

FIGURE 211 IRMA STERN'S *ARUM LILIES*. This picture, painted a decade after Stern's visit to the Congo, incorporates the West African stool ('ethnography') in the oil painting ('art').

247

The babel of voices in the hallowed precincts of the Royal Academy provides a signpost to Africa's archaeology in the third millennium – to the ways which the discipline may follow in its continuing exploration of the continent's past, and in the exploration of its own past as a discipline.

For one thing, it is unlikely that there will be an 'African archaeology'.

As Kwame Anthony Appiah pointed out in his review of *Africa: The Art of a Continent*, the notion of 'Africa' was itself an invention of Europe (Appiah 1995). In the nineteenth century, the image of the continent was pinned down by evolutionary assumptions of savagery, barbarism and cultural superiority, as popularly expressed in the novels of Joseph Conrad, Rider Haggard and others. Through the twentieth century, this frame was kept intact by the universalising assumptions of modernism: Africa was the 'other' against which Europe could define itself. But the motif of the twenty-first century, already established, is of disintegration and diversity. 'Archaeology Africa' is a transitory concept that is already being replaced by regional styles of research into the past and different forms of engagement with the present.

Such fragmentation is consistent with cosmopolitan trends in archaeological theory. The 'New Archaeology' of the 1960s claimed to be an objective, global philosophy of practice that would establish the discipline as a science,

offering the reward of truth. These claims were looking battered by the 1970s; today they are in ruins. Although archaeology still uses, to great benefit, a wide array of scientific techniques, these are laboratory tools – the artefacts of the trade. Archaeological theory, understood as a set of propositions about how the past worked, is today diverse and contradictory. We can expect such diversity and contradiction to increase in the twenty-first century.

'To take African history seriously requires a careful and cautious scrutiny of the distinct and sometimes disparate contexts of particular African traditions, rituals, kinship networks, patronage relations and disciplines of craftsmanship. This kind of historicist enquiry – with its stress on the complex interplay of the local with the regional, continental and global forces at work – enables us to highlight the specific ways in which African artists, critics, patrons and communities create, sustain and deploy art-objects' (West 1995: 9).

FIGURE 212 ARCHAEOLOGY IN POPULAR VIEW. One of the carved soapstone birds from Great Zimbabwe is now a national emblem and is incorporated in Zimbabwe's flag.

Further, the future will probably see a closing of the traditional divide between the expert – the respected authority on the past – and the ordinary consumer of archaeological knowledge. Again, such a trend is part of the character of our post-modernist world, in which popular culture has staked its claim and 'high art' is in decline. This is already reflected in the widespread debates about the place of archaeology in popular consciousness, whatever the medium of communication may be.

These are exciting trends. Archaeology in the third millennium will have new questions and new sorts of answers to give. It will be about many Africas and, at the same time, about the common history of the human species.

A fitting closing image is a Yoruba wood carving of a man travelling to market with trade goods stacked high on his head and a bicycle firmly by his side, an image Appiah took as a point of departure for his essay on Africa in the post-modern world (Appiah 1992). Appiah (the son of a Nigerian father and English mother) and Irma Stern (self-exiled from Germany to South Africa, and in search of the essential Africa) were hybrids, as indeed we all are today. And like Stern's King of the Bakubas with his Remington typewriter, the *Man with a Bicycle* brings the global and the local together, and uses them to go places.

'... a figure who is polyglot – speaking Yoruba and English, probably some Hausa and a little French for his trips to Cotonou or Cameroon ... what we should learn from is the imagination that produced it. The "Man with a Bicycle" is produced by someone who does not care that the bicycle is the Whiteman's invention – it is not there to be Other to the Yoruba Self; it is there because someone cared for its solidity; it is there because it will take us further than our feet will take us' (Appiah 1992: 254).

FIGURE 213 GOING PLACES. Yoruba Village Dignitary with Bicycle.

The language of archaeology

absolute date an estimate of the age of an artefact or archaeological unit expressed in calendar years.

accelerator dating a technique of radiocarbon dating (*q.v.*) which makes use of very small samples, allowing animal bones, for example, to be dated directly rather than by their association with larger charcoal samples.

Acheulean a division of the Early Stone Age (*see* Stone Age).

activity site a place where there is archaeological evidence for specialised behaviour such as butchering or iron smelting, as opposed to a general living site (*see* factory site).

adze a small, Late Stone Age tool which, it is generally accepted, was used for woodworking (*see* Late Stone Age).

aerial photography photographs taken from the air by a variety of means (from balloons, kites or aeroplanes, for example) and used in the search for archaeological sites, or to record and investigate complex architectural features.

aerial survey the process of searching for archaeological sites from the air (*see* aerial photography).

aggregation site a place where hunter–gatherers lived during that part of their annual cycle of movement across the landscape when they came together in larger social groups (*see* dispersal site).

agricultural revolution *see* Neolithic Revolution.

agropastoralism a composite term for farming practices that include both plant cultivation and the husbandry of domestic animals.

alluvium fine-grained and often fertile soil deposited by flowing water on floodplains, in estuaries and in river valleys.

altered consciousness a trance or trance-like state of mind in which a range of images is substituted for reality. In rock-art studies, many paintings have been seen as a record of states of altered consciousness and the work of shamans (*q.v.*).

amino-acid racemisation a method of absolute dating bone samples. This technique is based on the observation that the amino acids present in bone protein contain L-enantiomers that change into D-enantiomers at a known rate (enantiomers are mirror-image forms of the amino acid).

analogy a form of reasoning in which a similarity between two or more things is inferred from a known similarity between them in other respects. In archaeology, ethnoarchaeology and similar approaches to understanding the past depend on arguments by analogy (*see* ethnoarchaeology, palaeoethnobotany).

androcentrism an attitude which assumes that men must be central in society and history.

anthropology the study of humanity, in the broadest sense, including social and cultural behaviour, the past, and physical characteristics (*see* physical anthropology, social anthropology).

anthropomorphism the attribution of human form to something; for example, an artefact, animal or god.

antiquarianism the collection and study of artefacts without due regard for the context in which they are found (*see* context).

apartheid the system of legalised racial discrimination that structured South African society between 1948 and 1994.

archaeological record the combined archaeological evidence for the nature of the past.

archaeology the study of the material remains of the human past, ranging from the earliest bones and stone tools to things that are buried or thrown away in the present day.

archaeometry the application of the techniques of physics and chemistry to archaeological research problems.

architecture the design, erection and style of buildings and other structures.

archive a collection of documents.

arithmetic mean the sum of all the scores in a sample, divided by the number of cases.

artefact something fashioned by a person or people, ranging from the smallest tools to entire landscapes.

assemblage a group of artefacts; the term can be used to describe the complete collection from an archaeological site, and also collections from the same class of material from a given time period.

attribute strictly speaking, a minimal characteristic of an artefact that cannot be further subdivided; but in practice, 'attribute' is used for composite characteristics as well.

Australopithecus the earliest genus of hominid that evolved some five million years ago; the name means 'southern ape'.

band a form of social organisation in which there are no formal leaders, few marked disparities in status between individuals and, usually, complex mechanisms of sharing that prevent the accumulation of wealth.

barbarism a now-discredited stage in human evolution postulated by nineteenth-century theorists (*see* savagery, civilisation, social evolution).

barter a form of trade that involves the exchange of items considered equivalent in value, rather than through the use of a system of currency (*see* trade).

before the present (**BP**) a convention used for absolute dates (*q.v.*) which expresses the age estimate in years before 1950 (the 'present', and the year that radiocarbon dating became available to archaeologists).

bellows bags, often made of animal skins, that are used to pump air into a clay furnace during iron smelting (*see* bloomery process, smelting, *tuyère*).

Bergmann's Rule the proposition that the mean body size of animals varies in relation to changing temperature regimes.

biota the plant and animal life of a particular region or period.

bloomery process a technique of iron working, in which a cylindrical or conical clay furnace is charged with charcoal and iron ore, and air is pumped into the fire using bellows and *tuyères* to reach the temperature required to reduce iron ore in the solid state (*see* bellows, *tuyère*, smelting).

blower a large suction tube used in underwater archaeology to lift sand from an area that is being excavated (*see* hand fanning).

bone date a technique of relative dating in which the chemical composition of bones from archaeological sites – nitrogen, fluorine and uranium – is used to establish whether the bones were deposited in the archaeological site at the same time.

bonfire kiln a kiln for firing pottery; pots are stacked in the smouldering embers from slow-burning wood.

boskopoid a racial category (no longer in use) for a human physical type including a number of fossil remains and the Khoisan people of southern Africa.

breeding population see Mendelian population.

Broca's Area that part of the brain primarily responsible for communication skills.

Bronze Age a division in Thomsen's Three Age System (*q.v.*), designating a technological stage in Europe's archaeological sequence when the manufacture of bronze artefacts was important.

bulb of percussion in stone-tool technology, a distinctive bulge on the inner surface of a flake beneath the striking platform (*q.v.*), caused by shock waves travelling through the core (*q.v.*).

burin a specialised form of stone tool, often used in working bone.

Bushman a general term for the living and historically known hunter–gatherer communities of southern Africa; long considered a term of abuse, the term has now begun to regain respectability (*see* Khoisan, San).

butchery the set of activities involved in dismembering an animal carcass.

calendar date a date given in terms of a precise calendrical system, such as the Jewish, Islamic or Christian calendars, as opposed to a chronometric age estimate (*see* chronometric date).

calibration the adjustment of radiocarbon age estimations, involving the use of samples from tree rings of known age, to correct for natural variations in the amount of carbon-14 in the earth's atmosphere (*see* radiocarbon dating, dendrochronology).

calorie a unit of heat, used to express the energy value of food.

Cape Dutch architecture an older term used for the eighteenth-century colonial architecture of the Cape, South Africa.

carbon pathway characteristic ratios between carbon isotopes which are established by plants during photosynthesis, and which are passed on up the food chain to herbivores and carnivores. By identifying the carbon pathways of bone residues from archaeological sites, archaeologists can make inferences about past diets (*see* isotope, photosynthesis).

catchment area in archaeology, the territory within which the occupants of an archaeological site normally obtained essential food and raw materials (*see* site catchment analysis).

Caucasian a racial classification, now no longer much in use, for a person from Europe or Western Asia.

Central Place Theory a technique of spatial analysis developed to study the spacing and functioning of European industrial cities. Central Place Theory assumes that there will be a hierarchy of settlements, with smaller sites positioned in a regular relationship to regional centres, which in their turn will be placed logically in relation to a single 'central place'.

ceramics fired clay vessels used for purposes such as storage, carrying water, cooking and other domestic tasks.

chiefdom a form of social and political organisation in which there is a tension between the forces of centralisation, which allow individuals to build up political and economic power, and the tendency towards fragmentation.

chronology the determination of the sequence of past events.

chronometric date a term sometimes used for absolute dates (*q.v.*), so as to distinguish them from calendar dates.

civilisation in archaeology, a term used by nineteenth-century social evolution theorists to describe the final, and most advanced, stage of history. Although the concepts of social evolutionism have now been discredited, the term 'civilisation' is still used, albeit somewhat loosely (*see* barbarism, savagery, social evolution).

climatology the study of climate (*see* palaeoclimatology).

cluster analysis any technique for studying the way in which objects (artefacts, features or archaeological sites) are arranged in the dimension of space.

cobble tool a roughly fashioned implement, particularly associated with the earliest stages of human tool-making (*see* Stone Age).

cognitive archaeology an approach to archaeological interpretation which stresses the symbolic and cognitive aspects of material culture, as distinct from functionalist explanations.

cognitive map a concept used in the study of early hominid behaviour – evidence that early people were thinking in terms of regular shapes, standardised in stone-tool forms that were not entirely determined by functional necessity.

cognitive structure the way in which people conceptualise the world. The identification of cognitive structures is a central part of structuralist archaeology (*see* structuralism).

comparative collection a reference collection that is used to identify assemblages from archaeological sites. Reference collections are crucial in archaeological specialisations such as faunal analysis and palynology (*see* faunal analysis, palynology).

confirmatory data analysis (CDA) the stage in the statistical analysis of evidence that follows exploratory data analysis (*q.v.*). Confirmatory data analysis involves the application of a range of statistical techniques.

context the associations between artefacts from an archaeological site, and their position in time and space. Also, the set of beliefs and perspectives in which an archaeologist frames questions and interpretations of the past.

contextual archaeology a school of interpretation which sees the meaning of artefacts as residing in their total contexts, including the background and attitudes of the archaeologist as well.

Coordinated Universal Time a convention, adopted in 1964, which recognises a common system of time zones for the whole world.

core in stone-tool technology, a piece of stone from which flakes or blades are struck.

core concept as used in ceramic analysis, a basic set of attributes, definitive of a ceramic tradition (*see* tradition).

corm the reproductive organ in some plants, which grows beneath the ground surface as a swollen stem base surrounded by papery leaves.

correlation coefficient a statistical technique that measures the degree of correlation between two sets of observations.

correspondence analysis a computer-based, statistical technique that evaluates the degree of similarity between samples by means of a range of variables; it can be used for the purposes of seriation (*see* seriation).

cortex in archaeology, the outer layer of a cobble used to make a stone tool, distinguished by physical changes to the cobble's surface that have resulted from weathering.

cosmic radiation high energy radiation from outer space.

cosmology a comprehensive system of belief.

craniology a now-discredited discipline that was based on the proposition that human races could be studied by means of the size and shape of the skull.

cranium the skull.

Critical Theory a philosophical approach to understanding reality that stresses the intimate connection between the observer and that which is observed (*see* post-processualism).

cultural anthropology *see* social anthropology.

cultural formation processes the ways in which human actions have affected an artefact between the time that it was first used and the moment when it is recovered by an archaeologist; the complex history through which something made and used in the past becomes part of our history.

Cultural Resource Management (CRM) the safeguarding of an archaeological heritage through education, legislation, protective measures and the emergency excavation of sites threatened by development projects.

culture as used in archaeology, this term implies a social entity (such as a band, chiefdom or state) marked in the archaeological record by the use of similar artefacts.

Darwinianism *see* evolution.

data a series of observations, measurements or other facts.

datum point a fixed marker on an archaeological site (or in the sample area for a regional site survey) to which all horizontal and vertical measurements are referred.

debitage stone chips, discarded during the manufacture of stone tools.

deduction a process of reasoning in which a general proposition (or hypothesis) is used to infer specific consequences.

dendrochronology a technique of absolute dating that makes use of the fact that some long-lived tree species have discernible annual growth rings. By matching the width pattern in a set of tree rings belonging to a piece of timber from an archaeological site, and comparing this pattern with a key sequence from a long-lived tree in which annual growth rings have been counted back from the present day, archaeologists can calculate the date when the tree used on the site was felled (*see* calibration).

dendroclimatology plotting past climatic changes by measuring variations in the annual growth increments of long-lived trees (*see* dendrochronology).

deposit any accumulation of soil, sediment, sand, ash, etc., at an archaeological site.

determinism in archaeology, the belief that human actions are generally determined by the physical environment, and therefore that the past can be explained by looking for correlations between the archaeological record and environmental evidence.

diffusionism the now-redundant proposition that major discoveries in the past were unique, and that knowledge of them must have spread outwards from single centres of origin (*see* Neolithic Revolution).

dispersal site a place where hunter–gatherers lived

during that part of their annual cycle of movement across the landscape when they broke up into smaller social groups (*see* aggregation site).

domestication the process by which human communities selected and propagated advantageous features of wild plants and animals, thereby changing the course of their evolution and producing crops and livestock suitable for farmers' needs.

drip line the edge of the floor of a rock shelter, marked by water dripping from the edge of the overhang above.

Dutch East India Company the major agency of Dutch colonial expansion in the seventeenth and eighteenth centuries, responsible for the initial colonial settlement in Table Bay, South Africa; the administrative authority in South Africa from 1652 until 1795.

Early Iron Age a division of the Iron Age (*q.v.*).

Early Stone Age a division of the Stone Age (*q.v.*).

earthenware pottery made of baked clay (*see* ceramics).

ecofact an archaeological neologism for evidence of human ecological relationships.

ecology the study of the relations between living organisms and their environments (*see* palaeoecology).

economic territory *see* catchment area.

economy in archaeology, the ways in which people in the past obtained food and essential raw materials; 'trade' in the conventional sense.

ecosystem the system of interactions between plants and animals and their non-living environment (*see* ecology).

ecotone a boundary zone at the junction of two or more ecosystems, combining some of the characteristics of each with some features of its own.

Egyptology the study of written texts and archaeological evidence for the period of the Pharaohs in the Nile Valley, beginning in about 3100 BC and ending with the conquest of Egypt by Alexander in 332 BC. Egyptologists also study the period before the rise of the first Egyptian kingdoms (from about 4500 BC) onwards; nevertheless, Egyptology has long been considered a separate discipline in its own right.

electron a stable particle present in all atoms, orbiting the nucleus (*see* proton).

electron spin resonance dating a technique of absolute dating that measures the unpaired electrons trapped within bone and shell samples.

empiricism the belief that archaeological evidence has its own, inherent patterning that will become self-evident during the course of research; the opposite of processualism (*q.v.*).

endocast a cast of the inside of the cranium (or skull), showing details of its bony structure and therefore the shape of the brain's surface.

entoptic phenomena geometric shapes, including zigzags, chevrons, dots and grids, painted on the walls of rock shelters, which have been interpreted as representations of visual disturbances experienced by shamans in early stages of the trance (*see* rock art, shaman, trance dance).

entrepôt a conveniently located trading centre where goods are imported and re-exported.

ethnicity a sense of cultural identity based on language, customs, religion, physical appearance and other traits, individually or in combination.

ethnoarchaeology the systematic study of modern communities in order to discover the ways in which material culture is used in the contemporary world. The results of ethnoarchaeological research are used to deduce past patterns of behaviour from the fragmentary traces of the archaeological record.

ethnobotany the study of modern-day uses of plant foods (*see* ethnoarchaeology, palaeoethnobotany).

ethnography the study of contemporary cultures through first-hand experience (*see* social anthropology).

eugenics a now-discredited discipline that studies methods of improving human 'races', especially by selective breeding.

evolution the process of growth and development, accompanied by increasing complexity. In biology, nineteenth-century theories were brought together by Charles Darwin, forming the basis of modern evolutionary biology.

excavation the systematic uncovering of artefacts by removing soil and other deposits covering and accompanying them (*see* context, deposit).

exchange networks a regularised system in which commodities pass from person to person, either as gifts or in trade and barter (*see* barter, *hxaro*, trade).

exine *see* pollen grain.

experimental archaeology the attempt to re-create aspects of past life-styles by using the same materials, techniques and strategies believed to have been employed in the past.

exploratory data analysis (EDA) a statistical approach which starts by displaying evidence in rough, unanalysed form in order to show its major characteristics; a stage prior to confirmatory data analysis (*q.v.*).

factory site a specialised archaeological site where a specific set of technological activities has taken place; usually used to describe places where stone tools were made (*see* activity site).

false colour images *see* LANDSAT.

faunal analysis the study of animal, fish, shellfish, bird and fish bones from an archaeological site (*see* zooarchaeology).

faunal assemblage a collection of animal, fish or bird bones from an archaeological site.

faunal dating a technique of relative dating in which the range and abundance of animals are used as indicators of environmental conditions, and are matched with similar profiles from other sites.

feature a non-movable artefact on an archaeological site, such as a hearth, wall foundation or pit.

fetishism the belief that an artefact is the embodiment of a spirit, or that it has magical powers.

field recording any process of recording archaeological information in its original context (*see* fieldwork).

fieldwork any activity involving the collection of archaeological information in its original context.

figurine a small carved or moulded figure.

firki a West African term for clay soils which dry hard and crack in the dry season, thereby allowing dry grass to fall in and fertilise the land in the rainy season that follows.

fission track dating a technique of absolute dating, based on the measurement of traces of the spontaneous fission of an isotope of uranium.

flake-blade in stone-tool technology, a flake more than twice as long as it is broad, with either parallel or convergent sides; particularly characteristic of the Middle Stone Age.

flake scar in stone-tool technology, the negative image of a flake which is left on a core (*q.v.*) after the flake has been struck from the core.

flake tool in stone-tool technology, a flake struck from a core (*q.v.*) and used with or without retouch (*q.v.*).

flora plant life.

foodway a system of procedures which ensures that nutritional needs are met, and which also expresses cultural connections between people.

foraging searching for food, as opposed to cultivation and animal husbandry.

foraminifera small, single-celled organisms that are sensitive to change in sea temperatures, which affect their oxygen isotope ratios. Foraminifera are studied in order to establish past variations in climate.

forces of production in Marxism, the technology that is available to a human community (*see* Marxism, mode of production, relations of production).

forging the process of reheating and working a smelted 'bloom' of iron into an implement (*see* smelting).

formation processes the combined influences that affect artefacts; these must be taken into account in their interpretation (*see* cultural formation processes, natural formation processes).

fossil the remnants of a plant or animal surviving in a mineralised form (*see* palaeontology).

frequency distribution the presentation of information in graphic forms such as bar diagrams and graphs, showing major trends in the evidence.

functionalism an approach to interpretation which starts from the proposition that a society is a system of parts that work to maintain one another, ideally in a state of equilibrium. In more limited studies, an emphasis on the utilitarian properties of artefacts.

fynbos a Mediterranean-type heathland characteristic of the Western Cape, South Africa.

Geiger counter an instrument for measuring the amount of radioactivity in a sample (*see* isotope).

genetics the study of inheritance and variability in organisms.

genotype the genetic constitution of an organism (*see* phenotype).

genus in biology, a taxonomic group containing one or more species (*see* species).

Geographical Information System (GIS) a computer database designed to record geographical information in a wide range of different scales, allowing easy access and facilitating studies of distribution patterns.

geomagnetic reversal the periodic, complete reversal of the earth's magnetic field; a phenomenon used in archaeological dating techniques (*see* geomagnetism).

geomagnetism the magnetic field of the earth.

geomorphology the form of the landscape and the history of its development.

geophyte a plant in which the bud grows underground. Geophytes include plants with bulbs, corms, tubers, rhizomes and rootstocks, and were the mainstay of many hunter–gatherer diets in the Middle and Late Stone Ages.

glacial a cold phase, during which glaciers advanced during the Pleistocene (*see* glacier, interglacial, Pleistocene).

glacier a slowly moving mass of ice, originating in snowfalls.

Global Positioning System (GPS) a positioning system used in surveying which establishes a precise location by picking up signals from three or more satellites.

grave goods artefacts buried with a person.

grid a set of rectangular units laid out across the surface of an excavation or a sample area in order to maintain horizontal control.

grindstone a stone, showing characteristic wear patterns, used for grinding some substance or food.

haematite an iron-oxide mineral.

half-life the time taken for half the amount of an unstable isotope to decay (*see* isotope).

handaxe a flake or core tool made by fashioning a cobble (*see* Stone Age).

hand fanning the technique of excavating underwater in which the diver creates water currents to remove sand from artefacts (*see* blower).

harmattan a dry, dusty wind blowing from the Sahara Desert.

hieroglyph a symbol used in Egyptian and other North African writing systems, and based on pictures that represent the objects they stand for or sounds and groups of sounds.

hinterland the area in which a settlement is situated, and which is connected with the activities that happen there (*see* catchment area).

historical archaeology a branch of archaeology in which material culture is studied in conjunction with documentary sources.

Holocene the most recent geological time period, beginning with the end of the last glaciation about 10 000 years ago; a subdivision of the Quaternary period (*see* Quaternary, Pleistocene).

home base a term, used particularly in hominid studies, to indicate a living site.

hominid a general term for human-like higher primates that includes anatomically modern people, and also their earliest direct ancestors living some 5 million years ago.

Homo the genus to which we all belong. The earliest members of this line are known as *Homo habilis*, because they were distinguished by their use of stone tools. *Homo habilis* evolved from the earlier australopithecines some 2 million years ago.

horizon a discernible surface in an archaeological excavation.

hunter–gathering a way of living by gathering wild plant foods and hunting and scavenging for meat (*see* foraging).

hxaro a custom of reciprocal gift exchange which establishes partnerships between people who often live a long way apart, practised by the San of the Kalahari.

hydrology the study of the distribution and use of water.

hypothetico-deductive method characteristic of New Archaeology (*q.v.*), this approach to interpreting the past was developed from a school of thought in the philosophy of science which held that new knowledge could only be gained by framing hypotheses prior to research, and then by testing these against the archaeological evidence (*see* deduction).

Ice Age *see* Pleistocene.

iconography the meaning of a system of symbols.

ideology a body of ideas, a system of beliefs.

initiation the process of admitting a new member to a society, or to a new status and standing in society.

in situ in place; undisturbed.

interglacial a long, warmer interlude between cold phases or glacial periods (*see* glacial, Pleistocene).

interpluvial a supposed dry stage in Africa's climatic sequence that corresponds to an interglacial period in Europe. It is now recognised that simple correlations such as this did not occur (*see* pluvial).

intertidal zone that part of the shoreline between high- and low-water marks, exposed during low tides.

inventory in documentary research, a list of possessions, most often taken after a person's death as part of the process of settling the estate.

inverse stratigraphy the effect that occurs when earlier stratified deposits on an archaeological site are dug out and re-deposited, with the result that the uppermost layers are apparently moved to the bottom of the sequence (*see* stratigraphy).

irrigation the supply of water to fields by means of artificial channels and other technology.

Iron Age in African archaeology, synonymous with the advent of the farming way of life, and following directly from the Stone Age (*q.v.*). The Iron Age is marked both by the use and manufacture of iron, and by characteristic types of pottery. An adaptation of the European Three Age System (*q.v.*).

isometric a method of drawing that shows an object in three dimensions.

isotope atoms of the same chemical element which have slightly different physical characteristics. Isotopes are either 'stable', existing in elements in almost unvarying proportions, or 'unstable', in which case they break down at known rates and are radioactive (*see* half-life, radiometric clock).

isotopic fractionation characteristic alterations in the ratios of isotopes of an element. For the isotopes of hydrogen, nitrogen, carbon and oxygen, these alterations occur during photosynthesis and other chemical reactions within living organisms, providing an archaeometric basis for assessing human and animal diets from samples of bone.

Khoikhoi a collective term for the indigenous pastoralist communities of southern Africa. Meaning 'Men of men', Khoikhoi in the strict sense was the name of only a single chiefdom (*see* Khoisan).

Khoisan a collective term for both the Khoikhoi (pastoralist) and San (hunter–gatherer) communities of southern Africa (*see* San, Khoikhoi).

knapping the process of making stone tools.

kraal an enclosure for animals.

LANDSAT a satellite system in which records of reflected light and infra-red radiation from the surface of the earth are transmitted back to ground stations from satellites. These records can be converted into 'false colour' images that look like photographs, but which are rather impressions of changes in the nature of the earth's surfaces.

language the patterned use of sound as symbols.

Late Iron Age a division of the Iron Age (*q.v.*).

Late Stone Age a division of the Stone Age (*q.v.*).

layer a horizontal unit in an archaeological excavation, usually continuous over all or most of the excavated area (*see* stratigraphy, lens).

lens a discontinuous horizontal unit in an archaeological excavation (*see* stratigraphy, layer).

linguistics the study of language.

lithology the study of the general characteristics of rocks.

livestock domesticated animals.

longhouse in the South African context, a form of colonial architecture, particularly in the Western Cape region, in which rectangular thatched cottages were expanded to meet the changing needs of family groups.

Lower Palaeolithic a division of the Palaeolithic (*q.v.*).

macrofauna the larger mammals in a faunal assemblage from an archaeological site.

maize originally a wild cereal, and brought into domestication in Middle America. Introduced into Africa by Portuguese colonial settlers in the sixteenth century (*see* domestication).

mandible the lower jaw-bone in a vertebrate (*see* maxilla).

manuport an object brought to an archaeological site by human agency, and not necessarily fashioned into an artefact.

maritime archaeology the study of the archaeology of seafaring, including underwater archaeology (*q.v.*).

Marxism an economic, social and political theory of human society which privileges economic factors over other determinants and which sees the role of class and class struggle as central (*see* forces of production, mode of production, relations of production).

material culture the artefacts that constitute the material trace of a society (*see* culture).

maxilla the upper jaw-bone in vertebrates (*see* mandible).

mean *see* arithmetic mean.

Meat Weight Estimate the conversion of MNI or NISP counts for a faunal assemblage into an estimate of meat available to the past group of people who used the archaeological site; the calculation takes into account the average amount of meat that each different species could have contributed (*see* faunal analysis, Minimum Number of Individuals, Number of Identified Specimens).

medicine people *see* shaman.

member in geology, a stratigraphic unit.

Mendelian population the group of individuals within which most matings will take place for geographical or social reasons.

Meroitic a system of writing used in the Nubian state of Meroë from about the second century BC until the fourth century AD. Still not deciphered.

metal detector an instrument used to indicate the presence of metallic objects beneath the ground surface.

metallography the study of the composition and structure of metals and alloys.

microenvironment the environment in the immediate vicinity of an archaeological site or within part of a site.

microfauna the bones of small animals found in archaeological excavations, and often brought to the site by natural agents such as small carnivores and birds. The varying abundance of such small animals can be used to reconstruct past environments around the site.

microlith a small stone tool, often carefully retouched.

micromammal *see* microfauna.

microwear small-scale and often microscopic damage to the surfaces of artefacts (generally stone tools) when they were used for different purposes in the past.

midden the accumulation of debris from human occupation of a site or from the repeated use of a particular locality.

Middle Palaeolithic a division of the Palaeolithic (*q.v.*).

Middle Stone Age a division of the Stone Age (*q.v.*).

millet an African plant domesticate, probably first cultivated in the Ethiopian highlands (*see* domestication).

Minimum Number of Individuals (MNI) a measure of abundance used in faunal analysis (*q.v.*). The MNI count for a faunal assemblage gives the minimum numbers of individuals necessary to account for the faunal assemblage.

model part of the methodology of the New Archaeology (*q.v.*). A model is a set of propositions about how a hypothesis might be met by the archaeological record – a prediction set up for the purposes of testing.

mode of production in Marxism, the combination of the forces of production and the relations of production (*see* forces of production, relations of production, Marxism).

Mongoloid a now-redundant term for a major racial division of humankind.

monument any substantial or prominent artefact, particularly a building.

morphology the form and structure of an organism or of any artefact.

motif a minimal unit of decoration, often used in the study of ceramics from archaeological sites (*see* attribute).

mud brick bricks used in building and made of mud baked in the sun.

multidimensional scaling (MDS) a technique of cluster analysis (*q.v.*).

nationalism a common cultural identity that binds people to a particular country.

natural formation processes the environmental factors that contribute to the history of artefacts between the time they are discarded and the time they are excavated or described by an archaeologist.

Nearest Neighbour Analysis a technique of spatial analysis that starts with the proposition that the distances between settlements reflect the intensity of economic and social interaction between them.

Negritude a cultural movement that began among French-speaking African and Caribbean writers, as a protest against French colonial rule. It stressed the superiority of African culture, its mystical connections with the past, and its superiority over corrupt European materialism.

Negro a term used in nineteenth-century racial classification, now of little value in human biology, that classified people according to physical characteristics, particularly skin colour.

Neolithic a division of the Stone Age in Thomsen's Three Age System (*q.v.*). Neolithic means 'New Stone Age', and groups together the ground stone tools made by early farmers in Europe and Asia. Not generally used in African archaeology.

Neolithic Revolution an earlier theory of plant and animal domestication which saw the farming way of life developing in a single centre in the Near East and then spreading to other parts of the world. It is now known that farming developed independently in different areas (*see* domestication).

New Archaeology an approach, which developed in the US and Europe in the early 1960s, based on the proposition that the past can only be understood as a dynamic process (*see* processualism), and that research must proceed by the formulation of prior research hypotheses and their testing against the archaeological record (*see* hypothetico-deductive method).

niche a particular, defined position within an ecosystem (*q.v.*).

nomad a person who moves from place to place, following the needs of livestock for pasturage.

normal distribution a particular pattern of symmetrical distribution in a sample around its mean, producing a bell-shaped curve that can be defined by a specific equation.

nuclear family a minimal family unit, consisting of parent(s) and offspring.

Number of Identified Specimens (NISP) a measure of abundance used in faunal analysis (*q.v.*). The NISP count for a faunal assemblage gives the absolute numbers of animal bones identified for each animal species.

obsidian hydration dating a technique of absolute dating that measures the amount of hydration that has taken place on the exposed surfaces of obsidian through water absorption.

occupation horizon *see* horizon.

ochre a natural earth containing ferric oxide and silica; used as a pigment.

oral history stories and traditions passed from generation to generation by word of mouth.

osteoarthritis chronic inflammation of the bone joints.

overburden the deposit on the surface of an archaeological excavation that is not considered significant and is discarded.

palaeoclimatology the study of past climates (*see* climatology).

palaeoecology the study of past ecological relationships (*see* ecology).

palaeoenvironment the past environment.

palaeoethnobotany the application of the results of

ethnobotanical studies in the interpretation of the plant residues from archaeological sites (*see* ethnobotany).

Palaeolithic a division of the Stone Age in Thomsen's Three Age System (*q.v.*). Palaeolithic means 'Old Stone Age', and groups together all the stone tools made before the origins of agriculture.

palaeontology the study of fossils (*see* fossil).

palynology the reconstruction of past environments by identifying and counting the relative frequencies of fossil pollen grains.

papyrus paper made from the stem and pith of a tall aquatic reed, *Cyperus papyrus*, and used for writing in early Egypt.

patriarchy a form of social organisation in which descent and title are traced through the male line.

petrography the description and classification of rocks.

petrology the study of the physical characteristics of rock.

Pharaoh king of Egypt.

phase in archaeology, a unit of time, often an amalgamation of several stratigraphic units from an excavation.

phenotype the physical form of an organism, as determined by the interaction between its genetically inherited constitution and its environment (*see* genotype).

photosynthesis the synthesis of organic compounds from carbon dioxide and water, using light energy.

physical anthropology the study of the biology of the human species and of its hominid ancestors (*see* anthropology).

phytolith a small silica particle derived from a plant cell that survives after the organism has been burnt or has decomposed; common in ash layers on archaeological sites.

Piltdown man a notorious British archaeological fraud in which a human skull, orangutan jaw and some teeth were 'excavated' from an archaeological site and used to argue for the 'missing link' in human evolution. The Piltdown hoax was revealed by bone dates (*q.v.*).

Pleistocene a geological division of time, and a subdivision of the Quaternary. The Pleistocene began about 2 million years ago, and ended with the end of the last glaciation, about 10 000 years ago (*see* Quaternary, Holocene).

pluvial a supposed wet stage in Africa's climatic sequence that corresponds to a glacial period in Europe. It is now recognised that simple correlations such as this did not occur (*see* interpluvial).

polity a general term for a system of social organisation, used without implying the nature or scale of such social organisation.

pollen grain the very small, male reproductive organ of a flowering plant. Pollen grains have a hard outer shell (the exine) which can survive in certain sediments for a very long period of time (*see* palynol-

ogy).

pollen rain the dispersed pollen in the atmosphere at any one time. Understanding the nature of the pollen rain in the past is crucial in using fossil pollen grains to reconstruct environments (*see* palynology).

pollen sum the full range of pollens used to construct a pollen diagram in a palynological study (*see* palynology).

polysemy multiple meanings.

post-modernism more a range of reactions than a coherent body of theory, post-modernism is closely connected to a decline in confidence in the West's cultural superiority, and a scepticism about generalising approaches such as functionalism, Marxism and structuralism.

post-processualism a post-modernist (*q.v.*) approach to archaeology which views archaeological interpretation as an inherently political process that weaves the position of the archaeologist into the way that he or she writes about the past. Post-processualists particularly reject the claim of New Archaeology (*q.v.*) to be 'doing science', as well as the generalising claims of structuralism (*q.v.*).

post-structuralism an approach to archaeological interpretation which recognises the insights from structuralist explanations, but favours individualised explanations rather than having recourse to generalised laws (*see* structuralism).

potassium–argon dating a technique of absolute dating ´ (*q.v.*) which measures the decay of the radioactive isotope potassium-40 to the inert gas argon-40.

Potomac Typological System (POTS) a ceramic typology developed for the historical archaeology of the eastern seaboard of the United States. It is based on the classification system used by early European colonists themselves.

precipitation the total moisture available in an ecosystem. Precipitation includes rainfall, mists and fogs, and condensation.

pre-colonial in African archaeology, that part of history which pre-dates the beginning of European colonial settlement in a specific area.

prehistory that part of the past which pre-dates the use of written records in a specific area.

primary enclosure a term used to describe the first circular stone livestock enclosures built during the construction of Iron Age farming settlements in the higher grasslands of southern Africa (*see* secondary enclosure).

principal components analysis a technique of cluster analysis (*q.v.*).

probate record *see* inventory.

processualism the belief that archaeological interpretations can only come from studying the way, or 'process', by which the archaeological record has been formed. Processualism defines New Archaeology (*q.v.*) and can be considered the opposite of empiricism (*q.v.*).

projectile point any stone, glass or metal implement made to be hafted, forming a spear or an arrow.

protein compounds, made up of amino acids, that are essential constituents of all living organisms (*see* amino acid).

protohistory that part of the past in a specific region where documentary records are just beginning to come into use.

proton a stable elementary particle found in the nucleus of an atom (*see* electron).

proton induced X-ray emission spectroscopy (PIXE) an analytical technique for ceramics which produces a profile of the chemical composition of the clay used in potting, by bombarding the ceramic sample with a stream of protons in a Van de Graaff accelerator.

proton magnetometer an instrument used in subsurface detection which identifies and records variations in the earth's magnetic field.

quadrat a square sample area (*see* sample, transect).

Quaternary the most recent period in the geological time scale, beginning about 2 million years ago, and following the Tertiary period (*see* Holocene, Pleistocene).

race a classification of people made in terms of their physical characteristics.

racism discrimination on the basis of physical characteristics; the belief that these characteristics render one group of people inherently inferior to another.

radiocarbon dating a technique of absolute dating (*q.v.*) that makes use of the fact that the unstable carbon isotope, carbon-14, decays at a steady rate with a half-life (*q.v.*) of 5730 years.

radiometric clock time estimated from the amount of radioactive decay in a sample (*see* chronometric date).

raised beach the beach remaining from a time when the level of the sea was higher than that of the present day, or else the result of tectonic movement (*see* tectonic movement).

randomness in statistics, the quality of an object chosen without regard to any of its characteristics, so that any member of the group of objects has an equal chance of being chosen.

random numbers a sequence of numbers that do not form any progression, used to facilitate unbiased sampling.

random sampling *see* sampling, random.

range in statistics, the distance between the smallest and largest measurements in a sample.

reduction sequence the sequence of stages in the production of a stone tool in which a core is reduced to a set of flakes or blades and waste material.

relations of production in Marxism, the way in which people organise themselves in order to make use of technology (*see* forces of production, Marxism, mode of production).

relative date the age of an artefact or other archaeological unit, expressed as older or younger than another artefact or archaeological unit.

relativism the belief that there is no fixed or 'correct' interpretation of the past, but rather an infinite sequence of readings.

retouch in stone-tool technology, the secondary flaking and working of the edges of a flake or blade to make a more sophisticated artefact.

rift valley a long, narrow valley that results from the subsidence of land between two parallel geological faults.

river terrace a level of deposits, often gravels, left behind when a river was at a higher level than the present day.

rock art paintings on the walls of rock shelters or boulders, and engravings on stone. In southern Africa these are widely accepted as the work of shamans remembering experiences of altered states of consciousness (*see* trance dance, shaman).

rock shelter a rock overhang, providing shelter from the weather.

Sahel the broad band of arid savanna to the south and west of the Sahara Desert.

sample a set of items (for example, artefacts or sites) selected in a way that interpretations may be made about the nature of the larger population from which the set has been drawn.

sampling strategy the programme for sampling an archaeological site or a study area which is devised before fieldwork begins, taking into account the problems that are being investigated and the nature of the evidence that is likely to become available.

sampling, random a method of sampling in which sample points or blocks are fixed by coordinates that have been chosen from a table of randomly generated numbers.

sampling, stratified random a method of sampling in which the study area is first divided into zones (decided by the nature of the research problem), and each zone is subsequently sampled by means of sample points or blocks that have been positioned at random.

sampling, systematic a method of sampling in which a grid of equally spaced points or blocks is set up over an area and information is collected from within these sample units.

San a term for the contemporary and historically known hunter–gatherer communities of southern Africa. Long considered preferable to the term Bushman, 'San' can itself be a derogatory term (*see* Bushman, Khoisan).

savagery a now-discredited stage in human evolution postulated by nineteenth-century theorists (*see* barbarism, civilisation, social evolution).

savanna open grassland, with scattered bushes and trees.

scanning electron microscope an instrument that makes use of electrons to generate a three-dimensional computer image of an object.

schlep effect the patterning in a faunal assemblage from a living site that results when hunters butcher an animal carcass at the point of the kill and bring home only selected cuts of meat.

scraper a stone tool with a working edge retouched so as to be useful for preparing animal skins.

sea-level the average level of the sea at any one time.

seasonality in archaeology, patterns of human subsistence behaviour which are adapted to the changing availability of plant and animal foods at different times of the year.

secondary enclosure a term used to describe the circular stone livestock enclosures built to link together primary enclosures, thus forming a central area, during the construction of Iron Age farming settlements in the higher grasslands of southern Africa (*see* primary enclosure).

section the side of an archaeological excavation, usually straight but sometimes deliberately stepped or sloped, which is used to record stratigraphic sequences and relationships (*see* stratigraphy).

sediment material that has been deposited by water, ice or wind.

sedimentology the study of the structure and texture of sediments.

semiotics the study of signs and symbols.

seriation a method of relative dating which is based on the chronological ordering of a group of artefacts or assemblages; the most similar are placed adjacent to each other in the series.

settlement in archaeology, any place where people have lived, or the process of inhabiting a region.

settlement mound an artificial hill, resulting from the repeated occupation of the same place (see *tell*).

shaman a medicine person; in southern African San communities, a person who acquired healing and other powers by entering an altered state of consciousness through the trance dance. Many rock paintings in southern Africa were probably painted by shamans as remembered trance experiences (*see* trance dance).

sherd a piece of broken pottery.

sidescan sonar a survey method used in underwater archaeology in which sound waves are transmitted from an instrument towed on the water surface, and their 'echoes' are used to locate objects on the sea-bed.

sieving the process of looking for smaller objects, such as beads or small animal bones, by passing deposits from an archaeological excavation through a wire mesh.

sign an arbitrary or conventional mark that stands for something else.

signifier something that stands as a symbol or a sign (*see* sign, symbol).

site a place where artefacts occur, and where archaeologists work.

site catchment analysis a method of spatial analysis that is based on the observation that distance has an economic cost, and therefore settlements will tend to be placed in a logical relationship to natural resources such as grazing land, agricultural soils and water supplies (*see* catchment area).

slag the waste from an iron-smelting furnace (*see* bloomery process).

smelting the process of producing iron from iron ore and charcoal (*see* bellows, bloomery process, forging, *tuyère*).

social anthropology the study of the non-biological, behavioural aspects of society (*see* anthropology).

social evolution the now-discredited nineteenth-century theory that all history could be understood in terms of the universal stages of savagery, barbarism and civilisation (*see* barbarism, civilisation, savagery).

socio-political system the combined organising structure of a society.

soil stain a soil discoloration, indicating a feature such as a pit, burial or the one-time position of a wooden post.

sorghum originally a wild grass, brought into domestication by early farmers, probably in the Sahel regions to the south of the Sahara (*see* domestication).

sourveld grasslands on poorer soils, usually near the coast or in mountain areas, that have been leached of essential nutrients by heavy seasonal rains. Sourveld can support comparatively high densities of animals in the short spring growing season only (*see* sweetveld).

Southern Bantu Cattle Pattern a structuralist interpretation of Iron Age settlement patterns, which sees villages laid out as systems of polar oppositions that reflect gender and status distinctions within society (*see* structuralism).

southern highveld the extensive area of high grassland that covers South Africa's inner plateau.

spatial analysis the study of the distribution of artefacts; usually the study of the dispersal of settlements.

species in biology, any of the taxonomic groups into which a genus is divided (*see* genus).

spirit medium a person with the power to communicate with the spirits of the ancestors.

spit an arbitrary, horizontal excavation unit, used either for subdivision within the natural layering of the site, or in situations where no natural layering can be discerned (*see* layer, stratigraphy).

spoil tip the deposits from an archaeological excavation, dumped after excavation has been completed.

stalactite a conical mass of calcium carbonate hanging from the roof of a limestone cave (*see* stalagmite).

stalagmite a conical mass of calcium carbonate that

has accumulated on the floor of a limestone cave.

standard deviation a statistical measure of the dispersion of a sample around its arithmetic mean (*q.v.*).

state a form of social, political and economic organisation represented archaeologically by the stratification of settlements into clear hierarchies and by evidence for wealth and status differences, expressed in material culture.

steppe an extensive grassy plain with few or no trees.

Stone Age derived from Thomsen's Three Age System (*q.v.*), and used in Africa to group together hunting and gathering societies which depended principally on stone tools for their technology.

stratification the successive layering of deposits in an archaeological site (*see* stratigraphy).

stratified sampling *see* sampling, stratified random.

stratigraphy the layering of an archaeological site, reflecting a series of events and processes that resulted in the formation of the site through time (*see* inverse stratigraphy, stratigraphy).

stratum an individual layer in an archaeological stratigraphy (*q.v.*).

striking platform in stone-tool technology, the point of impact where the hammer stone impacts with the core to produce a flake or a blade.

structuralism an approach to interpretation that works from the proposition that human actions are guided by recurrent, innate patterns of thought which are organised as pairs of polar opposites.

style variations in the form of material culture that serve to identify both the individual identity of the maker and user, and the general identity of the social group.

sweetveld grasslands on high-quality soils, often in areas of lower rainfall. Sweetveld can be grazed by animals all the year, but needs careful management if it is not to be over-exploited (*see* sourveld).

symbol something that is used to represent something else.

symbolism the communication of meaning, either through language as a set of sound symbols or through material culture.

systematic sampling *see* sampling, systematic.

taphonomy the study of the processes which have affected organic materials in archaeological sites.

technology the system of rules and procedures that lies behind the manufacture and use of an artefact.

techno-organic evolution the replacement of the entirely biological adaptation of Darwinian evolution with adaptation and evolution through a combination of biological transformation and technology.

tectonic movement displacements of the plates that make up the earth's crust (*see* raised beach).

tell a settlement mound, the site of a town or village, where successive occupations have resulted in the build-up of an artificial hill (*see* settlement mound).

temper inclusions in clay used for pottery, to give vessels extra strength when they have been fired.

theodolite a surveying instrument for measuring horizontal and vertical angles.

thermoluminescence dating (TL) a technique of absolute dating (*q.v.*) which measures the emission of thermoluminescent light from electrons, themselves displaced by unstable isotopes in materials with a crystalline structure, notably clay used in making ceramics.

Thiessen Polygons a technique of spatial analysis that models the relationships between settlements by dividing up the landscape into the most logical territories for each.

Three Age System developed in Denmark by C. J. Thomsen and first published in 1836, the Three Age System recognised that Europe's archaeology could be divided into three chronological stages: a Stone Age, Bronze Age and Iron Age.

topography the land forms and other surface features of a region.

trade a general term for the exchange of commodities, either through barter (where objects considered of similar value are exchanged) or through the use of a system of currency (*see* barter).

tradition as used in archaeology, a tradition is a seriated sequence of artefact assemblages, particularly ceramics.

trance dance practised by San communities in the Kalahari today, and described by nineteenth-century informants as well, the trance dance is a community ritual in which altered states of consciousness are achieved by hyperventilation, intense concentration and rhythmic dancing. Many rock paintings were probably remembered trance experiences (*see* shaman).

transect an elongated, rectangular sample area (*see* sample, quadrat).

transhumance the regular movement by animals and human communities between summer and winter living areas.

travertine calcium carbonate, deposited as flow stone.

trigonometrical grid the system of surveying reference points set up across a landscape to facilitate map-making.

trigonometrical survey the process of establishing a grid of reference points for the purposes of map-making.

type a class of artefacts, defined by the consistent occurrence of a set of attributes.

type site an archaeological site from which a definitive set of artefacts has been described.

typology the systematic organisation and classification of artefacts into categories on the basis of attributes they share.

tuyère the clay pipe through which air is pumped from a bellows into a clay furnace during smelting (*see* bellows, bloomery process, smelting).

underwater archaeology the set of survey and excavation techniques used in the case of submerged sites and deposits, including those on sea-beds and lake and river beds (*see* maritime archaeology).

uniformitarianism the principle that ancient geological processes were the same as (uniform with) processes that can be observed in the present day. Uniformitarianism is largely accepted as self-evident today, but in the nineteenth century it was a key concept in the challenge to the biblical creationist view of the origins of life, and had an important influence on archaeology in its formative years.

Upper Palaeolithic a division of the Palaeolithic (*q.v.*).

uranium series dating a method of absolute dating based on the radioactive decay of uranium isotopes.

urbanism the set of historical processes by which city and town life began and developed.

Urban Revolution an earlier theory for the origins of towns and cities which saw urbanism developing at a single centre in the Near East and then spreading to other parts of the world. It is now known that urbanism developed independently in different areas (see Neolithic Revolution, urbanism).

Van de Graaff accelerator *see* proton induced X-ray emission spectroscopy.

vitrification conversion into a glass or glassy substance.

water flotation a method of obtaining plant samples, particularly carbonised seeds, by passing samples through water disturbed by compressed air.

zooarchaeology the study of animal remains from archaeological sites (*see* faunal analysis).

Bibliography

Abungu, G. and H. Mutoro. 1993. 'Coast–interior settlements and social relations in the Kenya coastal hinterland.' In: T. Shaw, P. Sinclair, B. Andah and A. Okpoko (eds.) *The Archaeology of Africa: Food, Metals and Towns*: 694-703. London: Routledge.

Achebe, C. 1991. 'African literature as restoration of celebration.' In: K. H. Petersen and A. Rutherford (eds.) *Chinua Achebe: A Celebration*: 1-10. Portsmouth: Heinemann.

Agorsah, E. K. 1990. 'Ethnoarchaeology: the search for a self-corrective approach to the study of past human behaviour.' *African Archaeological Review* 8: 189-208.

Aldred, C. 1984. *The Egyptians*. London: Thames and Hudson.

Ambrose, S. H. and M. J. DeNiro. 1986. 'Reconstruction of African human diet using bone collagen carbon and nitrogen isotope ratios.' *Nature* 319: 321-324.

Andah, B. W. 1990. 'The oral versus the written word in the cognitive revolution: language, culture and literacy.' *West African Journal of Archaeology* 20: 18-45.

Andah, B. W. 1993. 'Identifying early farming traditions of West Africa.' In: T. Shaw, P. Sinclair, B. Andah and A. Okpoko (eds.) *The Archaeology of Africa: Food, Metals and Towns*: 240-254. London: Routledge.

Angas, G. F. 1849. *The Kafirs Illustrated*. London: Hogarth.

Anquandah, J. 1993. 'The Kintampo complex: a case study of early sedentism and food production in sub-Sahelian West Africa.' In: T. Shaw, P. Sinclair, B. Andah and A. Okpoko (eds.) *The Archaeology of Africa: Food, Metals and Towns*: 255-260. London: Routledge.

Appiah, K. A. 1992. *In My Father's House: Africa in the Philosophy of Culture*. London: Methuen.

Appiah, K. A. 1995. 'Why Africa? Why art?' In: T. Phillips (ed.) *Africa: The Art of a Continent*: 21-26. London: Royal Academy of Arts.

Archer, F. M. 1982. ''n Voorstudie in verband met die eetbare plante van die Kamiesberge.' *Journal of South African Botany* 48(4): 433-449.

Asante, M. K. 1991. 'Afrocentrism in a multicultural democracy.' *American Visions* 6(4): 21.

Asombang, R. N. 1990. 'Museums and African

identity: the museum in Cameroon – a critique.' *West African Journal of Archaeology* 20: 188-198.

Avery, D. M. 1982. 'The micromammalian fauna from Border Cave, KwaZulu, South Africa.' *Journal of Archaeological Science* 9(2): 187-204.

Avery, D. M. 1987. 'Late Pleistocene coastal environment of the southern Cape Province of South Africa: micromammals from Klasies River Mouth.' *Journal of Archaeological Science* 14: 405-421.

Avery, G. 1987. 'Coastal birds and prehistory in the Western Cape.' In: J. Parkington and M. Hall (eds.) *Papers in the Prehistory of the Western Cape*: 164-191. Oxford: British Archaeological Reports.

Bada, J. L. and L. Deems. 1975. 'Accuracy of dates beyond the C-14 dating limit using the aspartic acid racemization reaction.' *Nature* 255: 218-219.

Bailey, G. and J. Parkington. 1988. 'The archaeology of prehistoric coastlines. An introduction.' In: G. Bailey and J. Parkington (eds.) *The Archaeology of Prehistoric Coastlines*: 1-10. Cambridge: Cambridge University Press.

Barnham, L. S. 1992. 'Let's walk before we run: an appraisal of historical materialist approaches to the Later Stone Age.' *South African Archaeological Bulletin* 47: 44-51.

Bassey-Duke, B. E. 1981. 'The experimental archaeological reserve. An experiment in decay at Adesina Oja, Ibadan, Nigeria.' *West African Journal of Archaeology* 11: 53-73.

Beaudry, M. C., J. Long, H. M. Miller, D. N. Fraser and G. Wheeler Stone. 1983. 'A vessel typology for early Chesapeake ceramics: the Potomac Typological System.' *Historical Archaeology* 17(1): 18-43.

Beaumont, P. B., H. de Villiers and J. C. Vogel. 1978. 'Modern man in sub-Saharan Africa prior to 49000 years BP: a review and evaluation with particular reference to Border Cave.' *South African Journal of Science* 74: 409-419.

Becker, M. and F. Wendorf. 1993. 'A microwear study of a Late Pleistocene Qadan assemblage from southern Egypt.' *Journal of Field Archaeology* 20: 389-398.

Bent, J. T. 1969. *The Ruined Cities of Mashonaland*. Bulawayo: Books of Rhodesia.

Bernal, M. 1991a. *Black Athena: The Afroasiatic Roots of Classical Civilization*. Volume 1: *The Fabrication of Ancient Greece, 1785–1985*. London: Vintage.

Bernal, M. 1991b. *Black Athena: The Afroasiatic Roots of Classical Civilization*. Volume 2: *The Archaeological and Documentary Evidence*. London: Free Association Books.

Biesele, M. 1993. *Women Like Meat: The Folklore and Foraging Ideology of the Kalahari Ju/'hoan*. Johannesburg: Witwatersrand University Press.

Binford, L. R. 1984. *Faunal Remains from Klasies River Mouth*. London: Academic Press.

Binford, L. R. and S. R. Binford (eds.) 1968. *New Perspectives in Archaeology*. Chicago: Aldine.

Binneman, J. 1984. 'Mapping and interpreting wear traces on stone implements: a case study from Boomplaas Cave.' In: M. Hall, G. Avery, D. M. Avery, M. L. Wilson and A. J. B. Humphreys (eds.) *Frontiers: Southern African Archaeology Today*: 143-151. Oxford: British Archaeological Reports.

Binneman, J. and J. Deacon. 1986. 'Experimental determination of use wear on stone adzes from Boomplaas Cave, South Africa.' *Journal of Archaeological Science* 13(3): 219-228.

Brain, C. K. 1974. 'Human food remains from the Iron Age at Zimbabwe.' *South African Journal of Science* 70: 303-309.

Brain, C. K. 1981. *The Hunters or the Hunted? An Introduction to African Cave Taphonomy*. Chicago: University of Chicago Press.

Brain, C. K. and A. Sillen. 1988. 'Evidence from the Swartkrans Cave for the earliest use of fire.' *Nature* 336: 464-466.

Brewer, J. and R. Porter. 1993. 'Introduction.' In: J. Brewer and R. Porter (eds.) *Consumption and the World of Goods*: 1-18. London: Routledge.

Bunn, H., J. W. K. Harris, G. Isaac, Z. Kaufulu, E. Kroll, K. Schick, N. Toth and A. K. Behrensmeyer. 1980. 'FxJi50: an Early Pleistocene site in northern Kenya.' *World Archaeology* 12(2): 109-136.

Burke, E. E. (ed.) 1969. *The Journals of Carl Mauch, 1869–1872*. Salisbury: National Archives of Rhodesia.

Caton-Thompson, G. 1931. *The Zimbabwe Culture: Ruins and Reactions*. Oxford: Clarendon Press.

Caton-Thompson, G. 1983. *Mixed Memoirs*. Gateshead: Paradigm Press.

Childe, G. 1936. *Man Makes Himself*. London: Watts.

Childs, S. T. and P. R. Schmidt. 1985. 'Experimental iron smelting: the genesis of a hypothesis with implications for African prehistory and history.' In: R. Haaland and P. Shinnie (eds.) *African Iron Working: Ancient and Traditional*. Oslo: Norwegian University Press.

Chippindale, C. 1992. 'Grammars of archaeological design: a generative and geometrical approach to the form of artifacts.' In: J.-C. Gardin and C. Peebles (eds.) *Representations in Archaeology*: 251-276. Bloomington: Indiana University Press.

Chittick, H. N. 1974. *Kilwa: An Islamic Trading City on the East African Coast*. Nairobi: British Institute in Eastern Africa.

Clark, J. D. 1990. 'A personal memoir.' In: P. Robertshaw (ed.) *A History of African Archaeology*: 189-204. London: James Currey.

Clark, J. D. and K. D. Williamson. 1984. 'A Middle Stone Age occupation site at Porc Epic Cave, Dire Dawa (east-central Ethiopia). Part I.' *African Archaeological Review* 2: 37-64.

Clarke, D. 1968. *Analytical Archaeology*. London: Methuen.

Cohen, R. and E. R. Service (eds.) 1978. *Origins of*

the State: The Anthropology of Political Evolution. Philadelphia: Institute for the Study of Human Issues.

Collinson, R. 1867. *The Three Voyages of Martin Frobisher*. New York: Burt Franklin.

Conkey, M. and J. Gero. 1991. 'Tension, pluralities, and engendering archaeology: an introduction.' In: J. Gero and M. Conkey (eds.) *Engendering Archaeology: Women and Prehistory*: 3-30. Oxford: Blackwell.

Conkey, M. and R. Tringham. 1995. 'Archaeology and the Goddess: exploring the contours of feminist archaeology.' In: D. Stanton and A. Stewart (eds.) *Feminisms in the Academy: Rethinking the Disciplines*: 199-247. Ann Arbor: University of Michigan Press.

Connah, G. 1981. *Three Thousand Years in Africa: Man and his Environment in the Lake Chad Region of Nigeria*. Cambridge: Cambridge University Press.

Connah, G. 1987. *African Civilizations. Precolonial Cities and States in Tropical Africa: An Archaeological Perspective*. Cambridge: Cambridge University Press.

Conrad, J. 1971. *Heart of Darkness*. New York: W. W. Norton.

Daniel, G. E. 1980. *A Short History of Archaeology*. London: Thames and Hudson.

Dart, R. A. 1925. 'Australopithecus africanus: the man-ape of South Africa.' *Nature* 115: 195-199.

Darwin, C. 1871. *The Descent of Man and Selection in Relation to Sex*. London: John Murray.

Deacon, H. J. 1976. *Where Hunters Gathered: A Study of Holocene Stone Age People in the Eastern Cape.* Cape Town: South African Archaeological Society.

Deacon, H. J. 1985. 'Review of Binford, "Faunal remains from Klasies River Mouth".' *South African Archaeological Bulletin* 40: 59-60.

Deacon, H. J. 1989. 'Late Pleistocene palaeoecology and archaeology in the southern Cape, South Africa.' In: P. Mellars and C. Stringer (eds.) *The Human Revolution*: 547-564. Edinburgh: Edinburgh University Press.

Deacon, H. J. 1992. 'Southern Africa and modern human origins.' *Philosophical Transactions of the Royal Society of London* 337: 177-183.

Deacon, H. J. 1993. 'Planting an idea: an archaeology of Stone Age gatherers in South Africa.' *South African Archaeological Bulletin* 48: 86-93.

Deacon, H. J. and V. B. Geleijnse. 1988. 'The stratigraphy and sedimentology of the Main Site sequence, Klasies River, South Africa.' *South African Archaeological Bulletin* 43: 5-14.

Deacon, H. J., Q. B. Hendey and J. J. N. Lambrechts (eds.) 1983a. *Fynbos Palaeoecology: A Preliminary Synthesis*. Pretoria: Council for Scientific and Industrial Research.

Deacon, H. J., A. Scholtz and L. D. Daitz. 1983b. 'Fossil charcoals as a source of palaeoecological information in the fynbos region.' In: H. J. Deacon,

Q. B. Hendey and J. J. N. Lambrechts (eds.) *Fynbos Palaeoecology: A Preliminary Synthesis*: 174-182. Pretoria: Council for Scientific and Industrial Research.

Deacon, J. 1984. *The Later Stone Age of Southernmost Africa*. Oxford: British Archaeological Reports.

Deacon, J. 1986. 'Editorial.' *South African Archaeological Bulletin* 41: 3-4.

Deacon, J. 1990. 'Weaving the fabric of Stone Age research in southern Africa.' In: P. Robertshaw (ed.) *A History of African Archaeology*: 39-58. London: James Currey.

Deacon, J. and N. Lancaster. 1988. *Late Quaternary Palaeoenvironments of Southern Africa*. Oxford: Clarendon Press.

De Barros, P. 1990. 'Changing paradigms, goals and methods in the archaeology of francophone West Africa.' In: P. Robertshaw (ed.) *A History of African Archaeology*: 155-172. London: James Currey.

DeCorse, C. R. 1989. 'Material aspects of Limba, Yalunka and Kuranko ethnicity: archaeological research in northeastern Sierra Leone.' In: S. J. Shennan (ed.) *Archaeological Approaches to Cultural Identity*: 125-140. London: Unwin Hyman.

Deetz, J. 1977. *In Small Things Forgotten: The Archaeology of Early American Life*. New York: Anchor Books.

Deetz, J. 1990. 'Landscapes as cultural statements.' In: W. M. Kelso and R. Most (eds.) *Earth Patterns: Essays in Landscape Archaeology*: 1-4. Charlottesville: University Press of Virginia.

De Maret, P. 1990. 'Phases and facies in the archaeology of Central Africa.' In: P. Robertshaw (ed.) *A History of African Archaeology*: 109-134. London: James Currey.

Denbow, J. R. 1984. 'Cows and kings: a spatial and economic analysis of a hierarchical Early Iron Age settlement system in eastern Botswana.' In: M. Hall, G. Avery, D. M. Avery, M. L. Wilson and A. J. B. Humphreys (eds.) *Frontiers: Southern African Archaeology Today*: 24-39. Oxford: British Archaeological Reports.

Diop, C. A. 1979. *Nations, Nègres et Culture*. Paris: Présence Africaine.

Dowden, R. 1995. 'Africa and its art may be a PC fiction created by the West's guilty conscience.' *Spectator* (London), October 1995.

Dowson, T. and D. Lewis-Williams (eds.) 1994a. *Contested Images: Diversity in Southern African Rock Art Research*. Johannesburg: Witwatersrand University Press.

Dowson, T. and D. Lewis-Williams. 1994b. 'Diversity in southern African rock art research.' In: T. Dowson and D. Lewis-Williams (eds.) *Contested Images: Diversity in Southern African Rock Art Research*: 1-8. Johannesburg: Witwatersrand University Press.

Duco, D. H. 1987. *De Nederlandse Kleipijp: Handboek voor Dateren en Determineren*. Leiden:

Pijpenkabinet.

Duncan, D. D. 1968. *Picasso's Picassos*. New York: Ballantine Books.

Effah-Gyamfi, K. 1980. 'Traditional pottery technology at Krobo, Takyman (Techiman), Ghana: an ethnoarchaeological study.' *West African Journal of Archaeology* 10: 103-116.

Eluyemi, O. 1989. 'The archaeology of the Yoruba: problems and possibilities.' In: S. J. Shennan (ed.) *Archaeological Approaches to Cultural Identity*: 207-209. London: Unwin Hyman.

Evers, T. M. 1979. 'Salt and soapstone bowl factories at Harmony, Letaba district, north-east Transvaal.' *South African Archaeological Society Goodwin Series* 3: 94-107.

Evers, T. M. 1982. 'Excavations at the Lydenburg Heads site, Eastern Transvaal, South Africa.' *South African Archaeological Bulletin* 37: 16-33.

Fagan, B. M. 1961. 'Radiocarbon dates for sub-Saharan Africa (from *c.* 1000 B.C.) – I.' *Journal of African History* 11(1): 137-139.

Fagan, B. M. 1977. *The Rape of the Nile: Tomb Robbers, Tourists and Archaeologists in Egypt*. London: Macdonald and Jane.

Fagan, B. M., D. W. Phillipson and S. G. H. Daniels. 1969. *Iron Age Cultures in Zambia*. Volume 2. London: Chatto and Windus.

Fairbanks, R. G. 1993. 'Flip-flop end to last Ice Age.' *Nature* 362: 495.

Foley, R. 1987. *Another Unique Species: Patterns in Human Evolutionary Ecology*. London: Longman.

Fransen, H. and M. A. Cook. 1980. *The Old Buildings of the Cape*. Cape Town: Balkema.

Frederikse, J. 1982. *None but Ourselves: Masses vs. Media in the Making of Zimbabwe*. Johannesburg: Ravan Press.

Freeman-Grenville, G. P. S. 1962. *The East African Coast: Select Documents from the First to the Earlier Nineteenth Century*. Oxford: Clarendon Press.

Garba, A. 1994. 'The origin of the stone raw materials from Borno and the problem of far-reaching contacts in prehistory.' *West African Journal of Archaeology* 24: 67-75.

Garlake, P. 1973. *Great Zimbabwe*. London: Thames and Hudson.

Garlake, P. S. 1982. *Great Zimbabwe Described and Explained*. Harare: Zimbabwe Publishing House.

Godby, M. and S. Klopper. 1996. 'The art of Willie Bester.' *African Arts* 29: forthcoming.

Goodwin, A. J. H. 1953. *Method in Prehistory: An Introduction to the Discipline of Prehistoric Archaeology with Special Reference to South African Conditions*. Cape Town: South African Archaeological Society.

Goodwin, A. J. H. and C. van Riet Lowe. 1929. 'The Stone Age cultures of South Africa.' *Annals of the South African Museum* 27: 1-289.

Gordon-Brown, A. 1975. *Pictorial Africana*. Cape Town: Balkema.

Gould, S. J. 1981. *The Mismeasure of Man*. New York: W. W. Norton.

Gowlett, J. 1984. *Ascent to Civilization: The Archaeology of Early Man*. New York: Knopf.

Gowlett, J. A. J. 1990. 'Archaeological studies of human origins and early prehistory in Africa.' In: P. Robertshaw (ed.) *A History of African Archaeology*: 13-38. London: James Currey.

Gribble, J. 1989. 'Verlorenvlei vernacular: a structuralist analysis of Sandveld folk architecture.' MA dissertation, University of Cape Town.

Griffiths, I. 1984. *An Atlas of African Affairs*. London: Routledge.

Grove, A. T. 1993. 'Africa's climate in the Holocene.' In: T. Shaw, P. Sinclair, B. Andah and A. Okpoko (eds.) *The Archaeology of Africa: Food, Metals and Towns*: 32-42. London: Routledge.

Haas, J. 1982. *The Evolution of the Prehistoric State*. New York: Columbia University Press.

Haggard, H. R. 1885. *King Solomon's Mines*. London: MacDonald.

Hall, J. 1995. 'It's hard not to see African art through modernist European eyes.' *Weekly Mail and Guardian* (Johannesburg), 20 October 1995.

Hall, M. 1981. *Settlement Patterns in the Iron Age of Zululand*. Oxford: British Archaeological Reports.

Hall, M. 1982. 'Quantifying trends in site location with multidimensional scaling.' *World Archaeology* 14(1): 131-152.

Hall, M. 1984a. 'Man's historical and traditional use of fire in southern Africa.' In: P. de V. Booysen and N. M. Tainton (eds.) *Ecological Effects of Fire in South African Ecosystems*: 39-52. Berlin: Springer-Verlag.

Hall, M. 1984b. 'The burden of tribalism: the social context of southern African Iron Age studies.' *American Antiquity* 49(3): 455-467.

Hall, M. 1987. *The Changing Past: Farmers, Kings and Traders in Southern Africa, 200–1860*. Cape Town: David Philip, and London: James Currey.

Hall, M. 1990. '"Hidden history". Iron Age archaeology in southern Africa.' In: P. Robertshaw (ed.) *A History of African Archaeology*: 59-77. London: James Currey.

Hall, M. 1991. 'At the frontier: some arguments against hunter–gatherer and farming modes of production in southern Africa.' In: T. Ingold, D. Riches and J. Woodburn (eds.) *Hunters and Gatherers*. Volume 1: *History, Evolution and Social Change*: 137-147. New York: Berg.

Hall, M. 1992. 'Small things and the mobile, conflictual fusion of power, fear and desire.' In: A. Yentsch and M. Beaudry (eds.) *The Art and Mystery of Historical Archaeology: Essays in Honor of James Deetz*: 373-399. Boca Raton, Florida: CRC Press.

Hall, M. 1993. 'The archaeology of colonial settlement in southern Africa.' *Annual Review of Anthropology* 22: 177-200.

Hall, M. 1995. 'The Legend of the Lost City; or, The Man with Golden Balls.' *Journal of Southern African Studies* 21(2): 179-199.

Hall, M., D. Halkett, J. Klose and G. Ritchie. 1990. 'The Barrack Street well: images of a Cape Town household in the nineteenth century.' *South African Archaeological Bulletin* 45(152): 73-92.

Hall, M. and K. Mack. 1983. 'The outline of an eighteenth century economic system in south-east Africa.' *Annals of the South African Museum* 91(2): 163-194.

Hall, M. and J. C. Vogel. 1980. 'Some recent radio-carbon dates from southern Africa.' *Journal of African History* 21: 431-455.

Hall, R. N. 1905. *Great Zimbabwe, Mashonaland, Rhodesia: An Account of Two Years Examination Work in 1902-4 on Behalf of the Government of Rhodesia*. London: Methuen.

Hall, R. N. 1909. *Prehistoric Rhodesia: An Examination of the Historical, Ethnological and Archaeological Evidences as to the Origin and Age of the Rock Lines and Stone Buildings with a Gazetteer of Mediaeval South-east Africa, 915 AD to 1750 AD and the Countries of the Monomotapa, Manica, Sabia, Quiteve, Sofala and Mozambique*. London: Fisher Unwin.

Hall, R. N. and W. G. Neal. 1902. *The Ancient Ruins of Rhodesia*. London: Methuen.

Hall, S. L. 1986. 'Pastoral adaptations and forager reactions in the Eastern Cape.' *South African Archaeological Society Goodwin Series* 5: 42-49.

Hall, S. L. 1990. 'Hunter–gatherer–fishers of the Fish River Basin: a contribution to the Holocene prehistory of the Eastern Cape.' Ph.D. dissertation, University of Stellenbosch.

Hall, S. L. and J. Binneman. 1987. 'Later Stone Age burial variability in the Cape: a social interpretation.' *South African Archaeological Bulletin* 42: 140-152.

Hanisch, E. O. M. 1981. 'Schroda: a Zhizo site in the Northern Transvaal.' In: E. A. Voigt (ed.) *Guide to Archaeological Sites in the Northern and Eastern Transvaal*: 37-54. Pretoria: Southern African Association of Archaeologists.

Harrison, G. A., J. S. Weiner, J. M. Tanner and N. A. Barnicot. 1977. *Human Biology: An Introduction to Human Evolution, Variation, Growth and Ecology*. Oxford: Oxford University Press.

Hassan, F. A. 1993. 'Town and village in ancient Egypt: ecology, society and urbanization.' In: T. Shaw, P. Sinclair, B. Andah and A. Okpoko (eds.) *The Archaeology of Africa: Food, Metals and Towns*: 551-569. London: Routledge.

Henderson, Z. 1992. 'The context of some Middle Stone Age hearths at Klasies River Shelter 1B: implications for understanding human behaviour.' *Southern African Field Archaeology* 1(1): 14-26.

Hendey, Q. B. and T. P. Volman. 1986. 'Last interglacial sea levels and coastal caves in the Cape Province, South Africa.' *Quaternary Research* 25: 189-198.

Higgs, E. S. (ed.) 1974. *Palaeoeconomy*. Cambridge: Cambridge University Press.

Higgs, E. S. and C. Vita-Finzi. 1972. 'Prehistoric economies: a territorial approach.' In: E. S. Higgs (ed.) *Papers in Economic Prehistory*: 27-36. Cambridge: Cambridge University Press.

Hodder, I. 1982. *Symbols in Action: Ethnoarchaeological Studies of Material Culture*. Cambridge: Cambridge University Press.

Hodder, I. 1989. 'Post-modernism, post-structuralism and post-processual archaeology.' In: I. Hodder (ed.) *The Meaning of Things: Material Culture and Symbolic Expression*: 64-78. London: Harper Collins.

Hodder, I. 1991. *Reading the Past: Current Approaches to Interpretation in Archaeology*. Cambridge: Cambridge University Press.

Holl, A. 1990. 'West African archaeology: colonialism and nationalism.' In: P. Robertshaw (ed.) *A History of African Archaeology*: 296-308. London: James Currey.

Horton, M. 1994. 'Swahili architecture, space and social structure.' In: M. Parker Pearson and C. Richards (eds.) *Architecture and Order: Approaches to Social Space*: 147-169. London: Routledge.

Huffman, T. N. 1978. 'The origins of Leopard's Kopje: an 11th century difaqane.' *Arnoldia (Rhodesia)* 7(7): 1-12.

Huffman, T. N. 1980. 'Ceramics, classification and Iron Age entities.' *African Studies* 39: 123-174.

Huffman, T. N. 1981. 'Snakes and birds: expressive space at Great Zimbabwe.' *African Studies* 40(2): 131-150.

Huffman, T. N. 1982. 'Archaeology and ethnohistory of the African Iron Age.' *Annual Review of Anthropology* 11: 133-150.

Huffman, T. N. 1984. 'Where you are the girls gather to play: the Great Enclosure at Great Zimbabwe.' In: M. Hall, G. Avery, D. M. Avery, M. L. Wilson and A. J. B. Humphreys (eds.) *Frontiers: Southern African Archaeology Today*: 252-265. Oxford: British Archaeological Reports.

Huffman, T. N. and J. C. Vogel. 1991. 'The chronology of Great Zimbabwe.' *South African Archaeological Bulletin* 46: 61-70.

Ibeanu, A. M. 1992. 'Pottery function: an indispensable criterion in Igbo pottery classification.' *West African Journal of Archaeology* 22: 159-164.

Isaac, G. 1976. 'Stages of cultural elaboration in the Pleistocene: possible archaeological indications of the development of language capabilities.' In: S. R. Harnad, H. D. Stekelis and J. Lancaster (eds.) *Origins and Evolution of Language and Speech*: 275-288. New York: New York Academy of Sciences.

Jacobson, L., J. H. N. Loubser, M. Peisach, C. A. Pineda and W. van der Westhuizen. 1991. 'PIXE analysis of pre-European pottery from the Northern Transvaal and its relevance to the distribution of ceramic styles and social interaction.' *South African Archaeological Bulletin* 46: 19-24.

Jaume, D., G. Pons, M. Palmer, M. McMinn, J. A. Alcover and G. Politis. 1992. 'Racism, archaeology and museums: the strange case of the stuffed African male in the Darder Museum, Banyoles (Catalonia), Spain.' *World Archaeological Bulletin* 6: 113-118.

Jenkins, S. 1995. 'Out of Africa and out of context. Why is the Royal Academy using artefacts of African life to adorn walls that have hung Rembrandt and Titian?' *The Times* (London), 7 October 1995.

Jenkins, T., H. Harpending and G. T. Nurse. 1978. 'Genetic distances among certain southern African populations.' In: R. J. Meier, C. M. Otten and F. Abdel-Hameed (eds.) *Evolutionary Models and Studies in Human Diversity*: 227-243. The Hague: Mouton.

Jung, C. C. 1973. *Memories, Dreams, Reflections*. London: Random House.

Karega-Munene 1992. 'Dissemination of archaeological information: the East African experience.' In: P. Reilly and S. Rahtz (eds.) *Archaeology in the Information Age*: 41-46. London: Routledge.

Kassam, A. and G. Megersa. 1989. 'Iron and beads: male and female symbols of creation. A study of ornament among Booran Oromo.' In: I. Hodder (ed.) *The Meaning of Things: Material Culture and Symbolic Expression*: 23-32. London: Unwin Hyman.

Kaufulu, Z. M. 1987. 'Formation and preservation of some Earlier Stone Age sites at Koobi Fora, northern Kenya.' *South African Archaeological Bulletin* 42: 23-33.

Keeley, L. H. 1980. *Experimental Determination of Stone Tool Uses: A Microwear Analysis*. Chicago: University of Chicago Press.

Kense, F. 1990. 'Archaeology in anglophone West Africa.' In: P. Robertshaw (ed.) *A History of African Archaeology*: 135-154. London: James Currey.

Kinahan, J. 1991. 'The historical archaeology of nineteenth century fisheries at Sandwich Harbour on the Namib coast.' *Cimbebasia* 13: 1-27.

Kiyaga-Mulindwa, D. 1982. 'Social and demographic changes in the Birim Valley, southern Ghana, *c*.1450 to *c*.1800.' *Journal of African History* 23: 63-82.

Kiyaga-Mulindwa, D. 1993. 'The Iron Age peoples of east-central Botswana.' In: T. Shaw, P. Sinclair, B. Andah and A. Okpoko (eds.) *The Archaeology of Africa: Food, Metals and Towns*: 386-390. London: Routledge.

Klein, R. G. 1976. 'The mammalian fauna of the Klasies River Mouth sites, southern Cape Province, South Africa.' *South African Archaeological Bulletin* 31: 75-98.

Klein, R. G. 1983. 'Palaeoenvironmental implications of Quaternary large mammals in the fynbos region.' In: H. J. Deacon, Q. B. Hendey and J. J. N. Lambrechts (eds.) *Fynbos Palaeoecology: A Preliminary Synthesis*: 116-138. Pretoria: Council for Scientific and Industrial Research.

Klein, R. G. and K. Cruz-Uribe. 1984. *The Analysis of Animal Bones from Archaeological Sites*. Chicago: University of Chicago Press.

Klein, R. G. and K. Cruz-Uribe. 1991. 'The bovids from Elandsfontein, South Africa, and their implications for the age, palaeoenvironment, and origins of the site.' *African Archaeological Review* 9: 21-79.

Kolb, P. 1968. *Present State of the Cape of Good Hope*. 2 volumes (facsimile reprint, originally published London, 1731). New York: Johnson Reprint Corporation.

Krafchik, B. 1994a. 'Introduction.' In: B. Krafchik (ed.) *The South African Museum and Its Public: Negotiating Partnerships*: 1-2. Cape Town: South African Museum.

Krafchik, B. (ed.) 1994b. *The South African Museum and Its Public: Negotiating Partnerships*. Cape Town: South African Museum.

Kuper, A. 1980. 'Symbolic dimensions of the Southern Bantu homestead.' *Africa* 50(1): 8-23.

Lavine, S. D. and I. Karp. 1991. 'Museums and multiculturalism.' In: I. Karp and S. D. Lavine (eds.) *Exhibiting Cultures: The Poetics and Politics of Museum Display*: 1-9. Washington: Smithsonian Institution.

Leakey, L. S. B. 1931. *The Stone Age Cultures of Kenya Colony*. Cambridge: Cambridge University Press.

Lee, R. B. and I. DeVore (eds.) 1968. *Man the Hunter*. Chicago: Aldine.

Leone, M. 1988. 'The Georgian order as the order of merchant capitalism in Annapolis, Maryland.' In: M. Leone and P. Potter (eds.) *The Recovery of Meaning: Historical Archaeology in the Eastern United States*: 235-261. Washington: Smithsonian Institution.

Levtzion, N. 1973. *Ancient Ghana and Mali*. London: Methuen.

Lewis-Williams, J. D. 1981. *Believing and Seeing: Symbolic Meanings in Southern San Rock Paintings*. London: Academic Press.

Lewis-Williams, J. D. 1983. *The Rock Art of Southern Africa*. Cambridge: Cambridge University Press.

Lewis-Williams, J. D. and T. Dowson. 1989. *Images of Power*. Johannesburg: Southern Book Publishers.

Livingstone, D. A. 1971. 'A 22,000-year pollen record from the plateau of Zambia.' *Limnology and Oceanography* 16(2): 349-356.

McBurney, C. B. M. 1960. *The Stone Age of Northern Africa*. Harmondsworth: Penguin.

McGuire, R. 1991. 'Building power in the cultural landscape of Broome County, New York 1880–1940.' In: R. McGuire and R. Paynter (eds.) *The Archaeology of Inequality*: 102-124. Oxford: Blackwell.

McIntosh, R. J. and S. K. McIntosh. 1981. 'The

Inland Niger Delta before the Empire of Mali: evidence from Jenne-Jeno.' *Journal of African History* 22(1): 1-22.

McIntosh, S. K. and R. J. McIntosh. 1979. 'Initial perspectives on prehistoric subsistence in the Inland Niger Delta (Mali).' *World Archaeology* 11(2): 227-243.

McIntosh, S. K. and R. J. McIntosh. 1980. *Prehistoric Investigations in the Region of Jenne, Mali: A Study in the Development of Urbanism in the Sahel*. Oxford: British Archaeological Reports.

McIntosh, S. K. and R. J. McIntosh. 1984. 'The early city in West Africa: towards an understanding.' *African Archaeological Review* 2: 73-98.

Maggs, T. 1976. *Iron Age Communities of the Southern Highveld*. Pietermaritzburg: Natal Museum.

Maggs, T. 1980a. 'Msuluzi Confluence: a seventh century Early Iron Age site on the Tugela River.' *Annals of the Natal Museum* 24(1): 111-146.

Maggs, T. 1980b. 'Mzonjani and the beginnings of the Iron Age in Natal.' *Annals of the Natal Museum* 24(1): 71-96.

Maggs, T. 1982a. 'Mgoduyanuka: terminal Iron Age settlement in the Natal grasslands.' *Annals of the Natal Museum* 25(1): 83-114.

Maggs, T. 1982b. 'Mabhija: pre-colonial industrial development in the Tugela Basin.' *Annals of the Natal Museum* 25(1): 123-141.

Maggs, T. 1984a. 'Ndondondwane: a preliminary report on an Early Iron Age site on the Lower Tugela River.' *Annals of the Natal Museum* 26(1): 71-93.

Maggs, T. 1984b. 'The Iron Age south of the Zambezi.' In: R. G. Klein (ed.) *Southern African Prehistory and Palaeoenvironments*: 329-360. Rotterdam: Balkema.

Maggs, T. and P. Davison. 1981. 'The Lydenburg Heads.' *African Arts* 14(2): 28-33.

Maggs, T. and V. Ward. 1980. 'Driel Shelter: rescue at a Late Stone Age site on the Tugela River.' *Annals of the Natal Museum* 24(1): 35-70.

Manhire, A. H., J. Parkington and R. Yates. 1985. 'Nets and fully recurved bows: rock paintings and hunting methods in the Western Cape, South Africa.' *World Archaeology* 17: 161-174.

Markell, A. 1993. 'Building on the past: the architecture and archaeology of Vergelegen.' *South African Archaeological Society Goodwin Series* 7: 71-83.

Marshall, F. 1991. 'Mammalian fauna from Gogo Falls.' *Azania* 26: 175-179.

Martin, M. 1993. 'Foreword.' In: M. Payne (ed.) *Face Value: Old Heads in Modern Masks*. Exhibition Catalogue: 4-5. Cape Town: Axeage Private Press.

Marx, K. 1974. *Capital: A Critical Analysis of Capitalist Production*. London: Lawrence and Wishart.

Mazel, A. D. 1989. 'Changing social relations in the Thukela Basin, Natal 7000–2000 BP.' *South African Archaeological Society Goodwin Series* 6: 33-41.

Metelerkamp, W. and J. Sealy. 1983. 'Some edible and medicinal plants of the Doorn Karoo.' *Veld and Flora* 69(1): 4-8.

Metz, G. 1994. 'Working with communities in Botswana.' In: B. Krafchik (ed.) *The South African Museum and Its Public: Negotiating Partnerships*: 11-14. Cape Town: South African Museum.

Miller, D. 1987. *Material Culture and Mass Consumption*. Oxford: Blackwell.

Miller, D. and G. Whitelaw. 1994. 'Early Iron Age metal working from the site of KwaGandaganda, Natal, South Africa.' *South African Archaeological Bulletin* 49: 79-89.

Miller, D. E., R. J. Yates, J. E. Parkington and J. C. Vogel. 1993. 'Radiocarbon-dated evidence relating to a mid-Holocene relative high sea-level on the south-western Cape coast, South Africa.' *South African Journal of Science* 89(1): 35-44.

Molino, J. 1992. 'Archaeology and symbol systems.' In: J.-C. Gardin and C. Peebles (eds.) *Representations in Archaeology*: 15-29. Bloomington: Indiana University Press.

Morais, J. 1984. 'Mozambican archaeology: past and present.' *African Archaeological Review* 2: 113-128.

Morris, A. G. 1992. *The Skeletons of Contact: A Study of Prehistoric Burials from the Lower Orange River Valley, South Africa*. Johannesburg: Witwatersrand University Press.

Morrison, M. E. S. 1968. 'Vegetation and climate in the uplands of south-western Uganda during the later Pleistocene period. 1. Muchoya Swamp, Kigezi District.' *Journal of Ecology* 56: 363-384.

Munjeri, D. 1991. 'Refocusing or reorientation? The exhibit or the populace: Zimbabwe on the threshold.' In: I. Karp and S. D. Lavine (eds.) *Exhibiting Cultures: The Poetics and Politics of Museum Display*: 444-456. Washington: Smithsonian Institution.

Nackerdien, R. 1993. *Faizal's Journey: Discovering the Past through Objects*. Cape Town: Community Education Resources, University of Cape Town.

Noli, D. 1985. 'Low altitude aerial photography from a tethered balloon.' *Journal of Field Archaeology* 12(4): 497-501.

Nott, J. C. and G. R. Gliddon. 1868. *Indigenous Races of the Earth*. Philadelphia.

Nurse, G. T., J. Weiner and T. Jenkins. 1985. *The Peoples of Southern Africa and Their Affinities*. Oxford: Oxford University Press.

Nzewunwa, N. 1980. *The Niger Delta: Aspects of Its Prehistoric Economy and Culture*. Oxford: British Archaeological Reports.

Nzewunwa, N. 1990. 'Archaeology in Nigerian education.' In: P. Stone and R. Mackenzie (eds.) *The Excluded Past: Archaeology in Education*: 33-42. London: Unwin Hyman.

O'Connor, D. 1990. 'Egyptology and archaeology: an African perspective.' In: P. Robertshaw (ed.) *A History of African Archaeology*: 236-251. London: James Currey.

Ogundele, S. O. 1993. 'Archaeological reconnaissance and excavations in parts of Tivland.' *West African Journal of Archaeology* 23: 67-91.

Okpoko, A. I. 1987. 'The early urban centres and states of West Africa.' *West African Journal of Archaeology* 17: 243-265.

Okpoko, A. I. 1989. 'The use of ethnography in archaeological investigations (ethnoarchaeology).' *West African Journal of Archaeology* 19: 65-82.

Olaniyan, T. 1995. 'Afrocentrism.' *Social Dynamics* 21(2): 91-105.

Olsen, B. 1990. 'Roland Barthes: from sign to text.' In: C. Tilley (ed.) *Reading Material Culture: Structuralism, Hermeneutics and Post-structuralism*: 163-205. Oxford: Blackwell.

Parkington, J. 1980. 'Time and place: some observations on spatial and temporal patterning in the Later Stone Age sequence in southern Africa.' *South African Archaeological Bulletin* 35: 73-83.

Parkington, J. 1981. 'The effects of environmental change on the scheduling of visits to the Elands Bay Cave, Cape Province, South Africa.' In: I. Hodder (ed.) *Pattern of the Past: Studies in Honour of David Clarke*: 341-359. Cambridge: Cambridge University Press.

Parkington, J. 1991. 'Approaches to dietary reconstruction in the Western Cape: Are you what you have eaten?' *Journal of Archaeological Science* 18: 331-342.

Parkington, J. and A. H. Manhire. 1996. 'Processions and groups: human figures, ritual occasions and social categories in the rock paintings of the Western Cape.' In: M. C. Conkey, O. Soffer and D. Stratmann (eds.) *Beyond Art: Pleistocene Image and Symbol*. Berkeley: Californian Academy of Sciences and University of California Press.

Parkington, J., P. Nilssen, C. Reeler and C. Henshilwood. 1992. 'Making sense of space at Dunefield Midden campsite, Western Cape, South Africa.' *Southern African Field Archaeology* 1(2): 63-70.

Parkington, J. and C. Poggenpoel. 1971. 'A Late Stone Age burial from Clanwilliam.' *South African Archaeological Bulletin* 26: 82-84.

Parkington, J., C. Poggenpoel, B. Buchanan, T. Robey, A. H. Manhire and J. Sealy. 1988. 'Holocene coastal settlement patterns in the Western Cape.' In: G. Bailey and J. Parkington (eds.) *The Archaeology of Prehistoric Coastlines*: 22-41. Cambridge: Cambridge University Press.

Payne, S. 1972. 'Partial recovery and sample bias: the results of some sieving experiments.' In: E. S. Higgs (ed.) *Papers in Economic Prehistory*: 49-64. Cambridge: Cambridge University Press.

Peires, J. B. 1981. *The House of Phalo: A History of the Xhosa People in the Days of Their Independence*. Johannesburg: Ravan Press.

Phillips, T. 1995. 'Introduction.' In: T. Phillips (ed.) *Africa: The Art of a Continent*: 11-20. London: Royal Academy of Arts.

Phillipson, D. W. 1970. 'Notes on the later prehistoric radiocarbon chronology of eastern and southern Africa.' *Journal of African History* 11(1): 1-15.

Phillipson, D. W. 1985. *African Archaeology*. Cambridge: Cambridge University Press.

Pikirayi, I. 1993. *The Archaeological Identity of the Mutapa State: Towards an Historical Archaeology of Northern Zimbabwe*. Uppsala: Societas Archaeologica Upsaliensis.

Plug, I. 1981. 'Some research results on the Late Pleistocene and Early Holocene deposits of Bushman Rock Shelter, Eastern Transvaal.' *South African Archaeological Bulletin* 36: 14-21.

Plug, I. and R. Engela. 1992. 'The macrofaunal remains from recent excavations at Rose Cottage Cave, Orange Free State.' *South African Archaeological Bulletin* 47: 16-25.

Poggenpoel, C. A. 1987. 'The implications of fish bone assemblages from Eland's Bay Cave, Tortoise Cave and Diepkloof Rock Shelter for changes in the Holocene history of the Verlorenvlei.' In: J. Parkington and M. Hall (eds.) *Papers in the Prehistory of the Western Cape*: 212-236. Oxford: British Archaeological Reports.

Randall-MacIver, D. 1906. *Mediaeval Rhodesia*. London: Macmillan.

Rathje, W. L. and M. B. Schiffer. 1982. *Archaeology*. New York: Harcourt Brace Jovanovich.

Renfrew, C. 1982. *Towards an Archaeology of Mind*. Cambridge: University of Cambridge.

Renfrew, C. and P. Bahn. 1991. *Archaeology: Theories, Methods and Practice*. London: Thames and Hudson.

Rightmire, G. P. and H. J. Deacon. 1991. 'Comparative studies of Late Pleistocene human remains from Klasies River Mouth, South Africa.' *Journal of Human Evolution* 20: 131-156.

Roberts, A. F. 1984. '"Fishers of men": religion and political economy among colonized Tabwa.' *Africa* 54: 49-70.

Robertshaw, P. 1990. 'The development of archaeology in East Africa.' In: P. Robertshaw (ed.) *A History of African Archaeology*: 78-94. London: James Currey.

Robertshaw, P. 1991. 'Gogo Falls: a complex site east of Lake Victoria.' *Azania* 26: 63-174.

Rowlands, M. 1989. 'The archaeology of colonialism and constituting the African peasantry.' In: D. Miller, M. Rowlands and C. Tilley (eds.) *Domination and Resistance*. London: Unwin Hyman.

Sackett, J. R. 1982. 'Approaches to style in lithic archaeology.' *Journal of Anthropological Archaeology* 1(1): 59-112.

Sadr, K. 1991. *The Development of Nomadism in Ancient Northeast Africa*. Philadelphia: University of

Pennsylvania Press.

Saitowitz, S. 1990. 'Nineteenth century glass trade beads from two Zulu royal residences.' MA dissertation, University of Cape Town.

Saitowitz, S., U. Seemann and M. Hall. 1993. 'The development of Cape Town's waterfront in the earlier nineteenth century: history and archaeology of the North Wharf.' *South African Archaeological Society Goodwin Series* 7: 98-103.

Sampson, C. G. 1988. 'Practical politics in the wilderness of mirrors.' *South African Archaeological Bulletin* 43: 60-63.

Schick, K. D. and N. Toth. 1993. *Making Silent Stones Speak: Human Evolution and the Dawn of Technology.* New York: Simon and Schuster.

Schrire, C., J. Deetz, D. Lubinsky and C. Poggenpoel. 1990. 'The chronology of Oudepost I, Cape, as inferred from an analysis of clay pipes.' *Journal of Archaeological Science* 17: 269-300.

Scott, L. 1984. 'Palynological evidence for Quaternary paleoenvironments in southern Africa.' In: R. G. Klein (ed.) *Southern African Prehistory and Paleoenvironments*: 65-80. Rotterdam: Balkema.

Sealy, J. and R. Yates. 1994. 'The chronology of the introduction of pastoralism to the Cape, South Africa.' *Antiquity* 68: 58-67.

Sealy, J. C., A. G. Morris, R. Armstrong, A. Markell and C. Schrire. 1993. 'An historic skeleton from the slave lodge at Vergelegen.' *South African Archaeological Society Goodwin Series* 7: 84-91.

Sealy, J. C. and N. J. van der Merwe. 1986. 'Isotope assessment and the seasonal mobility hypothesis in the southwestern Cape of South Africa.' *Current Anthropology* 27(2): 135-150.

Sealy, J. C. and N. J. van der Merwe. 1992. 'On "Approaches to dietary reconstruction in the Western Cape: Are you what you have eaten?" A reply to Parkington.' *Journal of Archaeological Science* 19: 459-466.

Shaw, T. 1990. 'A personal memoir.' In: P. Robertshaw (ed.) *A History of African Archaeology*: 205-220. London: James Currey.

Shaw, T., P. Sinclair, B. Andah and A. Okpoko (eds.) 1993. *The Archaeology of Africa: Food, Metals and Towns.* London: Routledge.

Shennan, S. 1988. *Quantifying Archaeology.* Edinburgh: Edinburgh University Press.

Shinnie, P. L. 1967. *Meroë: A Civilization of the Sudan.* London: Thames and Hudson.

Sinclair, P. 1982. 'Chibuene: an early trading site in southern Mozambique.' *Paideuma* 28: 150-164.

Sinclair, P. 1987. *Space, Time and Social Formation: A Territorial Approach to the Archaeology and Anthropology of Zimbabwe and Mozambique c. 0–1700 AD.* Uppsala: Societas Archaeologica Upsaliensis.

Sinclair, P., J. M. F. Morais, L. Adamowicz and R. T. Duarte. 1993a. 'A perspective on archaeological research in Mozambique.' In: T. Shaw, P. Sinclair, B. Andah and A. Okpoko (eds.) *The Archaeology of Africa: Food, Metals and Towns*: 409-431. London: Routledge.

Sinclair, P., I. Pikirayi, G. Pwiti and R. Soper. 1993b. 'Urban trajectories on the Zimbabwean plateau.' In: T. Shaw, P. Sinclair, B. Andah and A. Okpoko (eds.) *The Archaeology of Africa: Food, Metals and Towns*: 705-731. London: Routledge.

Singer, R. and J. Wymer. 1982. *The Middle Stone Age at Klasies River Mouth in South Africa.* Chicago: University of Chicago Press.

Smith, A. B. 1992. *Pastoralism in Africa: Origins and Development Ecology.* Johannesburg: Witwatersrand University Press.

Smith, W. 1972. *The Sunbird.* London: Heinemann.

Solomon, A. 1992. 'Gender, representation, and power in San ethnography and rock art.' *Journal of Anthropological Archaeology* 11: 291-329.

Sperber, D. 1975. *Rethinking Symbolism.* Cambridge: Cambridge University Press.

Stahl, A. B. 1993. 'Intensification in the West African Late Stone Age: a view from central Ghana.' In: T. Shaw, P. Sinclair, B. Andah and A. Okpoko (eds.) *The Archaeology of Africa: Food, Metals and Towns*: 261-273. London: Routledge.

Stern, I. 1943. *Congo.* Pretoria: Van Schaik.

Stewart, K. 1991. 'Fish remains from Gogo Falls.' *Azania* 26: 179-180.

Stiles, D. 1991. 'Early hominid behaviour and culture tradition: raw material studies in Bed II, Olduvai Gorge.' *African Archaeological Review* 9: 1-20.

Stow, G. W. 1905. *The Native Races of South Africa.* London: Swan Sonnenschein.

Summers, R. 1955. 'The dating of the Zimbabwe ruins.' *Antiquity* 29: 107-111.

Sutton, J. E. G. 1974. 'The aquatic civilization of middle Africa.' *Journal of African History* 15: 527-546.

Thackeray, A. I. 1989. 'Changing fashions in the Middle Stone Age: the stone artefact sequence from Klasies River Main Site, South Africa.' *African Archaeological Review* 7: 33-58.

Thackeray, A. I. and A. J. Kelly. 1988. 'A technological and typological analysis of Middle Stone Age assemblages antecedent to the Howiesons Poort at Klasies River Main Site.' *South African Archaeological Bulletin* 43: 15-26.

Thackeray, J. F. 1988. 'Molluscan fauna from Klasies River, South Africa.' *South African Archaeological Bulletin* 43: 27-32.

Thom, H. B. (ed.) 1954. *Journal of Jan van Riebeeck.* Volume 2: *1656–1658.* Cape Town: Balkema.

Thornton, R. 1988. 'Culture: a contemporary definition.' In: E. Boonzaier and J. Sharp (eds.) *South African Keywords: The Uses and Abuses of Political Concepts*: 17-28. Cape Town: David Philip.

Tilley, C. 1989. 'Interpreting material culture.' In: I.

Hodder (ed.) *The Meaning of Things: Material Culture and Symbolic Expression*: 185-194. London: Harper Collins.

Tilley, C. (ed.) 1990. *Reading Material Culture*. Oxford: Blackwell.

Tobias, P. V. 1974. 'The biology of the southern African Negro.' In: W. D. Hammond-Tooke (ed.) *The Bantu-speaking Peoples of Southern Africa*: 3-45. London: Routledge and Kegan Paul.

Trigger, B. 1990. 'The history of African archaeology in world perspective.' In: P. Robertshaw (ed.) *A History of African Archaeology*: 309-319. London: James Currey.

Tukey, J. W. 1977. *Exploratory Data Analysis*. Reading: Addison-Wesley.

Twagiramutara, P. 1989. 'Archaeological and anthropological hypotheses concerning the origin of ethnic divisions in sub-Saharan Africa.' In: R. Layton (ed.) *Conflict in the Archaeology of Living Traditions*: 88-96. London: Unwin Hyman.

Tyson, P. D. 1986. *Climatic Change and Variability in Southern Africa*. Cape Town: Oxford University Press.

Ucko, P. 1987. *Academic Freedom and Apartheid: The Story of the World Archaeological Congress*. London: Duckworth.

Van Andel, T. H. 1989. 'Late Quaternary sea-level changes and archaeology.' *Antiquity* 63: 733-745.

Van der Merwe, N. J. 1980. 'Production of high carbon steel in the African Iron Age: the direct steel process.' In: R. E. Leakey and B. A. Ogot (eds.) *Proceedings of the 8th Pan African Congress of Prehistory and Quaternary Studies*: 331-334. Nairobi: International Leakey Memorial Institute for African Prehistory.

Van der Merwe, N. J. and D. Killick. 1979. 'Square: an iron smelting site near Phalaborwa.' *South African Archaeological Society Goodwin Series* 3: 86-93.

Van der Merwe, N. J. and R. T. K. Scully. 1971. 'The Phalaborwa story: archaeological and ethnographic investigation of a South African Iron Age group.' *World Archaeology* 3(2): 178-196.

Van der Post, L. 1958. *The Lost World of the Kalahari*. New York: William Morrow.

Voigt, E. A. 1983. *Mapungubwe: An Archaeozoological Interpretation of an Iron Age Community*. Pretoria: Transvaal Museum.

Wadley, L. 1987. *Later Stone Age Hunters of the Southern Transvaal: Social and Ecological Interpretation*. Oxford: British Archaeological Reports.

Wadley, L. 1991. 'Rose Cottage Cave: background and a preliminary report on the recent excavations.' *South African Archaeological Bulletin* 46: 125-130.

Wandibba, S. 1990. 'Archaeology and education in Kenya.' In: P. Stone and R. Mackenzie (eds.) *The Excluded Past: Archaeology in Education*: 43-49. London: Unwin Hyman.

Weiss, M. L. and A. E. Mann. 1985. *Human Biology and Behavior: An Anthropological Perspective*. Boston: Little, Brown.

Wenner, D. B. and N. J. van der Merwe. 1987. 'Mining for the lowest grade ore: traditional iron production in northern Malawi.' *Geoarchaeology* 2(3): 199-216.

Werz, B. E. J. S. 1993a. 'Shipwrecks of Robben Island, South Africa: an exercise in cultural resource management in the underwater environment.' *International Journal of Nautical Archaeology* 22(3): 245-256.

Werz, B. E. J. S. 1993b. 'Maritime archaeological project Table Bay: aspects of the first field season.' *South African Archaeological Society Goodwin Series* 7: 33-39.

West, C. 1995. 'Preface.' In: T. Phillips (ed.) *Africa: The Art of a Continent*: 9-10. London: Royal Academy of Arts.

Wetterstrom, W. 1991. 'Plant remains from Gogo Falls.' *Azania* 26: 180-191.

Wharton, E. 1974. *The Age of Innocence*. Harmondsworth: Penguin.

White, T. D. 1987. 'Cannibalism at Klasies?' *Sagittarius* 2: 6-9.

Whitelaw, G. 1994. 'KwaGandaganda: settlement patterns in the Natal Early Iron Age.' *Natal Museum Journal of Humanities* 6: 1-64.

Wiessner, P. 1983. 'Style and social information in Kalahari San projectile points.' *American Antiquity* 48(2): 253-276.

Willey, G. R. and J. A. Sabloff. 1974. *A History of American Archaeology*. London: Thames and Hudson.

Wilmsen, E. N. 1989. *Land Filled with Flies: A Political Economy of the Kalahari*. Chicago: University of Chicago Press.

Winer, M. and J. Deetz. 1990. 'The transformation of British culture in the Eastern Cape, 1820–1860.' *Social Dynamics* 16(1): 55-75.

Yates, R., A. H. Manhire and J. Parkington. 1993. 'Colonial era paintings in the rock art of the southwestern Cape: some preliminary observations.' *South African Archaeological Society Goodwin Series* 7: 59-70.

Yates, R., S. Woodborne and M. Hall. 1995. 'The chronology of colonial settlement at the Cape of Good Hope: clay tobacco pipes.' Unpublished report, Department of Archaeology, University of Cape Town.

Young, R. 1990. *White Mythologies: Writing History and the West*. London: Routledge.

Index